S0-ALM-207

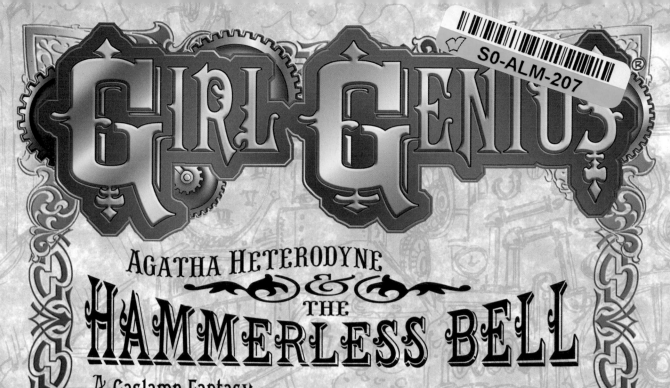

GIRL GENIUS

AGATHA HETERODYNE
&
THE
HAMMERLESS BELL

A Gaslamp Fantasy
with
ADVENTURE, ROMANCE & MAD SCIENCE

Story by Kaja & Phil Foglio
Pencils by Phil Foglio
Colors by Cheyenne Wright

AIRSHIP
ENTERTAINMENT

OTHER BOOKS FROM AIRSHIP ENTERTAINMENT AND STUDIO FOGLIO

Girl Genius® Graphic Novels

Other Graphic Novels

Girl Genius® is published by:
Airship Entertainment™: a happy part of Studio Foglio, LLC
2400 NW 80th St #129 Seattle WA 98117-4449, USA

Please visit our Web sites at www.airshipbooks.com and www.girlgenius.net

Girl Genius is a registered trademark of Studio Foglio, LLC. Girl Genius, the Girl Genius logos, Studio Foglio and the Studio Foglio logo, Airship Entertainment, Airship Books & Comics & the Airship logo, the Jägermonsters, Mr. Tock, the Heterodyne trilobite badge, the Jägermonsters' monster badge, the Wulfenbach badge, the Spark, Agatha Heterodyne, Trelawney Thorpe, the Heterodyne Boys, Transylvania Polygnostic, the Transylvania Polygnostic University arms, the Secret Cypher Society, Krosp, Castle Wulfenbach, Castle Heterodyne and all the Girl Genius characters are © & ™ 2000-2012 Studio Foglio.

All material ©2001–2012 Studio Foglio. All rights reserved. No part of this book may be reproduced in any form (including electronic) without permission in writing from the publisher except for brief passages in connection with a review.

This is a work of fiction and any resemblance herein to actual persons, events or institutions is purely coincidental.

Story by Phil & Kaja Foglio. Pencils by Phil Foglio. Colors by Cheyenne Wright. Selected spot illustrations colored by Kaja Foglio and/or Cheyenne Wright. Logos, Lettering, Artist Bullying & Book Design by Kaja. Fonts mostly by Comicraft– www.comicbookfonts.com.

This material originally appeared from November 2010 to November 2011 at www.girlgenius.net.

Published simultaneously in Hardcover (ISBN 978-1-890856-56-4)
and in Softcover (ISBN 978-1-890856-55-7) editions.

First Printing: June 2012   PRINTED IN THE USA

This book is dedicated to Maxine Danger Wright: girl genius and adorable baby *extraordinaire*.

PHIL FOGLIO

The co–chair of Transylvania Polygnostic University's Department of Very Nearly True History is internationally recognized for his fieldwork chronicling the early life of Agatha Heterodyne. Lately, due to a generous endowment from the "Jägerkin Fund for Education und Promotion Ov De Idea Dot Ve Iz Not Really Baby–Eating Monsters *All* De Time," his usual research has been sidetracked by an attempt to document all the instances when the Lady Heterodyne is known to have worn a hat.

KAJA FOGLIO

The Professoressa recently completed a six-month tour of the Paris Institute of Technology and Cuisine, The London Museum of Electromagnetic Atrocities & Chocolate Factory, and Prague University's Department of Egregious Experimentation & Distillery; all while continuing her award–winning work upon the Heterodyne saga. Unfortunately, she has lately been distracted by a new project which attempts to examine and catalog the number of major technological breakthroughs that the Lady Heterodyne made while eating scones. This is due to a timely research grant from the Mechanicsburg Elevenses, Luncheon and Teatime Society.

CHEYENNE WRIGHT

Transylvania Polygnostic's current Chief Chromatic Engineer, and also the person who has managed to survive the longest while working with the Professors on their continuing graphic biography–like chronicle of the adventures of Agatha Heterodyne. Due to certain conditions attached to a joint endowment from the Eastern European Council of Visible Light and The Noble Alliance of Higher Wavelengths, he has just completed a painstakingly documented record of every instance where the Lady Heterodyne wore pastel colors. He claims to have found the assignment: "profoundly nerve–racking, and far from the comfort zone of my people."

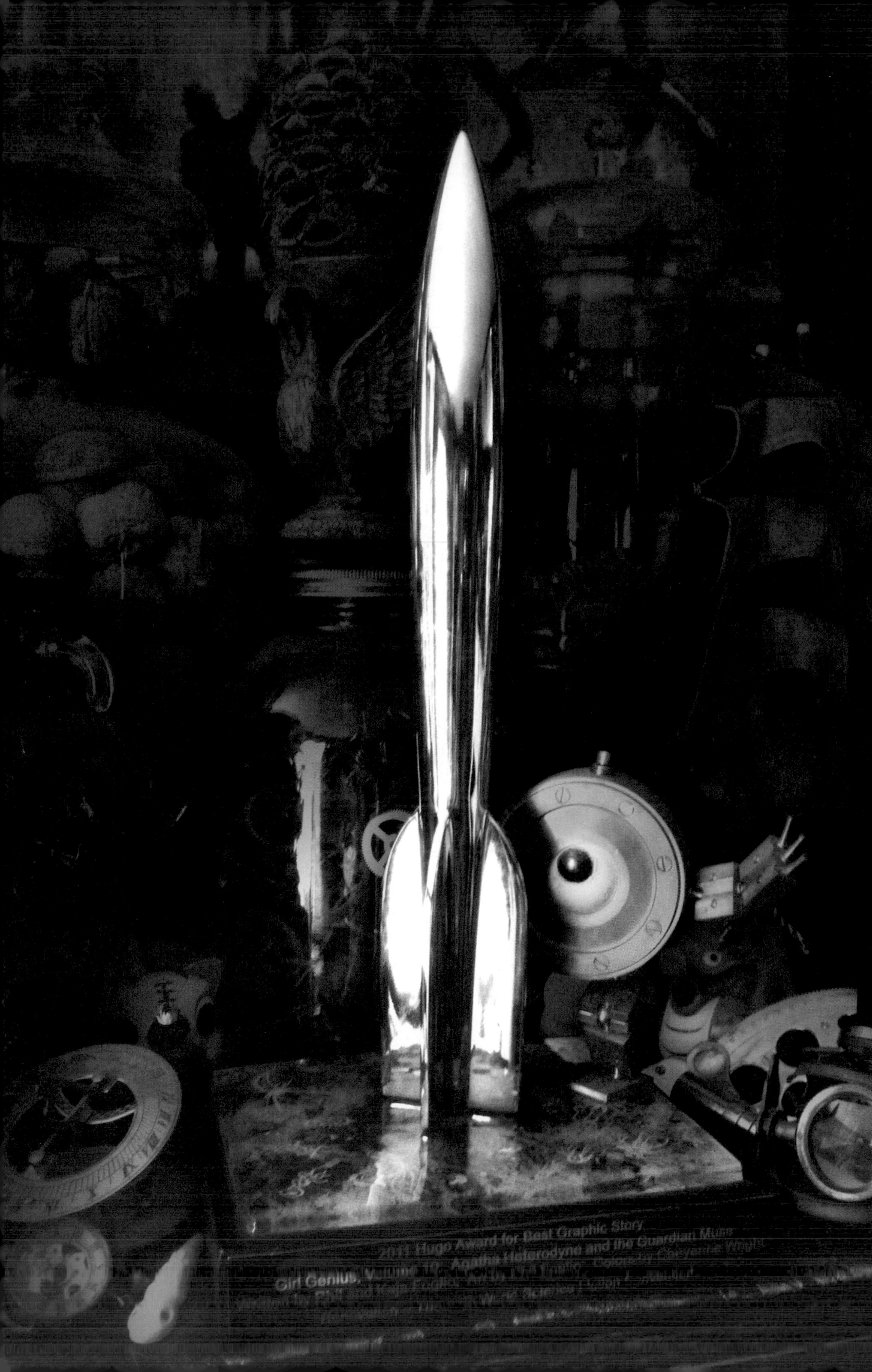
2011 Hugo Award for Best Graphic Story
Girl Genius, Volume 10: Agatha Heterodyne and the Guardian Muse

Photo by Kaja Foglio • Hugo Award Base by Marina Gélineau • Dingbot by Tiff Hudson

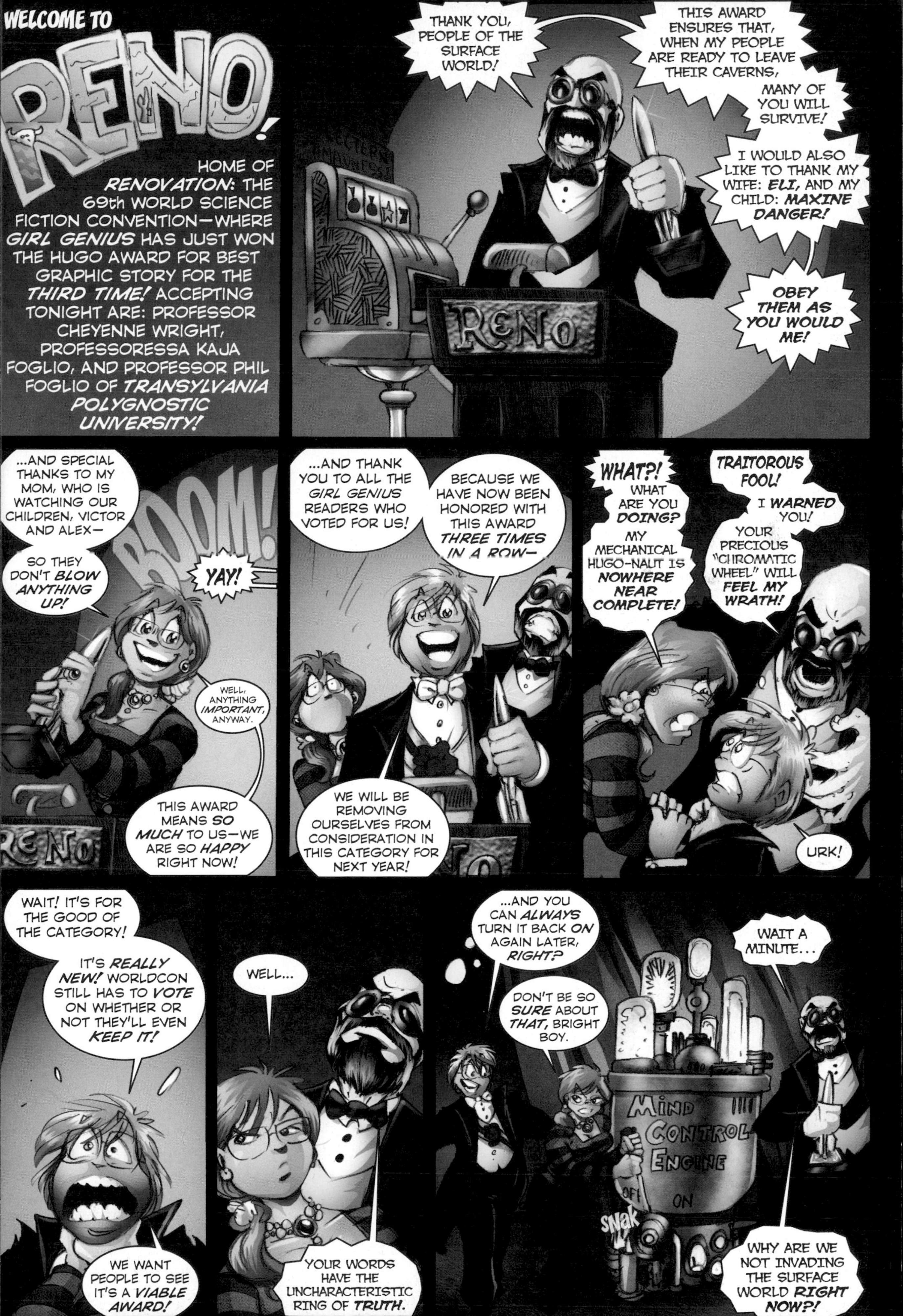
WELCOME TO
RENO!
HOME OF RENOVATION: THE 69th WORLD SCIENCE FICTION CONVENTION—WHERE GIRL GENIUS HAS JUST WON THE HUGO AWARD FOR BEST GRAPHIC STORY FOR THE THIRD TIME! ACCEPTING TONIGHT ARE: PROFESSOR CHEYENNE WRIGHT, PROFESSORESSA KAJA FOGLIO, AND PROFESSOR PHIL FOGLIO OF TRANSYLVANIA POLYGNOSTIC UNIVERSITY!
THANK YOU, PEOPLE OF THE SURFACE WORLD!
THIS AWARD ENSURES THAT, WHEN MY PEOPLE ARE READY TO LEAVE THEIR CAVERNS,
MANY OF YOU WILL SURVIVE!
I WOULD ALSO LIKE TO THANK MY WIFE: ELI, AND MY CHILD: MAXINE DANGER!
OBEY THEM AS YOU WOULD ME!
RENO
...AND SPECIAL THANKS TO MY MOM, WHO IS WATCHING OUR CHILDREN, VICTOR AND ALEX—
SO THEY DON'T BLOW ANYTHING UP!
BOOM!
YAY!
WELL, ANYTHING IMPORTANT, ANYWAY.
THIS AWARD MEANS SO MUCH TO US—WE ARE SO HAPPY RIGHT NOW!
...AND THANK YOU TO ALL THE GIRL GENIUS READERS WHO VOTED FOR US!
BECAUSE WE HAVE NOW BEEN HONORED WITH THIS AWARD THREE TIMES IN A ROW—
WE WILL BE REMOVING OURSELVES FROM CONSIDERATION IN THIS CATEGORY FOR NEXT YEAR!
WHAT?! WHAT ARE YOU DOING?
MY MECHANICAL HUGO-NAUT IS NOWHERE NEAR COMPLETE!
TRAITOROUS FOOL!
I WARNED YOU!
YOUR PRECIOUS "CHROMATIC WHEEL" WILL FEEL MY WRATH!
URK!
WAIT! IT'S FOR THE GOOD OF THE CATEGORY!
IT'S REALLY NEW! WORLDCON STILL HAS TO VOTE ON WHETHER OR NOT THEY'LL EVEN KEEP IT!
WE WANT PEOPLE TO SEE IT'S A VIABLE AWARD!
WELL...
YOUR WORDS HAVE THE UNCHARACTERISTIC RING OF TRUTH.
...AND YOU CAN ALWAYS TURN IT BACK ON AGAIN LATER, RIGHT?
DON'T BE SO SURE ABOUT THAT, BRIGHT BOY.
WAIT A MINUTE...
MIND CONTROL ENGINE
OFF
ON
SNAK
WHY ARE WE NOT INVADING THE SURFACE WORLD RIGHT NOW?!

• THE STORY SO FAR •

Agatha Clay was an unlucky student at Transylvania Polygnostic University, until an accident revealed her hidden "spark:" a capacity for mad science beyond the reach of all but the most gifted. This alone would have been enough to bring her to the attention of Baron Wulfenbach, the powerful Spark who holds the fractious ruling houses of Europa under his thumb, but Agatha is *also* the last of the famous Heterodyne family–beloved folk heroes who disappeared many years ago. In addition, the Baron now has excellent reason to believe that Agatha is actually a malevolent entity known as "The Other," who almost destroyed Europa twenty years before. He isn't entirely wrong, either. While held prisoner in the town of Sturmhalten, the personality of the "Other," actually Agatha's long-missing mother, took over Agatha's body. Agatha has managed to regain control, but the "Other" is still there, currently held in check by a clever device.

After many adventures, Agatha has made her way across Europa to Mechanicsburg, the ancestral home of the Heterodyne family–and she's not the only one. The Baron is also in the town–as a patient in Mechanicsburg's famous hospital. The Baron has been positioning his forces to destroy Castle Heterodyne, but now his son Gilgamesh has gone inside, hoping that his presence will stall his father's plans. Along with Gil has come a group of friends, also hoping to aid Agatha. Inside, they have encountered Zola, a charismatic girl claiming to be the lost Heterodyne heir–part of a larger plan to take control of the Baron's empire–and Prince Tarvek of Sturmhalten–formerly involved with the same plot but now fleeing both captors and coconspirators. Also in the Castle are a number of prisoners there to make repairs, and Othar Tryggvassen: "Gentleman Adventurer"–a Hero sent by the Baron to "rescue" his son.

The Castle itself is a self-aware mechanical fortress which was badly damaged in the war with the "Other." Agatha had managed to make the Castle accept her as the true Heterodyne, but was then quickly forced to shut it down to keep its out-of-control systems from harming her friends.

Agatha has now arrived at the heart of the Castle, hoping to reset its systems using the last, dying fragment of its mind. Zola is close behind–bent on killing Agatha to cement her power, while most of Agatha's friends are far away, working to save the life of the mysterious construct who once guarded the children of Castle Wulfenbach.

CPH

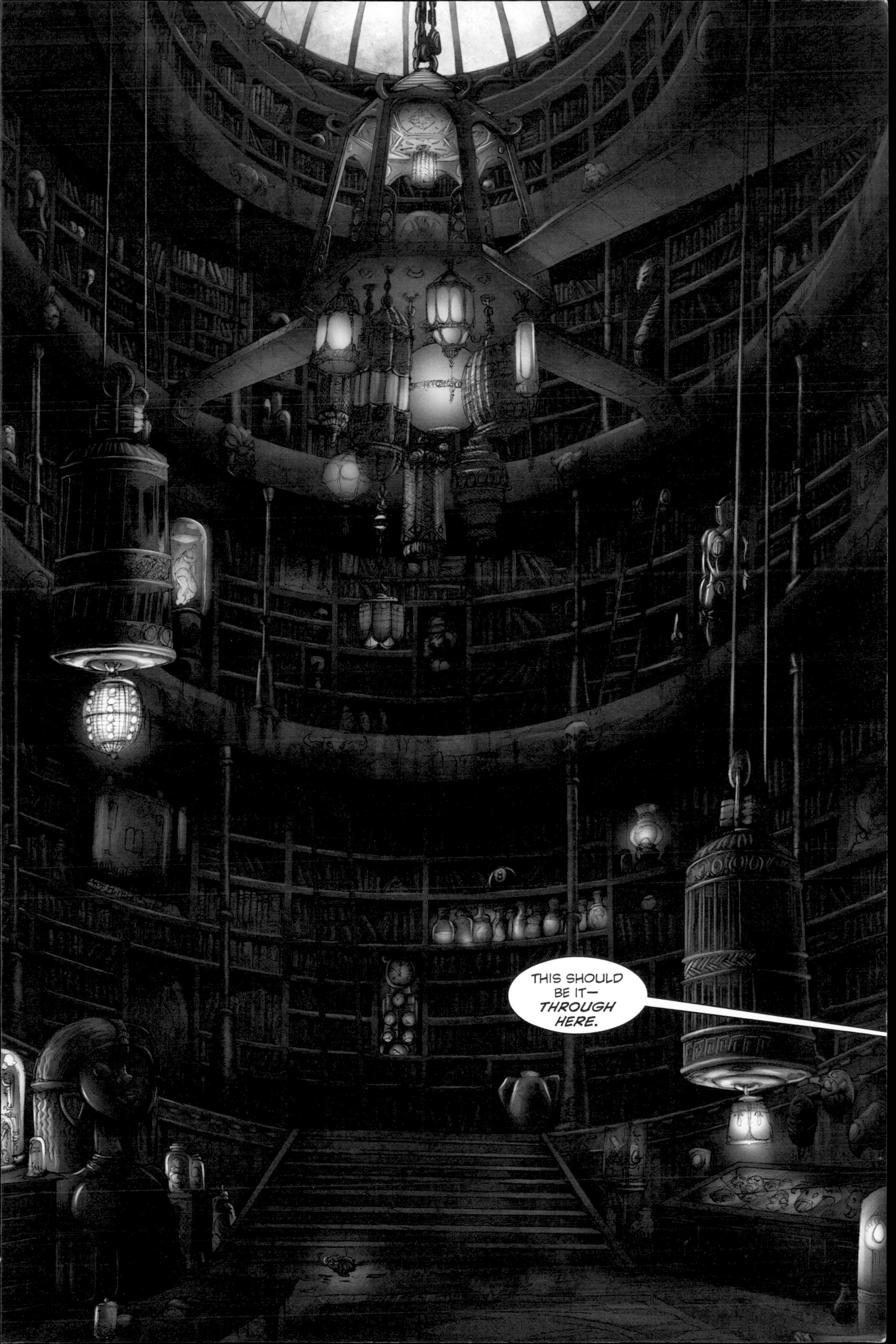
THIS SHOULD BE IT—*THROUGH HERE.*

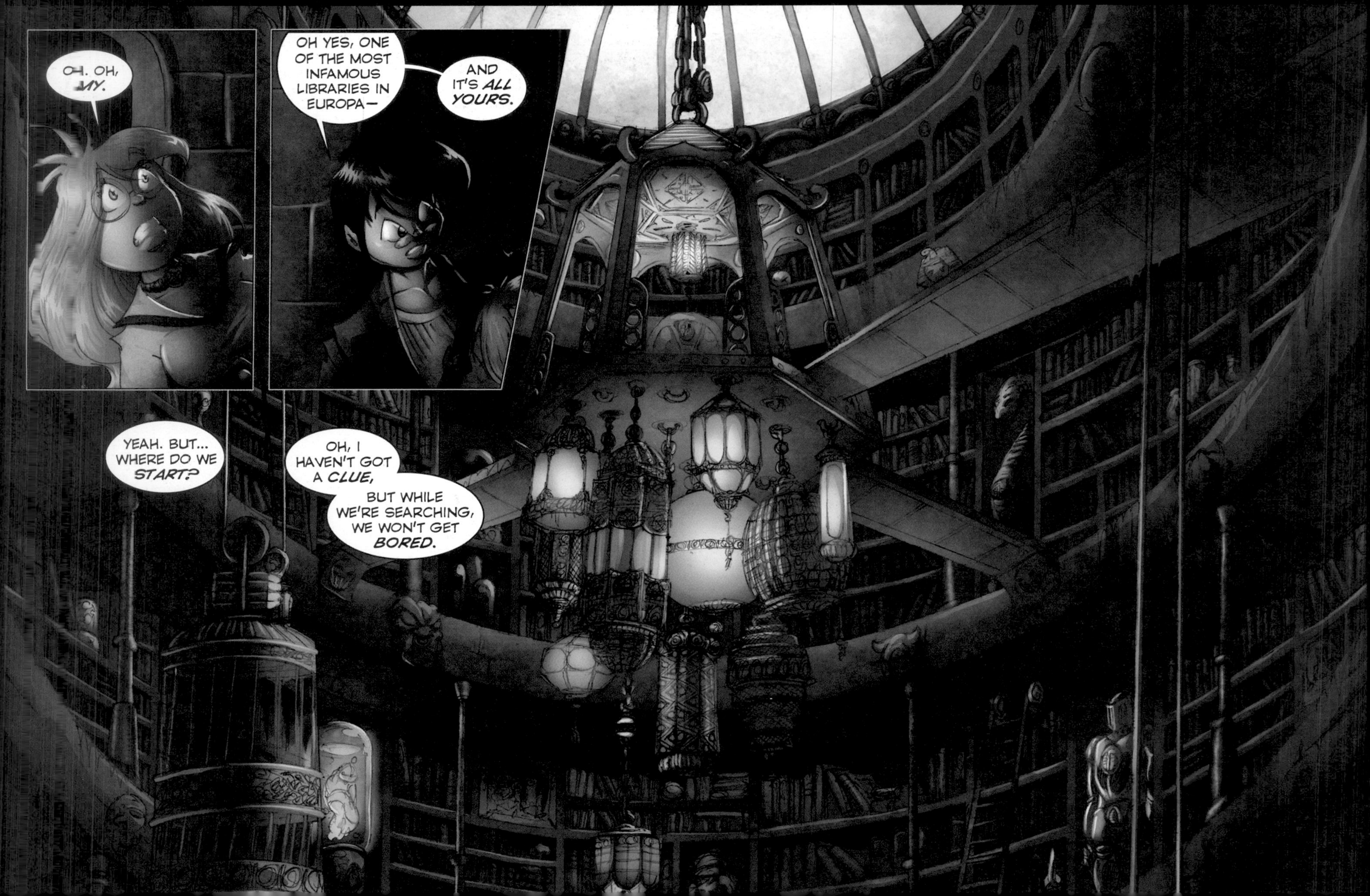
OH. OH, MY.
OH YES, ONE OF THE MOST INFAMOUS LIBRARIES IN EUROPA—
AND IT'S ALL YOURS.
YEAH. BUT... WHERE DO WE START?
OH, I HAVEN'T GOT A CLUE,
BUT WHILE WE'RE SEARCHING, WE WON'T GET BORED.

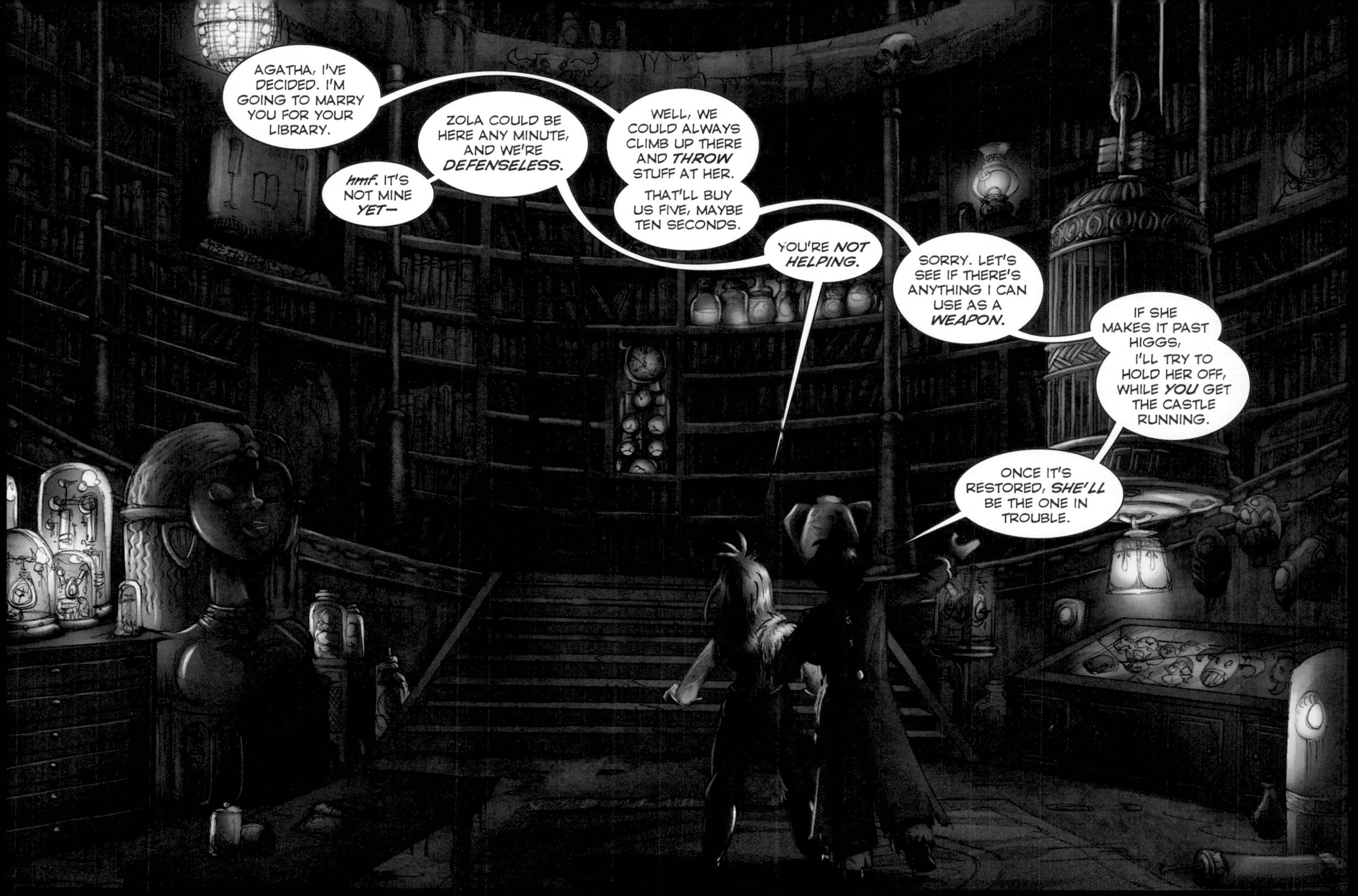
AGATHA, I'VE DECIDED. I'M GOING TO MARRY YOU FOR YOUR LIBRARY.
hmf. IT'S NOT MINE *YET—*
ZOLA COULD BE HERE ANY MINUTE, AND WE'RE *DEFENSELESS.*
WELL, WE COULD ALWAYS CLIMB UP THERE AND *THROW* STUFF AT HER.
THAT'LL BUY US FIVE, MAYBE TEN SECONDS.
YOU'RE *NOT HELPING.*
SORRY. LET'S SEE IF THERE'S ANYTHING I CAN USE AS A *WEAPON.*
IF SHE MAKES IT PAST HIGGS,
I'LL TRY TO HOLD HER OFF, WHILE *YOU* GET THE CASTLE RUNNING.
ONCE IT'S RESTORED, *SHE'LL* BE THE ONE IN TROUBLE.

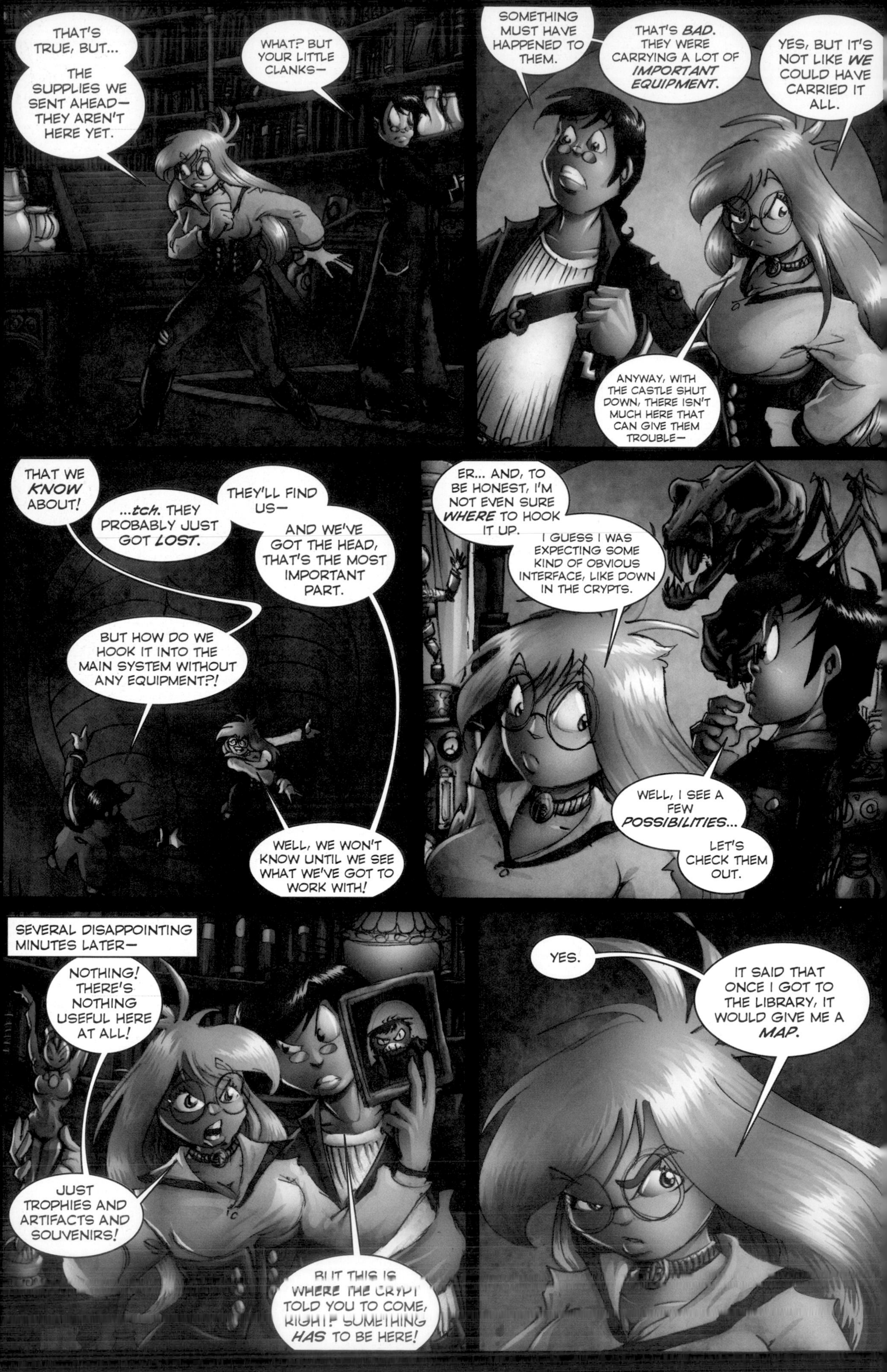
THAT'S TRUE, BUT...
THE SUPPLIES WE SENT AHEAD— THEY AREN'T HERE YET.
WHAT? BUT YOUR LITTLE CLANKS—
SOMETHING MUST HAVE HAPPENED TO THEM.
THAT'S BAD. THEY WERE CARRYING A LOT OF IMPORTANT EQUIPMENT.
YES, BUT IT'S NOT LIKE WE COULD HAVE CARRIED IT ALL.
ANYWAY, WITH THE CASTLE SHUT DOWN, THERE ISN'T MUCH HERE THAT CAN GIVE THEM TROUBLE—
THAT WE KNOW ABOUT!
...tch. THEY PROBABLY JUST GOT LOST.
THEY'LL FIND US—
AND WE'VE GOT THE HEAD, THAT'S THE MOST IMPORTANT PART.
BUT HOW DO WE HOOK IT INTO THE MAIN SYSTEM WITHOUT ANY EQUIPMENT?!
WELL, WE WON'T KNOW UNTIL WE SEE WHAT WE'VE GOT TO WORK WITH!
ER... AND, TO BE HONEST, I'M NOT EVEN SURE WHERE TO HOOK IT UP.
I GUESS I WAS EXPECTING SOME KIND OF OBVIOUS INTERFACE, LIKE DOWN IN THE CRYPTS.
WELL, I SEE A FEW POSSIBILITIES...
LET'S CHECK THEM OUT.
SEVERAL DISAPPOINTING MINUTES LATER—
NOTHING! THERE'S NOTHING USEFUL HERE AT ALL!
JUST TROPHIES AND ARTIFACTS AND SOUVENIRS!
BUT THIS IS WHERE THE CRYPT TOLD YOU TO COME, RIGHT? SOMETHING HAS TO BE HERE!
YES.
IT SAID THAT ONCE I GOT TO THE LIBRARY, IT WOULD GIVE ME A MAP.

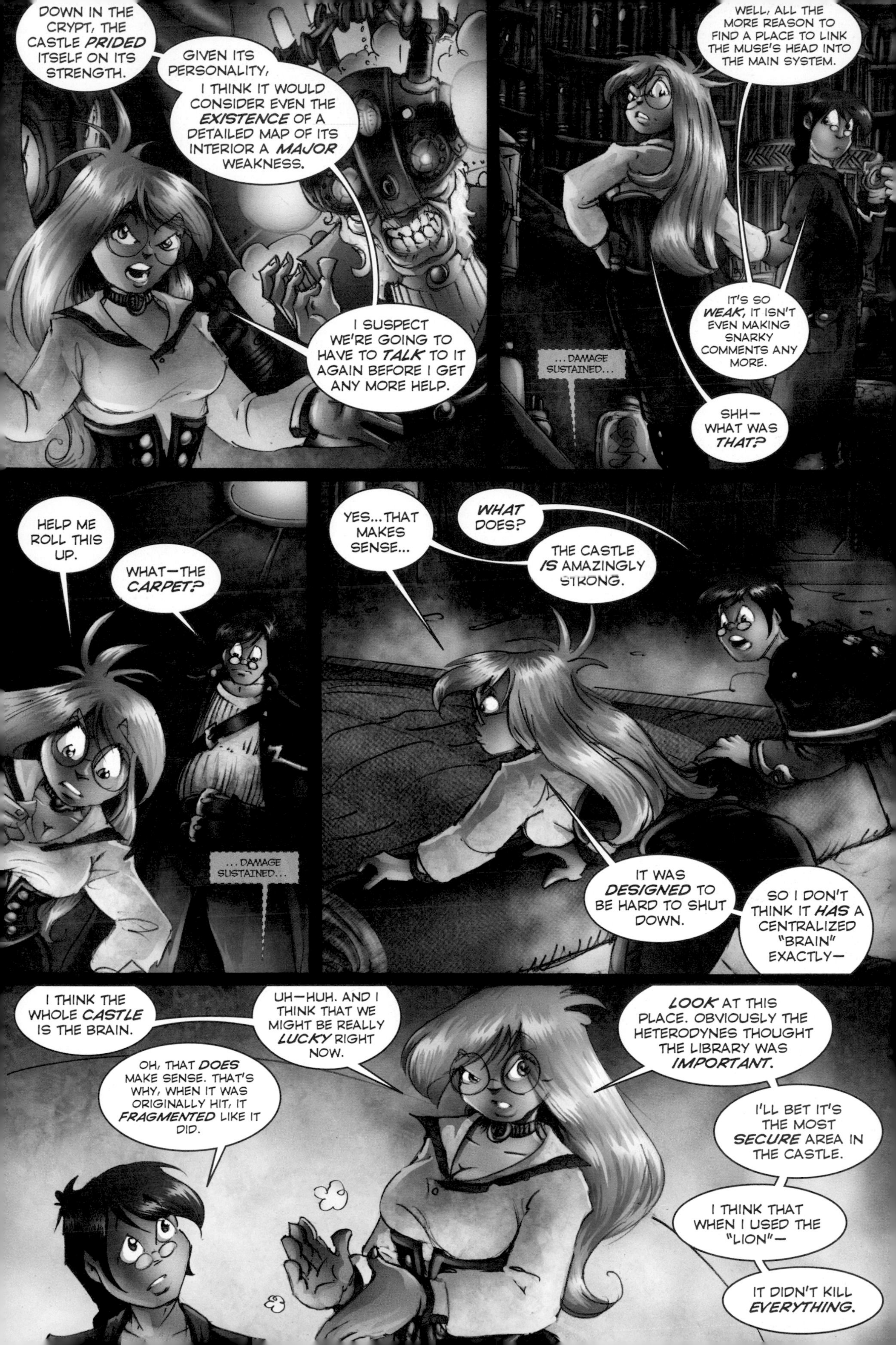
DOWN IN THE CRYPT, THE CASTLE PRIDED ITSELF ON ITS STRENGTH.
GIVEN ITS PERSONALITY, I THINK IT WOULD CONSIDER EVEN THE EXISTENCE OF A DETAILED MAP OF ITS INTERIOR A MAJOR WEAKNESS.
I SUSPECT WE'RE GOING TO HAVE TO TALK TO IT AGAIN BEFORE I GET ANY MORE HELP.
WELL, ALL THE MORE REASON TO FIND A PLACE TO LINK THE MUSE'S HEAD INTO THE MAIN SYSTEM.
IT'S SO WEAK, IT ISN'T EVEN MAKING SNARKY COMMENTS ANY MORE.
...DAMAGE SUSTAINED...
SHH— WHAT WAS THAT?
HELP ME ROLL THIS UP.
WHAT—THE CARPET?
...DAMAGE SUSTAINED...
YES...THAT MAKES SENSE...
WHAT DOES?
THE CASTLE IS AMAZINGLY STRONG.
IT WAS DESIGNED TO BE HARD TO SHUT DOWN.
SO I DON'T THINK IT HAS A CENTRALIZED "BRAIN" EXACTLY—
I THINK THE WHOLE CASTLE IS THE BRAIN.
OH, THAT DOES MAKE SENSE. THAT'S WHY, WHEN IT WAS ORIGINALLY HIT, IT FRAGMENTED LIKE IT DID.
UH—HUH. AND I THINK THAT WE MIGHT BE REALLY LUCKY RIGHT NOW.
LOOK AT THIS PLACE. OBVIOUSLY THE HETERODYNES THOUGHT THE LIBRARY WAS IMPORTANT.
I'LL BET IT'S THE MOST SECURE AREA IN THE CASTLE.
I THINK THAT WHEN I USED THE "LION"—
IT DIDN'T KILL EVERYTHING.

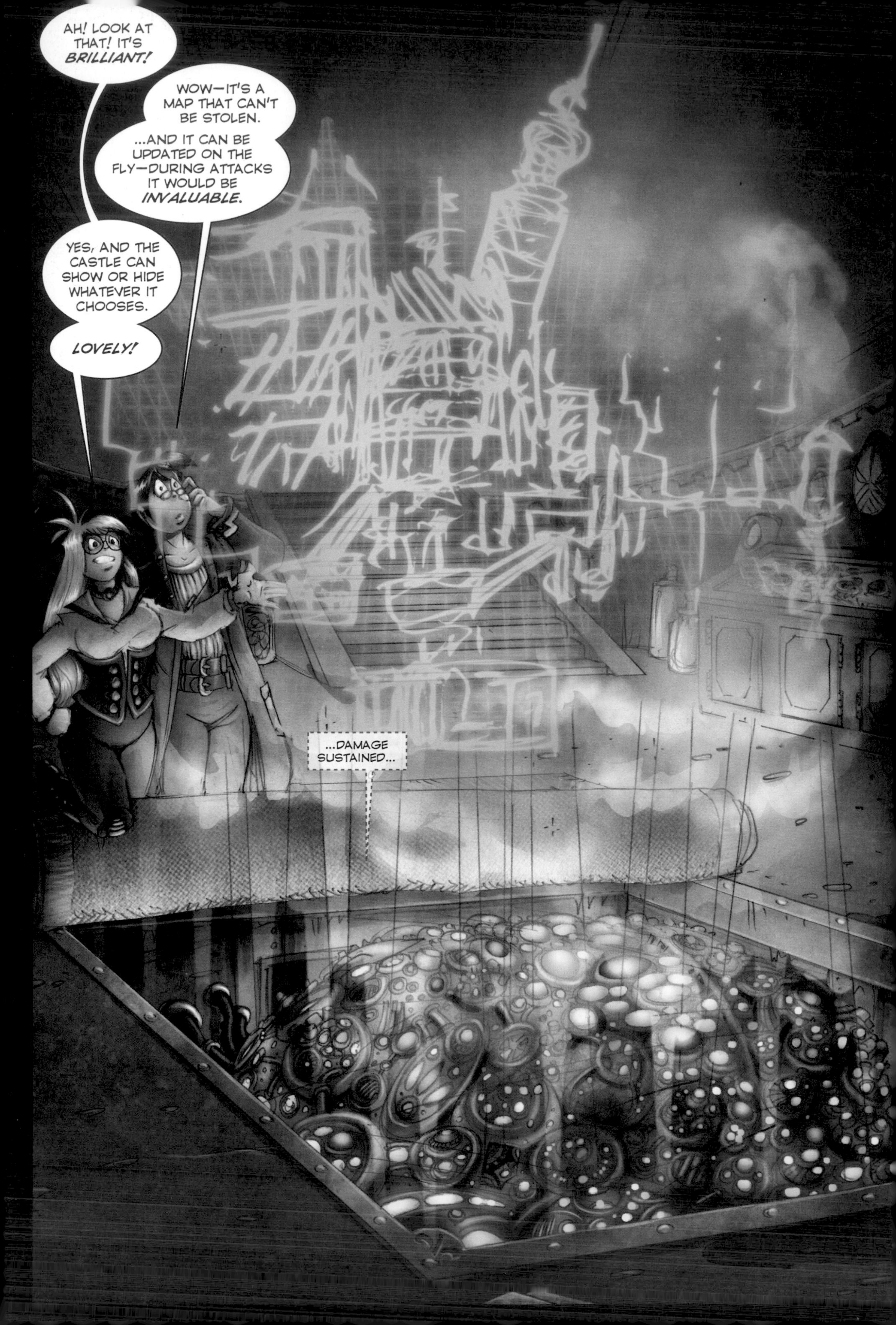
AH! LOOK AT THAT! IT'S *BRILLIANT!*
WOW—IT'S A MAP THAT CAN'T BE STOLEN.
...AND IT CAN BE UPDATED ON THE FLY—DURING ATTACKS IT WOULD BE *INVALUABLE*.
YES, AND THE CASTLE CAN SHOW OR HIDE WHATEVER IT CHOOSES.
LOVELY!
...DAMAGE SUSTAINED...

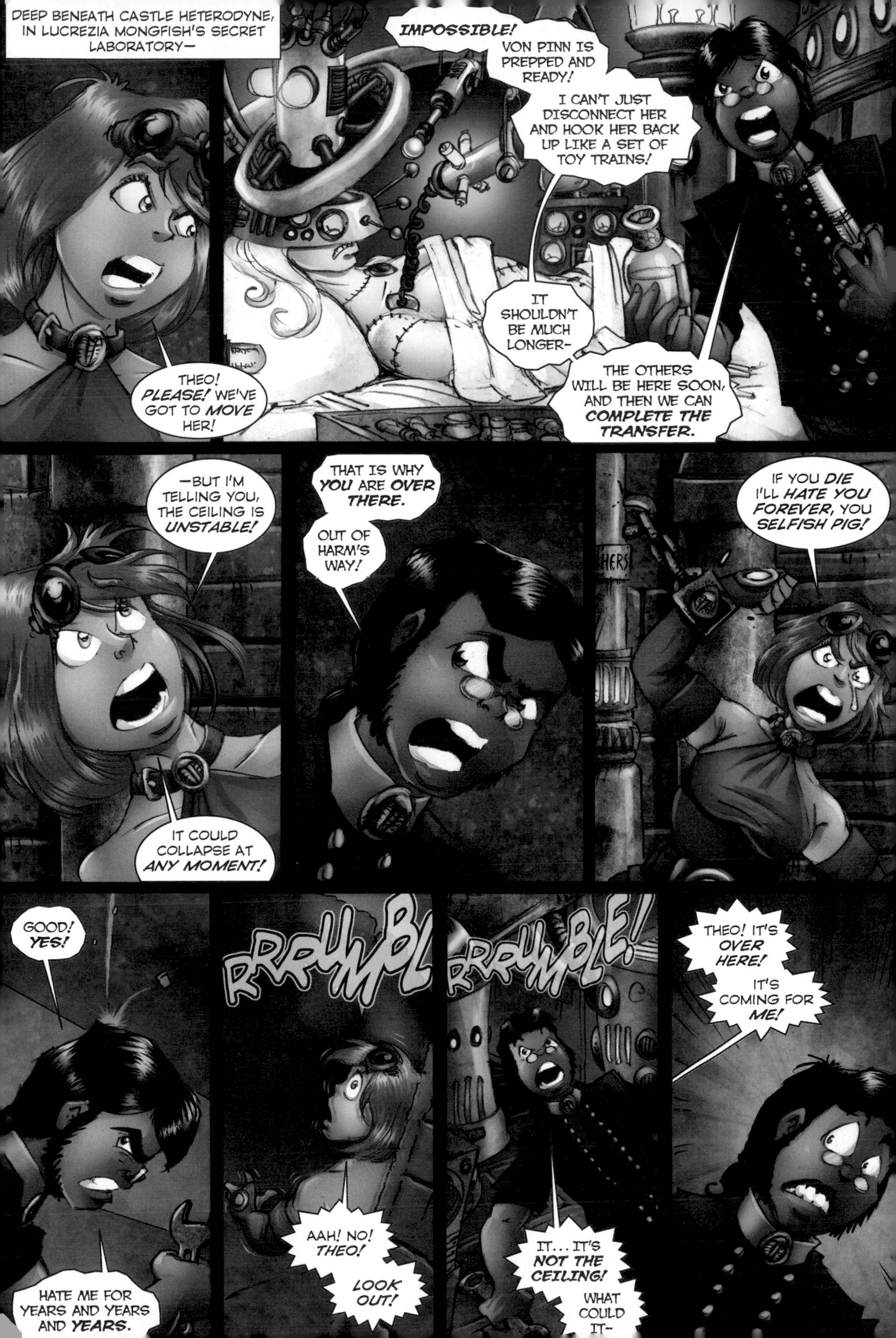
DEEP BENEATH CASTLE HETERODYNE, IN LUCREZIA MONGFISH'S SECRET LABORATORY—
THEO! PLEASE! WE'VE GOT TO MOVE HER!
IMPOSSIBLE!
VON PINN IS PREPPED AND READY!
I CAN'T JUST DISCONNECT HER AND HOOK HER BACK UP LIKE A SET OF TOY TRAINS!
IT SHOULDN'T BE MUCH LONGER-
THE OTHERS WILL BE HERE SOON, AND THEN WE CAN COMPLETE THE TRANSFER.
—BUT I'M TELLING YOU, THE CEILING IS UNSTABLE!
IT COULD COLLAPSE AT ANY MOMENT!
THAT IS WHY YOU ARE OVER THERE.
OUT OF HARM'S WAY!
IF YOU DIE I'LL HATE YOU FOREVER, YOU SELFISH PIG!
GOOD! YES!
HATE ME FOR YEARS AND YEARS AND YEARS.
RRRUMBL RRRUMBLE!
AAH! NO! THEO!
LOOK OUT!
IT... IT'S NOT THE CEILING!
WHAT COULD IT-
THEO! IT'S OVER HERE!
IT'S COMING FOR ME!

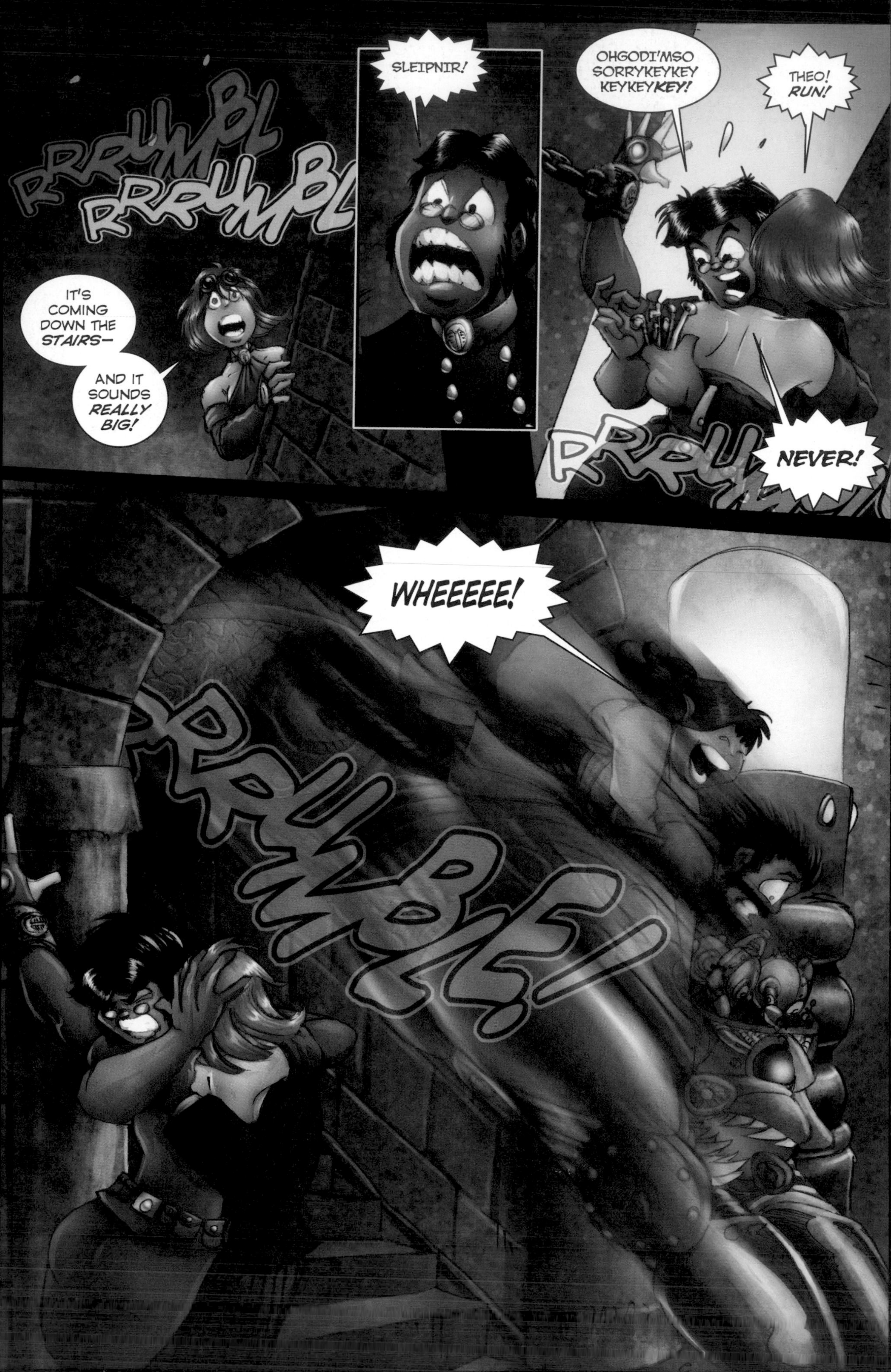
RRRUMBL RRRUMBL
IT'S COMING DOWN THE STAIRS—
AND IT SOUNDS REALLY BIG!
SLEIPNIR!
OHGODI'MSO SORRYKEYKEY KEYKEYKEY!
THEO! RUN!
NEVER!
RRRU
WHEEEEE!
RRRUMBLE!

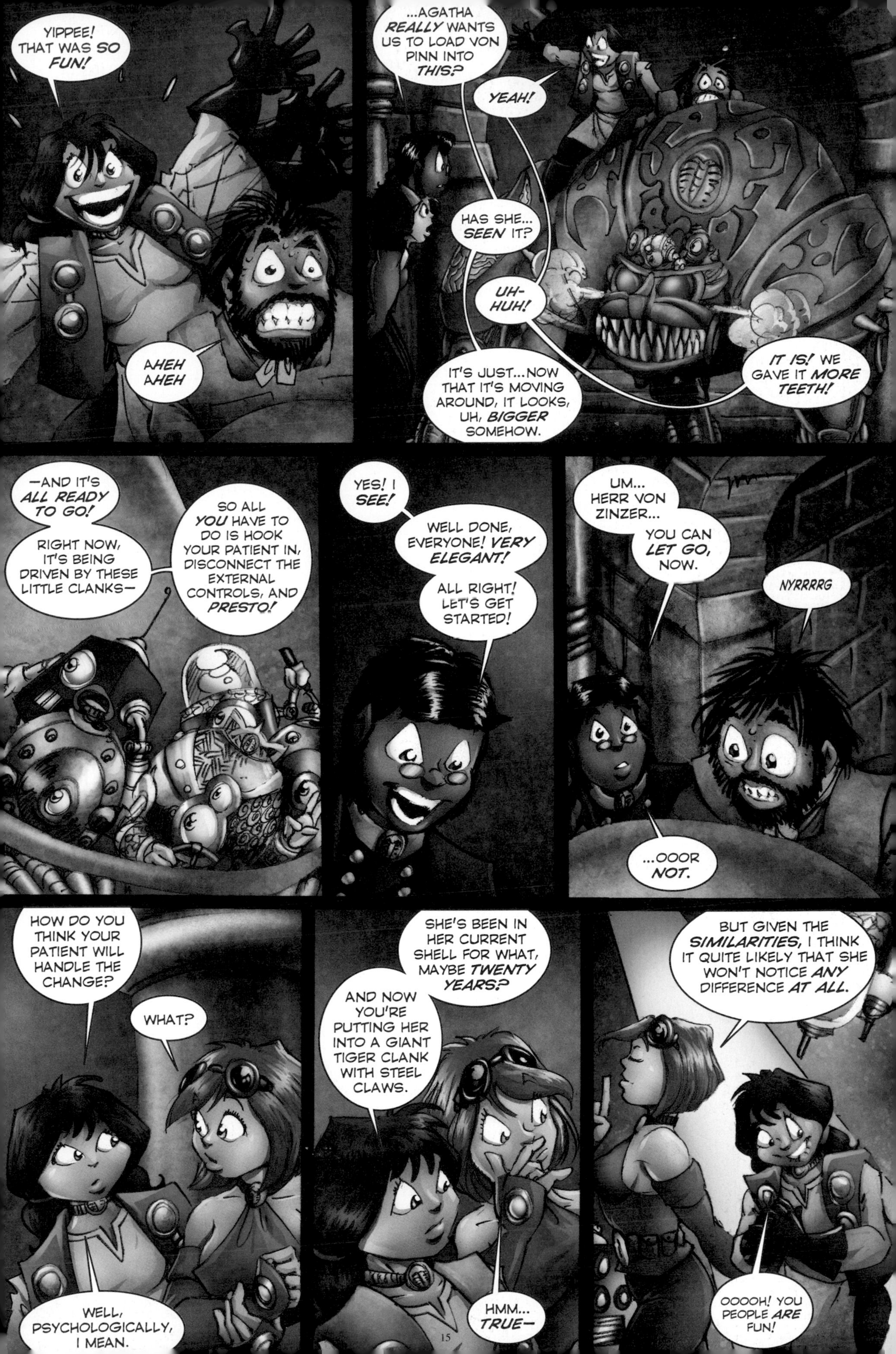
YIPPEE! THAT WAS SO FUN!
AHEH AHEH
...AGATHA REALLY WANTS US TO LOAD VON PINN INTO THIS?
YEAH!
HAS SHE... SEEN IT?
UH-HUH!
IT'S JUST...NOW THAT IT'S MOVING AROUND, IT LOOKS, UH, BIGGER SOMEHOW.
IT IS! WE GAVE IT MORE TEETH!
—AND IT'S ALL READY TO GO!
RIGHT NOW, IT'S BEING DRIVEN BY THESE LITTLE CLANKS—
SO ALL YOU HAVE TO DO IS HOOK YOUR PATIENT IN, DISCONNECT THE EXTERNAL CONTROLS, AND PRESTO!
YES! I SEE!
WELL DONE, EVERYONE! VERY ELEGANT!
ALL RIGHT! LET'S GET STARTED!
UM... HERR VON ZINZER...
YOU CAN LET GO, NOW.
NYRRRRG
...OOOR NOT.
HOW DO YOU THINK YOUR PATIENT WILL HANDLE THE CHANGE?
WHAT?
WELL, PSYCHOLOGICALLY, I MEAN.
SHE'S BEEN IN HER CURRENT SHELL FOR WHAT, MAYBE TWENTY YEARS?
AND NOW YOU'RE PUTTING HER INTO A GIANT TIGER CLANK WITH STEEL CLAWS.
HMM... TRUE—
BUT GIVEN THE SIMILARITIES, I THINK IT QUITE LIKELY THAT SHE WON'T NOTICE ANY DIFFERENCE AT ALL.
OOOOH! YOU PEOPLE ARE FUN!

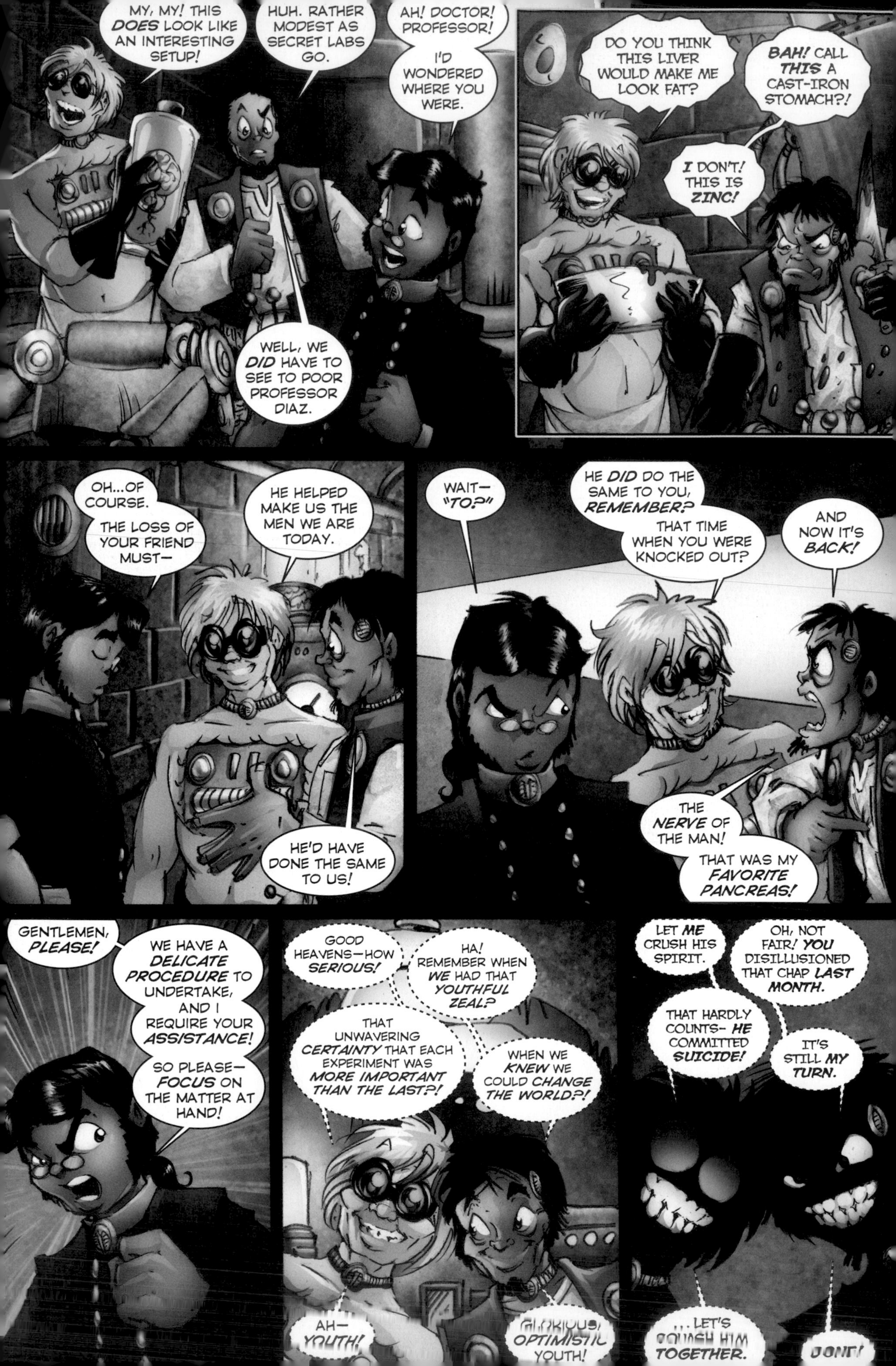

MY, MY! THIS *DOES* LOOK LIKE AN INTERESTING SETUP!
HUH. RATHER MODEST AS SECRET LABS GO.
AH! DOCTOR! PROFESSOR!
I'D WONDERED WHERE YOU WERE.
WELL, WE *DID* HAVE TO SEE TO POOR PROFESSOR DIAZ.
DO YOU THINK THIS LIVER WOULD MAKE ME LOOK FAT?
BAH! CALL *THIS* A CAST-IRON STOMACH?!
I DON'T! THIS IS *ZINC!*
OH...OF COURSE.
THE LOSS OF YOUR FRIEND MUST—
HE HELPED MAKE US THE MEN WE ARE TODAY.
HE'D HAVE DONE THE SAME TO US!
WAIT— *"TO?"*
HE *DID* DO THE SAME TO YOU, *REMEMBER?*
THAT TIME WHEN YOU WERE KNOCKED OUT?
AND NOW IT'S *BACK!*
THE *NERVE* OF THE MAN!
THAT WAS MY *FAVORITE PANCREAS!*
GENTLEMEN, *PLEASE!*
WE HAVE A *DELICATE PROCEDURE* TO UNDERTAKE, AND I REQUIRE YOUR *ASSISTANCE!*
SO PLEASE— *FOCUS* ON THE MATTER AT HAND!
GOOD HEAVENS—HOW *SERIOUS!*
HA! REMEMBER WHEN *WE* HAD THAT *YOUTHFUL ZEAL?*
THAT UNWAVERING *CERTAINTY* THAT EACH EXPERIMENT WAS *MORE IMPORTANT THAN THE LAST?!*
WHEN WE *KNEW* WE COULD *CHANGE THE WORLD?!*
AH— *YOUTH!*
OPTIMISTIC YOUTH!
LET *ME* CRUSH HIS SPIRIT.
OH, NOT FAIR! *YOU* DISILLUSIONED THAT CHAP *LAST MONTH.*
THAT HARDLY COUNTS- *HE* COMMITTED *SUICIDE!*
IT'S STILL *MY TURN.*
... LET'S SQUASH HIM *TOGETHER.*

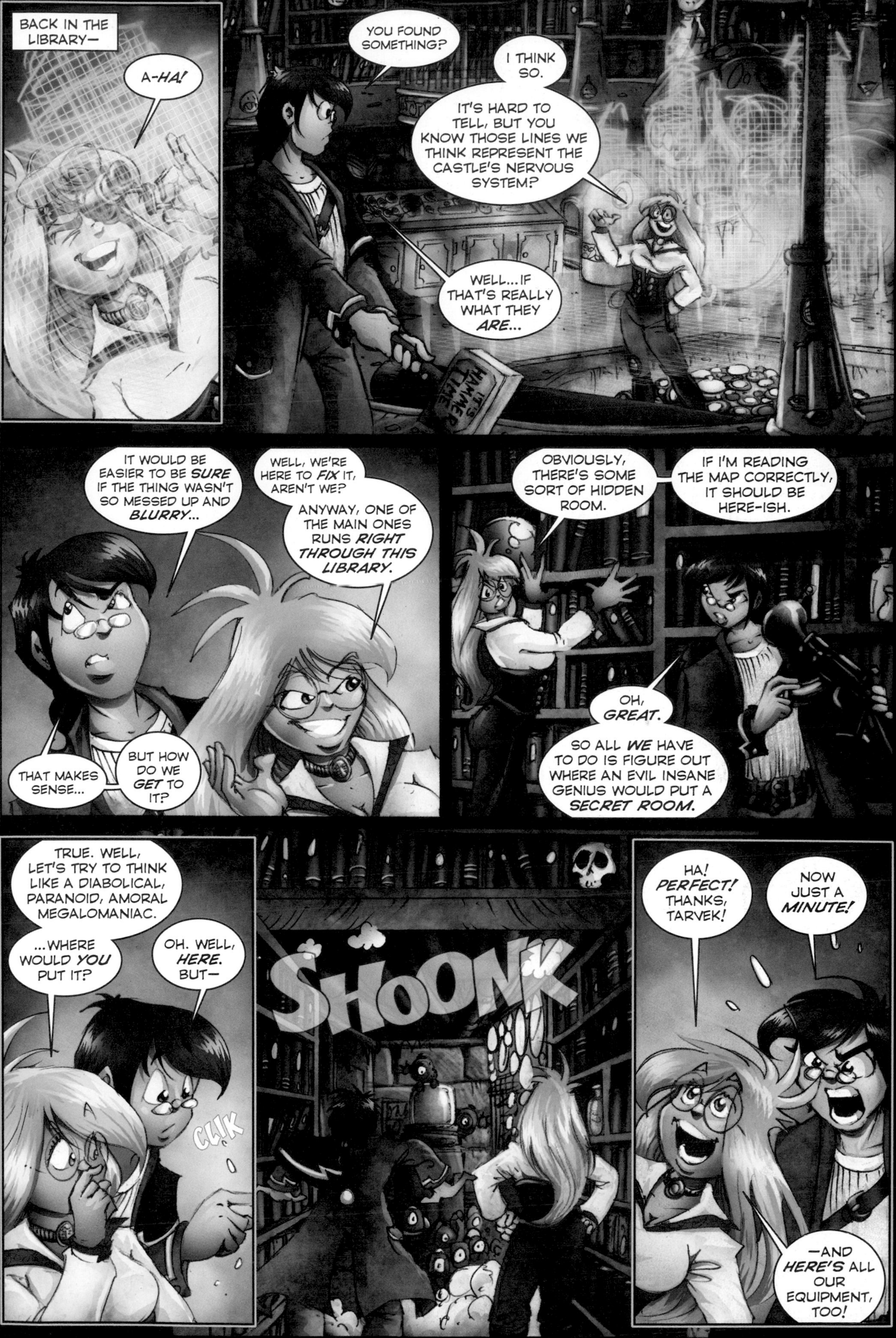
BACK IN THE LIBRARY—
A-*HA!*
YOU FOUND SOMETHING?
I THINK SO.
IT'S HARD TO TELL, BUT YOU KNOW THOSE LINES WE THINK REPRESENT THE CASTLE'S NERVOUS SYSTEM?
WELL... IF THAT'S REALLY WHAT THEY *ARE*...
IT'S HAMMER TIME
IT WOULD BE EASIER TO BE *SURE* IF THE THING WASN'T SO MESSED UP AND *BLURRY*...
WELL, WE'RE HERE TO *FIX* IT, AREN'T WE?
ANYWAY, ONE OF THE MAIN ONES RUNS *RIGHT THROUGH THIS LIBRARY.*
THAT MAKES SENSE...
BUT HOW DO WE *GET* TO IT?
OBVIOUSLY, THERE'S SOME SORT OF HIDDEN ROOM.
IF I'M READING THE MAP CORRECTLY, IT SHOULD BE HERE-ISH.
OH, *GREAT.*
SO ALL *WE* HAVE TO DO IS FIGURE OUT WHERE AN EVIL INSANE GENIUS WOULD PUT A *SECRET ROOM.*
TRUE. WELL, LET'S TRY TO THINK LIKE A DIABOLICAL, PARANOID, AMORAL MEGALOMANIAC.
...WHERE WOULD *YOU* PUT IT?
OH. WELL, *HERE.* BUT—
CLIK
SHOONK
HA! *PERFECT!* THANKS, TARVEK!
NOW JUST A *MINUTE!*
—AND *HERE'S* ALL OUR EQUIPMENT, TOO!

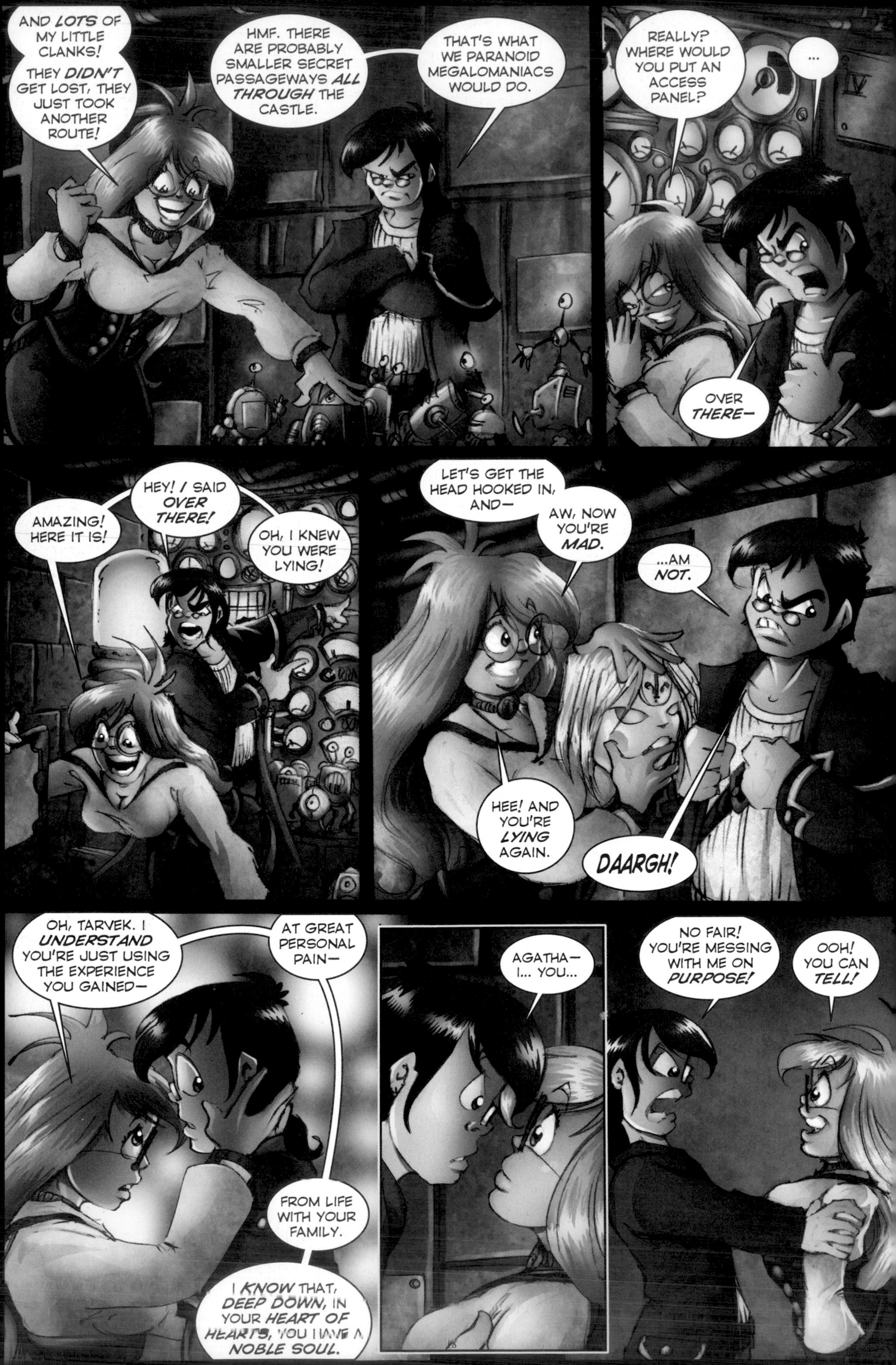

AND LOTS OF MY LITTLE CLANKS! THEY DIDN'T GET LOST, THEY JUST TOOK ANOTHER ROUTE!
HMF. THERE ARE PROBABLY SMALLER SECRET PASSAGEWAYS ALL THROUGH THE CASTLE.
THAT'S WHAT WE PARANOID MEGALOMANIACS WOULD DO.
REALLY? WHERE WOULD YOU PUT AN ACCESS PANEL?
...
OVER THERE—
AMAZING! HERE IT IS!
HEY! I SAID OVER THERE!
OH, I KNEW YOU WERE LYING!
LET'S GET THE HEAD HOOKED IN, AND—
AW, NOW YOU'RE MAD.
...AM NOT.
HEE! AND YOU'RE LYING AGAIN.
DAARGH!
OH, TARVEK. I UNDERSTAND YOU'RE JUST USING THE EXPERIENCE YOU GAINED—
AT GREAT PERSONAL PAIN—
FROM LIFE WITH YOUR FAMILY.
I KNOW THAT, DEEP DOWN, IN YOUR HEART OF HEARTS, YOU HAVE A NOBLE SOUL.
AGATHA— I... YOU...
NO FAIR! YOU'RE MESSING WITH ME ON PURPOSE!
OOH! YOU CAN TELL!

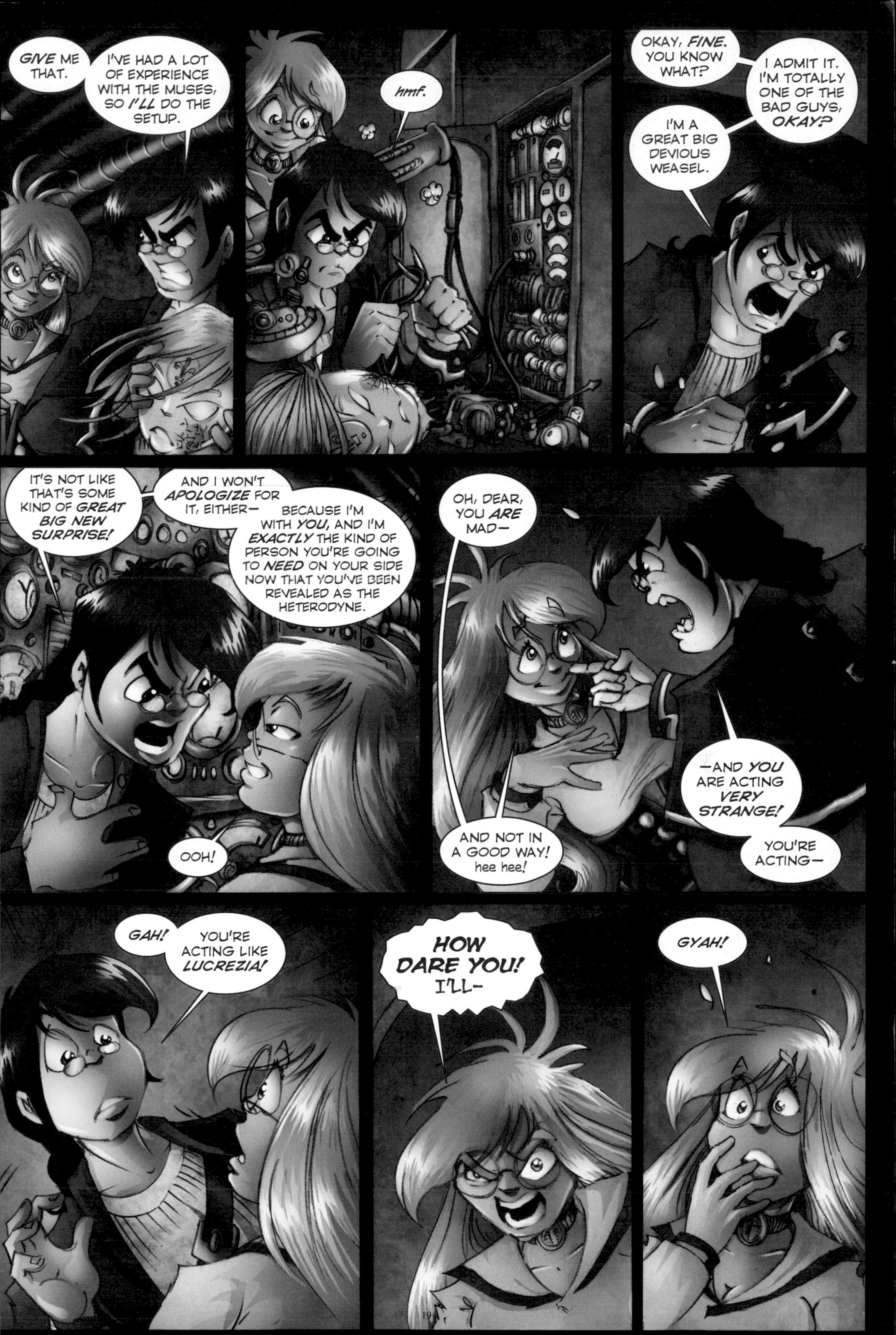
GIVE ME THAT.
I'VE HAD A LOT OF EXPERIENCE WITH THE MUSES, SO I'LL DO THE SETUP.
hmf.
OKAY, FINE. YOU KNOW WHAT?
I ADMIT IT. I'M TOTALLY ONE OF THE BAD GUYS, OKAY?
I'M A GREAT BIG DEVIOUS WEASEL.
IT'S NOT LIKE THAT'S SOME KIND OF GREAT BIG NEW SURPRISE!
AND I WON'T APOLOGIZE FOR IT, EITHER—
BECAUSE I'M WITH YOU, AND I'M EXACTLY THE KIND OF PERSON YOU'RE GOING TO NEED ON YOUR SIDE NOW THAT YOU'VE BEEN REVEALED AS THE HETERODYNE.
OOH!
OH, DEAR, YOU ARE MAD—
AND NOT IN A GOOD WAY! hee hee!
—AND YOU ARE ACTING VERY STRANGE!
YOU'RE ACTING—
GAH!
YOU'RE ACTING LIKE LUCREZIA!
HOW DARE YOU! I'LL-
GYAH!

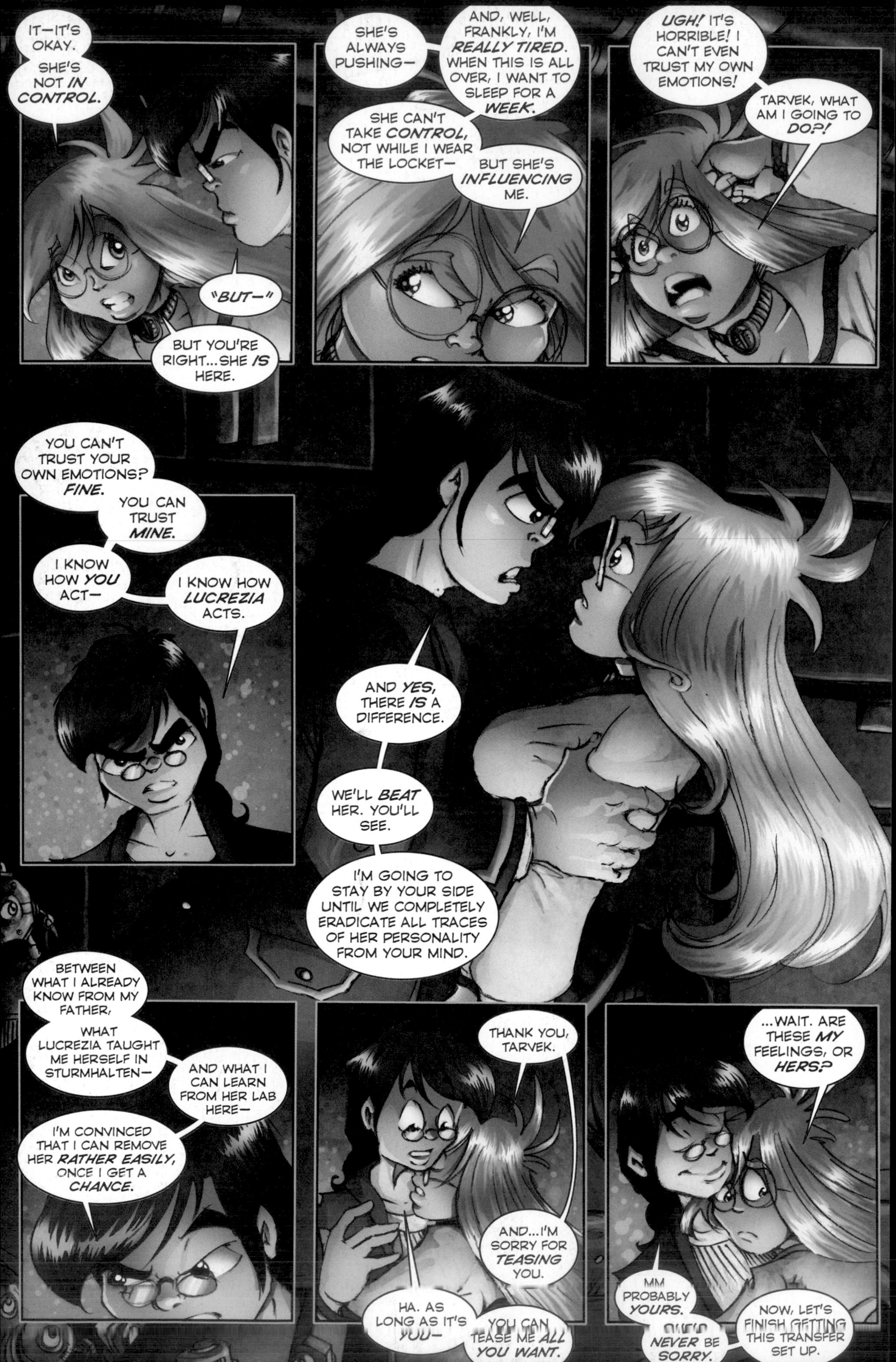

IT—IT'S OKAY.
SHE'S NOT IN CONTROL.
"BUT—"
BUT YOU'RE RIGHT...SHE IS HERE.
SHE'S ALWAYS PUSHING—
AND, WELL, FRANKLY, I'M REALLY TIRED. WHEN THIS IS ALL OVER, I WANT TO SLEEP FOR A WEEK.
SHE CAN'T TAKE CONTROL, NOT WHILE I WEAR THE LOCKET—
BUT SHE'S INFLUENCING ME.
UGH! IT'S HORRIBLE! I CAN'T EVEN TRUST MY OWN EMOTIONS!
TARVEK, WHAT AM I GOING TO DO?!
YOU CAN'T TRUST YOUR OWN EMOTIONS? FINE.
YOU CAN TRUST MINE.
I KNOW HOW YOU ACT—
I KNOW HOW LUCREZIA ACTS.
AND YES, THERE IS A DIFFERENCE.
WE'LL BEAT HER. YOU'LL SEE.
I'M GOING TO STAY BY YOUR SIDE UNTIL WE COMPLETELY ERADICATE ALL TRACES OF HER PERSONALITY FROM YOUR MIND.
BETWEEN WHAT I ALREADY KNOW FROM MY FATHER,
WHAT LUCREZIA TAUGHT ME HERSELF IN STURMHALTEN—
AND WHAT I CAN LEARN FROM HER LAB HERE—
I'M CONVINCED THAT I CAN REMOVE HER RATHER EASILY, ONCE I GET A CHANCE.
THANK YOU, TARVEK.
AND...I'M SORRY FOR TEASING YOU.
HA. AS LONG AS IT'S YOU—
YOU CAN TEASE ME ALL YOU WANT.
...WAIT. ARE THESE MY FEELINGS, OR HERS?
MM PROBABLY YOURS.
NEVER BE SORRY.
NOW, LET'S FINISH GETTING THIS TRANSFER SET UP.

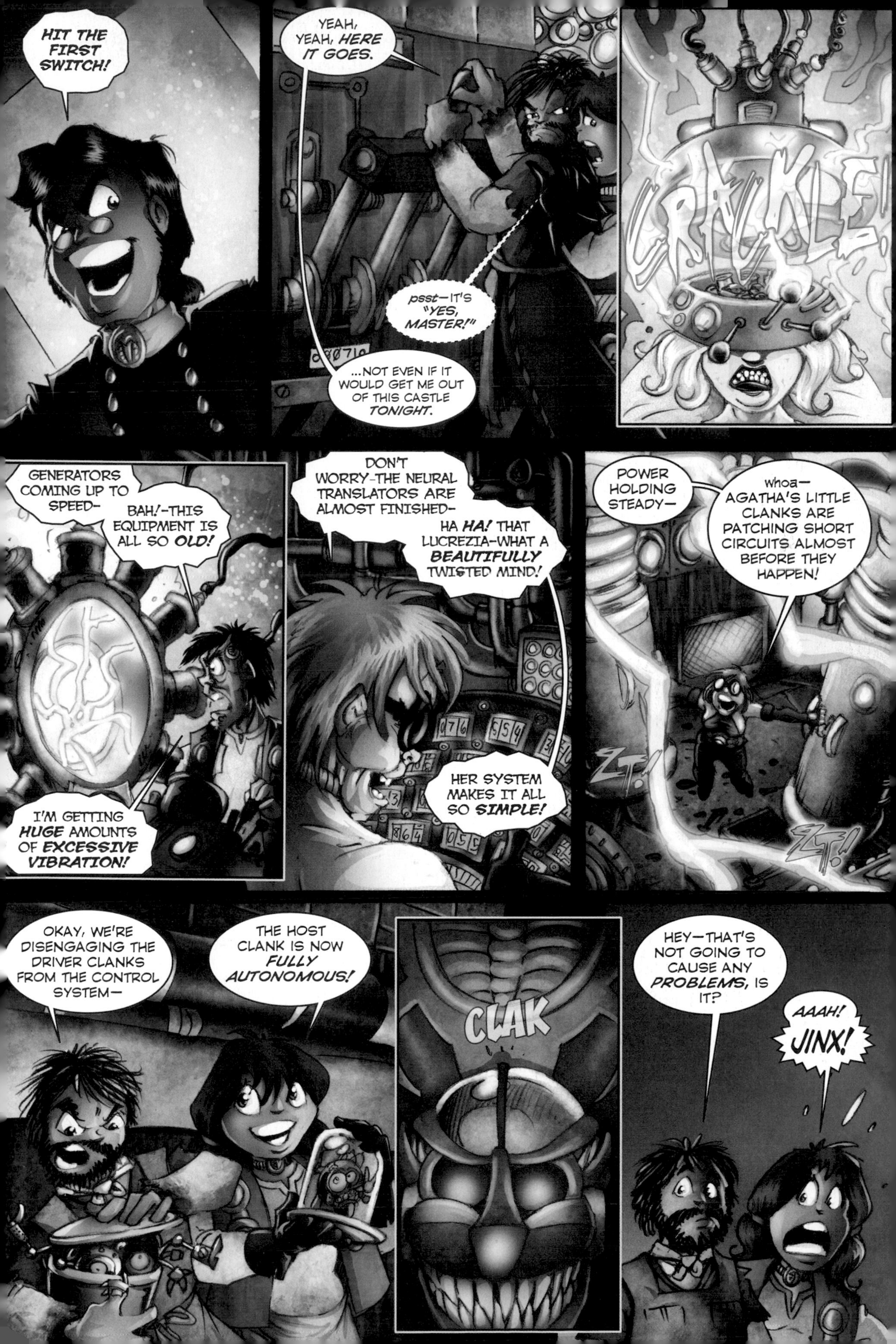
HIT THE FIRST SWITCH!
YEAH, YEAH, HERE IT GOES.
psst—IT'S "YES, MASTER!"
...NOT EVEN IF IT WOULD GET ME OUT OF THIS CASTLE TONIGHT.
CRACKLE!
GENERATORS COMING UP TO SPEED—
BAH!—THIS EQUIPMENT IS ALL SO OLD!
I'M GETTING HUGE AMOUNTS OF EXCESSIVE VIBRATION!
DON'T WORRY—THE NEURAL TRANSLATORS ARE ALMOST FINISHED—
HA HA! THAT LUCREZIA—WHAT A BEAUTIFULLY TWISTED MIND!
HER SYSTEM MAKES IT ALL SO SIMPLE!
POWER HOLDING STEADY—
whoa—AGATHA'S LITTLE CLANKS ARE PATCHING SHORT CIRCUITS ALMOST BEFORE THEY HAPPEN!
ZZT!
ZZT!
OKAY, WE'RE DISENGAGING THE DRIVER CLANKS FROM THE CONTROL SYSTEM—
THE HOST CLANK IS NOW FULLY AUTONOMOUS!
CLAK
HEY—THAT'S NOT GOING TO CAUSE ANY PROBLEMS, IS IT?
AAAH! JINX!

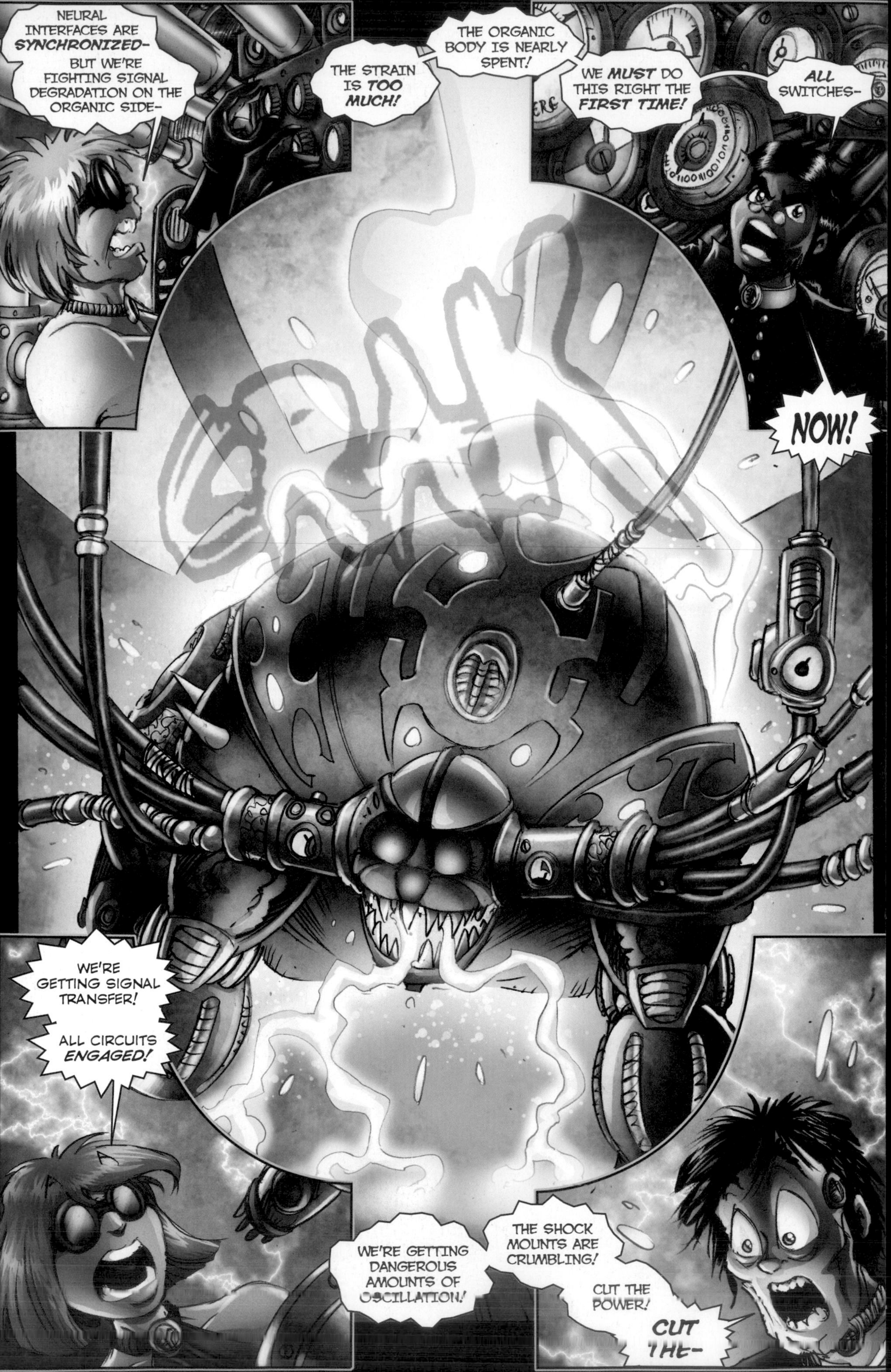
NEURAL INTERFACES ARE SYNCHRONIZED-
BUT WE'RE FIGHTING SIGNAL DEGRADATION ON THE ORGANIC SIDE-
THE STRAIN IS TOO MUCH!
THE ORGANIC BODY IS NEARLY SPENT!
WE MUST DO THIS RIGHT THE FIRST TIME!
ALL SWITCHES-
NOW!
WE'RE GETTING SIGNAL TRANSFER!
ALL CIRCUITS ENGAGED!
WE'RE GETTING DANGEROUS AMOUNTS OF OSCILLATION!
THE SHOCK MOUNTS ARE CRUMBLING!
CUT THE POWER!
CUT THE-

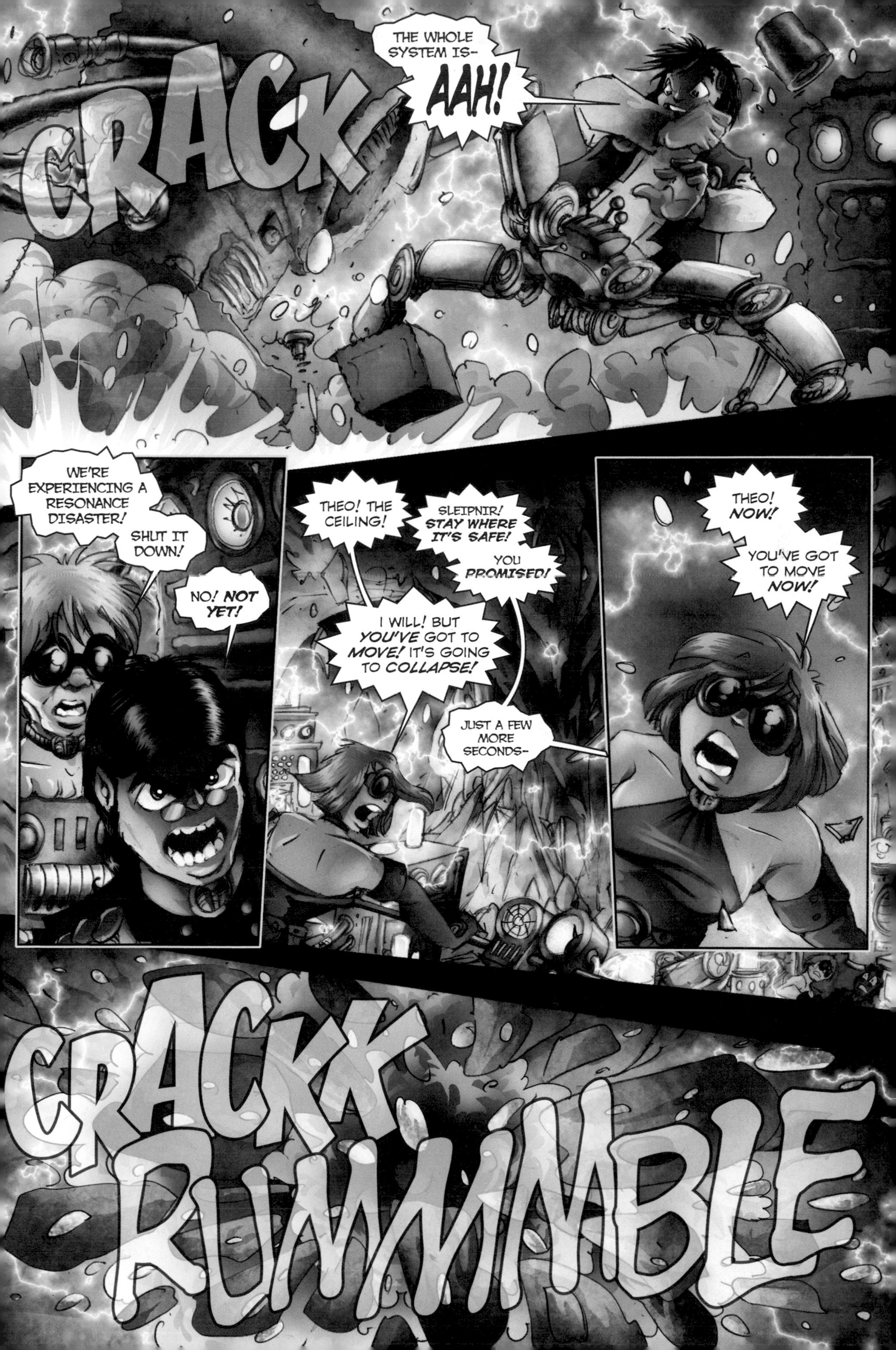
CRACK
THE WHOLE SYSTEM IS-
AAH!
WE'RE EXPERIENCING A RESONANCE DISASTER!
SHUT IT DOWN!
NO! NOT YET!
THEO! THE CEILING!
SLEIPNIR! STAY WHERE IT'S SAFE!
YOU PROMISED!
I WILL! BUT YOU'VE GOT TO MOVE! IT'S GOING TO COLLAPSE!
JUST A FEW MORE SECONDS-
THEO! NOW!
YOU'VE GOT TO MOVE NOW!
CRACKK
RUMMMBLE

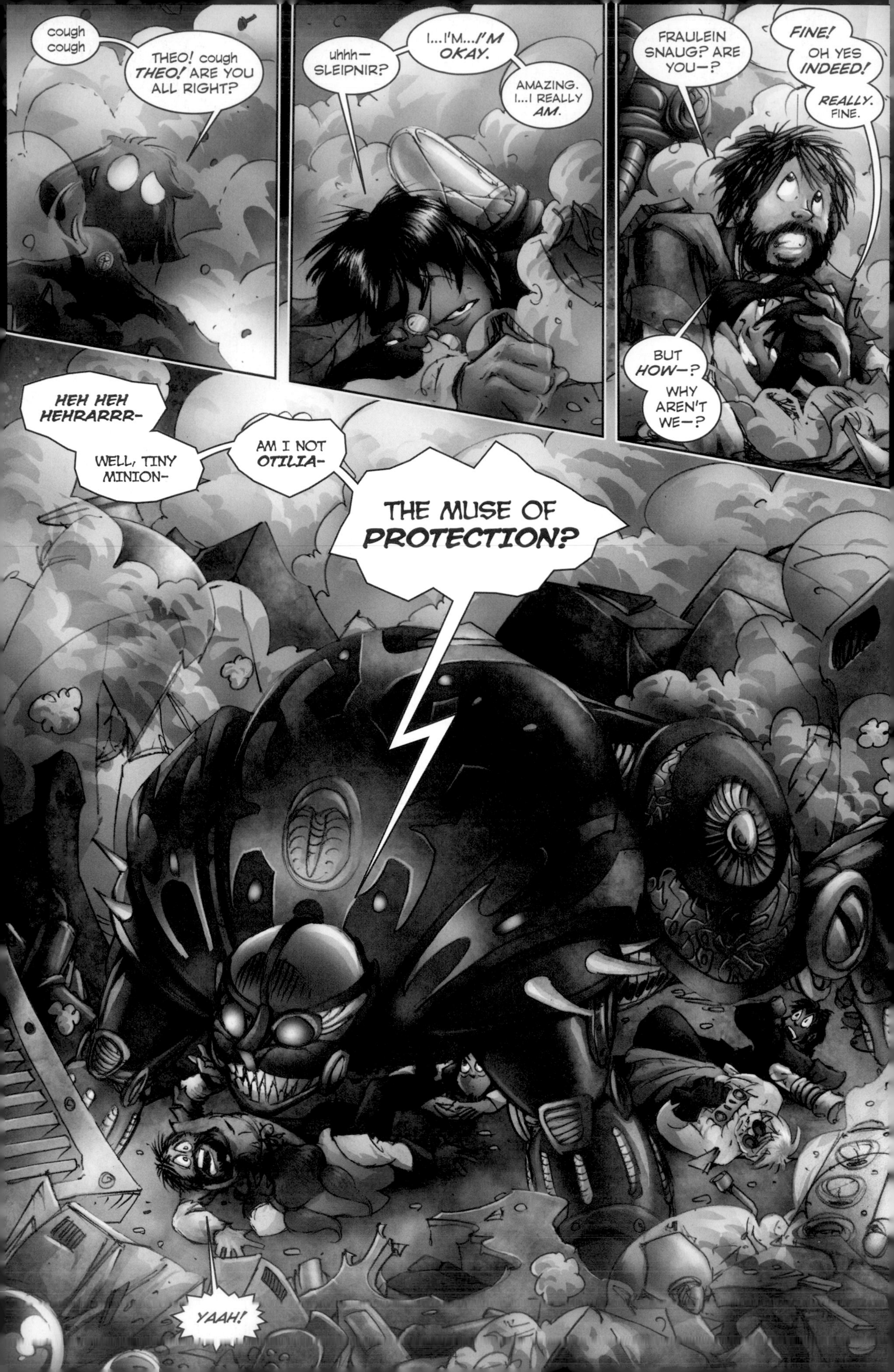
cough cough
THEO! cough THEO! ARE YOU ALL RIGHT?
uhhh— SLEIPNIR?
I...I'M...I'M OKAY.
AMAZING. I...I REALLY AM.
FRAULEIN SNAUG? ARE YOU—?
FINE! OH YES INDEED!
REALLY. FINE.
BUT HOW—? WHY AREN'T WE—?
HEH HEH HEHRARRR-
WELL, TINY MINION-
AM I NOT OTILIA-
THE MUSE OF PROTECTION?
YAAH!

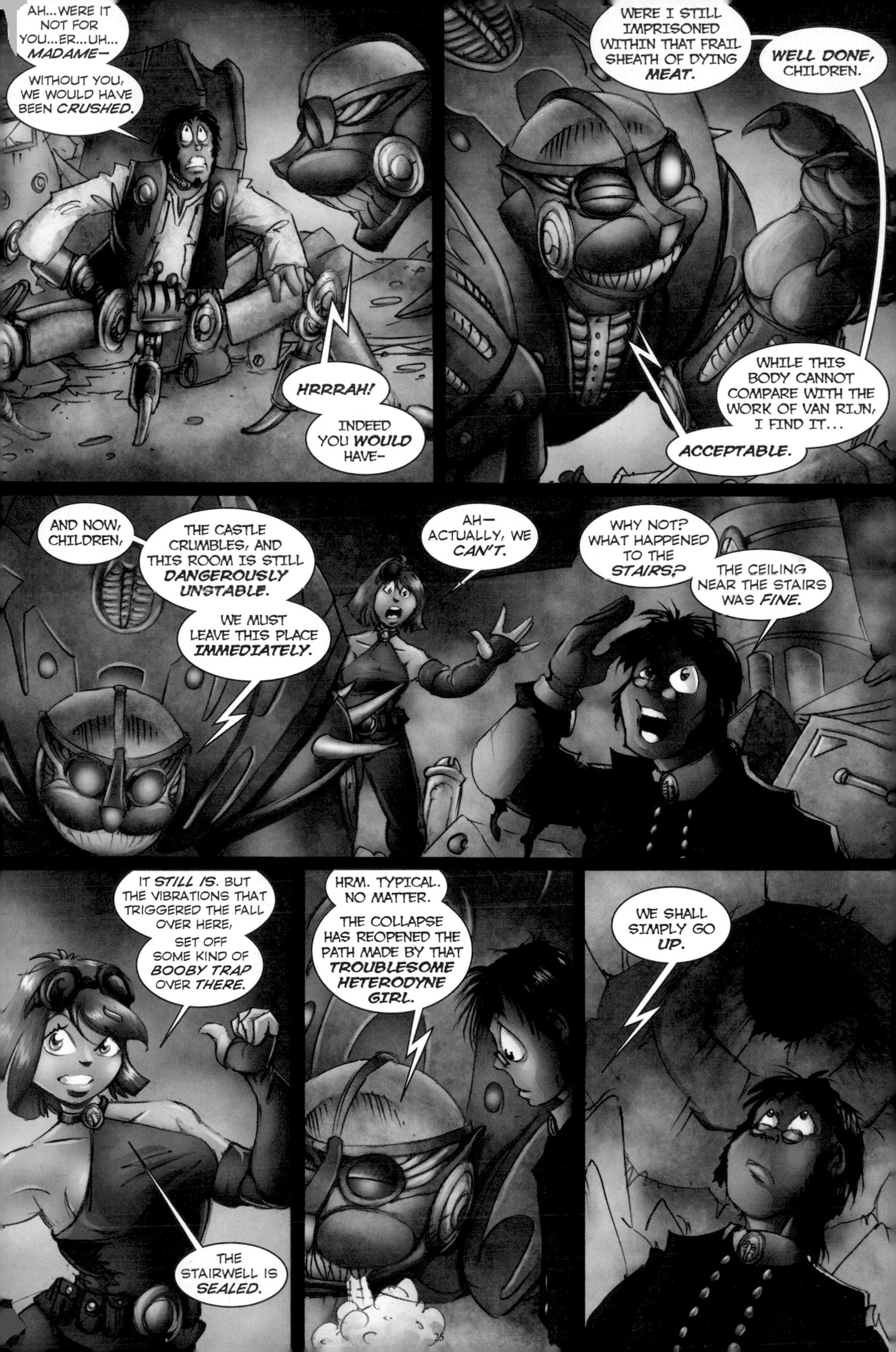

AH...WERE IT NOT FOR YOU...ER...UH... MADAME—
WITHOUT YOU, WE WOULD HAVE BEEN CRUSHED.
HRRRAH!
INDEED YOU WOULD HAVE-
WERE I STILL IMPRISONED WITHIN THAT FRAIL SHEATH OF DYING MEAT.
WELL DONE, CHILDREN.
WHILE THIS BODY CANNOT COMPARE WITH THE WORK OF VAN RIJN, I FIND IT...
ACCEPTABLE.
AND NOW, CHILDREN,
THE CASTLE CRUMBLES, AND THIS ROOM IS STILL DANGEROUSLY UNSTABLE.
WE MUST LEAVE THIS PLACE IMMEDIATELY.
AH— ACTUALLY, WE CAN'T.
WHY NOT? WHAT HAPPENED TO THE STAIRS?
THE CEILING NEAR THE STAIRS WAS FINE.
IT STILL IS. BUT THE VIBRATIONS THAT TRIGGERED THE FALL OVER HERE,
SET OFF SOME KIND OF BOOBY TRAP OVER THERE.
THE STAIRWELL IS SEALED.
HRM. TYPICAL. NO MATTER.
THE COLLAPSE HAS REOPENED THE PATH MADE BY THAT TROUBLESOME HETERODYNE GIRL.
WE SHALL SIMPLY GO UP.

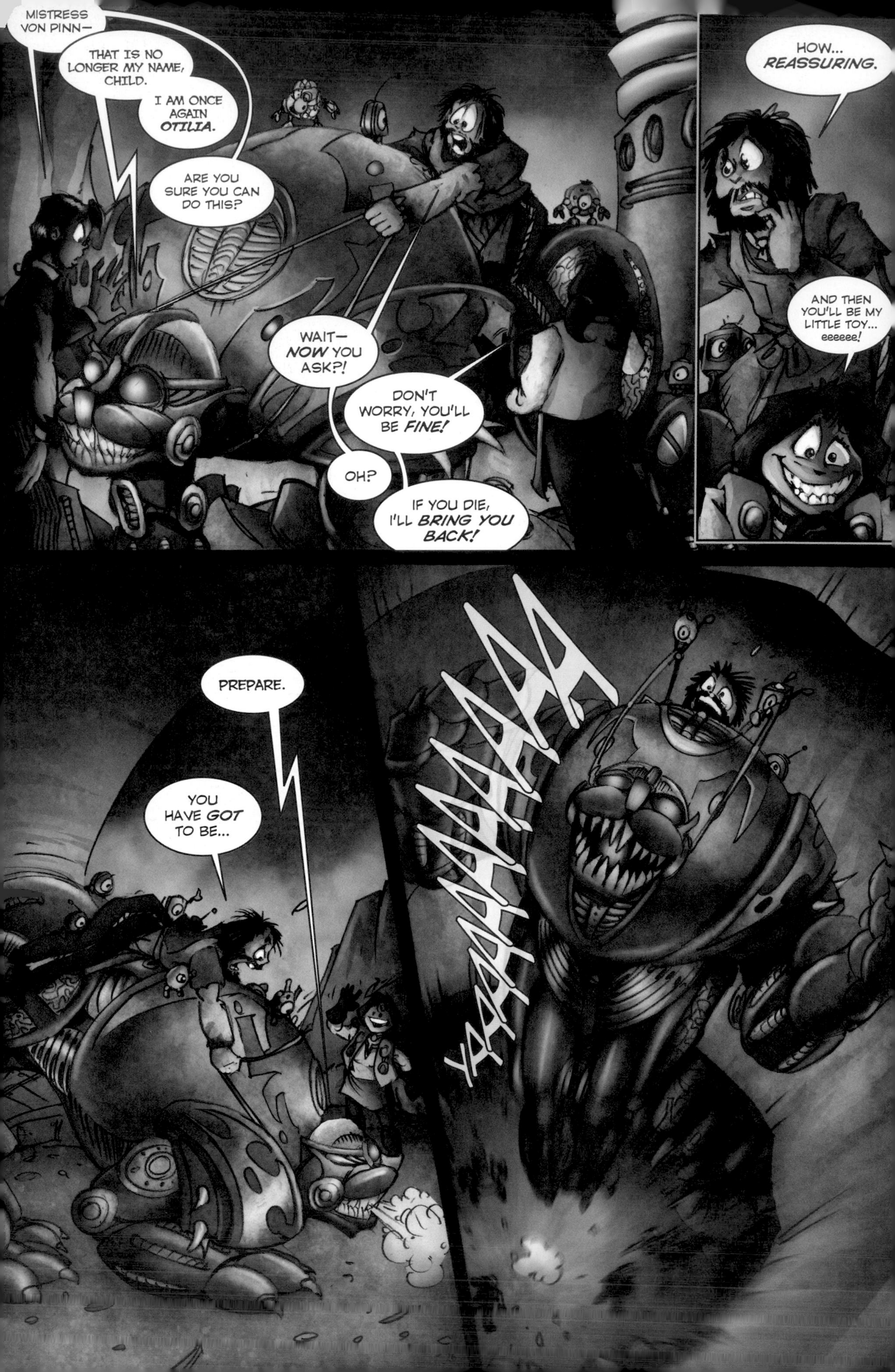
MISTRESS VON PINN—
THAT IS NO LONGER MY NAME, CHILD.
I AM ONCE AGAIN *OTILIA*.
ARE YOU SURE YOU CAN DO THIS?
WAIT— *NOW* YOU ASK?!
DON'T WORRY, YOU'LL BE *FINE!*
OH?
IF YOU DIE, I'LL *BRING YOU BACK!*
HOW... *REASSURING.*
AND THEN YOU'LL BE MY LITTLE TOY... eeeeee!
PREPARE.
YOU HAVE *GOT* TO BE...
YAAAAAAAAAHHHHHH

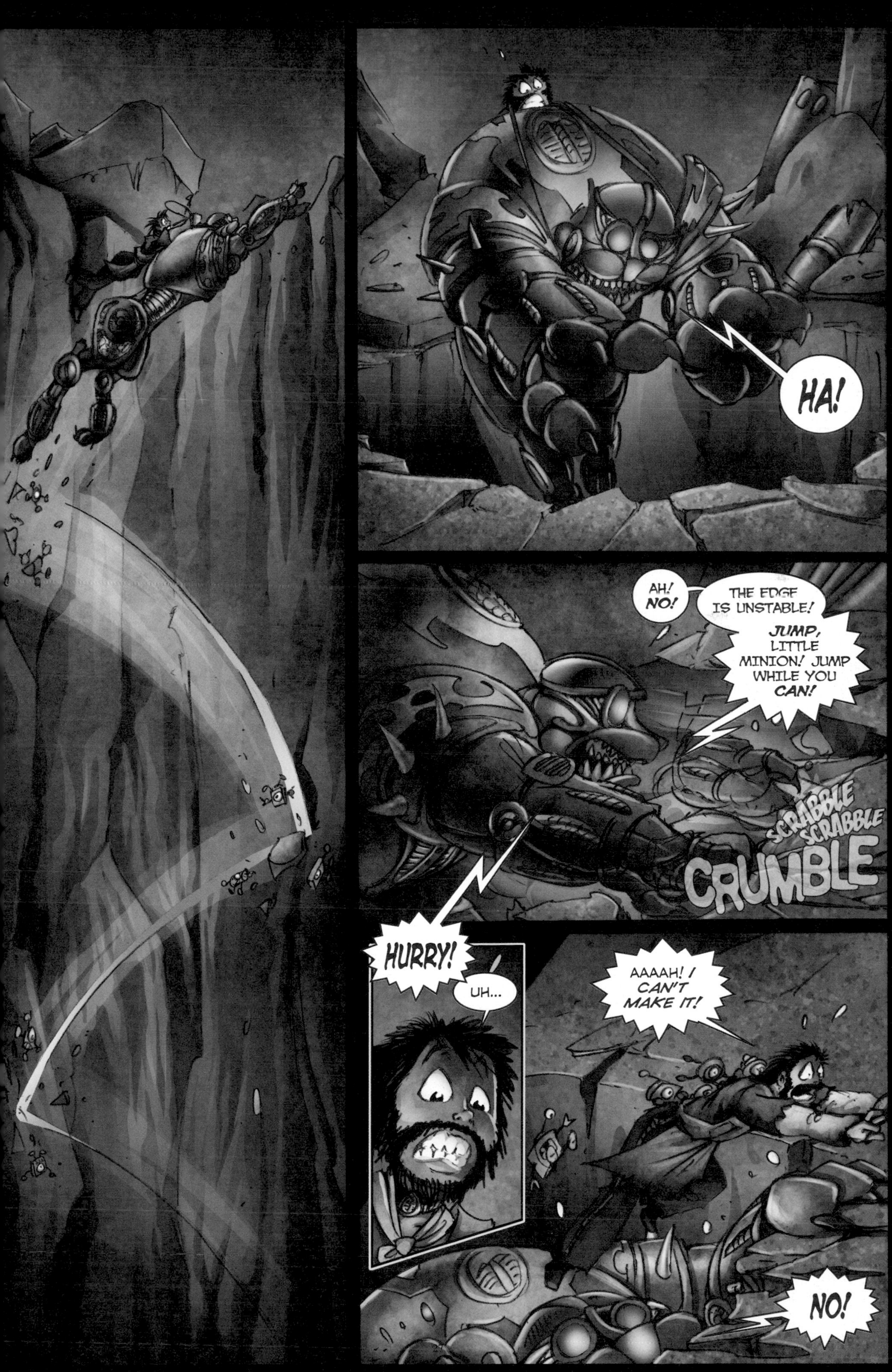
HA!
AH! NO!
THE EDGE IS UNSTABLE!
JUMP, LITTLE MINION! JUMP WHILE YOU CAN!
SCRABBLE SCRABBLE
CRUMBLE
HURRY!
UH...
AAAAH! I CAN'T MAKE IT!
NO!

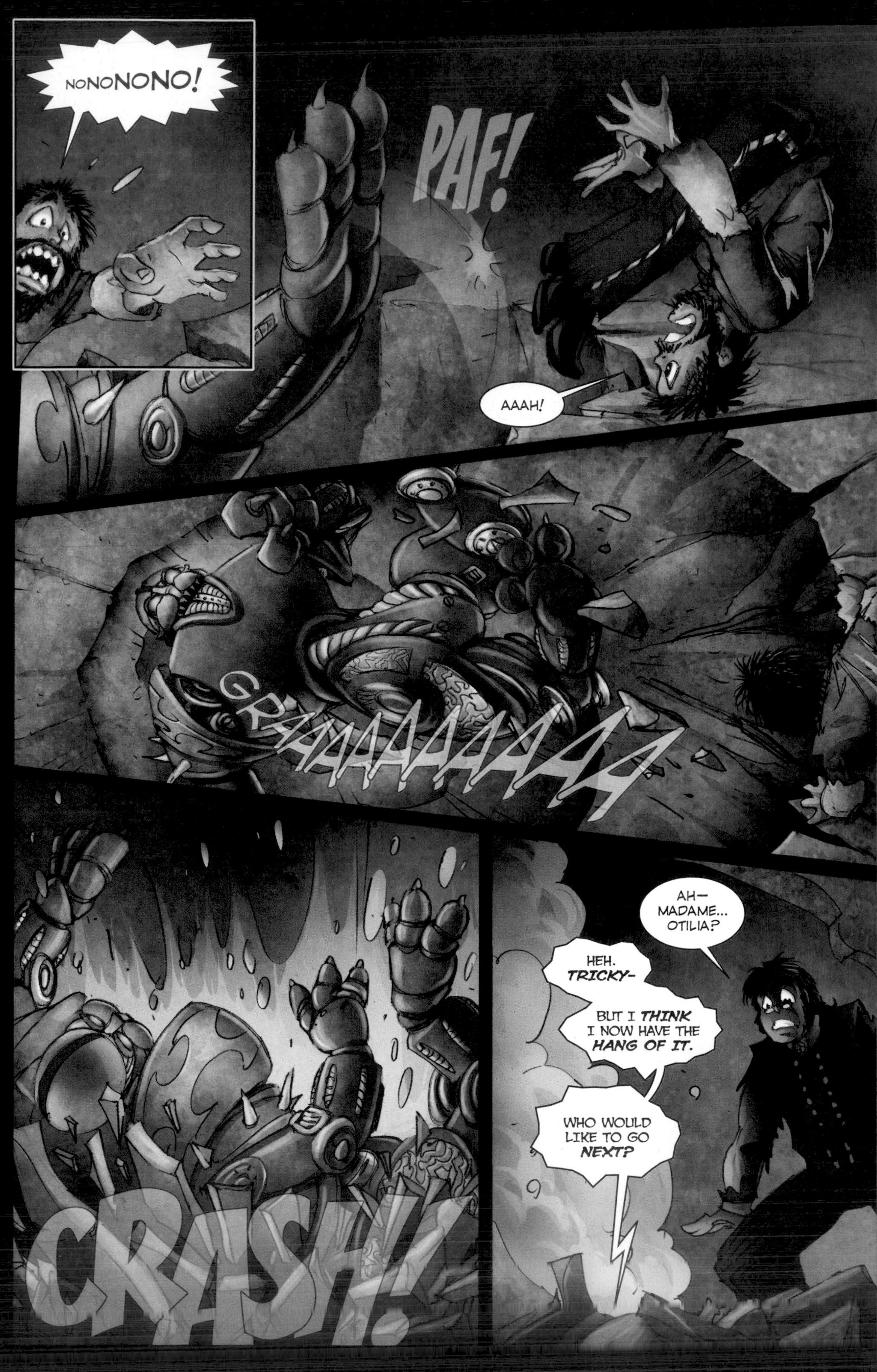
NONONONO!
PAF!
AAAH!
GRAAAAAAAAAA
CRASH!
AH— MADAME... OTILIA?
HEH. TRICKY-
BUT I THINK I NOW HAVE THE HANG OF IT.
WHO WOULD LIKE TO GO NEXT?

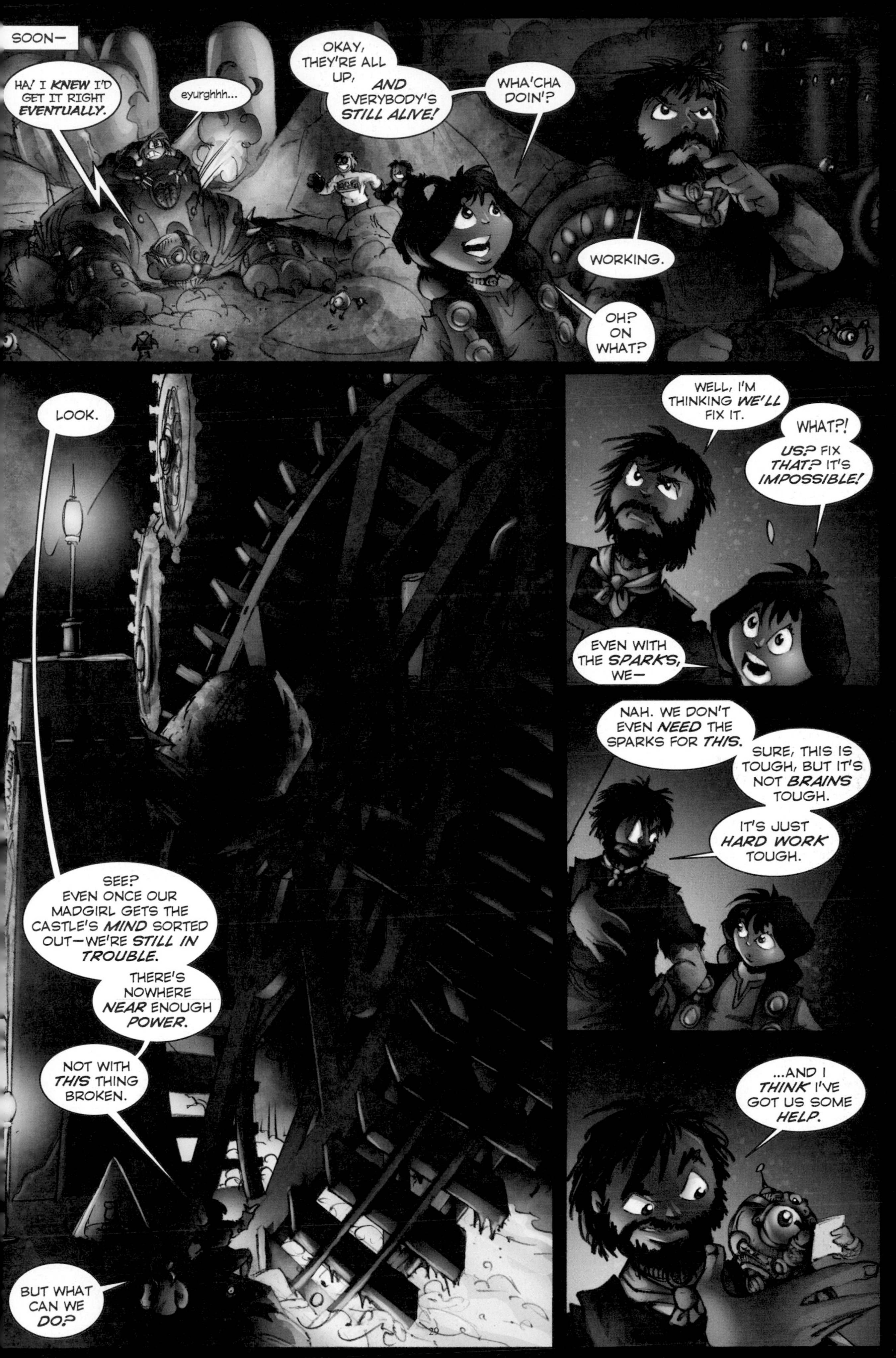
SOON—
HA! I KNEW I'D GET IT RIGHT EVENTUALLY.
eyurghhh...
OKAY, THEY'RE ALL UP, AND EVERYBODY'S STILL ALIVE!
WHA'CHA DOIN'?
WORKING.
OH? ON WHAT?
LOOK.
SEE? EVEN ONCE OUR MADGIRL GETS THE CASTLE'S MIND SORTED OUT—WE'RE STILL IN TROUBLE.
THERE'S NOWHERE NEAR ENOUGH POWER.
NOT WITH THIS THING BROKEN.
BUT WHAT CAN WE DO?
WELL, I'M THINKING WE'LL FIX IT.
WHAT?! US? FIX THAT? IT'S IMPOSSIBLE!
EVEN WITH THE SPARKS, WE—
NAH. WE DON'T EVEN NEED THE SPARKS FOR THIS.
SURE, THIS IS TOUGH, BUT IT'S NOT BRAINS TOUGH.
IT'S JUST HARD WORK TOUGH.
...AND I THINK I'VE GOT US SOME HELP.

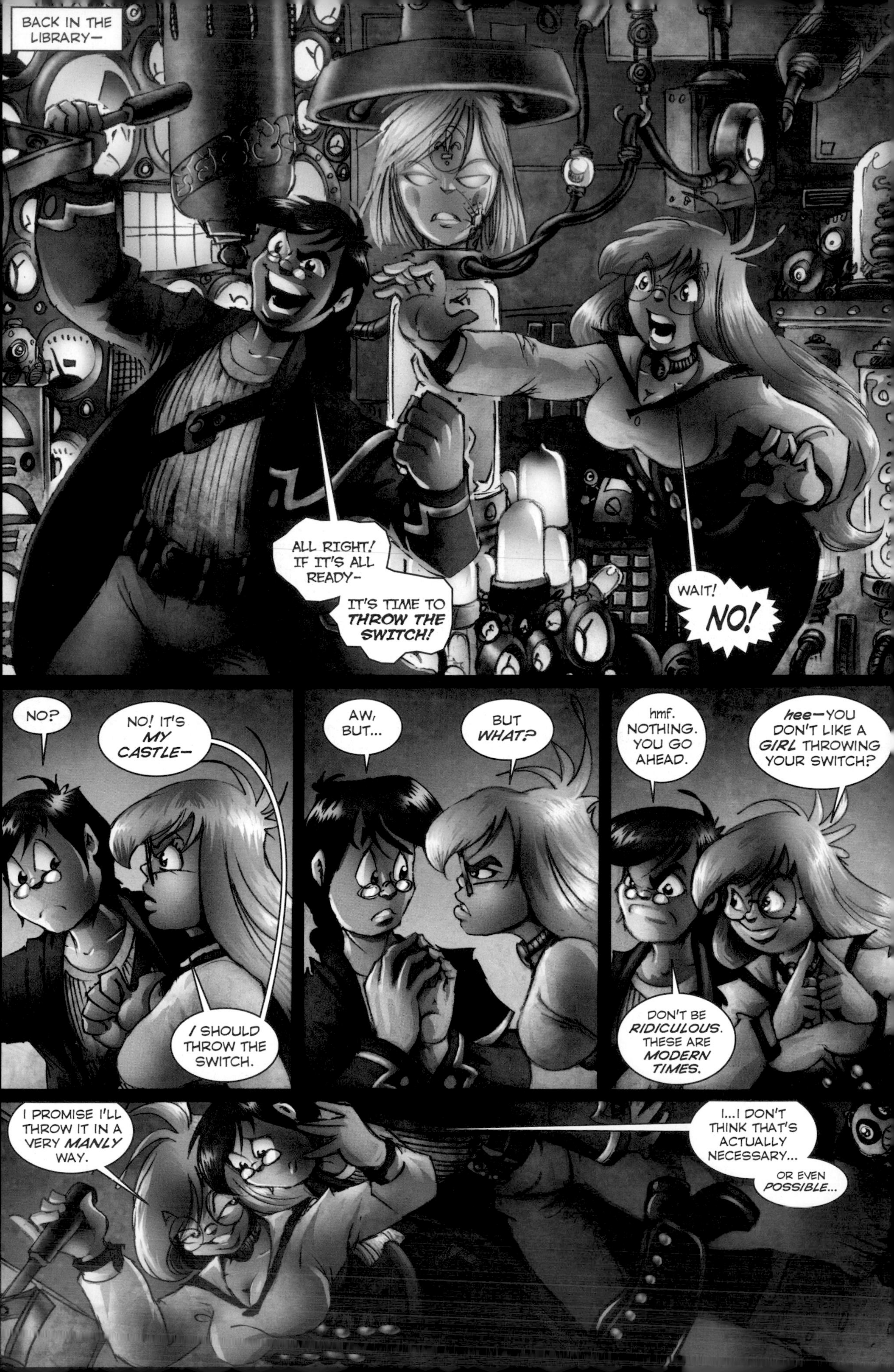
BACK IN THE LIBRARY—
ALL RIGHT! IF IT'S ALL READY-
IT'S TIME TO THROW THE SWITCH!
WAIT! NO!
NO?
NO! IT'S MY CASTLE—
I SHOULD THROW THE SWITCH.
AW, BUT...
BUT WHAT?
hmf. NOTHING. YOU GO AHEAD.
hee—YOU DON'T LIKE A GIRL THROWING YOUR SWITCH?
DON'T BE RIDICULOUS. THESE ARE MODERN TIMES.
I PROMISE I'LL THROW IT IN A VERY MANLY WAY.
I...I DON'T THINK THAT'S ACTUALLY NECESSARY...
OR EVEN POSSIBLE...

SKRACZ!
CHUNK
TIK TIK TIK TIK
THAT'S IT. THE SYSTEM'S SHUT DOWN.
THE TRANSFER *SHOULD* BE COMPLETE...
UM— *CASTLE?*
AHHHHH... I AM HERE.
...WAIT... I AM STILL ADJUSTING MY PARAMETERS...
IS SOMETHING *WRONG?*
AH. NOTHING WRONG, NO. *QUITE* THE *CONTRARY.*
ONLY...
MY PRISON WAS... SO *CONFINING...*
NOW, I AM... HOME... BUT IT IS *LARGE...*
SO MANY ROUTINES... CODES...
I FEEL... AS A RAINDROP RETURNED TO THE *OCEAN.*
WAIT-*YES.* WE SPOKE IN THE CRYPTS. YES.
AND NOW HERE YOU ARE... YOU'VE MADE IT TO THE LIBRARY... *WELL DONE.*
YESSS... I *REMEMBER* NOW.
HEH HEH *HEH.* THAT AND SO MUCH *MORE-*
THIS WILL TAKE... *SOME TIME...*
IS THERE ANYTHING I CAN DO TO *HELP?*
MMMMMM... *DUCK?*
WHAT?
AGATHA...
LOOK OU— *OOF!*
WHAK
SHOVE!
HEY!

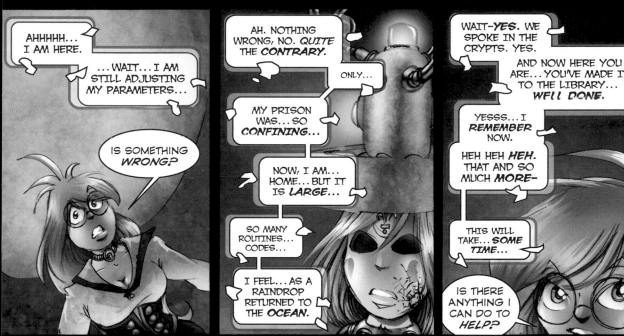

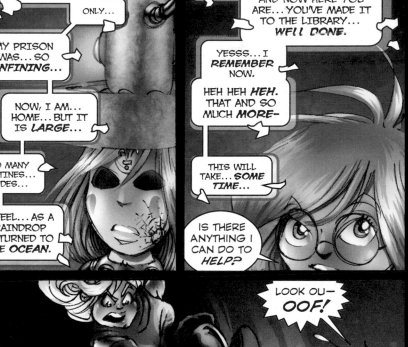

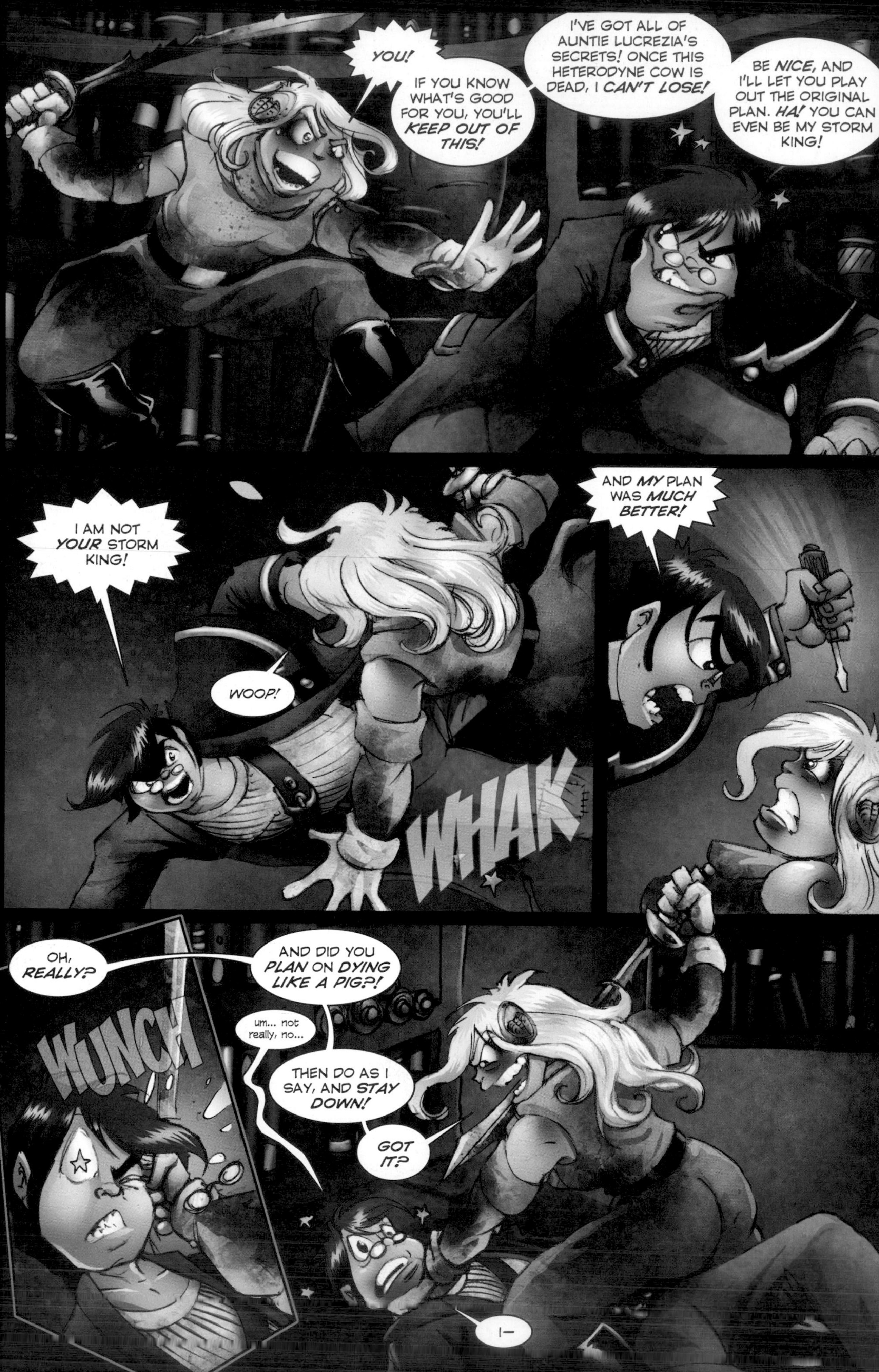
YOU!
IF YOU KNOW WHAT'S GOOD FOR YOU, YOU'LL KEEP OUT OF THIS!
I'VE GOT ALL OF AUNTIE LUCREZIA'S SECRETS! ONCE THIS HETERODYNE COW IS DEAD, I CAN'T LOSE!
BE NICE, AND I'LL LET YOU PLAY OUT THE ORIGINAL PLAN. HA! YOU CAN EVEN BE MY STORM KING!
I AM NOT YOUR STORM KING!
WOOP!
WHAK
AND MY PLAN WAS MUCH BETTER!
OH, REALLY?
WUNCH
AND DID YOU PLAN ON DYING LIKE A PIG?!
um... not really, no...
THEN DO AS I SAY, AND STAY DOWN!
GOT IT?
I—

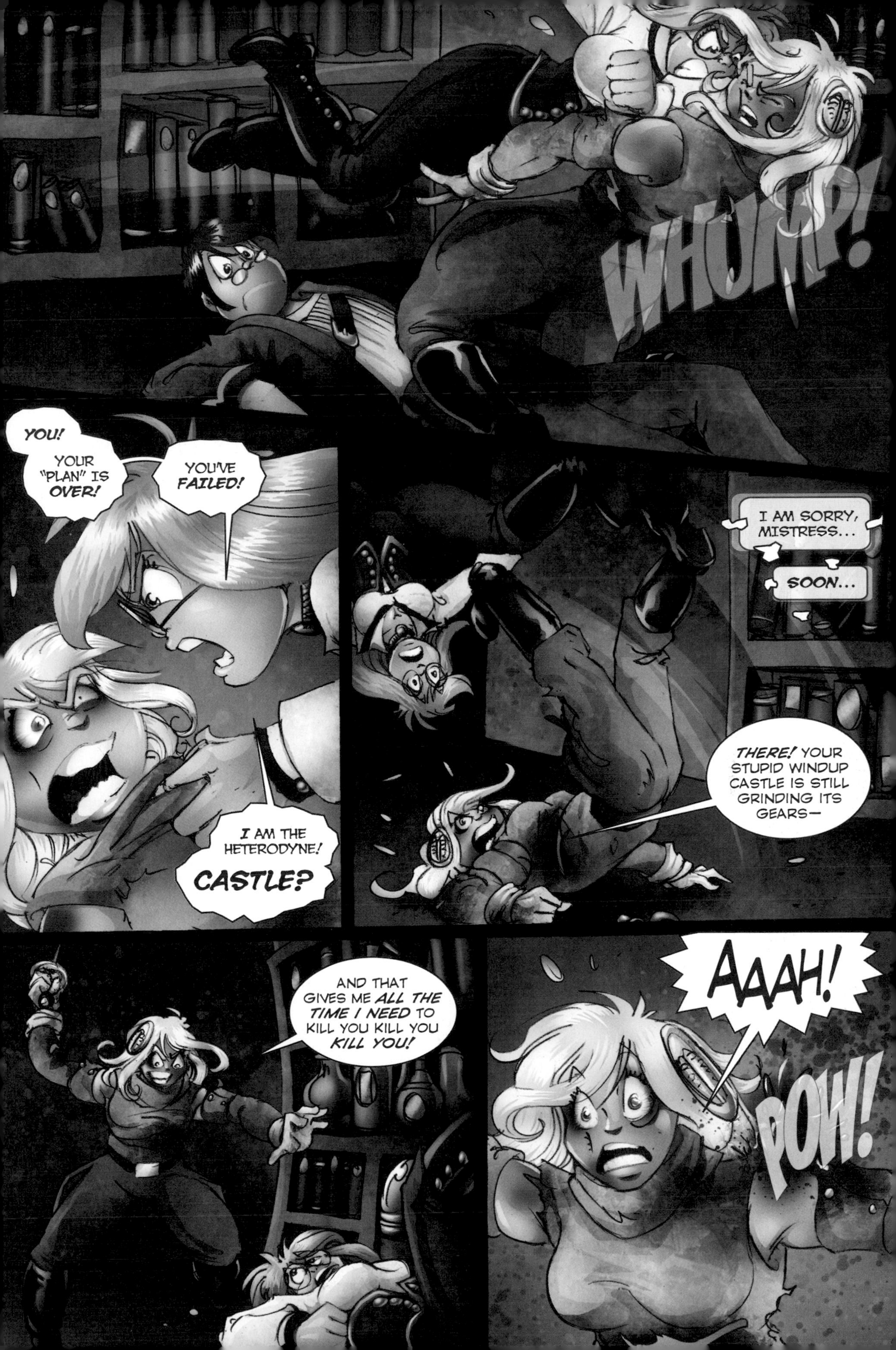
WHUMP!
YOU! YOUR "PLAN" IS OVER!
YOU'VE FAILED!
I AM THE HETERODYNE!
CASTLE?
I AM SORRY, MISTRESS...
SOON...
THERE! YOUR STUPID WINDUP CASTLE IS STILL GRINDING ITS GEARS—
AND THAT GIVES ME ALL THE TIME I NEED TO KILL YOU KILL YOU KILL YOU!
AAAH!
POW!

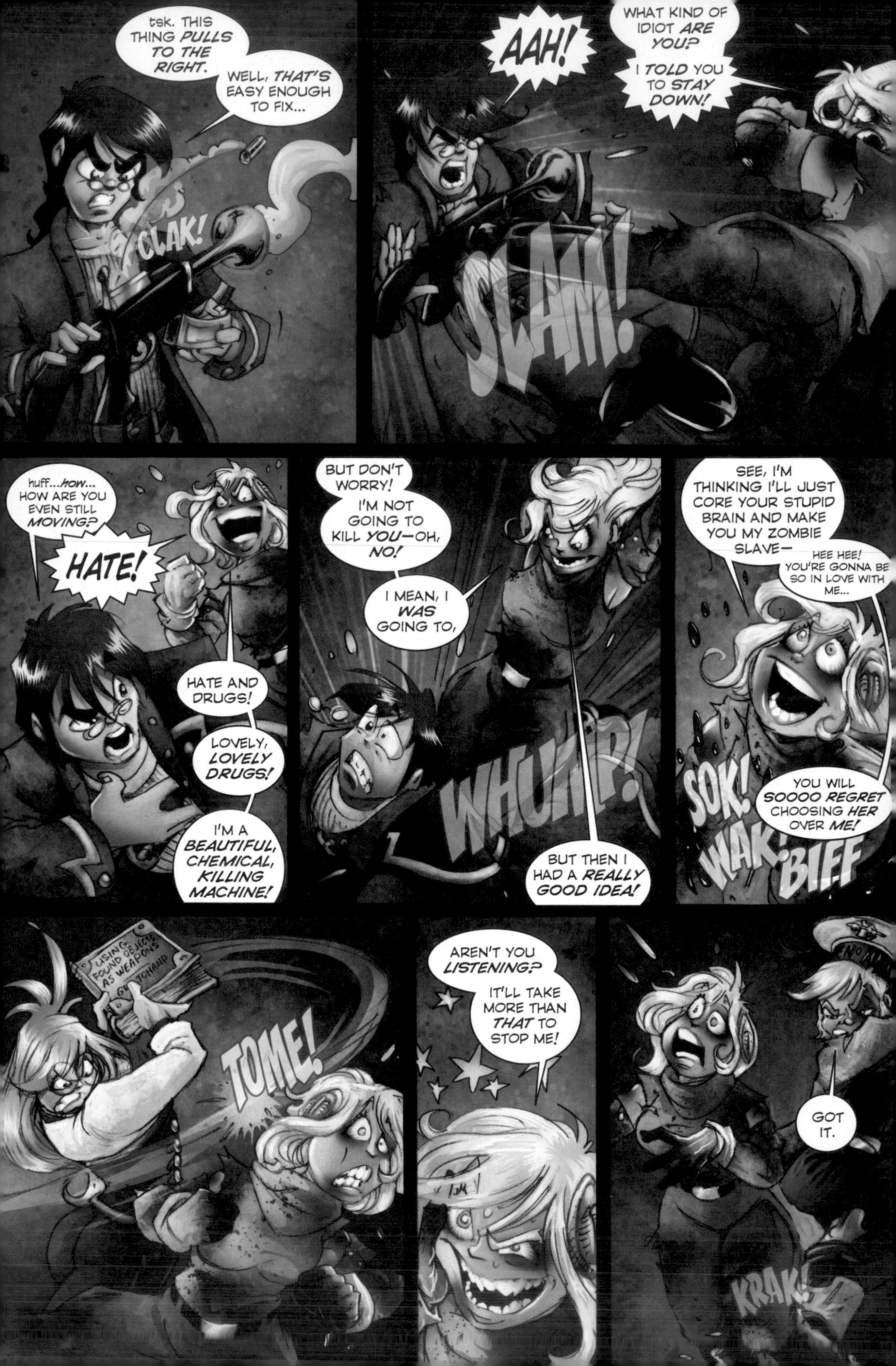
tsk. THIS THING PULLS TO THE RIGHT.
WELL, THAT'S EASY ENOUGH TO FIX...
CLAK!
AAH!
WHAT KIND OF IDIOT ARE YOU?
I TOLD YOU TO STAY DOWN!
SLAM!
huff...how... HOW ARE YOU EVEN STILL MOVING?
HATE!
HATE AND DRUGS!
LOVELY, LOVELY DRUGS!
I'M A BEAUTIFUL, CHEMICAL, KILLING MACHINE!
BUT DON'T WORRY!
I'M NOT GOING TO KILL YOU—OH, NO!
I MEAN, I WAS GOING TO,
WHUMP!
BUT THEN I HAD A REALLY GOOD IDEA!
SEE, I'M THINKING I'LL JUST CORE YOUR STUPID BRAIN AND MAKE YOU MY ZOMBIE SLAVE—
HEE HEE! YOU'RE GONNA BE SO IN LOVE WITH ME...
SOK!
WAK!
BIFF
YOU WILL SOOOO REGRET CHOOSING HER OVER ME!
USING FOUND OBJECTS AS WEAPONS
TOME!
AREN'T YOU LISTENING?
IT'LL TAKE MORE THAN THAT TO STOP ME!
GOT IT.
KRAK!

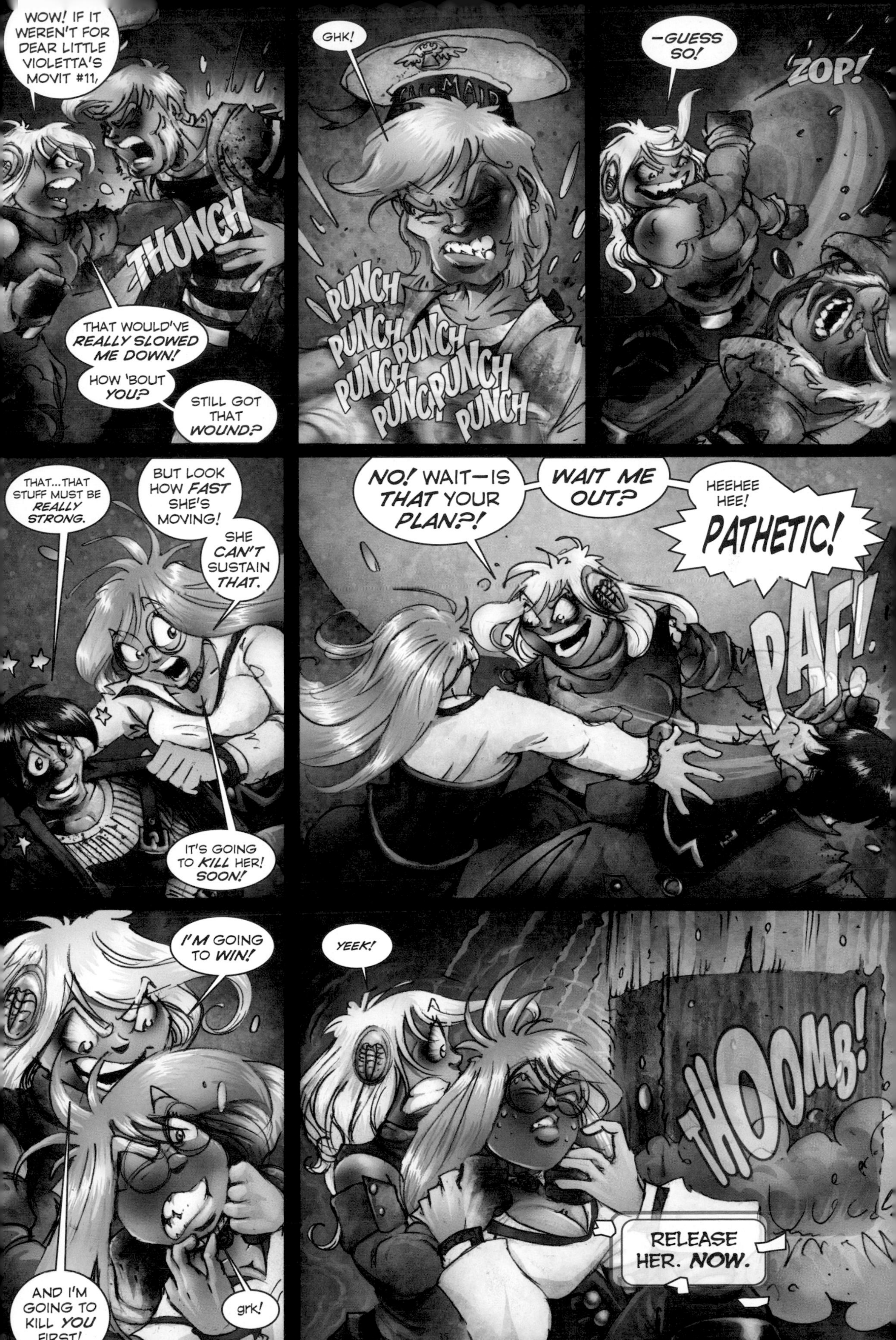
WOW! IF IT WEREN'T FOR DEAR LITTLE VIOLETTA'S MOVIT #11,
THUNCH
THAT WOULD'VE REALLY SLOWED ME DOWN!
HOW 'BOUT YOU?
STILL GOT THAT WOUND?
GHK!
PUNCH PUNCH PUNCH PUNCH PUNCH PUNCH PUNCH PUNCH
—GUESS SO!
ZOP!
THAT...THAT STUFF MUST BE REALLY STRONG.
BUT LOOK HOW FAST SHE'S MOVING!
SHE CAN'T SUSTAIN THAT.
IT'S GOING TO KILL HER! SOON!
NO! WAIT—IS THAT YOUR PLAN?!
WAIT ME OUT?
HEEHEE HEE!
PATHETIC!
PAF!
I'M GOING TO WIN!
AND I'M GOING TO KILL YOU FIRST!
grk!
YEEK!
WHOOMB!
RELEASE HER. NOW.

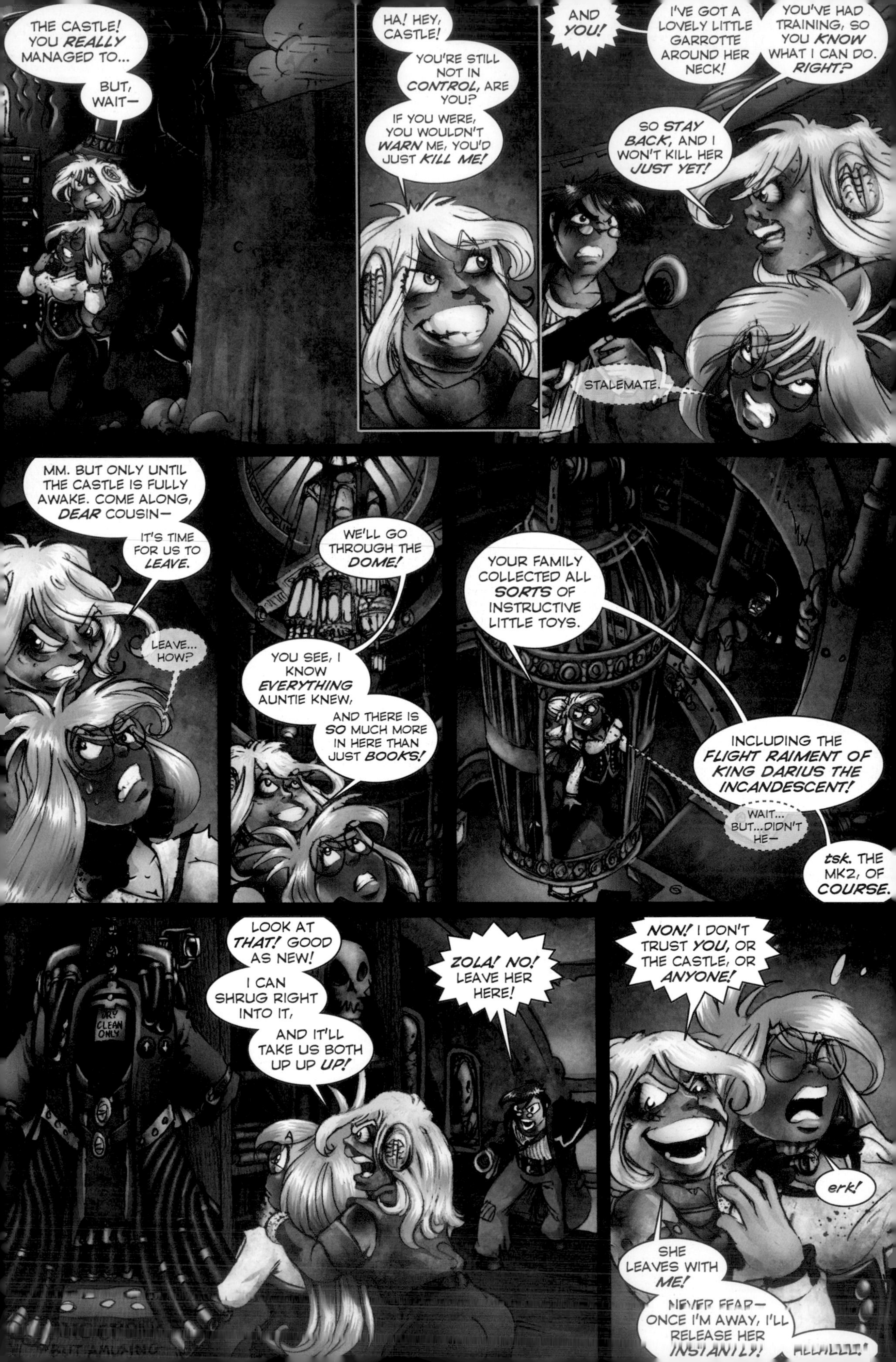

THE CASTLE! YOU *REALLY* MANAGED TO...
BUT, WAIT—
HA! HEY, CASTLE!
YOU'RE STILL NOT IN *CONTROL*, ARE YOU?
IF YOU WERE, YOU WOULDN'T *WARN* ME, YOU'D JUST *KILL ME!*
AND *YOU!*
I'VE GOT A LOVELY LITTLE GARROTTE AROUND HER NECK!
YOU'VE HAD TRAINING, SO YOU *KNOW* WHAT I CAN DO. *RIGHT?*
SO *STAY BACK*, AND I WON'T KILL HER *JUST YET!*
STALEMATE.
MM. BUT ONLY UNTIL THE CASTLE IS FULLY AWAKE. COME ALONG, *DEAR* COUSIN—
IT'S TIME FOR US TO *LEAVE*.
LEAVE... HOW?
WE'LL GO THROUGH THE *DOME!*
YOU SEE, I KNOW *EVERYTHING* AUNTIE KNEW,
AND THERE IS *SO* MUCH MORE IN HERE THAN JUST *BOOKS!*
YOUR FAMILY COLLECTED ALL *SORTS* OF INSTRUCTIVE LITTLE TOYS.
INCLUDING THE *FLIGHT RAIMENT OF KING DARIUS THE INCANDESCENT!*
WAIT... BUT...DIDN'T HE—
tsk. THE MK2, OF *COURSE*.
DRY CLEAN ONLY
LOOK AT *THAT!* GOOD AS NEW!
I CAN SHRUG RIGHT INTO IT,
AND IT'LL TAKE US BOTH UP UP *UP!*
ZOLA! NO! LEAVE HER HERE!
NON! I DON'T TRUST *YOU*, OR THE CASTLE, OR *ANYONE!*
erk!
SHE LEAVES WITH *ME!*
NEVER FEAR— ONCE I'M AWAY, I'LL RELEASE HER *INSTANTLY!*

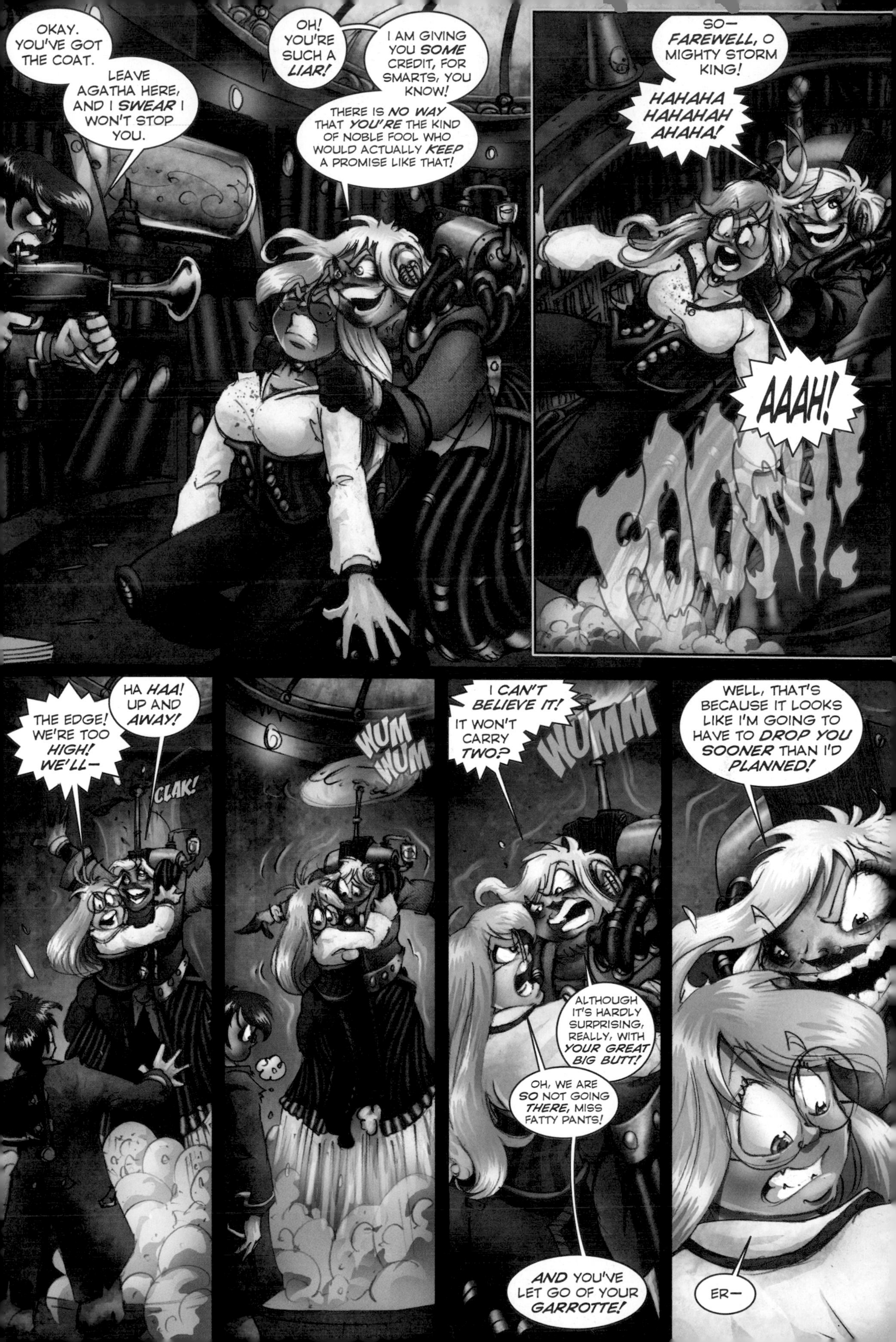
OKAY. YOU'VE GOT THE COAT.
LEAVE AGATHA HERE, AND I SWEAR I WON'T STOP YOU.
OH! YOU'RE SUCH A LIAR!
I AM GIVING YOU SOME CREDIT, FOR SMARTS, YOU KNOW!
THERE IS NO WAY THAT YOU'RE THE KIND OF NOBLE FOOL WHO WOULD ACTUALLY KEEP A PROMISE LIKE THAT!
SO— FAREWELL, O MIGHTY STORM KING!
HAHAHA HAHAHAH AHAHA!
AAAH!
BOOM!
HA HAA! UP AND AWAY!
THE EDGE! WE'RE TOO HIGH! WE'LL—
CLAK!
WUM WUM
I CAN'T BELIEVE IT!
IT WON'T CARRY TWO?
WUMM
ALTHOUGH IT'S HARDLY SURPRISING, REALLY, WITH YOUR GREAT BIG BUTT!
OH, WE ARE SO NOT GOING THERE, MISS FATTY PANTS!
AND YOU'VE LET GO OF YOUR GARROTTE!
WELL, THAT'S BECAUSE IT LOOKS LIKE I'M GOING TO HAVE TO DROP YOU SOONER THAN I'D PLANNED!
ER—

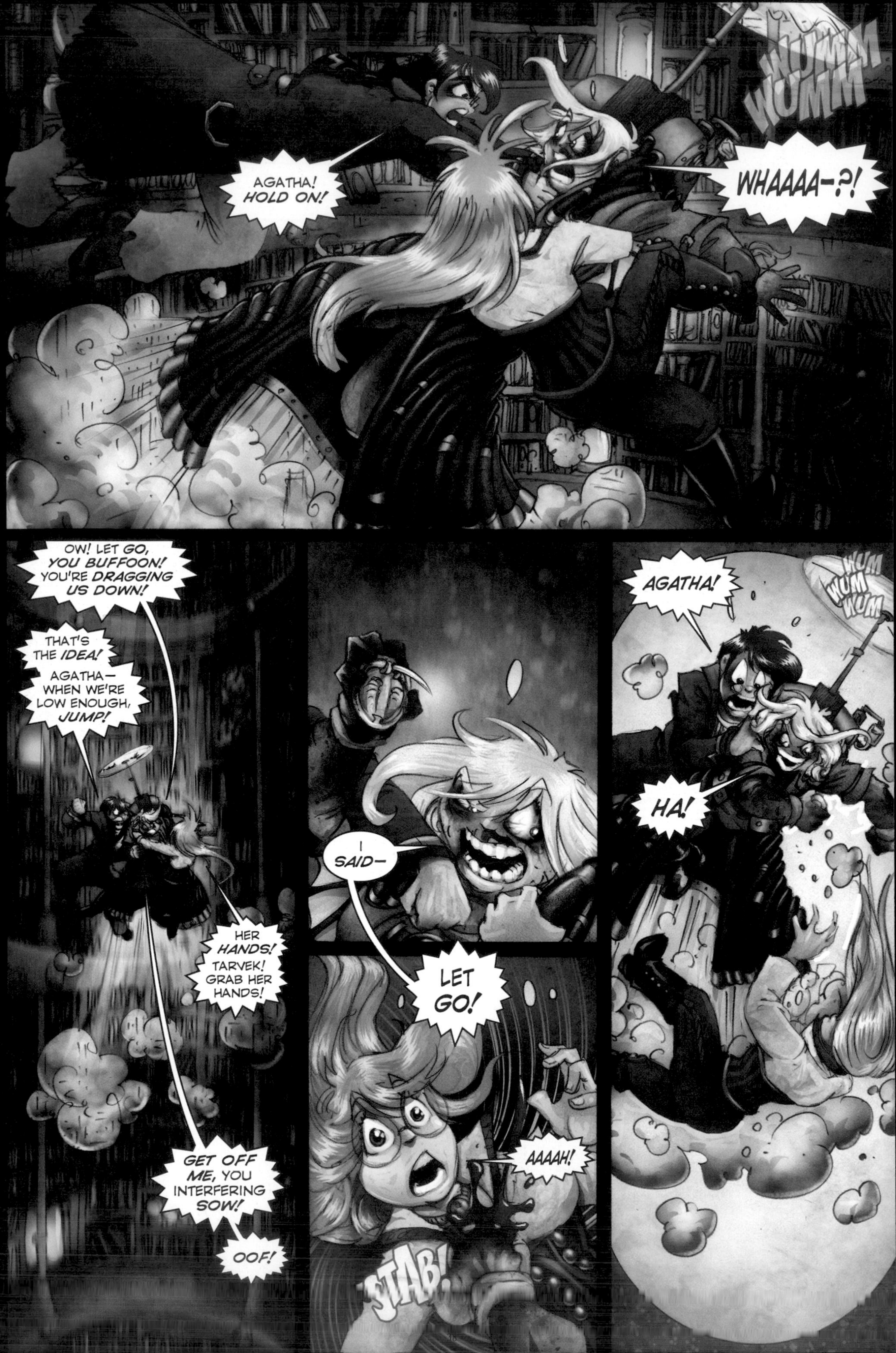
WUMM WUMM
AGATHA! HOLD ON!
WHAAAA-?!
OW! LET GO, YOU BUFFOON! YOU'RE DRAGGING US DOWN!
THAT'S THE IDEA!
AGATHA— WHEN WE'RE LOW ENOUGH, JUMP!
HER HANDS! TARVEK! GRAB HER HANDS!
GET OFF ME, YOU INTERFERING SOW!
OOF!
I SAID—
LET GO!
AAAAH!
STAB!
AGATHA!
WUM WUM WUM
HA!

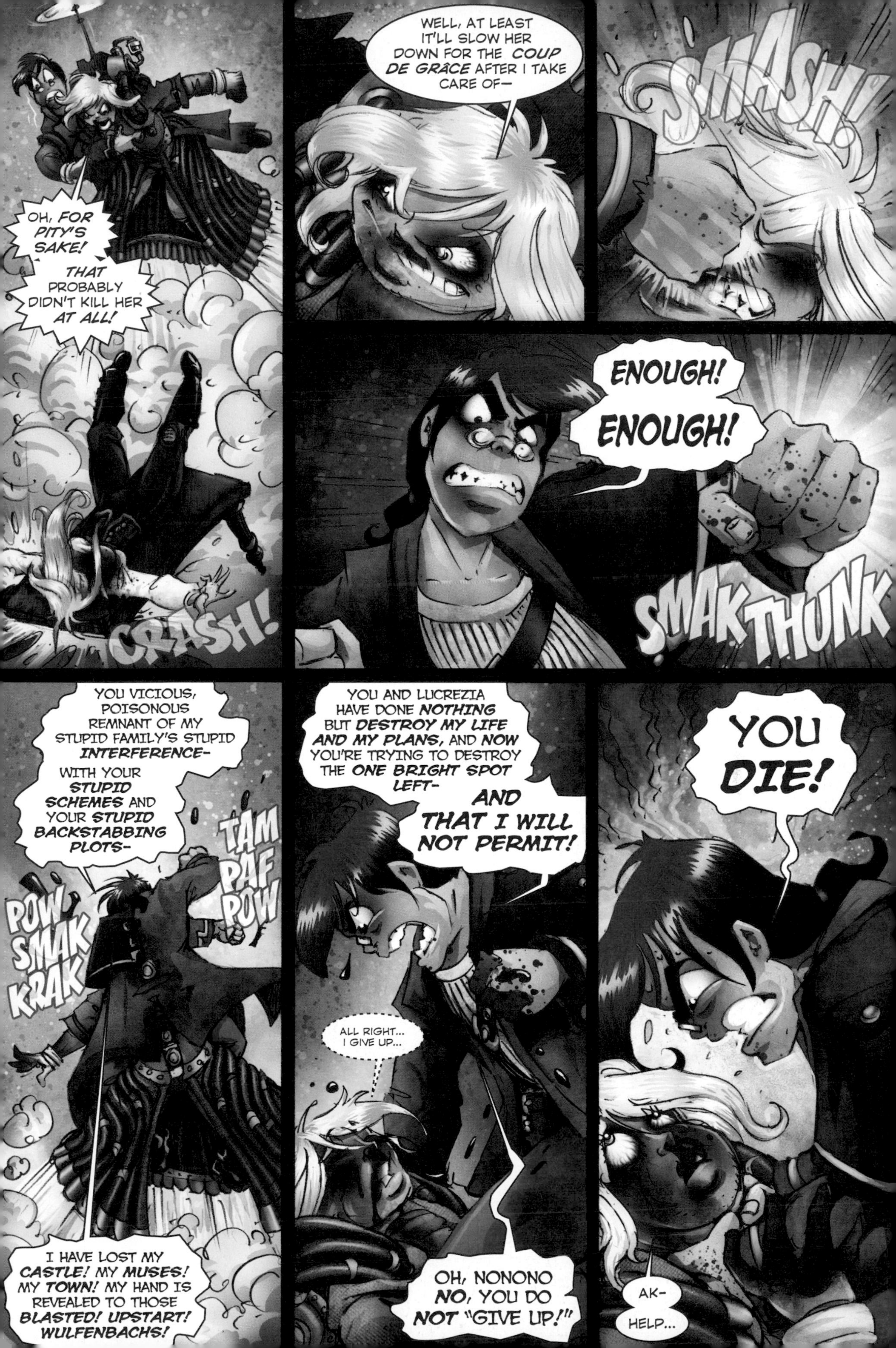
OH, FOR PITY'S SAKE!
THAT PROBABLY DIDN'T KILL HER AT ALL!
CRASH!
WELL, AT LEAST IT'LL SLOW HER DOWN FOR THE COUP DE GRÂCE AFTER I TAKE CARE OF—
SMASH!
ENOUGH!
ENOUGH!
SMAK THUNK
YOU VICIOUS, POISONOUS REMNANT OF MY STUPID FAMILY'S STUPID INTERFERENCE-
WITH YOUR STUPID SCHEMES AND YOUR STUPID BACKSTABBING PLOTS-
TAM PAF POW
POW SMAK KRAK
I HAVE LOST MY CASTLE! MY MUSES! MY TOWN! MY HAND IS REVEALED TO THOSE BLASTED! UPSTART! WULFENBACHS!
YOU AND LUCREZIA HAVE DONE NOTHING BUT DESTROY MY LIFE AND MY PLANS, AND NOW YOU'RE TRYING TO DESTROY THE ONE BRIGHT SPOT LEFT-
AND THAT I WILL NOT PERMIT!
ALL RIGHT... I GIVE UP...
OH, NONONO NO, YOU DO NOT "GIVE UP!"
YOU DIE!
AK-
HELP...

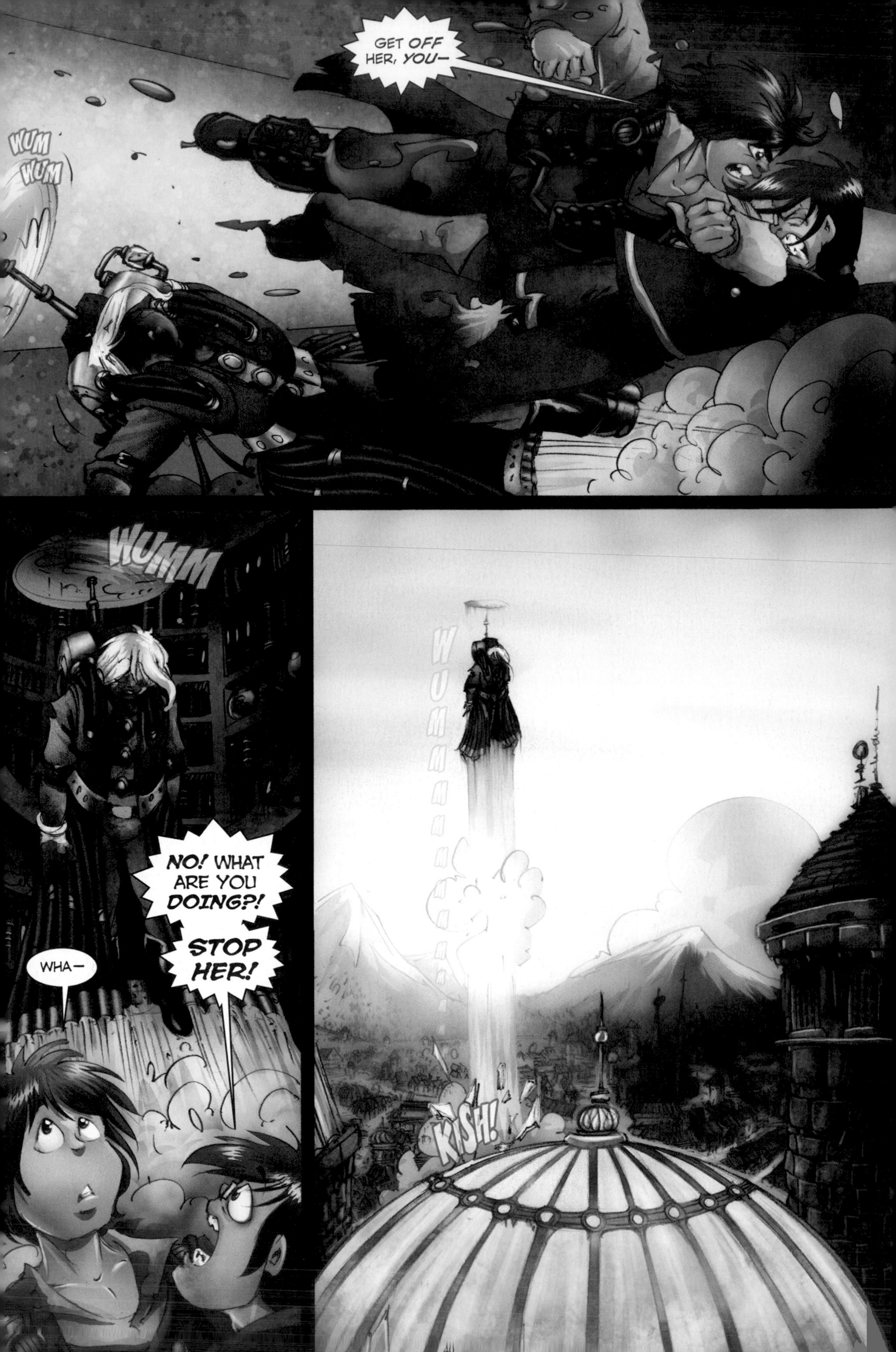
GET OFF HER, YOU—
WUM
WUM
WUMM
NO! WHAT ARE YOU DOING?!
WHA—
STOP HER!
WUMMMMMMMMMM
KRSH!

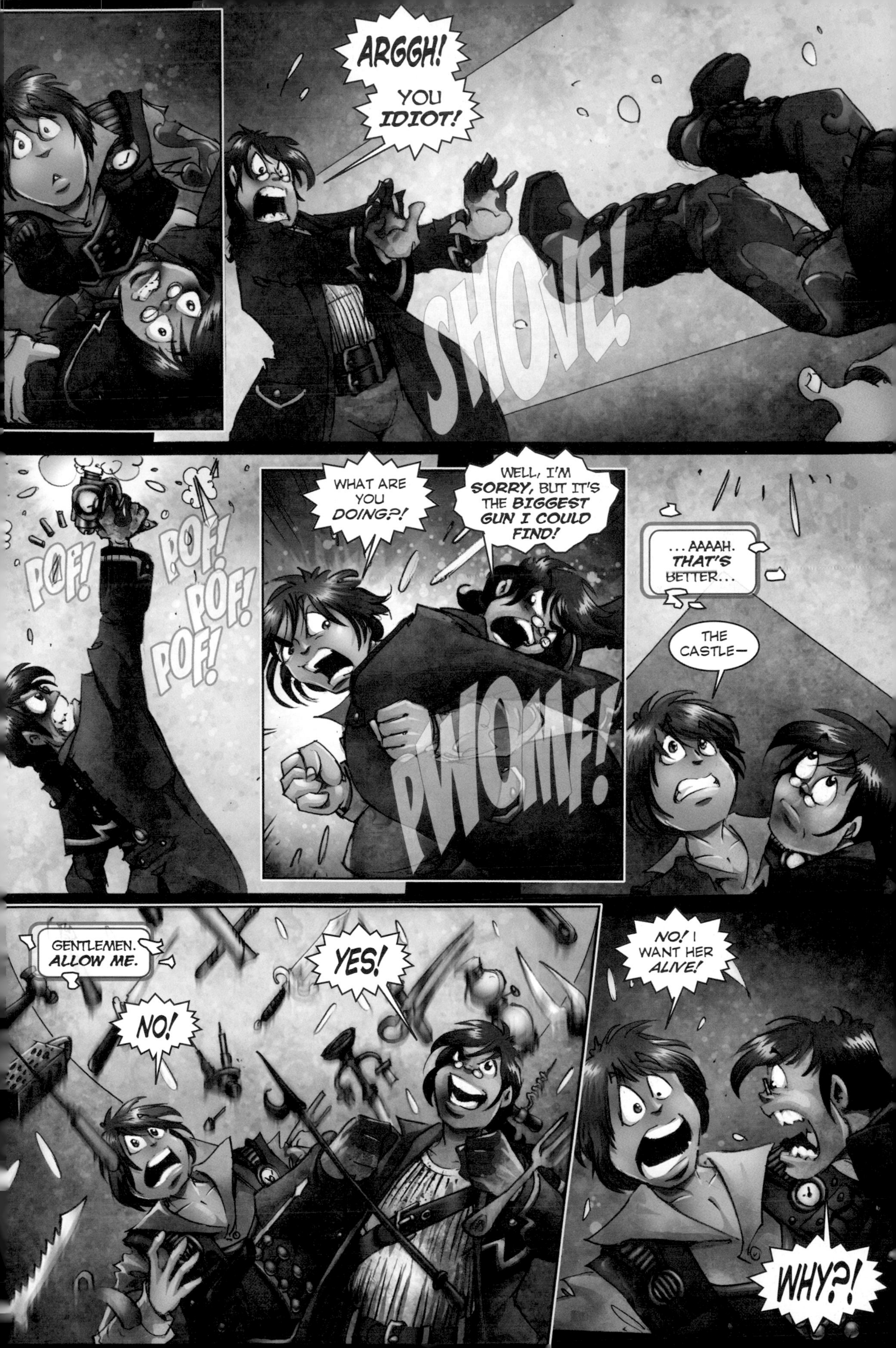
ARGGH!
YOU IDIOT!
SHOVE!
POF! POF! POF! POF!
WHAT ARE YOU DOING?!
WELL, I'M SORRY, BUT IT'S THE BIGGEST GUN I COULD FIND!
PWOMF!
...AAAAH. THAT'S BETTER...
THE CASTLE—
GENTLEMEN. ALLOW ME.
NO!
YES!
NO! I WANT HER ALIVE!
WHY?!

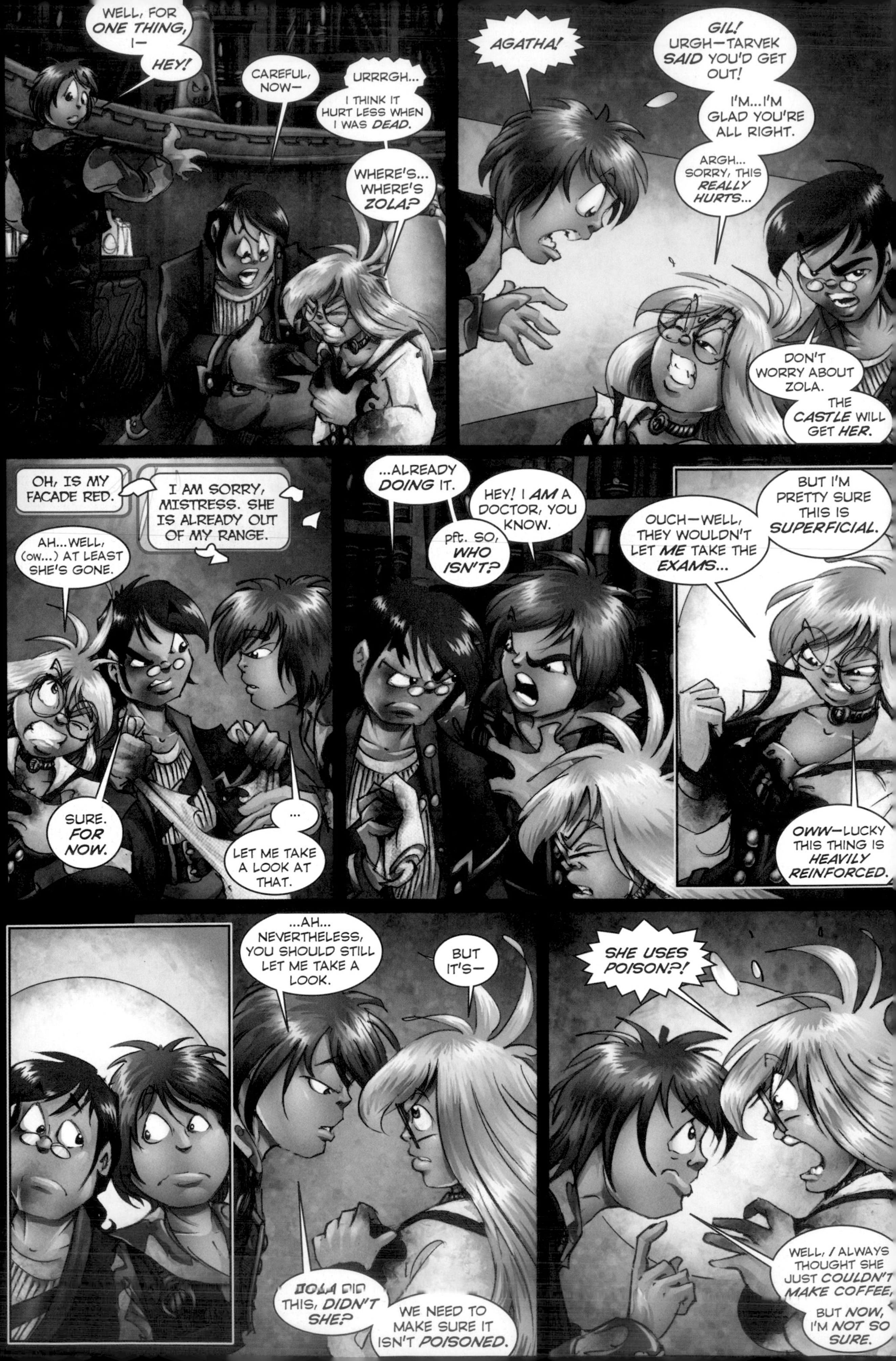
WELL, FOR ONE THING, I—
HEY!
CAREFUL, NOW—
URRRGH...
I THINK IT HURT LESS WHEN I WAS DEAD.
WHERE'S... WHERE'S ZOLA?
AGATHA!
GIL! URGH—TARVEK SAID YOU'D GET OUT!
I'M...I'M GLAD YOU'RE ALL RIGHT.
ARGH... SORRY, THIS REALLY HURTS...
DON'T WORRY ABOUT ZOLA.
THE CASTLE WILL GET HER.
OH, IS MY FACADE RED.
I AM SORRY, MISTRESS. SHE IS ALREADY OUT OF MY RANGE.
AH...WELL, (OW...) AT LEAST SHE'S GONE.
SURE. FOR NOW.
...
LET ME TAKE A LOOK AT THAT.
...ALREADY DOING IT.
pft. SO, WHO ISN'T?
HEY! I AM A DOCTOR, YOU KNOW.
OUCH—WELL, THEY WOULDN'T LET ME TAKE THE EXAMS...
BUT I'M PRETTY SURE THIS IS SUPERFICIAL.
OWW—LUCKY THIS THING IS HEAVILY REINFORCED.
...AH... NEVERTHELESS, YOU SHOULD STILL LET ME TAKE A LOOK.
BUT IT'S—
ZOLA DID THIS, DIDN'T SHE?
WE NEED TO MAKE SURE IT ISN'T POISONED.
SHE USES POISON?!
WELL, I ALWAYS THOUGHT SHE JUST COULDN'T MAKE COFFEE,
BUT NOW, I'M NOT SO SURE.

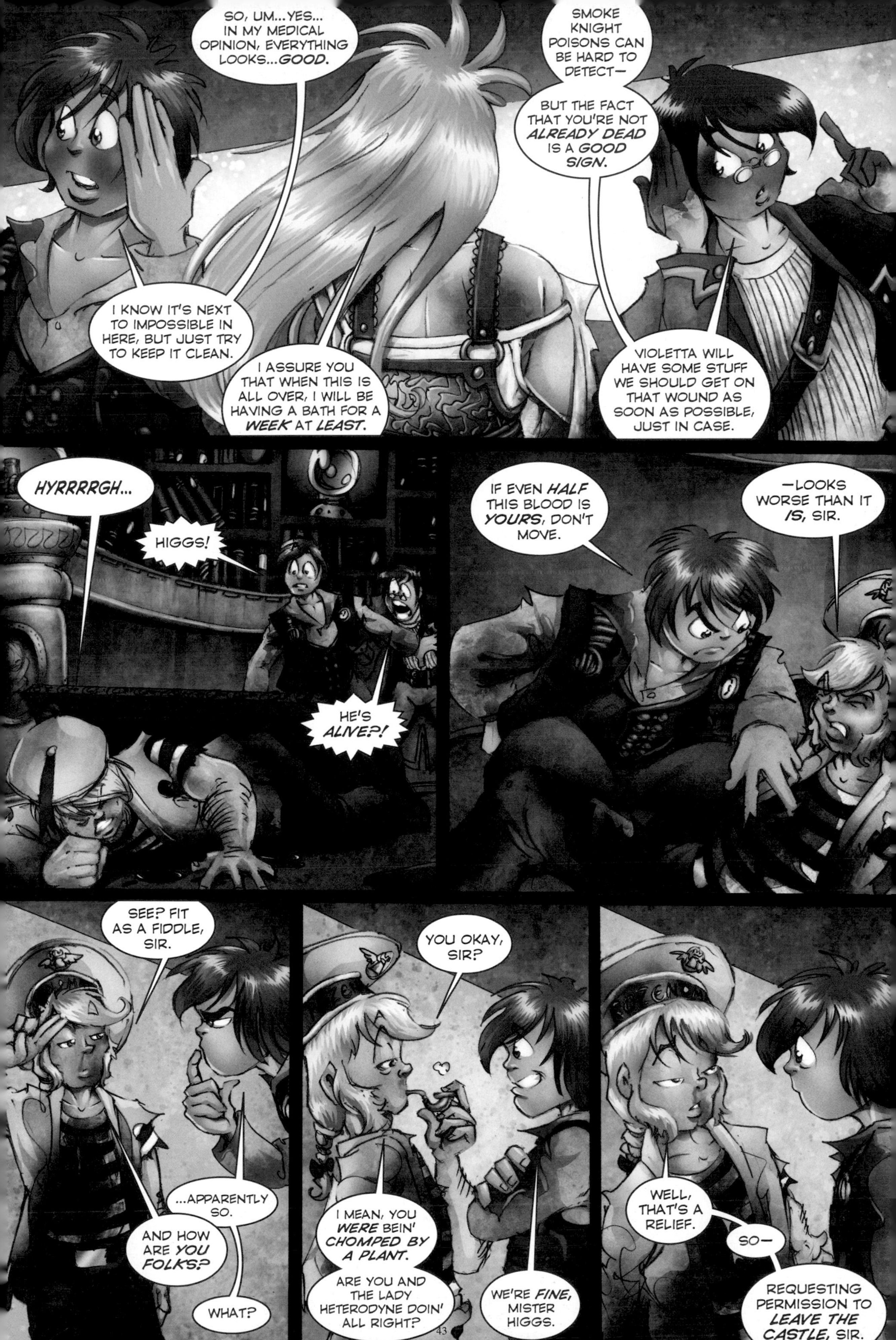
SO, UM...YES... IN MY MEDICAL OPINION, EVERYTHING LOOKS...*GOOD*.
I KNOW IT'S NEXT TO IMPOSSIBLE IN HERE, BUT JUST TRY TO KEEP IT CLEAN.
I ASSURE YOU THAT WHEN THIS IS ALL OVER, I WILL BE HAVING A BATH FOR A *WEEK* AT *LEAST*.
SMOKE KNIGHT POISONS CAN BE HARD TO DETECT—
BUT THE FACT THAT YOU'RE NOT *ALREADY DEAD* IS A *GOOD SIGN*.
VIOLETTA WILL HAVE SOME STUFF WE SHOULD GET ON THAT WOUND AS SOON AS POSSIBLE, JUST IN CASE.
HYRRRRGH...
HIGGS!
HE'S *ALIVE?!*
IF EVEN *HALF* THIS BLOOD IS *YOURS*, DON'T MOVE.
—LOOKS WORSE THAN IT *IS*, SIR.
SEE? FIT AS A FIDDLE, SIR.
...APPARENTLY SO.
AND HOW ARE *YOU FOLKS?*
WHAT?
YOU OKAY, SIR?
I MEAN, YOU *WERE* BEIN' *CHOMPED BY A PLANT*.
ARE YOU AND THE LADY HETERODYNE DOIN' ALL RIGHT?
WE'RE *FINE*, MISTER HIGGS.
WELL, THAT'S A RELIEF.
SO—
REQUESTING PERMISSION TO *LEAVE THE CASTLE*, SIR.

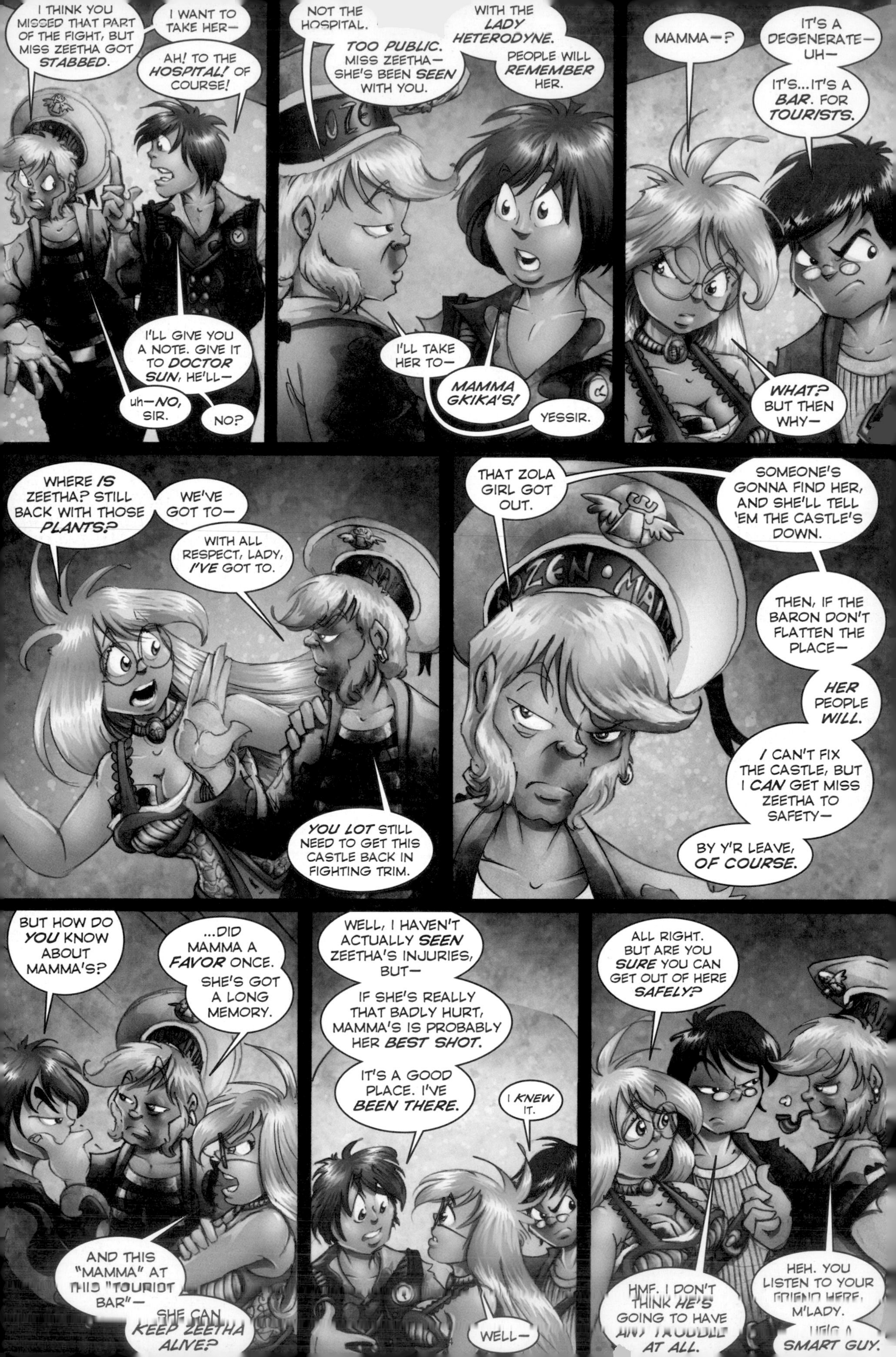
I THINK YOU MISSED THAT PART OF THE FIGHT, BUT MISS ZEETHA GOT ***STABBED***.
I WANT TO TAKE HER—
AH! TO THE ***HOSPITAL!*** OF COURSE!
I'LL GIVE YOU A NOTE. GIVE IT TO ***DOCTOR SUN***, HE'LL—
uh—***NO***, SIR.
NO?
NOT THE HOSPITAL.
TOO PUBLIC. MISS ZEETHA—SHE'S BEEN ***SEEN*** WITH YOU.
WITH THE ***LADY HETERODYNE***.
PEOPLE WILL ***REMEMBER*** HER.
I'LL TAKE HER TO—
MAMMA GKIKA'S!
YESSIR.
MAMMA—?
IT'S A DEGENERATE—UH—
IT'S...IT'S A ***BAR***. FOR ***TOURISTS***.
WHAT? BUT THEN WHY—
WHERE ***IS*** ZEETHA? STILL BACK WITH THOSE ***PLANTS?***
WE'VE GOT TO—
WITH ALL RESPECT, LADY, ***I'VE*** GOT TO.
YOU LOT STILL NEED TO GET THIS CASTLE BACK IN FIGHTING TRIM.
THAT ZOLA GIRL GOT OUT.
SOMEONE'S GONNA FIND HER, AND SHE'LL TELL 'EM THE CASTLE'S DOWN.
THEN, IF THE BARON DON'T FLATTEN THE PLACE—
HER PEOPLE ***WILL***.
I CAN'T FIX THE CASTLE, BUT I ***CAN*** GET MISS ZEETHA TO SAFETY—
BY Y'R LEAVE, ***OF COURSE***.
BUT HOW DO ***YOU*** KNOW ABOUT MAMMA'S?
...DID MAMMA A ***FAVOR*** ONCE.
SHE'S GOT A LONG MEMORY.
AND THIS "MAMMA" AT THIS "TOURIST" BAR"—
SHE CAN ***KEEP ZEETHA ALIVE?***
WELL, I HAVEN'T ACTUALLY ***SEEN*** ZEETHA'S INJURIES, BUT—
IF SHE'S REALLY THAT BADLY HURT, MAMMA'S IS PROBABLY HER ***BEST SHOT***.
IT'S A GOOD PLACE. I'VE ***BEEN THERE***.
I ***KNEW*** IT.
WELL—
ALL RIGHT. BUT ARE YOU ***SURE*** YOU CAN GET OUT OF HERE ***SAFELY?***
HMF. I DON'T THINK ***HE'S*** GOING TO HAVE ***ANY TROUBLE AT ALL***.
HEH. YOU LISTEN TO YOUR FRIEND HERE, M'LADY.
HE'S A ***SMART GUY***.

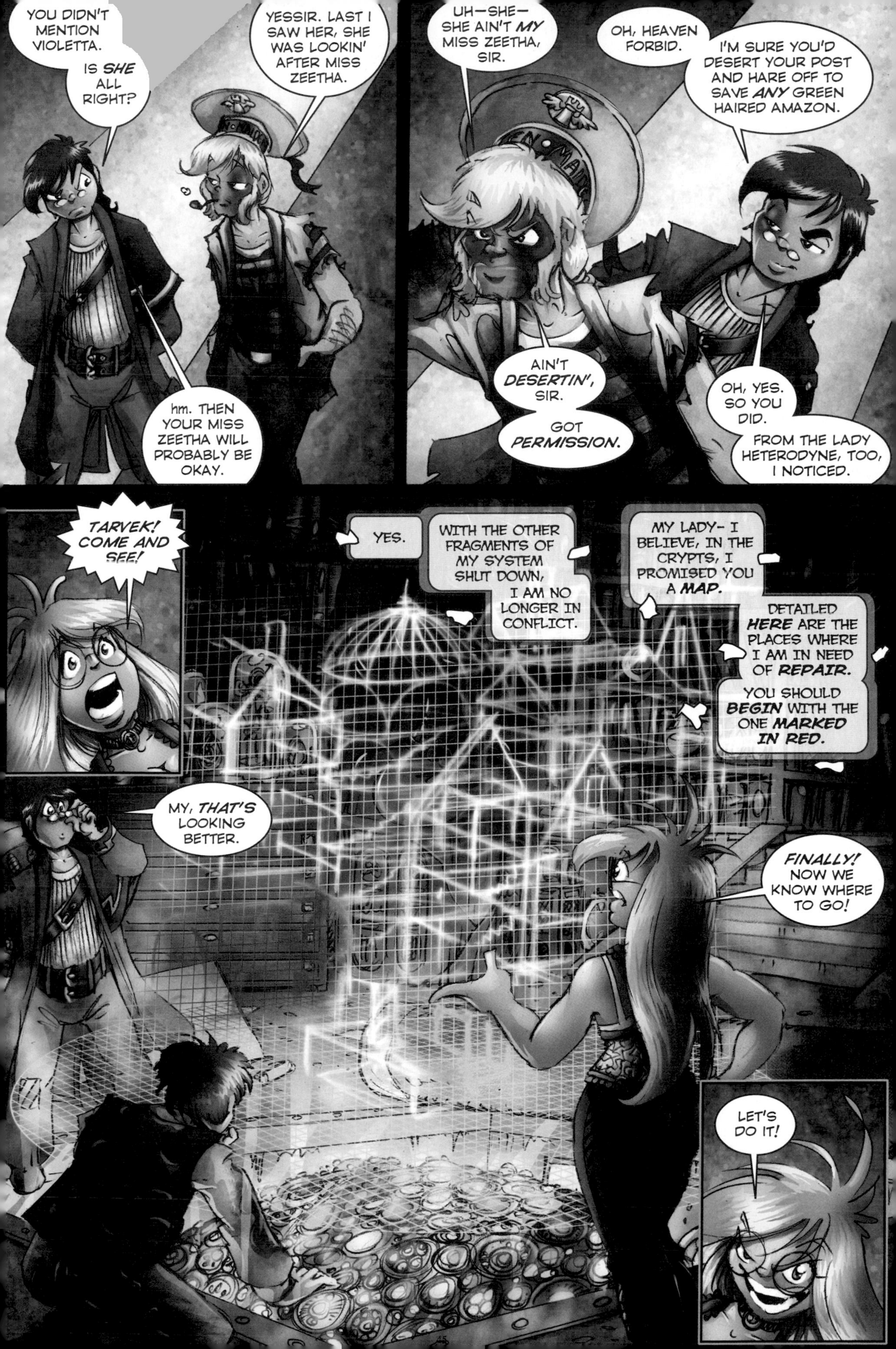
YOU DIDN'T MENTION VIOLETTA.
IS *SHE* ALL RIGHT?
YESSIR. LAST I SAW HER, SHE WAS LOOKIN' AFTER MISS ZEETHA.
hm. THEN YOUR MISS ZEETHA WILL PROBABLY BE OKAY.
UH—SHE— SHE AIN'T *MY* MISS ZEETHA, SIR.
OH, HEAVEN FORBID.
I'M SURE YOU'D DESERT YOUR POST AND HARE OFF TO SAVE *ANY* GREEN HAIRED AMAZON.
AIN'T *DESERTIN'*, SIR.
GOT *PERMISSION.*
OH, YES. SO YOU DID.
FROM THE LADY HETERODYNE, TOO, I NOTICED.
TARVEK! COME AND SEE!
YES.
WITH THE OTHER FRAGMENTS OF MY SYSTEM SHUT DOWN, I AM NO LONGER IN CONFLICT.
MY LADY- I BELIEVE, IN THE CRYPTS, I PROMISED YOU A *MAP.*
DETAILED *HERE* ARE THE PLACES WHERE I AM IN NEED OF *REPAIR.*
YOU SHOULD *BEGIN* WITH THE ONE *MARKED IN RED.*
MY, *THAT'S* LOOKING BETTER.
FINALLY! NOW WE KNOW WHERE TO GO!
LET'S DO IT!

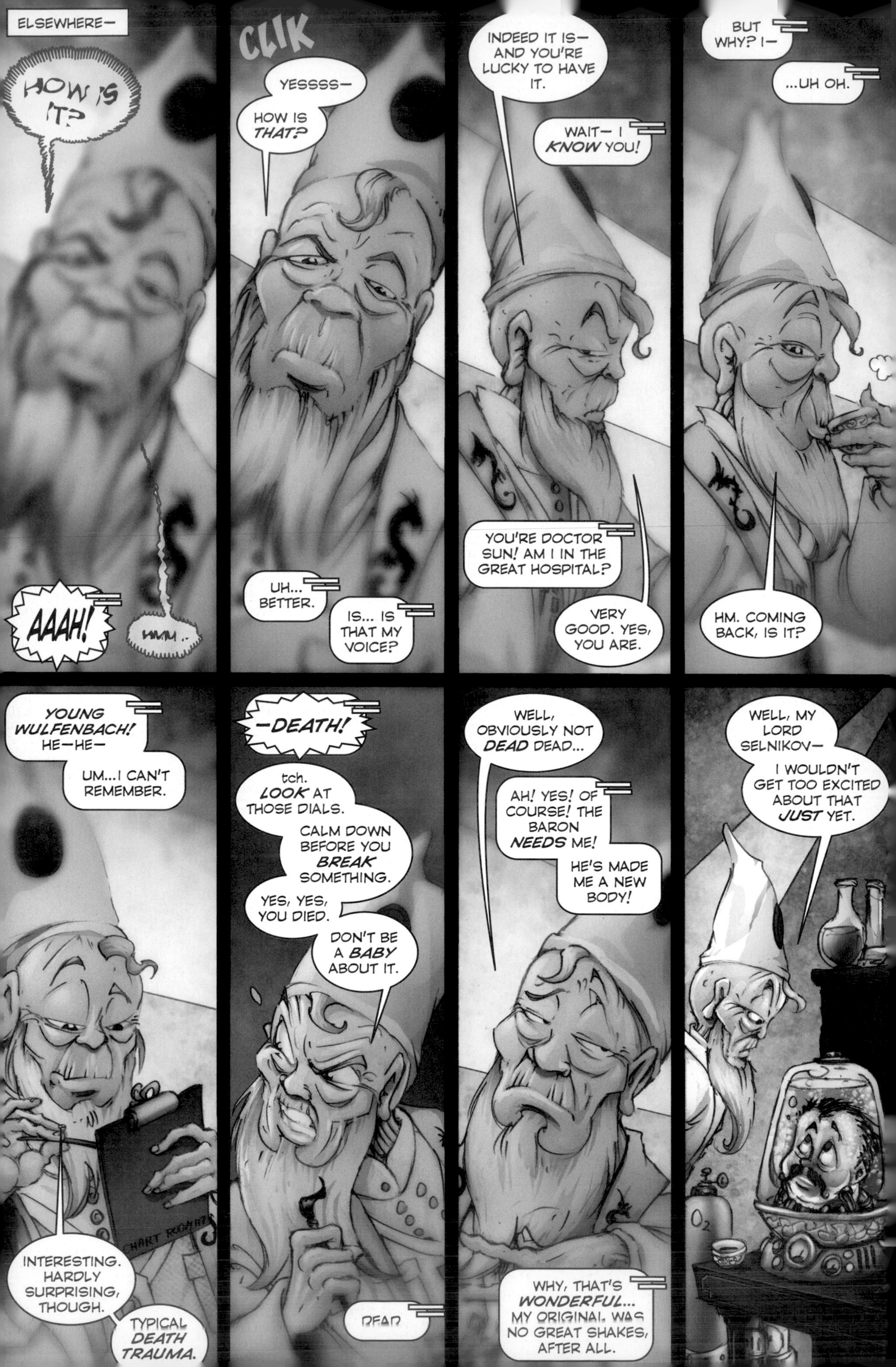
ELSEWHERE—
HOW IS IT?
AAAH!
CLIK
YESSSS—
HOW IS *THAT?*
UH... BETTER.
IS... IS THAT MY VOICE?
INDEED IT IS— AND YOU'RE LUCKY TO HAVE IT.
WAIT— I *KNOW* YOU!
YOU'RE DOCTOR SUN! AM I IN THE GREAT HOSPITAL?
VERY GOOD. YES, YOU ARE.
BUT WHY? I—
...UH OH.
HM. COMING BACK, IS IT?
YOUNG WULFENBACH! HE—HE—
UM...I CAN'T REMEMBER.
INTERESTING. HARDLY SURPRISING, THOUGH.
TYPICAL *DEATH TRAUMA.*
—DEATH!
tch. *LOOK* AT THOSE DIALS.
CALM DOWN BEFORE YOU *BREAK* SOMETHING.
YES, YES, YOU DIED.
DON'T BE A *BABY* ABOUT IT.
DEAD
WELL, OBVIOUSLY NOT *DEAD* DEAD...
AH! YES! OF COURSE! THE BARON *NEEDS* ME!
HE'S MADE ME A NEW BODY!
WHY, THAT'S *WONDERFUL*... MY ORIGINAL WAS NO GREAT SHAKES, AFTER ALL.
WELL, MY LORD SELNIKOV—
I WOULDN'T GET TOO EXCITED ABOUT THAT *JUST* YET.

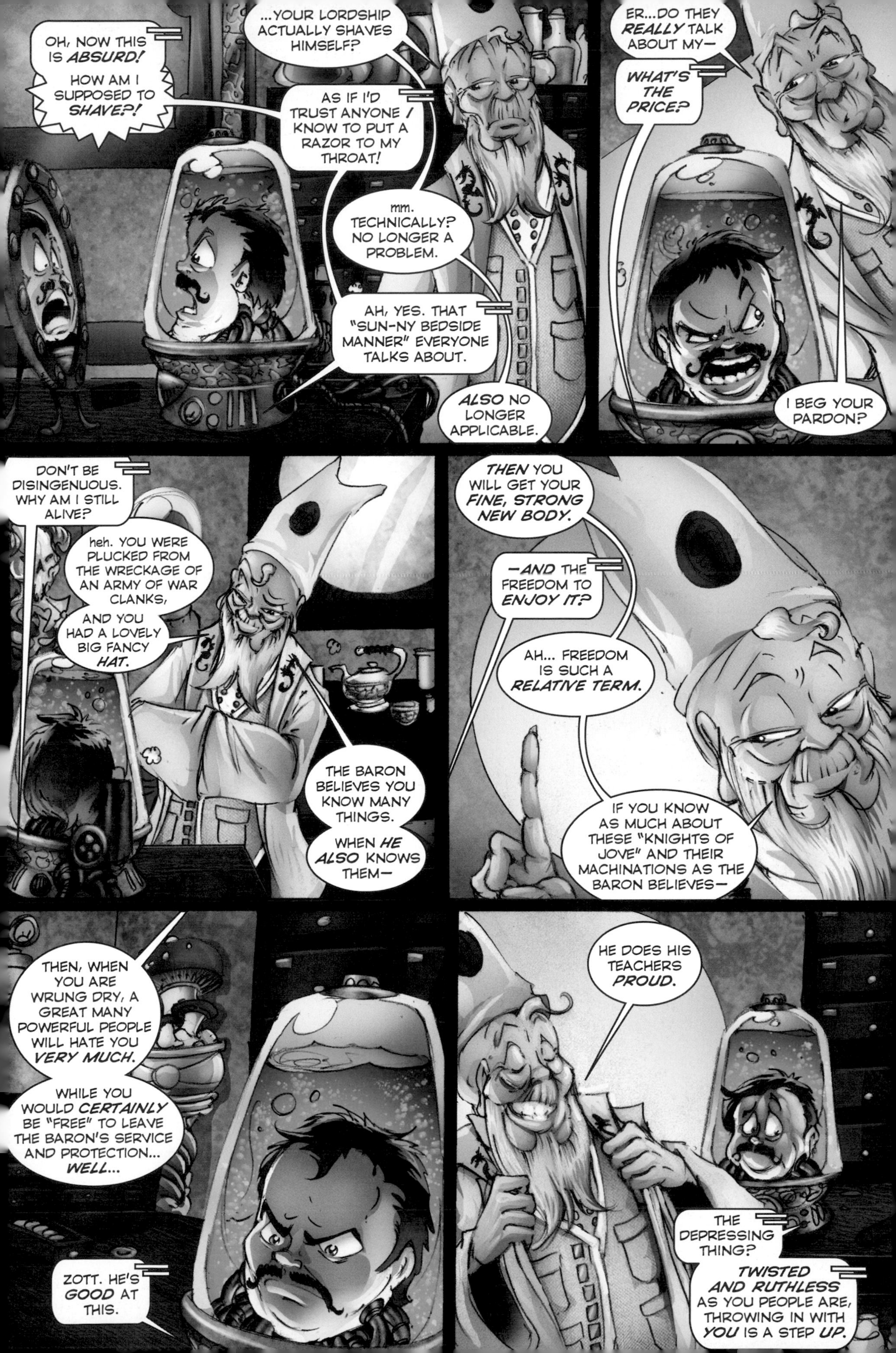
OH, NOW THIS IS ABSURD!
HOW AM I SUPPOSED TO SHAVE?!
...YOUR LORDSHIP ACTUALLY SHAVES HIMSELF?
AS IF I'D TRUST ANYONE I KNOW TO PUT A RAZOR TO MY THROAT!
mm. TECHNICALLY? NO LONGER A PROBLEM.
AH, YES. THAT "SUN-NY BEDSIDE MANNER" EVERYONE TALKS ABOUT.
ALSO NO LONGER APPLICABLE.
ER...DO THEY REALLY TALK ABOUT MY—
WHAT'S THE PRICE?
I BEG YOUR PARDON?
DON'T BE DISINGENUOUS. WHY AM I STILL ALIVE?
heh. YOU WERE PLUCKED FROM THE WRECKAGE OF AN ARMY OF WAR CLANKS,
AND YOU HAD A LOVELY BIG FANCY HAT.
THE BARON BELIEVES YOU KNOW MANY THINGS.
WHEN HE ALSO KNOWS THEM—
THEN YOU WILL GET YOUR FINE, STRONG NEW BODY.
—AND THE FREEDOM TO ENJOY IT?
AH... FREEDOM IS SUCH A RELATIVE TERM.
IF YOU KNOW AS MUCH ABOUT THESE "KNIGHTS OF JOVE" AND THEIR MACHINATIONS AS THE BARON BELIEVES—
THEN, WHEN YOU ARE WRUNG DRY, A GREAT MANY POWERFUL PEOPLE WILL HATE YOU VERY MUCH.
WHILE YOU WOULD CERTAINLY BE "FREE" TO LEAVE THE BARON'S SERVICE AND PROTECTION... WELL...
ZOTT. HE'S GOOD AT THIS.
HE DOES HIS TEACHERS PROUD.
THE DEPRESSING THING?
TWISTED AND RUTHLESS AS YOU PEOPLE ARE, THROWING IN WITH YOU IS A STEP UP.

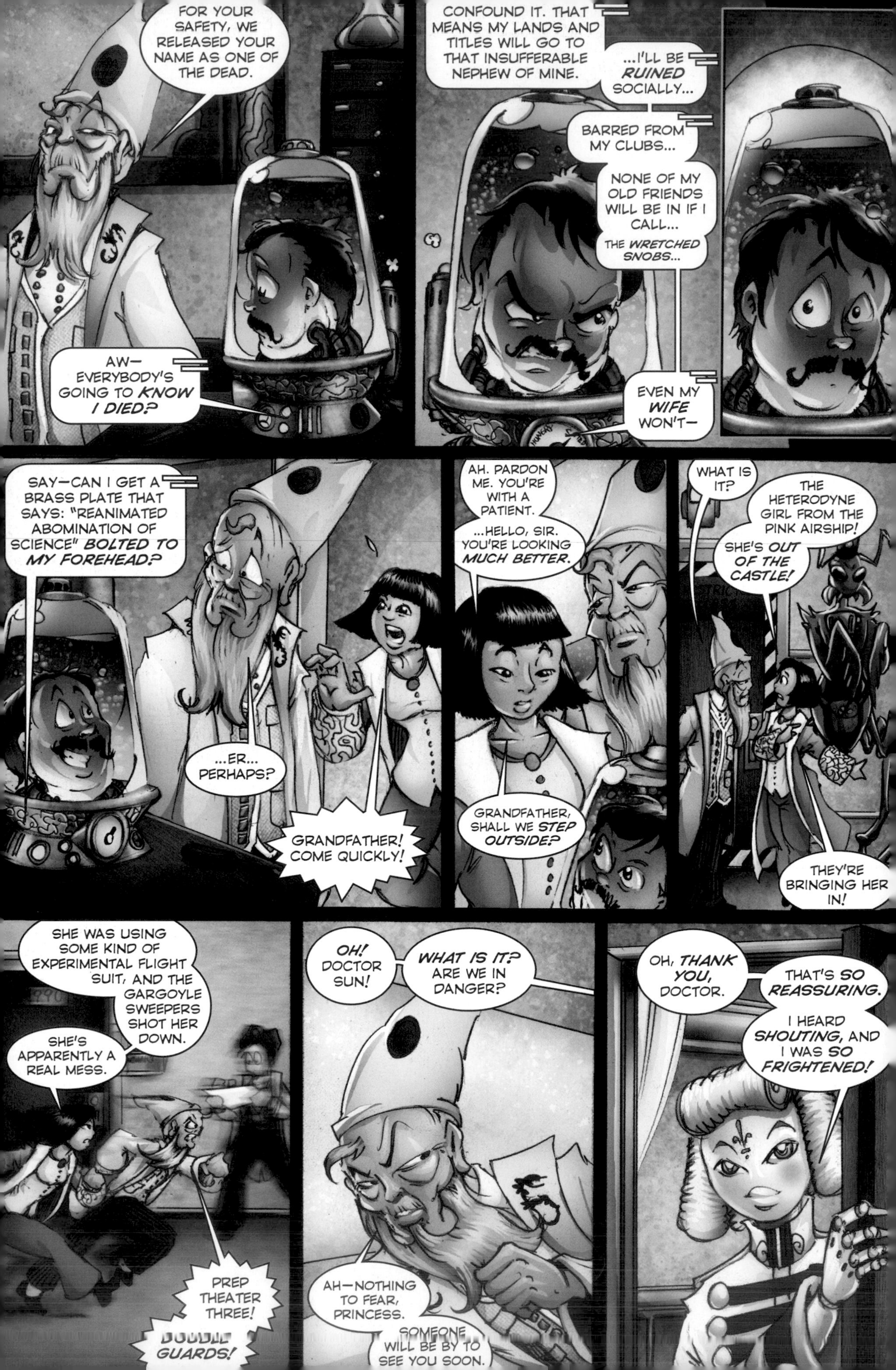
FOR YOUR SAFETY, WE RELEASED YOUR NAME AS ONE OF THE DEAD.
AW— EVERYBODY'S GOING TO *KNOW I DIED?*
CONFOUND IT. THAT MEANS MY LANDS AND TITLES WILL GO TO THAT INSUFFERABLE NEPHEW OF MINE.
...I'LL BE *RUINED* SOCIALLY...
BARRED FROM MY CLUBS...
NONE OF MY OLD FRIENDS WILL BE IN IF I CALL...
THE *WRETCHED SNOBS*...
EVEN MY *WIFE* WON'T—
SAY—CAN I GET A BRASS PLATE THAT SAYS: "REANIMATED ABOMINATION OF SCIENCE" *BOLTED TO MY FOREHEAD?*
...ER... PERHAPS?
GRANDFATHER! COME QUICKLY!
AH. PARDON ME. YOU'RE WITH A PATIENT.
...HELLO, SIR. YOU'RE LOOKING *MUCH BETTER.*
GRANDFATHER, SHALL WE *STEP OUTSIDE?*
WHAT IS IT?
THE HETERODYNE GIRL FROM THE PINK AIRSHIP!
SHE'S *OUT OF THE CASTLE!*
THEY'RE BRINGING HER IN!
SHE WAS USING SOME KIND OF EXPERIMENTAL FLIGHT SUIT, AND THE GARGOYLE SWEEPERS SHOT HER DOWN.
SHE'S APPARENTLY A REAL MESS.
PREP THEATER THREE!
GUARDS!
OH! DOCTOR SUN!
WHAT IS IT? ARE WE IN DANGER?
AH—NOTHING TO FEAR, PRINCESS.
SOMEONE WILL BE BY TO SEE YOU SOON.
OH, *THANK YOU,* DOCTOR.
THAT'S *SO REASSURING.*
I HEARD *SHOUTING,* AND I WAS *SO FRIGHTENED!*

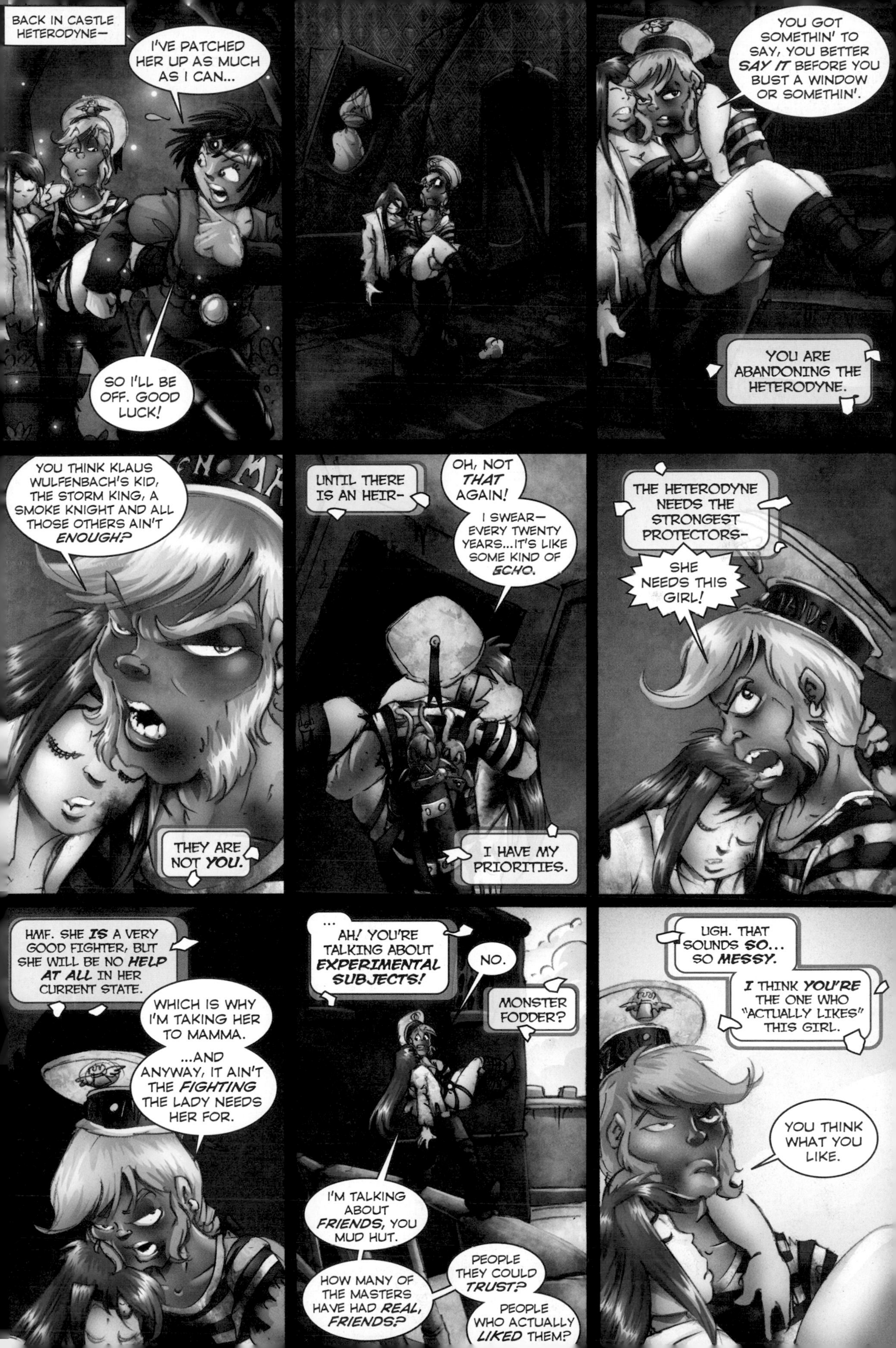

BACK IN CASTLE HETERODYNE—
I'VE PATCHED HER UP AS MUCH AS I CAN...
SO I'LL BE OFF. GOOD LUCK!
YOU GOT SOMETHIN' TO SAY, YOU BETTER SAY IT BEFORE YOU BUST A WINDOW OR SOMETHIN'.
YOU ARE ABANDONING THE HETERODYNE.
YOU THINK KLAUS WULFENBACH'S KID, THE STORM KING, A SMOKE KNIGHT AND ALL THOSE OTHERS AIN'T ENOUGH?
THEY ARE NOT YOU.
UNTIL THERE IS AN HEIR—
OH, NOT THAT AGAIN!
I SWEAR—EVERY TWENTY YEARS...IT'S LIKE SOME KIND OF ECHO.
I HAVE MY PRIORITIES.
THE HETERODYNE NEEDS THE STRONGEST PROTECTORS—
SHE NEEDS THIS GIRL!
HMF. SHE IS A VERY GOOD FIGHTER, BUT SHE WILL BE NO HELP AT ALL IN HER CURRENT STATE.
WHICH IS WHY I'M TAKING HER TO MAMMA.
...AND ANYWAY, IT AIN'T THE FIGHTING THE LADY NEEDS HER FOR.
... AH! YOU'RE TALKING ABOUT EXPERIMENTAL SUBJECTS!
NO.
MONSTER FODDER?
I'M TALKING ABOUT FRIENDS, YOU MUD HUT.
HOW MANY OF THE MASTERS HAVE HAD REAL, FRIENDS?
PEOPLE THEY COULD TRUST?
PEOPLE WHO ACTUALLY LIKED THEM?
UGH. THAT SOUNDS SO... SO MESSY.
I THINK YOU'RE THE ONE WHO "ACTUALLY LIKES" THIS GIRL.
YOU THINK WHAT YOU LIKE.

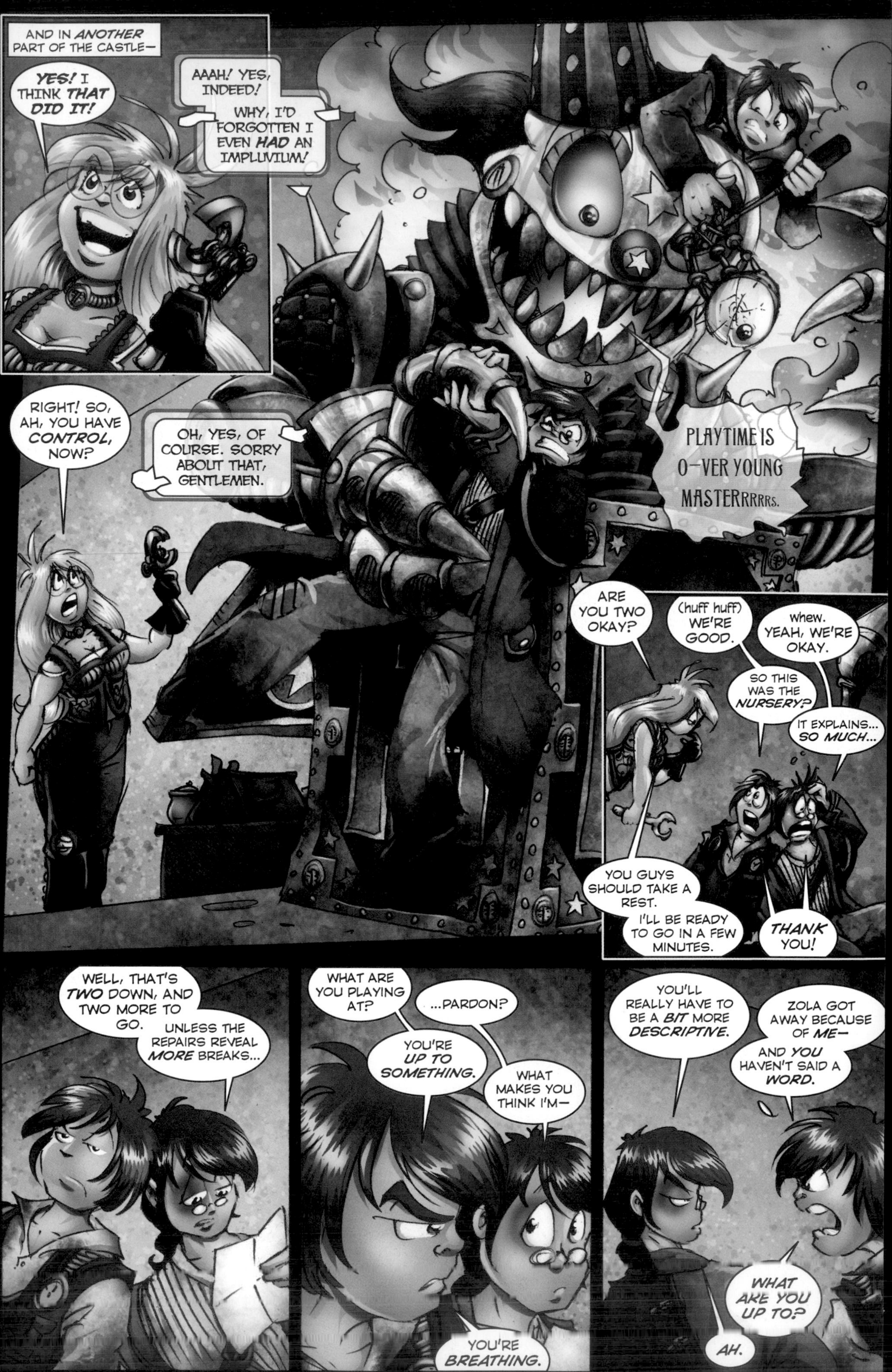

AND IN ANOTHER PART OF THE CASTLE—
YES! I THINK THAT DID IT!
AAAH! YES, INDEED!
WHY, I'D FORGOTTEN I EVEN HAD AN IMPLUVIUM!
RIGHT! SO, AH, YOU HAVE CONTROL, NOW?
OH, YES, OF COURSE. SORRY ABOUT THAT, GENTLEMEN.
PLAYTIME IS O—VER YOUNG MASTERRRRRS.
ARE YOU TWO OKAY?
(huff huff) WE'RE GOOD.
whew. YEAH, WE'RE OKAY.
SO THIS WAS THE NURSERY?
IT EXPLAINS... SO MUCH...
YOU GUYS SHOULD TAKE A REST.
I'LL BE READY TO GO IN A FEW MINUTES.
THANK YOU!
WELL, THAT'S TWO DOWN, AND TWO MORE TO GO.
UNLESS THE REPAIRS REVEAL MORE BREAKS...
WHAT ARE YOU PLAYING AT?
...PARDON?
YOU'RE UP TO SOMETHING.
WHAT MAKES YOU THINK I'M—
YOU'RE BREATHING.
YOU'LL REALLY HAVE TO BE A BIT MORE DESCRIPTIVE.
ZOLA GOT AWAY BECAUSE OF ME—
AND YOU HAVEN'T SAID A WORD.
WHAT ARE YOU UP TO?
AH.

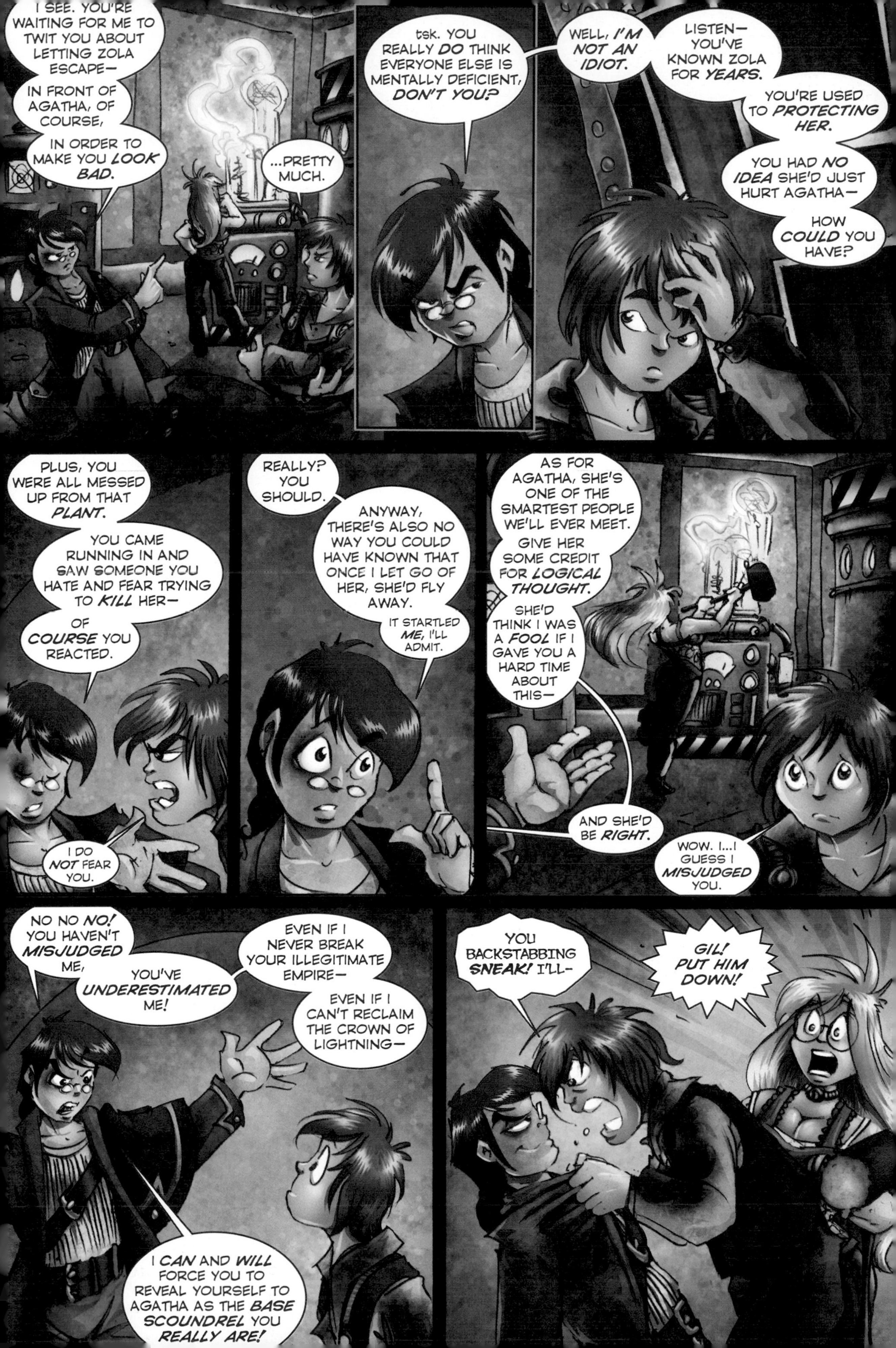

I SEE. YOU'RE WAITING FOR ME TO TWIT YOU ABOUT LETTING ZOLA ESCAPE—
IN FRONT OF AGATHA, OF COURSE,
IN ORDER TO MAKE YOU LOOK BAD.
...PRETTY MUCH.
tsk. YOU REALLY DO THINK EVERYONE ELSE IS MENTALLY DEFICIENT, DON'T YOU?
WELL, I'M NOT AN IDIOT.
LISTEN— YOU'VE KNOWN ZOLA FOR YEARS.
YOU'RE USED TO PROTECTING HER.
YOU HAD NO IDEA SHE'D JUST HURT AGATHA—
HOW COULD YOU HAVE?
PLUS, YOU WERE ALL MESSED UP FROM THAT PLANT.
YOU CAME RUNNING IN AND SAW SOMEONE YOU HATE AND FEAR TRYING TO KILL HER—
OF COURSE YOU REACTED.
I DO NOT FEAR YOU.
REALLY? YOU SHOULD.
ANYWAY, THERE'S ALSO NO WAY YOU COULD HAVE KNOWN THAT ONCE I LET GO OF HER, SHE'D FLY AWAY.
IT STARTLED ME, I'LL ADMIT.
AS FOR AGATHA, SHE'S ONE OF THE SMARTEST PEOPLE WE'LL EVER MEET.
GIVE HER SOME CREDIT FOR LOGICAL THOUGHT.
SHE'D THINK I WAS A FOOL IF I GAVE YOU A HARD TIME ABOUT THIS—
AND SHE'D BE RIGHT.
WOW. I...I GUESS I MISJUDGED YOU.
NO NO NO! YOU HAVEN'T MISJUDGED ME,
YOU'VE UNDERESTIMATED ME!
EVEN IF I NEVER BREAK YOUR ILLEGITIMATE EMPIRE—
EVEN IF I CAN'T RECLAIM THE CROWN OF LIGHTNING—
I CAN AND WILL FORCE YOU TO REVEAL YOURSELF TO AGATHA AS THE BASE SCOUNDREL YOU REALLY ARE!
YOU BACKSTABBING SNEAK! I'LL-
GIL! PUT HIM DOWN!

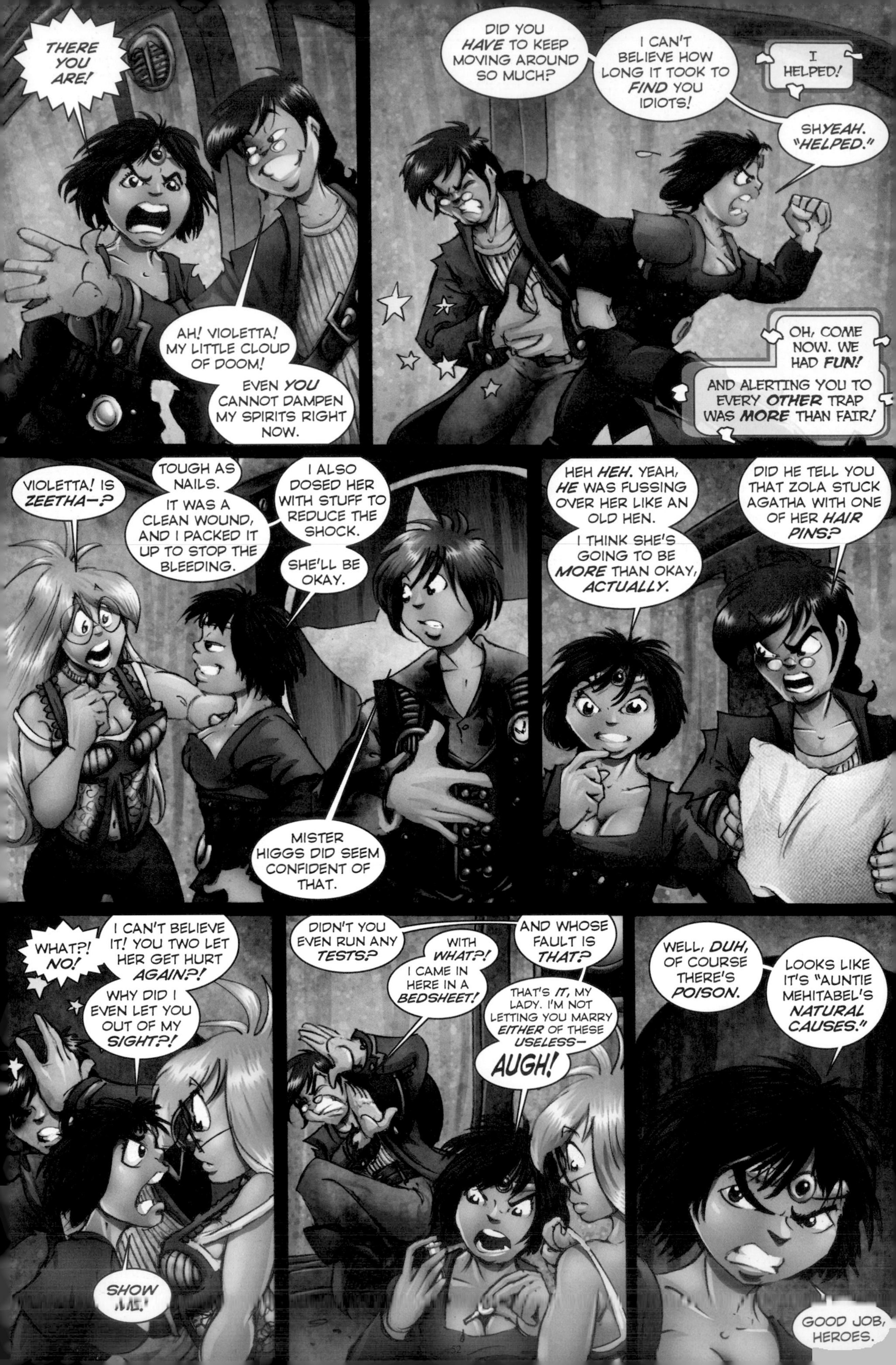
THERE YOU ARE!
AH! VIOLETTA! MY LITTLE CLOUD OF DOOM!
EVEN YOU CANNOT DAMPEN MY SPIRITS RIGHT NOW.
DID YOU HAVE TO KEEP MOVING AROUND SO MUCH?
I CAN'T BELIEVE HOW LONG IT TOOK TO FIND YOU IDIOTS!
I HELPED!
SHYEAH. "HELPED."
OH, COME NOW. WE HAD FUN!
AND ALERTING YOU TO EVERY OTHER TRAP WAS MORE THAN FAIR!
VIOLETTA! IS ZEETHA—?
TOUGH AS NAILS.
IT WAS A CLEAN WOUND, AND I PACKED IT UP TO STOP THE BLEEDING.
I ALSO DOSED HER WITH STUFF TO REDUCE THE SHOCK.
SHE'LL BE OKAY.
MISTER HIGGS DID SEEM CONFIDENT OF THAT.
HEH HEH. YEAH, HE WAS FUSSING OVER HER LIKE AN OLD HEN.
I THINK SHE'S GOING TO BE MORE THAN OKAY, ACTUALLY.
DID HE TELL YOU THAT ZOLA STUCK AGATHA WITH ONE OF HER HAIR PINS?
WHAT?! NO!
I CAN'T BELIEVE IT! YOU TWO LET HER GET HURT AGAIN?!
WHY DID I EVEN LET YOU OUT OF MY SIGHT?!
SHOW
DIDN'T YOU EVEN RUN ANY TESTS?
WITH WHAT?! I CAME IN HERE IN A BEDSHEET!
AND WHOSE FAULT IS THAT?
THAT'S IT, MY LADY. I'M NOT LETTING YOU MARRY EITHER OF THESE USELESS—
AUGH!
WELL, DUH, OF COURSE THERE'S POISON.
LOOKS LIKE IT'S "AUNTIE MEHITABEL'S NATURAL CAUSES."
GOOD JOB, HEROES.

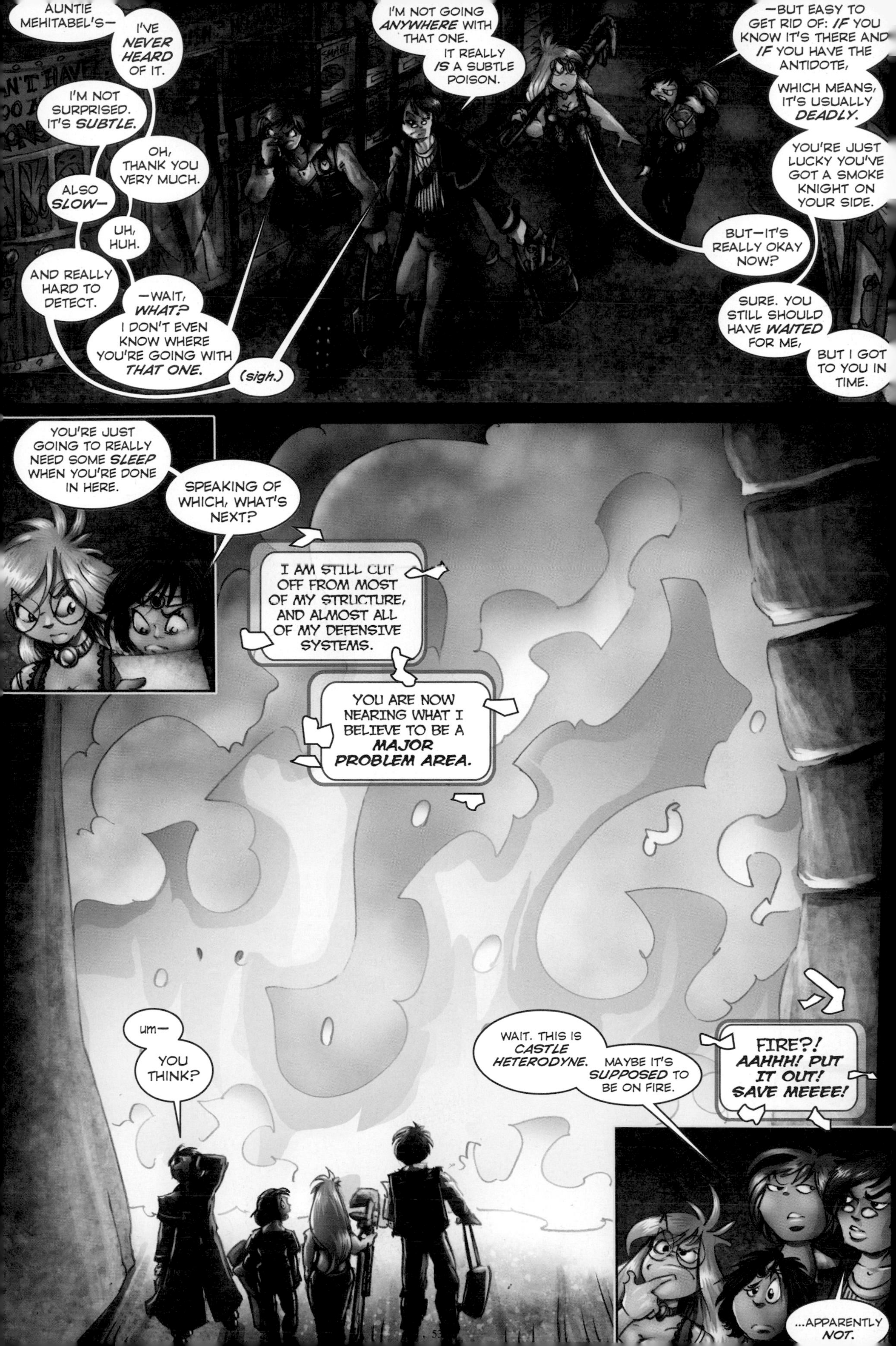
AUNTIE MEHITABEL'S—
I'VE NEVER HEARD OF IT.
I'M NOT SURPRISED. IT'S SUBTLE.
OH, THANK YOU VERY MUCH.
ALSO SLOW—
UH, HUH.
AND REALLY HARD TO DETECT.
—WAIT, WHAT? I DON'T EVEN KNOW WHERE YOU'RE GOING WITH THAT ONE.
(sigh.)
I'M NOT GOING ANYWHERE WITH THAT ONE.
IT REALLY IS A SUBTLE POISON.
—BUT EASY TO GET RID OF: IF YOU KNOW IT'S THERE AND IF YOU HAVE THE ANTIDOTE,
WHICH MEANS, IT'S USUALLY DEADLY.
YOU'RE JUST LUCKY YOU'VE GOT A SMOKE KNIGHT ON YOUR SIDE.
BUT—IT'S REALLY OKAY NOW?
SURE. YOU STILL SHOULD HAVE WAITED FOR ME,
BUT I GOT TO YOU IN TIME.
YOU'RE JUST GOING TO REALLY NEED SOME SLEEP WHEN YOU'RE DONE IN HERE.
SPEAKING OF WHICH, WHAT'S NEXT?
I AM STILL CUT OFF FROM MOST OF MY STRUCTURE, AND ALMOST ALL OF MY DEFENSIVE SYSTEMS.
YOU ARE NOW NEARING WHAT I BELIEVE TO BE A MAJOR PROBLEM AREA.
um—
YOU THINK?
WAIT. THIS IS CASTLE HETERODYNE.
MAYBE IT'S SUPPOSED TO BE ON FIRE.
FIRE?! AAHHH! PUT IT OUT! SAVE MEEEE!
...APPARENTLY NOT.

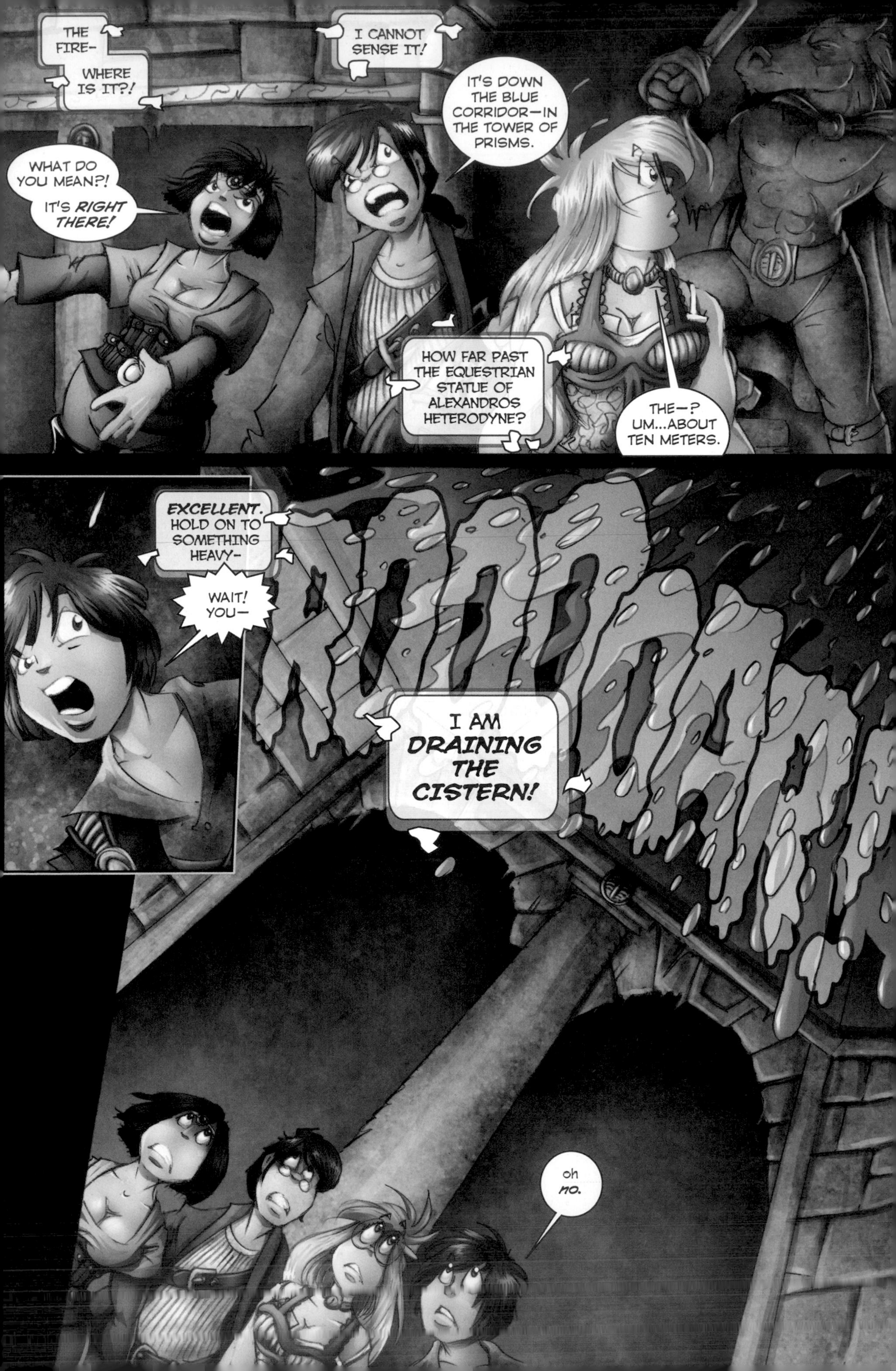

THE FIRE- WHERE IS IT?!
I CANNOT SENSE IT!
IT'S DOWN THE BLUE CORRIDOR—IN THE TOWER OF PRISMS.
WHAT DO YOU MEAN?! IT'S RIGHT THERE!
HOW FAR PAST THE EQUESTRIAN STATUE OF ALEXANDROS HETERODYNE?
THE—? UM...ABOUT TEN METERS.
EXCELLENT. HOLD ON TO SOMETHING HEAVY-
WAIT! YOU—
I AM DRAINING THE CISTERN!
oh no.

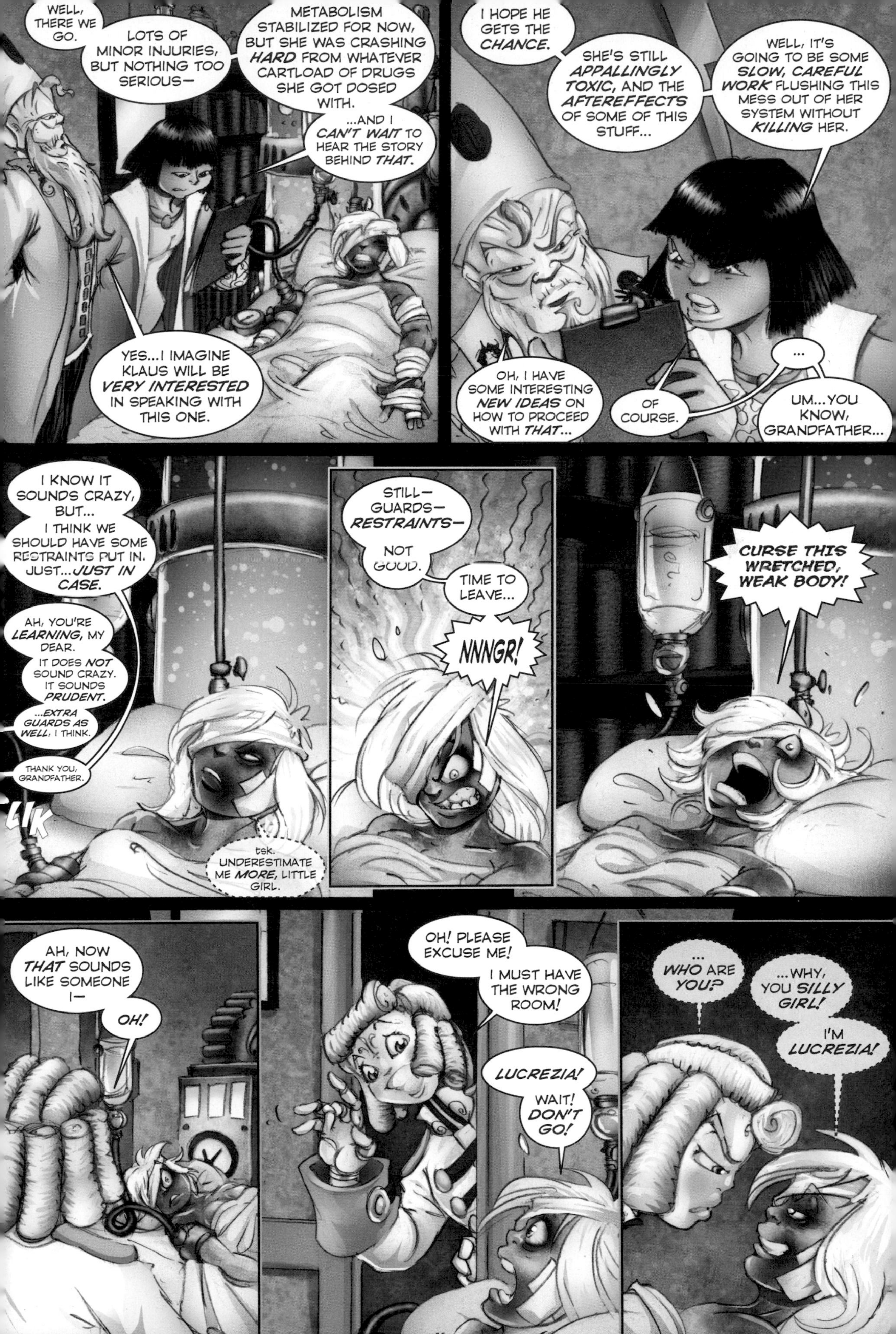

WELL, THERE WE GO.
LOTS OF MINOR INJURIES, BUT NOTHING TOO SERIOUS—
METABOLISM STABILIZED FOR NOW, BUT SHE WAS CRASHING HARD FROM WHATEVER CARTLOAD OF DRUGS SHE GOT DOSED WITH.
...AND I CAN'T WAIT TO HEAR THE STORY BEHIND THAT.
YES...I IMAGINE KLAUS WILL BE VERY INTERESTED IN SPEAKING WITH THIS ONE.
I HOPE HE GETS THE CHANCE.
SHE'S STILL APPALLINGLY TOXIC, AND THE AFTEREFFECTS OF SOME OF THIS STUFF...
WELL, IT'S GOING TO BE SOME SLOW, CAREFUL WORK FLUSHING THIS MESS OUT OF HER SYSTEM WITHOUT KILLING HER.
OH, I HAVE SOME INTERESTING NEW IDEAS ON HOW TO PROCEED WITH THAT...
OF COURSE.
...
UM...YOU KNOW, GRANDFATHER...
I KNOW IT SOUNDS CRAZY, BUT...
I THINK WE SHOULD HAVE SOME RESTRAINTS PUT IN. JUST...JUST IN CASE.
AH, YOU'RE LEARNING, MY DEAR.
IT DOES NOT SOUND CRAZY. IT SOUNDS PRUDENT.
...EXTRA GUARDS AS WELL, I THINK.
THANK YOU, GRANDFATHER.
LIK
tsk. UNDERESTIMATE ME MORE, LITTLE GIRL.
STILL— GUARDS— RESTRAINTS—
NOT GOOD.
TIME TO LEAVE...
NNNGR!
CURSE THIS WRETCHED, WEAK BODY!
AH, NOW THAT SOUNDS LIKE SOMEONE I—
OH!
OH! PLEASE EXCUSE ME!
I MUST HAVE THE WRONG ROOM!
LUCREZIA!
WAIT! DON'T GO!
...WHO ARE YOU?
...WHY, YOU SILLY GIRL!
I'M LUCREZIA!

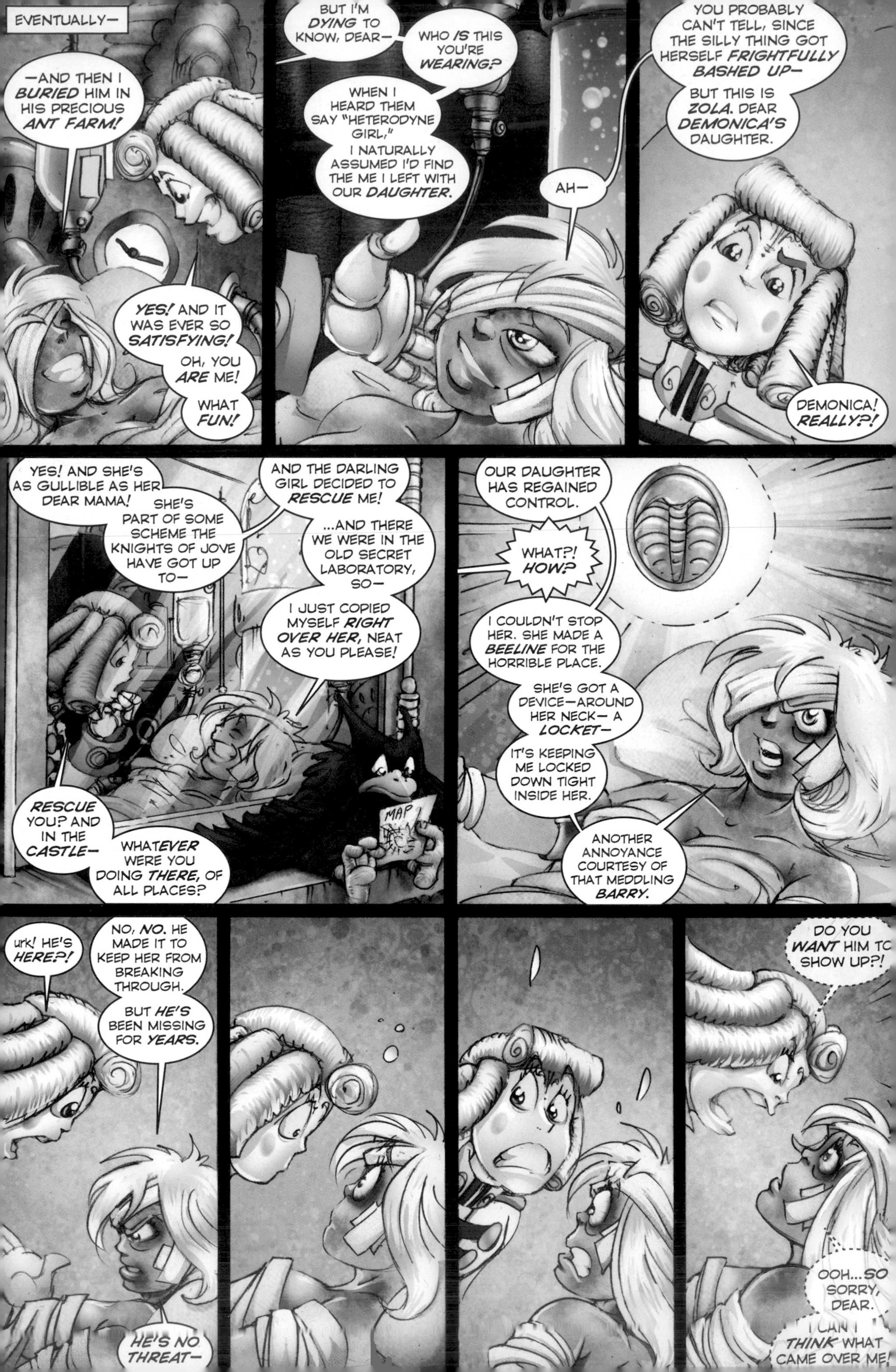
EVENTUALLY—
—AND THEN I BURIED HIM IN HIS PRECIOUS ANT FARM!
YES! AND IT WAS EVER SO SATISFYING!
OH, YOU ARE ME!
WHAT FUN!
BUT I'M DYING TO KNOW, DEAR—
WHO IS THIS YOU'RE WEARING?
WHEN I HEARD THEM SAY "HETERODYNE GIRL," I NATURALLY ASSUMED I'D FIND THE ME I LEFT WITH OUR DAUGHTER.
AH—
YOU PROBABLY CAN'T TELL, SINCE THE SILLY THING GOT HERSELF FRIGHTFULLY BASHED UP—
BUT THIS IS ZOLA. DEAR DEMONICA'S DAUGHTER.
DEMONICA! REALLY?!
YES! AND SHE'S AS GULLIBLE AS HER DEAR MAMA!
SHE'S PART OF SOME SCHEME THE KNIGHTS OF JOVE HAVE GOT UP TO—
AND THE DARLING GIRL DECIDED TO RESCUE ME!
...AND THERE WE WERE IN THE OLD SECRET LABORATORY, SO—
I JUST COPIED MYSELF RIGHT OVER HER, NEAT AS YOU PLEASE!
RESCUE YOU? AND IN THE CASTLE—
WHATEVER WERE YOU DOING THERE, OF ALL PLACES?
MAP
OUR DAUGHTER HAS REGAINED CONTROL.
WHAT?! HOW?
I COULDN'T STOP HER. SHE MADE A BEELINE FOR THE HORRIBLE PLACE.
SHE'S GOT A DEVICE—AROUND HER NECK— A LOCKET—
IT'S KEEPING ME LOCKED DOWN TIGHT INSIDE HER.
ANOTHER ANNOYANCE COURTESY OF THAT MEDDLING BARRY.
urk! HE'S HERE?!
NO, NO. HE MADE IT TO KEEP HER FROM BREAKING THROUGH.
BUT HE'S BEEN MISSING FOR YEARS.
HE'S NO THREAT—
DO YOU WANT HIM TO SHOW UP?!
OOH...SO SORRY, DEAR.
I CAN'T THINK WHAT CAME OVER ME!

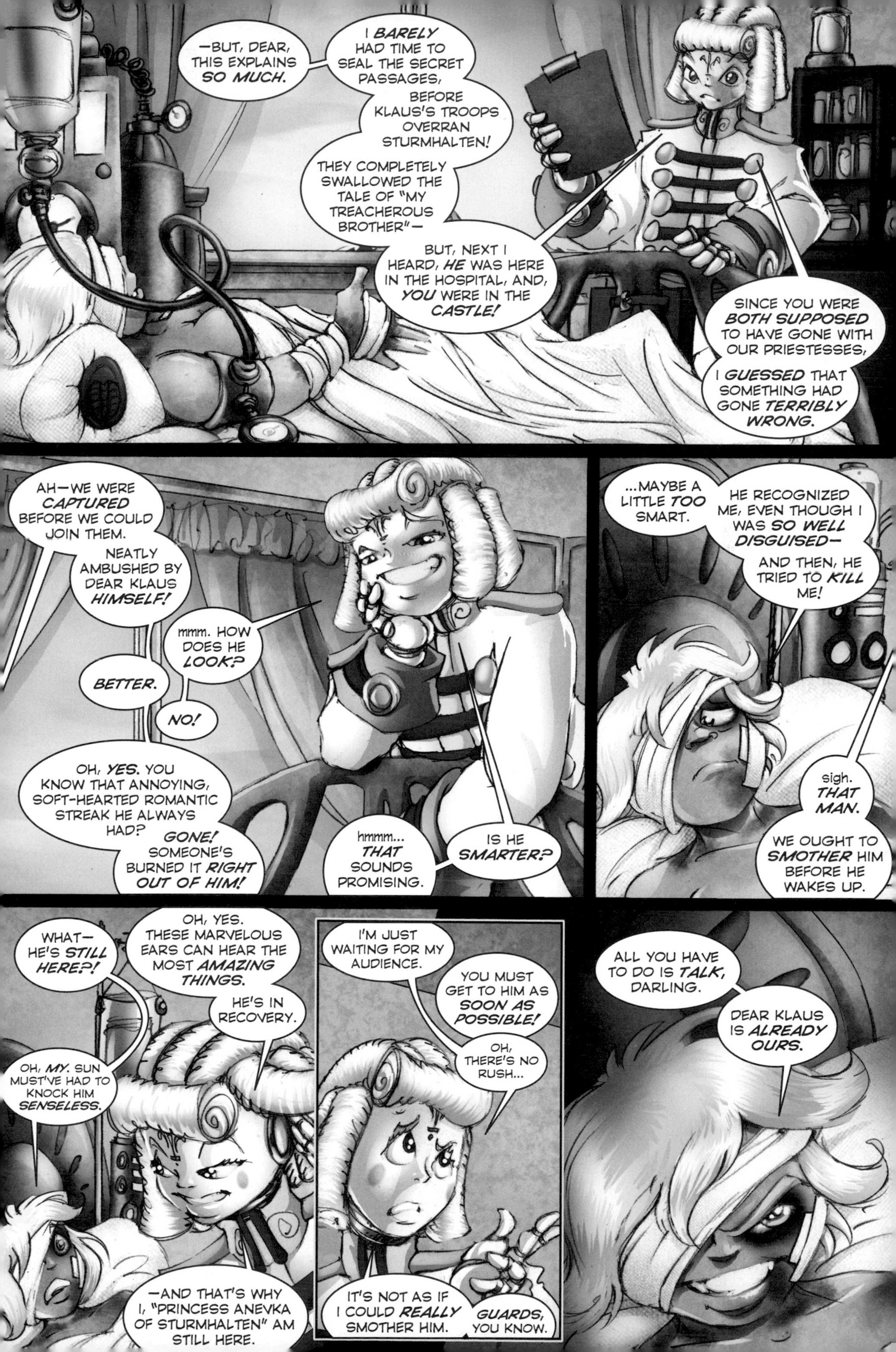
—BUT, DEAR, THIS EXPLAINS SO MUCH.
I BARELY HAD TIME TO SEAL THE SECRET PASSAGES,
BEFORE KLAUS'S TROOPS OVERRAN STURMHALTEN!
THEY COMPLETELY SWALLOWED THE TALE OF "MY TREACHEROUS BROTHER"—
BUT, NEXT I HEARD, HE WAS HERE IN THE HOSPITAL, AND, YOU WERE IN THE CASTLE!
SINCE YOU WERE BOTH SUPPOSED TO HAVE GONE WITH OUR PRIESTESSES,
I GUESSED THAT SOMETHING HAD GONE TERRIBLY WRONG.
AH—WE WERE CAPTURED BEFORE WE COULD JOIN THEM.
NEATLY AMBUSHED BY DEAR KLAUS HIMSELF!
mmm. HOW DOES HE LOOK?
BETTER.
NO!
OH, YES. YOU KNOW THAT ANNOYING, SOFT-HEARTED ROMANTIC STREAK HE ALWAYS HAD?
GONE! SOMEONE'S BURNED IT RIGHT OUT OF HIM!
hmmm... THAT SOUNDS PROMISING.
IS HE SMARTER?
...MAYBE A LITTLE TOO SMART.
HE RECOGNIZED ME, EVEN THOUGH I WAS SO WELL DISGUISED—
AND THEN, HE TRIED TO KILL ME!
sigh. THAT MAN.
WE OUGHT TO SMOTHER HIM BEFORE HE WAKES UP.
WHAT— HE'S STILL HERE?!
OH, YES. THESE MARVELOUS EARS CAN HEAR THE MOST AMAZING THINGS.
HE'S IN RECOVERY.
OH, MY. SUN MUST'VE HAD TO KNOCK HIM SENSELESS.
—AND THAT'S WHY I, "PRINCESS ANEVKA OF STURMHALTEN" AM STILL HERE.
I'M JUST WAITING FOR MY AUDIENCE.
YOU MUST GET TO HIM AS SOON AS POSSIBLE!
OH, THERE'S NO RUSH...
IT'S NOT AS IF I COULD REALLY SMOTHER HIM.
GUARDS, YOU KNOW.
ALL YOU HAVE TO DO IS TALK, DARLING.
DEAR KLAUS IS ALREADY OURS.

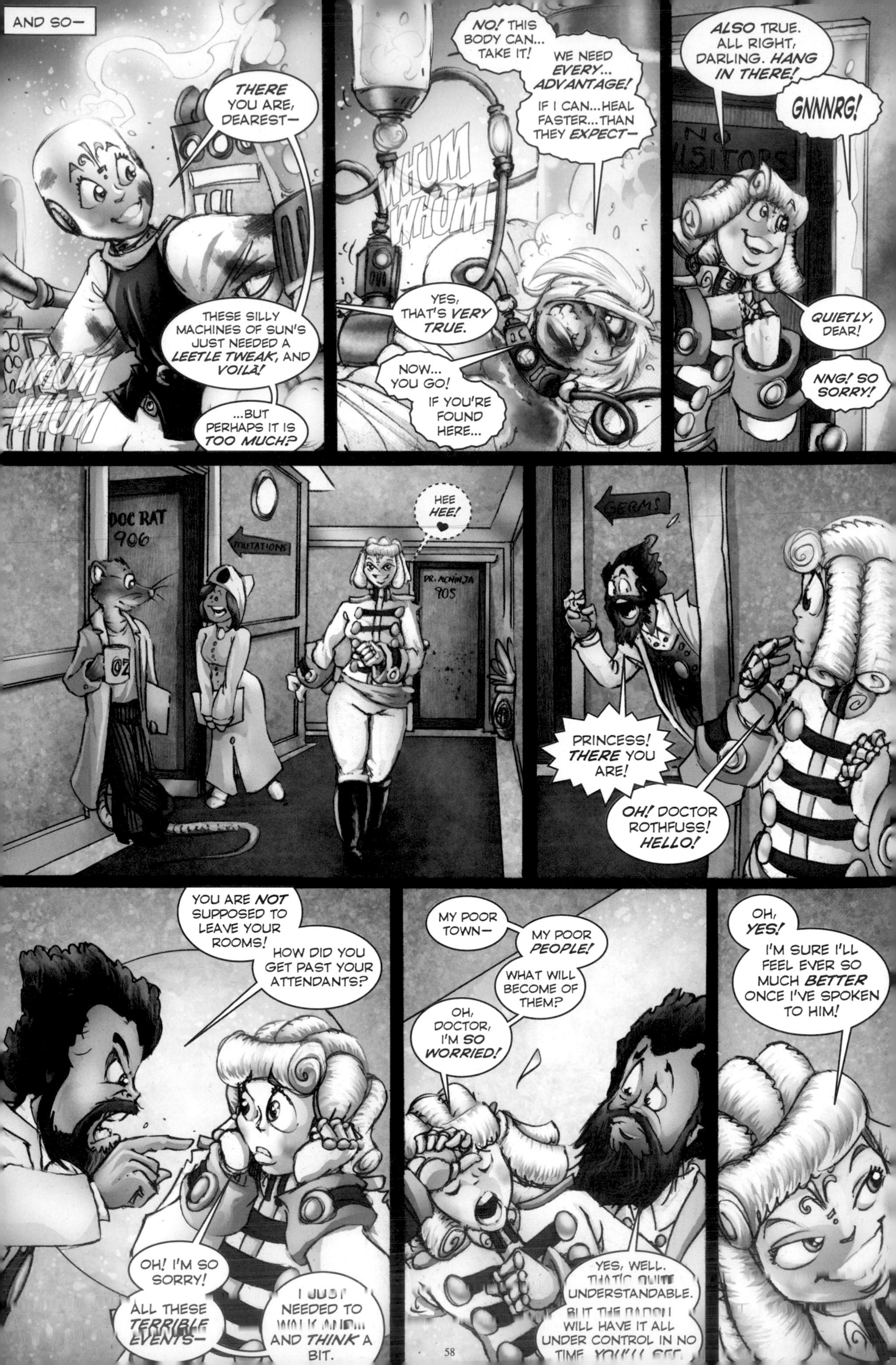
AND SO—
THERE YOU ARE, DEAREST—
THESE SILLY MACHINES OF SUN'S JUST NEEDED A LEETLE TWEAK, AND VOILÀ!
WHUM WHUM
...BUT PERHAPS IT IS TOO MUCH?
NO! THIS BODY CAN... TAKE IT!
WE NEED EVERY... ADVANTAGE!
IF I CAN...HEAL FASTER...THAN THEY EXPECT—
WHUM WHUM
YES, THAT'S VERY TRUE.
NOW... YOU GO!
IF YOU'RE FOUND HERE...
ALSO TRUE. ALL RIGHT, DARLING. HANG IN THERE!
GNNNRG!
NO VISITORS
QUIETLY, DEAR!
NNG! SO SORRY!
DOC RAT 906
MUTATIONS
HEE HEE!
DR. MCNINJA 905
GERMS
PRINCESS! THERE YOU ARE!
OH! DOCTOR ROTHFUSS! HELLO!
YOU ARE NOT SUPPOSED TO LEAVE YOUR ROOMS!
HOW DID YOU GET PAST YOUR ATTENDANTS?
OH! I'M SO SORRY!
ALL THESE TERRIBLE EVENTS—
NEEDED TO
AND THINK A BIT.
MY POOR TOWN—
MY POOR PEOPLE!
WHAT WILL BECOME OF THEM?
OH, DOCTOR, I'M SO WORRIED!
YES, WELL.
UNDERSTANDABLE.
WILL HAVE IT ALL UNDER CONTROL IN NO
OH, YES!
I'M SURE I'LL FEEL EVER SO MUCH BETTER ONCE I'VE SPOKEN TO HIM!

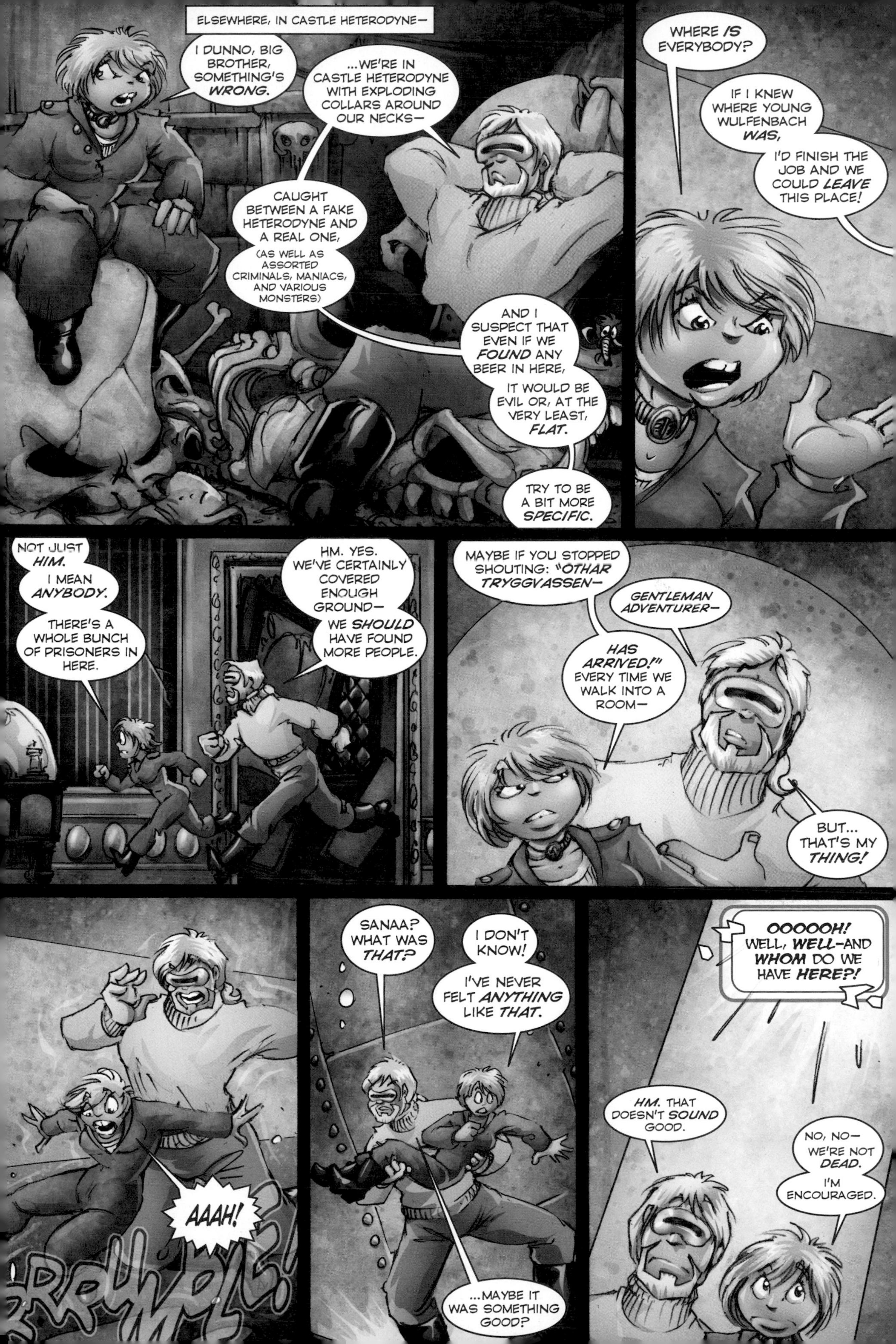
ELSEWHERE, IN CASTLE HETERODYNE—
I DUNNO, BIG BROTHER, SOMETHING'S *WRONG*.
...WE'RE IN CASTLE HETERODYNE WITH EXPLODING COLLARS AROUND OUR NECKS—
CAUGHT BETWEEN A FAKE HETERODYNE AND A REAL ONE,
(AS WELL AS ASSORTED CRIMINALS, MANIACS, AND VARIOUS MONSTERS)
AND I SUSPECT THAT EVEN IF WE *FOUND* ANY BEER IN HERE,
IT WOULD BE EVIL OR, AT THE VERY LEAST, *FLAT*.
TRY TO BE A BIT MORE *SPECIFIC*.
WHERE *IS* EVERYBODY?
IF I KNEW WHERE YOUNG WULFENBACH *WAS*,
I'D FINISH THE JOB AND WE COULD *LEAVE* THIS PLACE!
NOT JUST *HIM*.
I MEAN *ANYBODY*.
THERE'S A WHOLE BUNCH OF PRISONERS IN HERE.
HM. YES. WE'VE CERTAINLY COVERED ENOUGH GROUND—
WE *SHOULD* HAVE FOUND MORE PEOPLE.
MAYBE IF YOU STOPPED SHOUTING: "*OTHAR TRYGGVASSEN*—
GENTLEMAN ADVENTURER—
HAS ARRIVED!" EVERY TIME WE WALK INTO A ROOM—
BUT... THAT'S MY *THING!*
AAAH!
SANAA? WHAT WAS *THAT?*
I DON'T KNOW!
I'VE NEVER FELT *ANYTHING* LIKE *THAT*.
...MAYBE IT WAS SOMETHING GOOD?
OOOOOH! WELL, *WELL*—AND *WHOM* DO WE HAVE *HERE?!*
HM. THAT DOESN'T *SOUND* GOOD.
NO, NO— WE'RE NOT *DEAD*.
I'M ENCOURAGED.

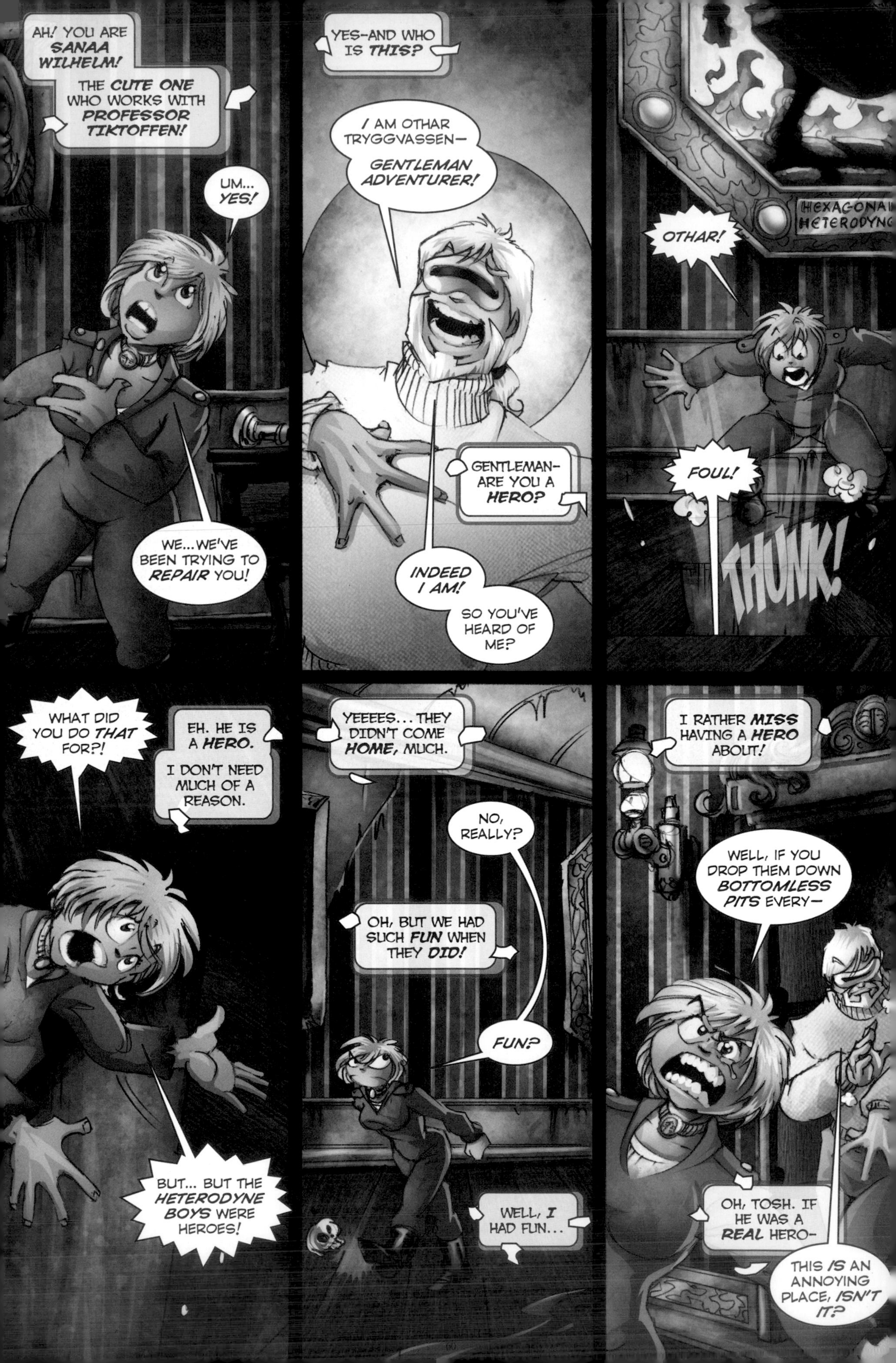

AH! YOU ARE SANAA WILHELM!
THE CUTE ONE WHO WORKS WITH PROFESSOR TIKTOFFEN!
UM... YES!
WE...WE'VE BEEN TRYING TO REPAIR YOU!
YES–AND WHO IS THIS?
I AM OTHAR TRYGGVASSEN—
GENTLEMAN ADVENTURER!
GENTLEMAN–ARE YOU A HERO?
INDEED I AM!
SO YOU'VE HEARD OF ME?
HEXAGONAL HETERODYNE
OTHAR!
FOUL!
THUNK!
WHAT DID YOU DO THAT FOR?!
EH. HE IS A HERO.
I DON'T NEED MUCH OF A REASON.
BUT... BUT THE HETERODYNE BOYS WERE HEROES!
YEEEES... THEY DIDN'T COME HOME, MUCH.
NO, REALLY?
OH, BUT WE HAD SUCH FUN WHEN THEY DID!
FUN?
WELL, I HAD FUN...
I RATHER MISS HAVING A HERO ABOUT!
WELL, IF YOU DROP THEM DOWN BOTTOMLESS PITS EVERY—
OH, TOSH. IF HE WAS A REAL HERO–
THIS IS AN ANNOYING PLACE, ISN'T IT?

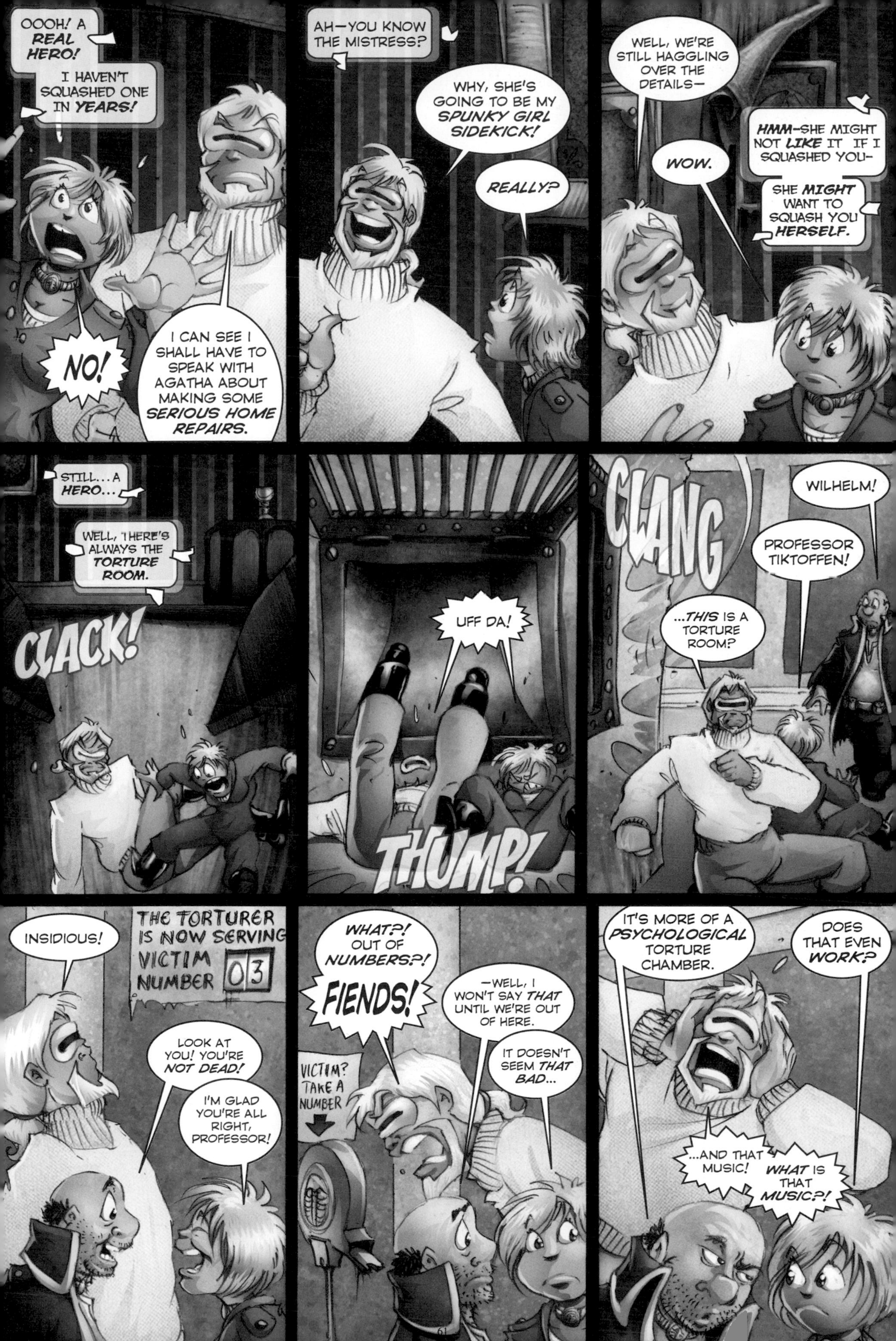
OOOH! A REAL HERO!
I HAVEN'T SQUASHED ONE IN YEARS!
NO!
I CAN SEE I SHALL HAVE TO SPEAK WITH AGATHA ABOUT MAKING SOME SERIOUS HOME REPAIRS.
AH—YOU KNOW THE MISTRESS?
WHY, SHE'S GOING TO BE MY SPUNKY GIRL SIDEKICK!
REALLY?
WELL, WE'RE STILL HAGGLING OVER THE DETAILS—
WOW.
HMM—SHE MIGHT NOT LIKE IT IF I SQUASHED YOU-
SHE MIGHT WANT TO SQUASH YOU HERSELF.
STILL... A HERO...
WELL, THERE'S ALWAYS THE TORTURE ROOM.
CLACK!
UFF DA!
THUMP!
CLANG
WILHELM!
PROFESSOR TIKTOFFEN!
...THIS IS A TORTURE ROOM?
THE TORTURER IS NOW SERVING VICTIM NUMBER 03
INSIDIOUS!
LOOK AT YOU! YOU'RE NOT DEAD!
I'M GLAD YOU'RE ALL RIGHT, PROFESSOR!
WHAT?! OUT OF NUMBERS?!
FIENDS!
—WELL, I WON'T SAY THAT UNTIL WE'RE OUT OF HERE.
VICTIM? TAKE A NUMBER
IT DOESN'T SEEM THAT BAD...
IT'S MORE OF A PSYCHOLOGICAL TORTURE CHAMBER.
DOES THAT EVEN WORK?
...AND THAT MUSIC!
WHAT IS THAT MUSIC?!

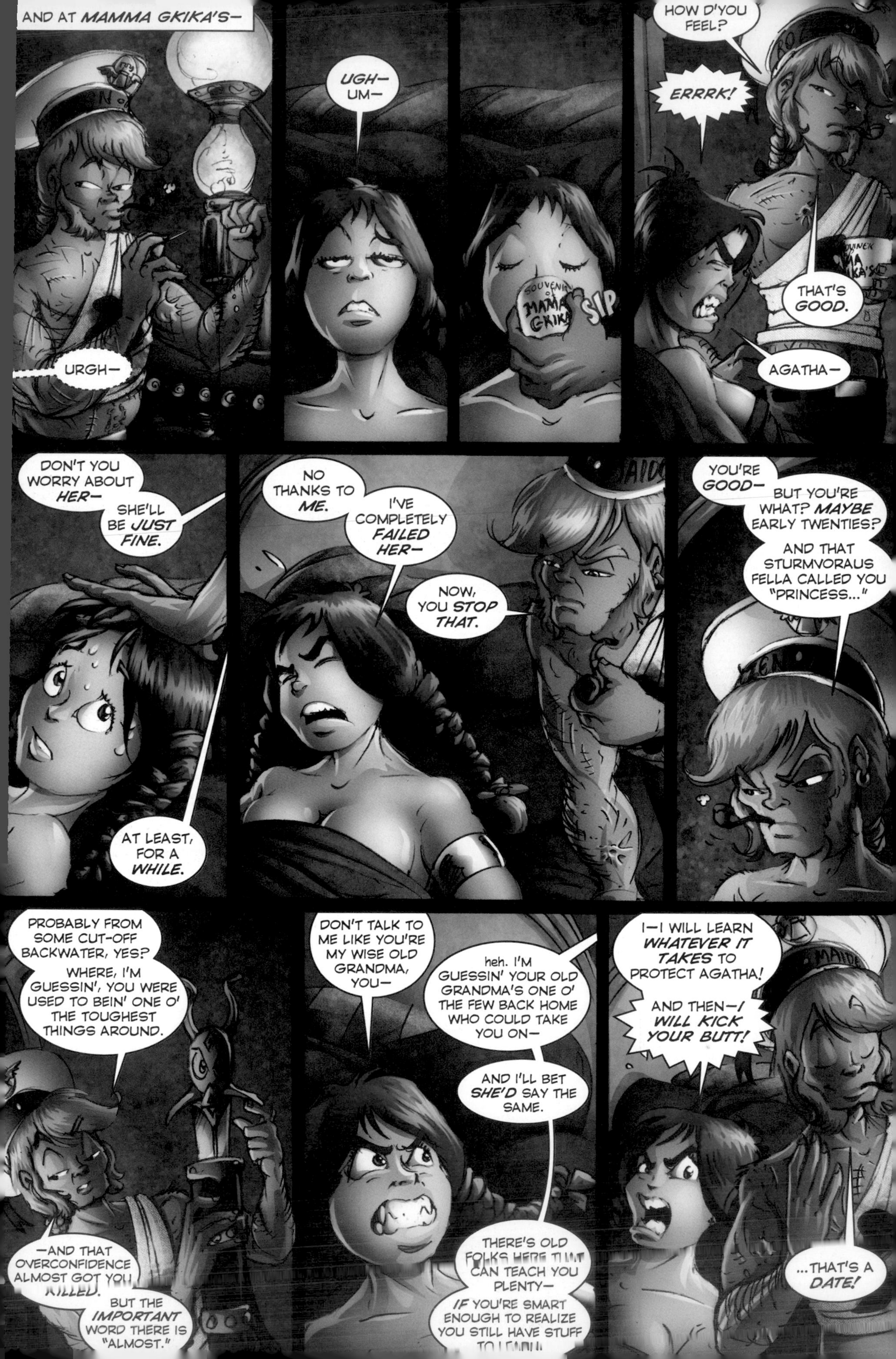
AND AT MAMMA GKIKA'S—
URGH—
UGH— UM—
SIP
HOW D'YOU FEEL?
ERRRK!
THAT'S GOOD.
AGATHA—
DON'T YOU WORRY ABOUT HER—
SHE'LL BE JUST FINE.
AT LEAST, FOR A WHILE.
NO THANKS TO ME.
I'VE COMPLETELY FAILED HER—
NOW, YOU STOP THAT.
YOU'RE GOOD—
BUT YOU'RE WHAT? MAYBE EARLY TWENTIES?
AND THAT STURMVORAUS FELLA CALLED YOU "PRINCESS..."
PROBABLY FROM SOME CUT-OFF BACKWATER, YES?
WHERE, I'M GUESSIN', YOU WERE USED TO BEIN' ONE O' THE TOUGHEST THINGS AROUND.
—AND THAT OVERCONFIDENCE ALMOST GOT YOU KILLED.
BUT THE IMPORTANT WORD THERE IS "ALMOST."
DON'T TALK TO ME LIKE YOU'RE MY WISE OLD GRANDMA, YOU—
heh. I'M GUESSIN' YOUR OLD GRANDMA'S ONE O' THE FEW BACK HOME WHO COULD TAKE YOU ON—
AND I'LL BET SHE'D SAY THE SAME.
THERE'S OLD FOLKS HERE THAT CAN TEACH YOU PLENTY—
IF YOU'RE SMART ENOUGH TO REALIZE YOU STILL HAVE STUFF
I—I WILL LEARN WHATEVER IT TAKES TO PROTECT AGATHA!
AND THEN—I WILL KICK YOUR BUTT!
...THAT'S A DATE!

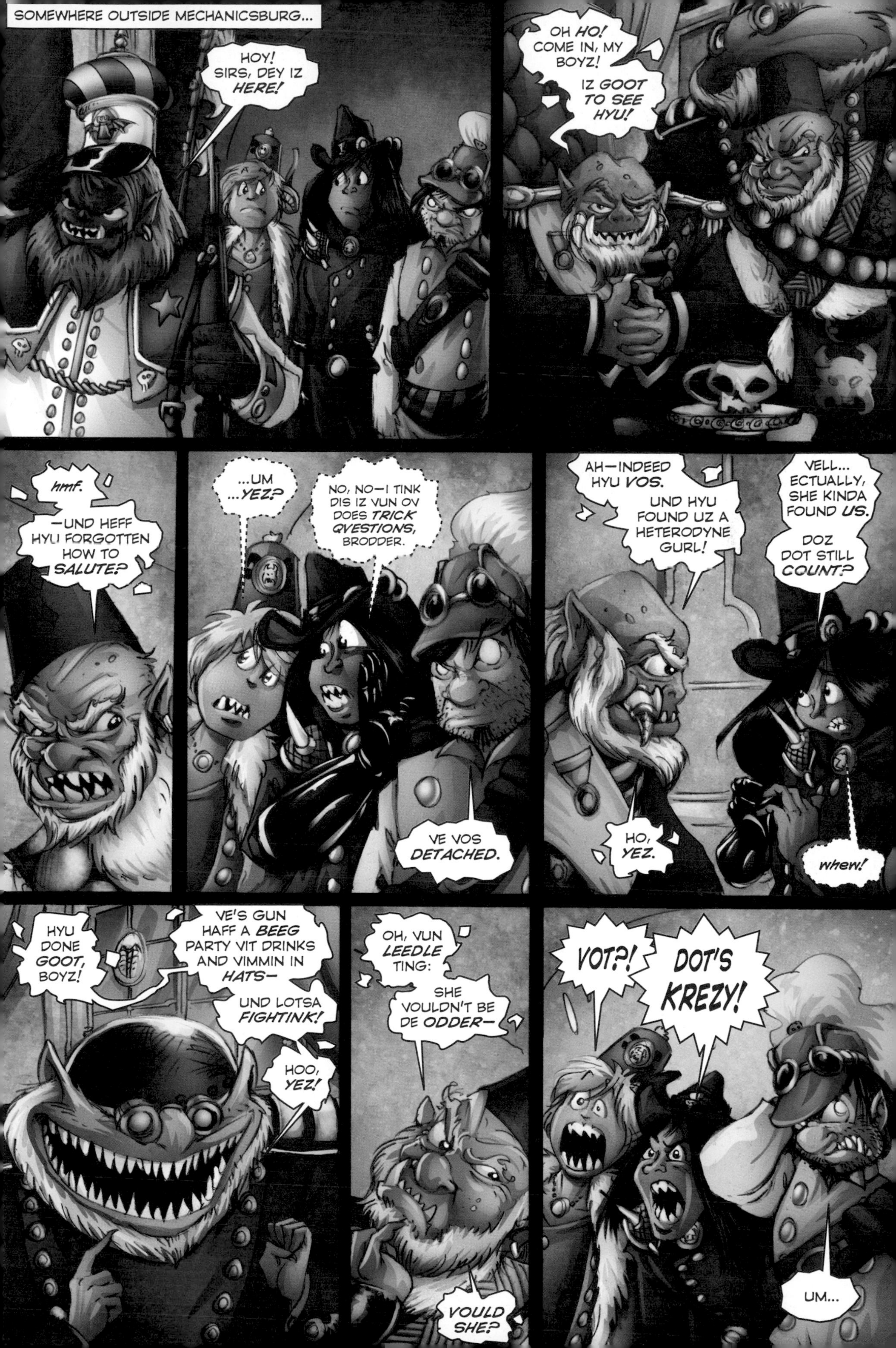
SOMEWHERE OUTSIDE MECHANICSBURG...
HOY! SIRS, DEY IZ HERE!
OH HO! COME IN, MY BOYZ!
IZ GOOT TO SEE HYU!
hmf.
—UND HEFF HYU FORGOTTEN HOW TO SALUTE?
...UM ...YEZ?
NO, NO—I TINK DIS IZ VUN OV DOES TRICK QVESTIONS, BRODDER.
VE VOS DETACHED.
AH—INDEED HYU VOS.
UND HYU FOUND UZ A HETERODYNE GURL!
HO, YEZ.
VELL... ECTUALLY, SHE KINDA FOUND US.
DOZ DOT STILL COUNT?
whew!
HYU DONE GOOT, BOYZ!
VE'S GUN HAFF A BEEG PARTY VIT DRINKS AND VIMMIN IN HATS—
UND LOTSA FIGHTINK!
HOO, YEZ!
OH, VUN LEEDLE TING:
SHE VOULDN'T BE DE ODDER—
VOULD SHE?
VOT?!
DOT'S KREZY!
UM...

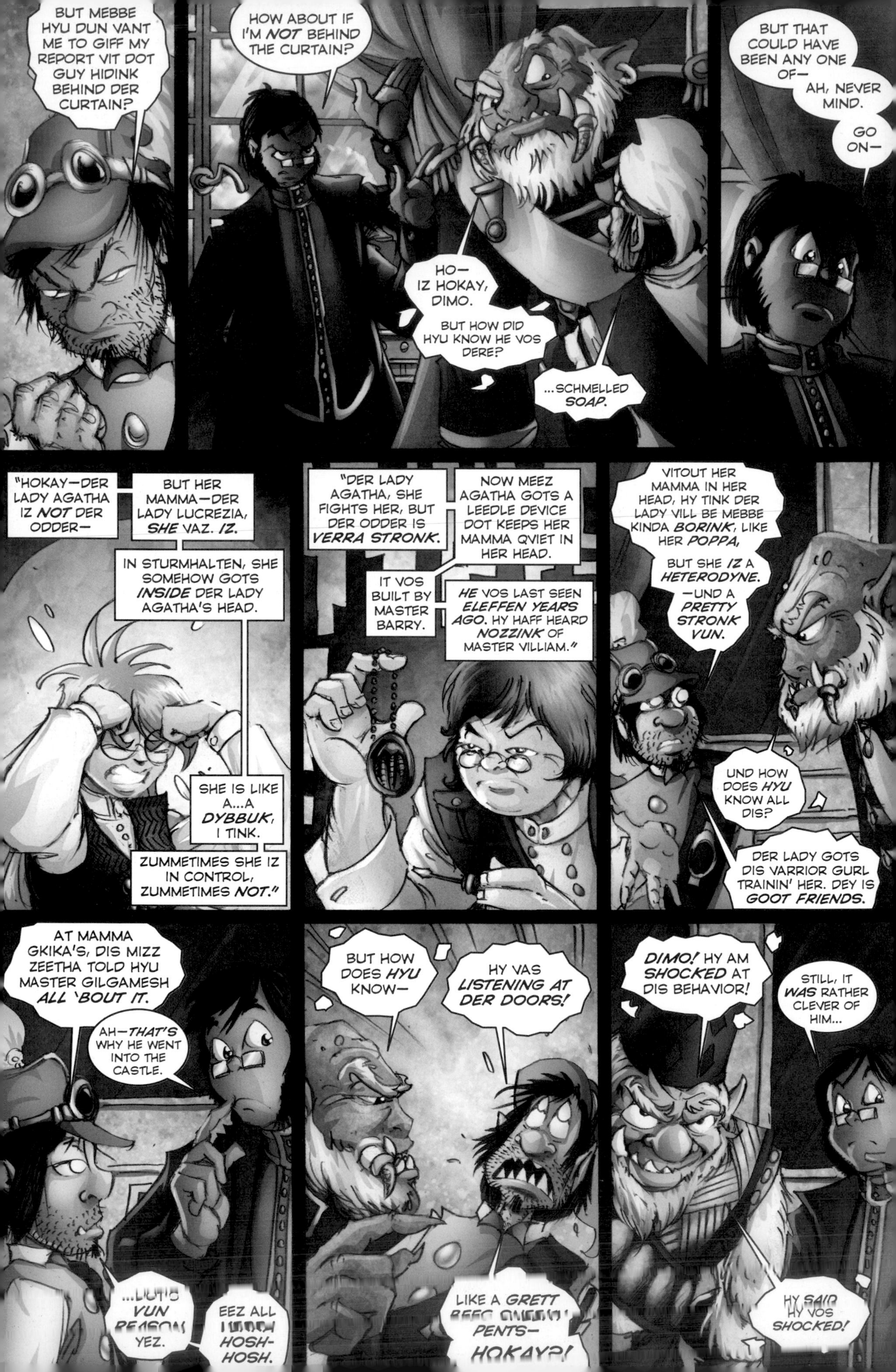

BUT MEBBE HYU DUN VANT ME TO GIFF MY REPORT VIT DOT GUY HIDINK BEHIND DER CURTAIN?
HOW ABOUT IF I'M *NOT* BEHIND THE CURTAIN?
HO— IZ HOKAY, DIMO.
BUT HOW DID HYU KNOW HE VOS DERE?
...SCHMELLED *SOAP*.
BUT THAT COULD HAVE BEEN ANY ONE OF—
AH, NEVER MIND.
GO ON—
"HOKAY—DER LADY AGATHA IZ *NOT* DER ODDER—
BUT HER MAMMA—DER LADY LUCREZIA, *SHE* VAZ. *IZ*.
IN STURMHALTEN, SHE SOMEHOW GOTS *INSIDE* DER LADY AGATHA'S HEAD.
SHE IS LIKE A...A *DYBBUK*, I TINK.
ZUMMETIMES SHE IZ IN CONTROL, ZUMMETIMES *NOT*."
"DER LADY AGATHA, SHE FIGHTS HER, BUT DER ODDER IS *VERRA STRONK*.
NOW MEEZ AGATHA GOTS A LEEDLE DEVICE DOT KEEPS HER MAMMA QVIET IN HER HEAD.
IT VOS BUILT BY MASTER BARRY.
HE VOS LAST SEEN *ELEFFEN YEARS AGO*. HY HAFF HEARD *NOZZINK* OF MASTER VILLIAM."
VITOUT HER MAMMA IN HER HEAD, HY TINK DER LADY VILL BE MEBBE KINDA *BORINK*, LIKE HER *POPPA*,
BUT SHE *IZ* A *HETERODYNE*.
—UND A *PRETTY STRONK VUN*.
UND HOW DOES *HYU* KNOW ALL DIS?
DER LADY GOTS DIS VARRIOR GURL TRAININ' HER. DEY IS *GOOT FRIENDS*.
AT MAMMA GKIKA'S, DIS MIZZ ZEETHA TOLD HYU MASTER GILGAMESH *ALL 'BOUT IT*.
AH—*THAT'S* WHY HE WENT INTO THE CASTLE.
VUN
YEZ.
EEZ ALL
HOSH-HOSH.
BUT HOW DOES *HYU* KNOW—
HY VAS *LISTENING AT DER DOORS!*
LIKE A *GRETT*
PENTS—
HOKAY?!
DIMO! HY AM *SHOCKED* AT DIS BEHAVIOR!
STILL, IT *WAS* RATHER CLEVER OF HIM...
HY *SAID* HY VOS *SHOCKED!*

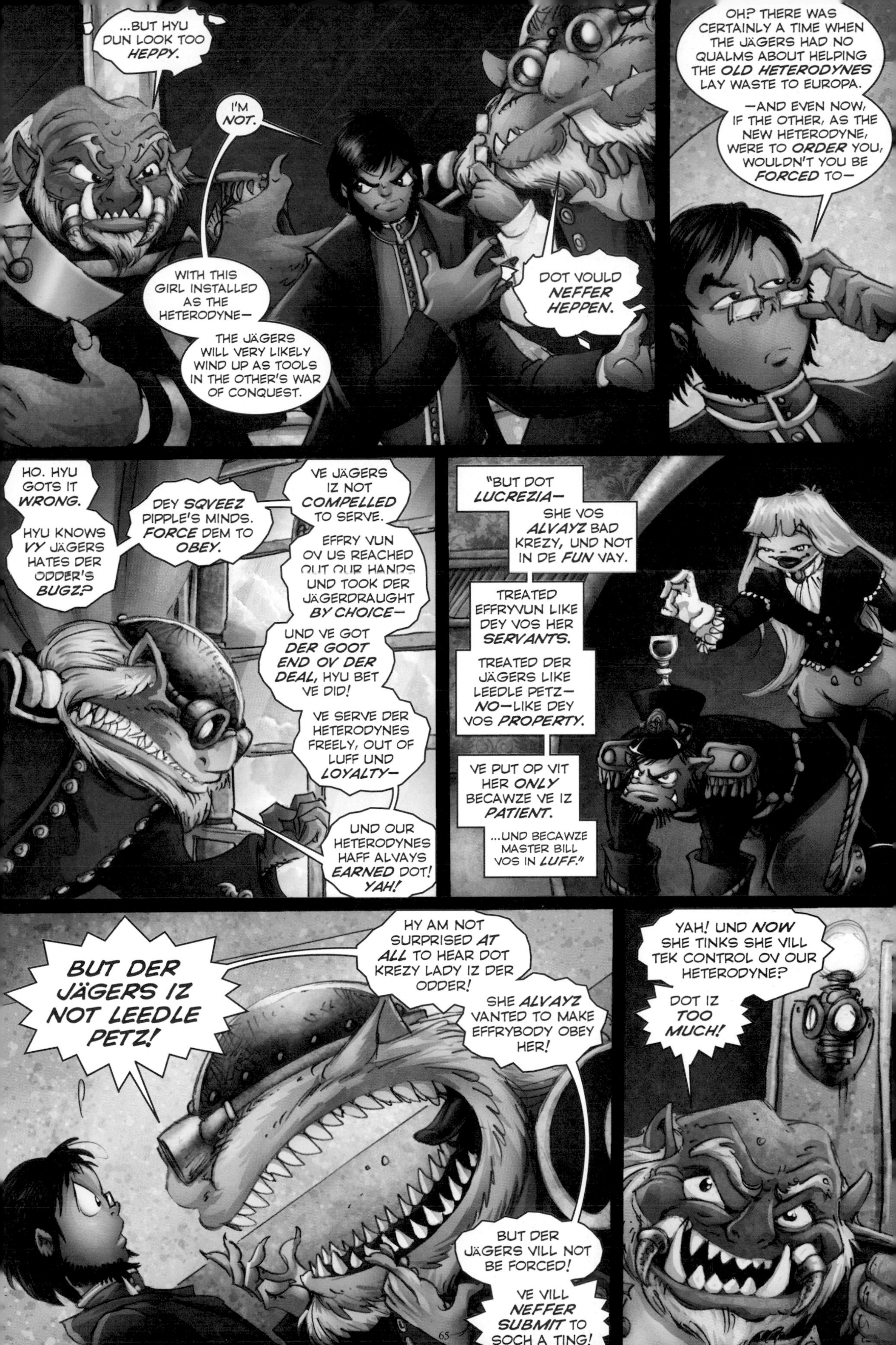

...BUT HYU DUN LOOK TOO *HEPPY*.
I'M *NOT*.
WITH THIS GIRL INSTALLED AS THE HETERODYNE—
THE JÄGERS WILL VERY LIKELY WIND UP AS TOOLS IN THE OTHER'S WAR OF CONQUEST.
DOT VOULD *NEFFER HEPPEN*.
OH? THERE WAS CERTAINLY A TIME WHEN THE JÄGERS HAD NO QUALMS ABOUT HELPING THE *OLD HETERODYNES* LAY WASTE TO EUROPA.
—AND EVEN NOW, IF THE OTHER, AS THE NEW HETERODYNE, WERE TO *ORDER* YOU, WOULDN'T YOU BE *FORCED* TO—
HO. HYU GOTS IT *WRONG*.
HYU KNOWS *VY* JÄGERS HATES DER ODDER'S *BUGZ?*
DEY *SQVEEZ* PIPPLE'S MINDS. *FORCE* DEM TO *OBEY*.
VE JÄGERS IZ NOT *COMPELLED* TO SERVE.
EFFRY VUN OV US REACHED OUT OUR HANDS UND TOOK DER JÄGERDRAUGHT *BY CHOICE*—
UND VE GOT *DER GOOT END OV DER DEAL*, HYU BET VE DID!
VE SERVE DER HETERODYNES FREELY, OUT OF LUFF UND *LOYALTY*—
UND OUR HETERODYNES HAFF ALVAYS *EARNED* DOT! *YAH!*
"BUT DOT *LUCREZIA*—
SHE VOS *ALVAYZ* BAD KREZY, UND NOT IN DE *FUN* VAY.
TREATED EFFRYVUN LIKE DEY VOS HER *SERVANTS*.
TREATED DER JÄGERS LIKE LEEDLE PETZ—*NO*—LIKE DEY VOS *PROPERTY*.
VE PUT OP VIT HER *ONLY* BECAWZE VE IZ *PATIENT*.
...UND BECAWZE MASTER BILL VOS IN *LUFF*."
BUT DER JÄGERS IZ NOT LEEDLE PETZ!
HY AM NOT SURPRISED *AT ALL* TO HEAR DOT KREZY LADY IZ DER ODDER!
SHE *ALVAYZ* VANTED TO MAKE EFFRYBODY OBEY HER!
BUT DER JÄGERS VILL NOT BE FORCED!
VE VILL *NEFFER SUBMIT* TO SOCH A TING!
YAH! UND *NOW* SHE TINKS SHE VILL TEK CONTROL OV OUR HETERODYNE?
DOT IZ *TOO MUCH!*

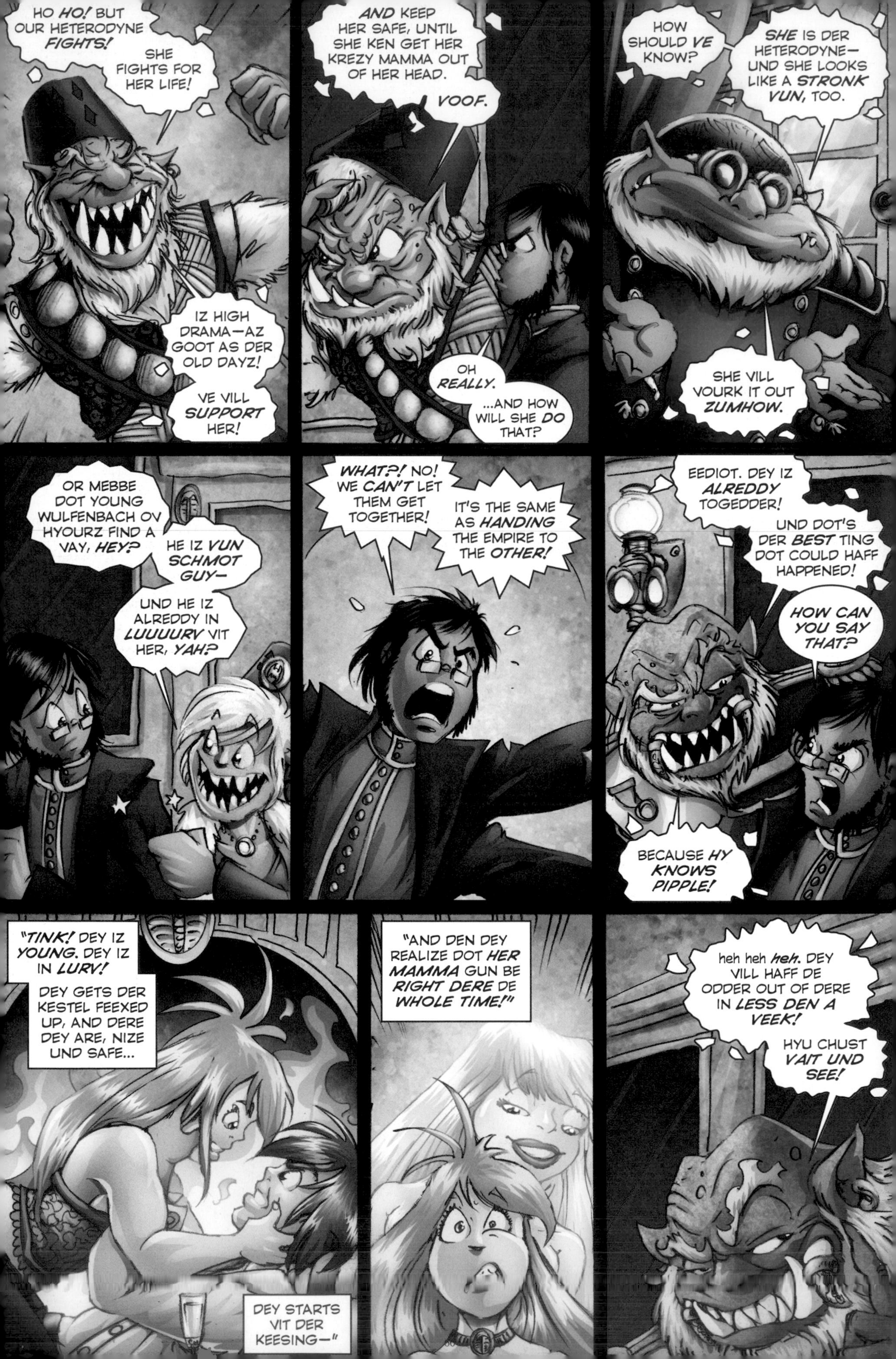
HO HO! BUT OUR HETERODYNE FIGHTS!
SHE FIGHTS FOR HER LIFE!
IZ HIGH DRAMA—AZ GOOT AS DER OLD DAYZ!
VE VILL SUPPORT HER!
AND KEEP HER SAFE, UNTIL SHE KEN GET HER KREZY MAMMA OUT OF HER HEAD.
VOOF.
OH REALLY.
...AND HOW WILL SHE DO THAT?
HOW SHOULD VE KNOW?
SHE IS DER HETERODYNE—UND SHE LOOKS LIKE A STRONK VUN, TOO.
SHE VILL VOURK IT OUT ZUMHOW.
OR MEBBE DOT YOUNG WULFENBACH OV HYOURZ FIND A VAY, HEY?
HE IZ VUN SCHMOT GUY—
UND HE IZ ALREDDY IN LUUUURV VIT HER, YAH?
WHAT?! NO! WE CAN'T LET THEM GET TOGETHER!
IT'S THE SAME AS HANDING THE EMPIRE TO THE OTHER!
EEDIOT. DEY IZ ALREDDY TOGEDDER!
UND DOT'S DER BEST TING DOT COULD HAFF HAPPENED!
HOW CAN YOU SAY THAT?
BECAUSE HY KNOWS PIPPLE!
"TINK! DEY IZ YOUNG. DEY IZ IN LURV!
DEY GETS DER KESTEL FEEXED UP, AND DERE DEY ARE, NIZE UND SAFE...
DEY STARTS VIT DER KEESING—"
"AND DEN DEY REALIZE DOT HER MAMMA GUN BE RIGHT DERE DE WHOLE TIME!"
heh heh heh. DEY VILL HAFF DE ODDER OUT OF DERE IN LESS DEN A VEEK!
HYU CHUST VAIT UND SEE!

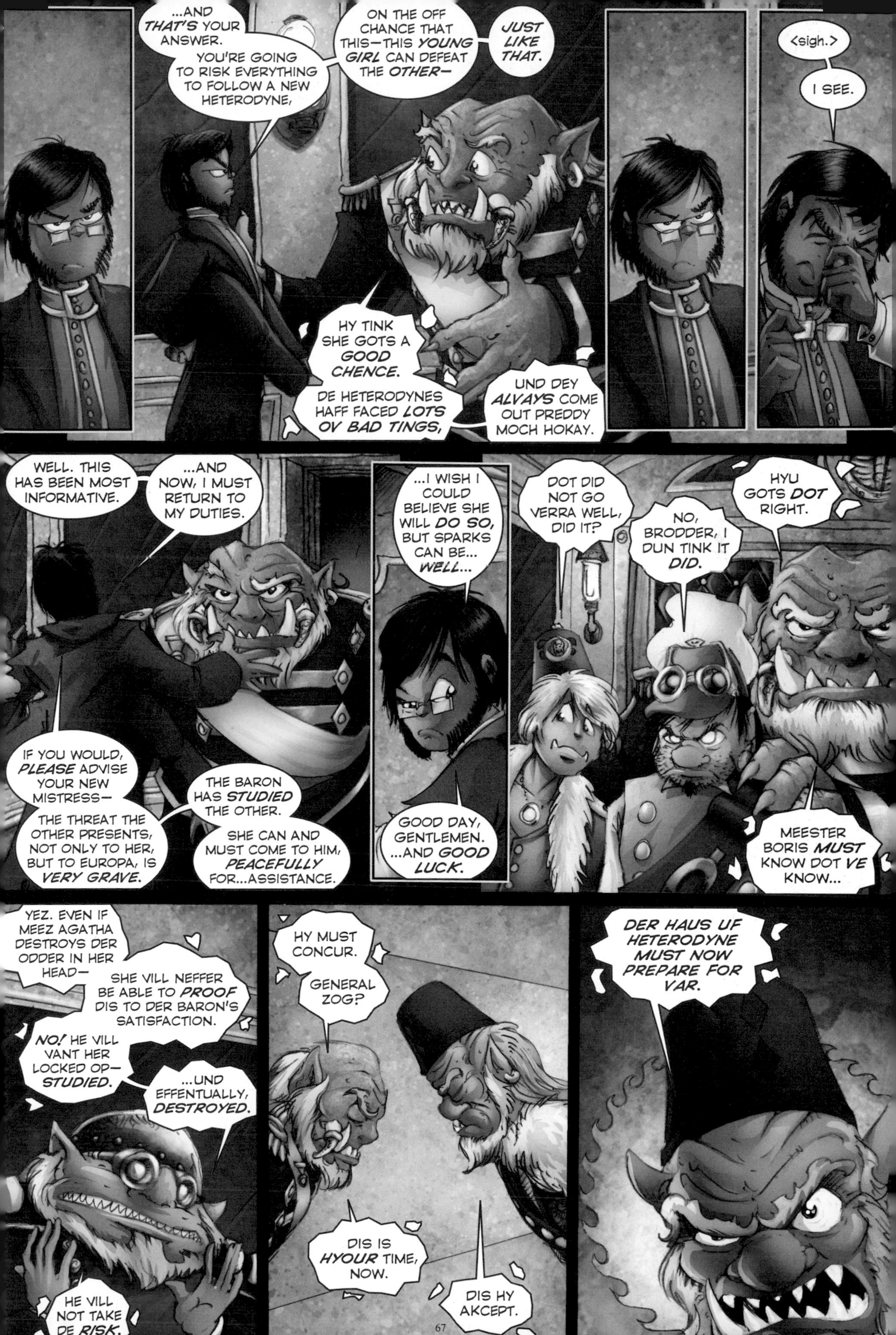
...AND THAT'S YOUR ANSWER.
YOU'RE GOING TO RISK EVERYTHING TO FOLLOW A NEW HETERODYNE,
ON THE OFF CHANCE THAT THIS—THIS YOUNG GIRL CAN DEFEAT THE OTHER—
JUST LIKE THAT.
HY TINK SHE GOTS A GOOD CHENCE.
DE HETERODYNES HAFF FACED LOTS OV BAD TINGS,
UND DEY ALVAYS COME OUT PREDDY MOCH HOKAY.
<sigh.>
I SEE.
WELL. THIS HAS BEEN MOST INFORMATIVE.
...AND NOW, I MUST RETURN TO MY DUTIES.
IF YOU WOULD, PLEASE ADVISE YOUR NEW MISTRESS—
THE THREAT THE OTHER PRESENTS, NOT ONLY TO HER, BUT TO EUROPA, IS VERY GRAVE.
THE BARON HAS STUDIED THE OTHER.
SHE CAN AND MUST COME TO HIM, PEACEFULLY FOR...ASSISTANCE.
...I WISH I COULD BELIEVE SHE WILL DO SO, BUT SPARKS CAN BE... WELL...
GOOD DAY, GENTLEMEN. ...AND GOOD LUCK.
DOT DID NOT GO VERRA WELL, DID IT?
NO, BRODDER, I DUN TINK IT DID.
HYU GOTS DOT RIGHT.
MEESTER BORIS MUST KNOW DOT VE KNOW...
YEZ. EVEN IF MEEZ AGATHA DESTROYS DER ODDER IN HER HEAD—
SHE VILL NEFFER BE ABLE TO PROOF DIS TO DER BARON'S SATISFACTION.
NO! HE VILL VANT HER LOCKED OP—STUDIED.
...UND EFFENTUALLY, DESTROYED.
HE VILL NOT TAKE DE RISK.
HY MUST CONCUR.
GENERAL ZOG?
DIS IS HYOUR TIME, NOW.
DIS HY AKCEPT.
DER HAUS UF HETERODYNE MUST NOW PREPARE FOR VAR.

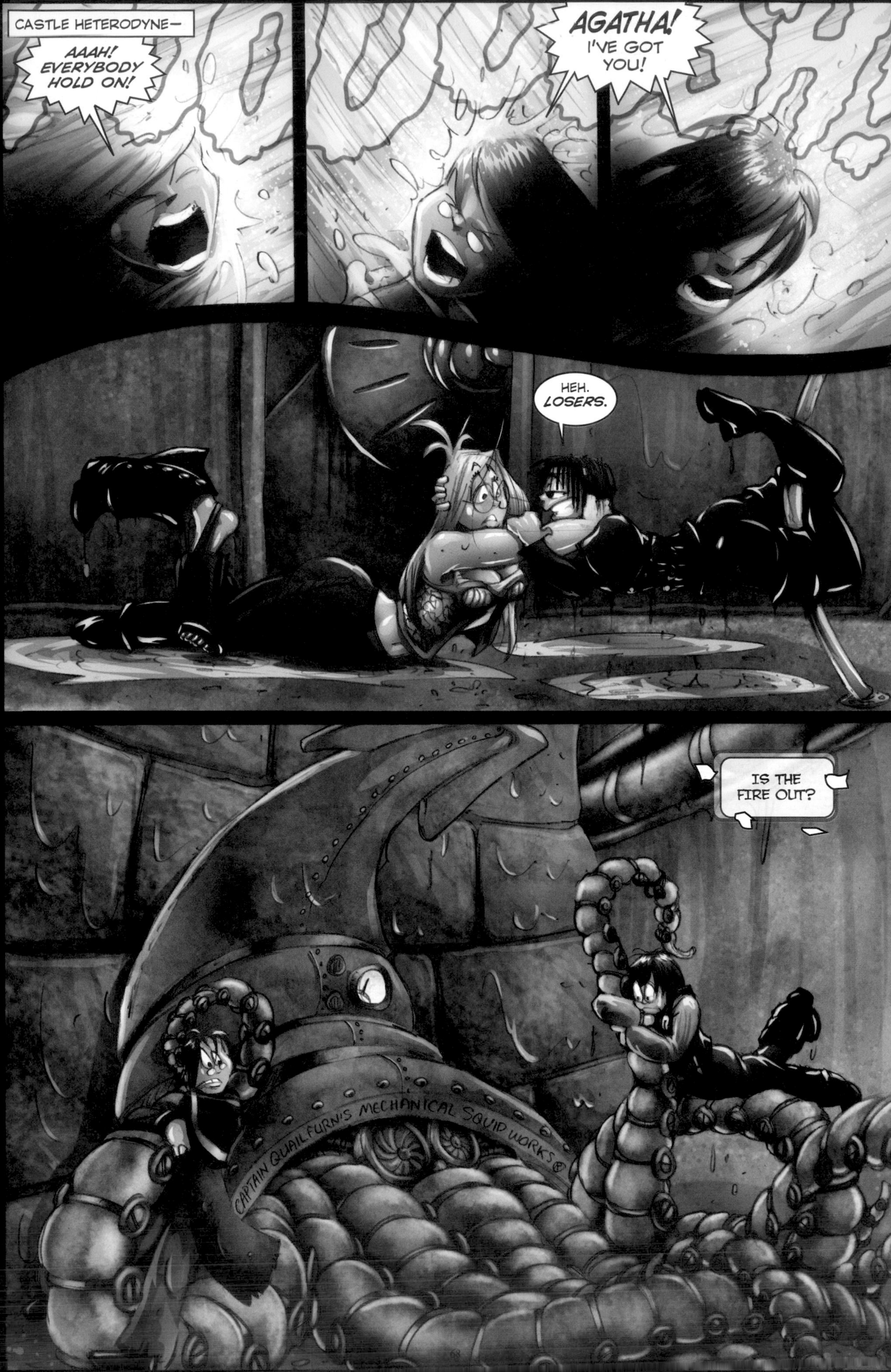

CASTLE HETERODYNE—
AAAH! EVERYBODY HOLD ON!
AGATHA! I'VE GOT YOU!
HEH. LOSERS.
IS THE FIRE OUT?
CAPTAIN QUAILFURN'S MECHANICAL SQUID WORKS

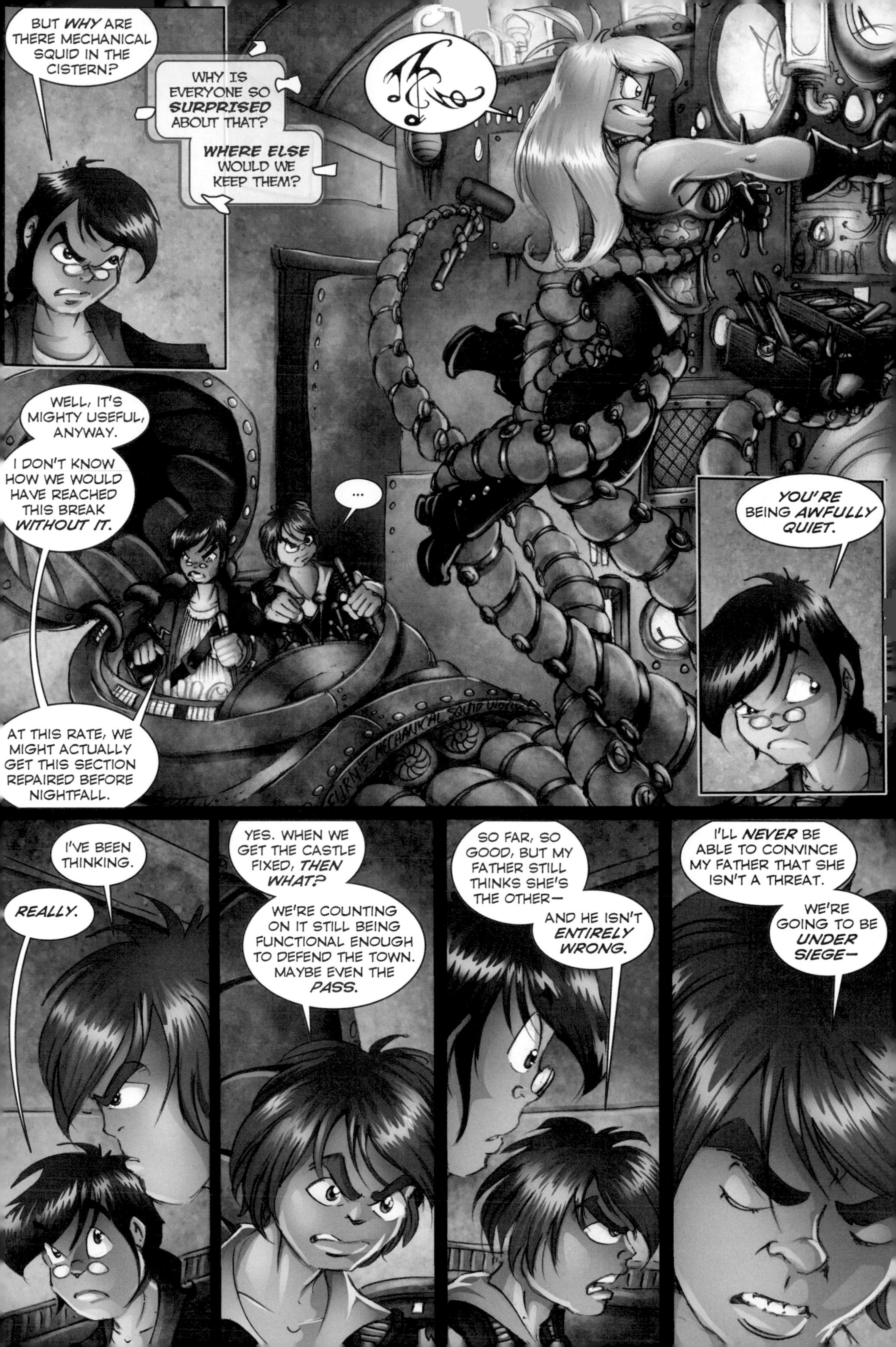
BUT WHY ARE THERE MECHANICAL SQUID IN THE CISTERN?
WHY IS EVERYONE SO SURPRISED ABOUT THAT?
WHERE ELSE WOULD WE KEEP THEM?
WELL, IT'S MIGHTY USEFUL, ANYWAY.
I DON'T KNOW HOW WE WOULD HAVE REACHED THIS BREAK WITHOUT IT.
AT THIS RATE, WE MIGHT ACTUALLY GET THIS SECTION REPAIRED BEFORE NIGHTFALL.
...
YOU'RE BEING AWFULLY QUIET.
I'VE BEEN THINKING.
REALLY.
YES. WHEN WE GET THE CASTLE FIXED, THEN WHAT?
WE'RE COUNTING ON IT STILL BEING FUNCTIONAL ENOUGH TO DEFEND THE TOWN. MAYBE EVEN THE PASS.
SO FAR, SO GOOD, BUT MY FATHER STILL THINKS SHE'S THE OTHER—
AND HE ISN'T ENTIRELY WRONG.
I'LL NEVER BE ABLE TO CONVINCE MY FATHER THAT SHE ISN'T A THREAT.
WE'RE GOING TO BE UNDER SIEGE—

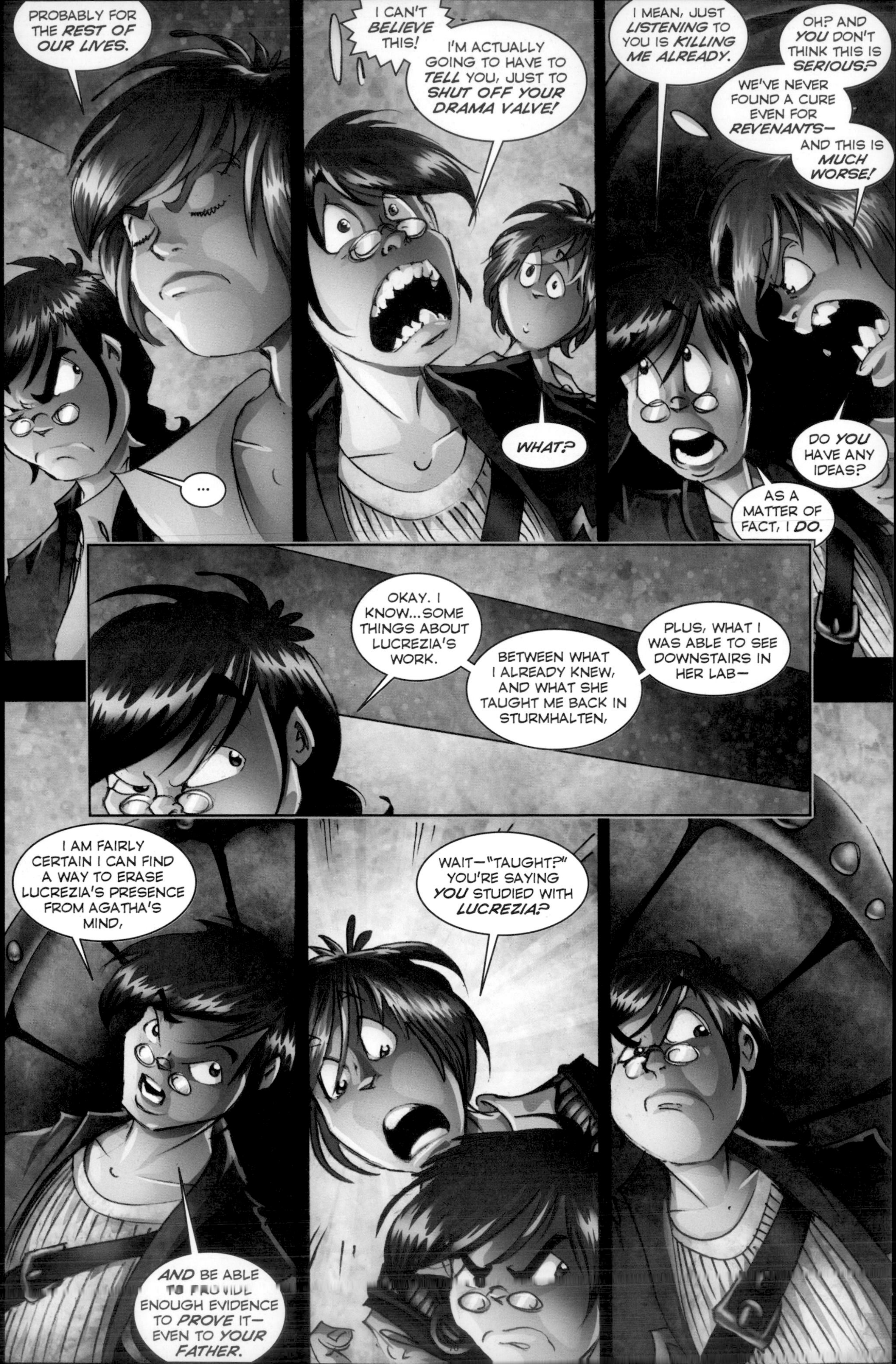
PROBABLY FOR THE REST OF OUR LIVES.
...
I CAN'T BELIEVE THIS!
I'M ACTUALLY GOING TO HAVE TO TELL YOU, JUST TO SHUT OFF YOUR DRAMA VALVE!
WHAT?
I MEAN, JUST LISTENING TO YOU IS KILLING ME ALREADY.
OH? AND YOU DON'T THINK THIS IS SERIOUS?
WE'VE NEVER FOUND A CURE EVEN FOR REVENANTS—
AND THIS IS MUCH WORSE!
DO YOU HAVE ANY IDEAS?
AS A MATTER OF FACT, I DO.
OKAY. I KNOW...SOME THINGS ABOUT LUCREZIA'S WORK.
BETWEEN WHAT I ALREADY KNEW, AND WHAT SHE TAUGHT ME BACK IN STURMHALTEN,
PLUS, WHAT I WAS ABLE TO SEE DOWNSTAIRS IN HER LAB—
I AM FAIRLY CERTAIN I CAN FIND A WAY TO ERASE LUCREZIA'S PRESENCE FROM AGATHA'S MIND,
AND BE ABLE TO PROVIDE ENOUGH EVIDENCE TO PROVE IT— EVEN TO YOUR FATHER.
WAIT—"TAUGHT?" YOU'RE SAYING YOU STUDIED WITH LUCREZIA?

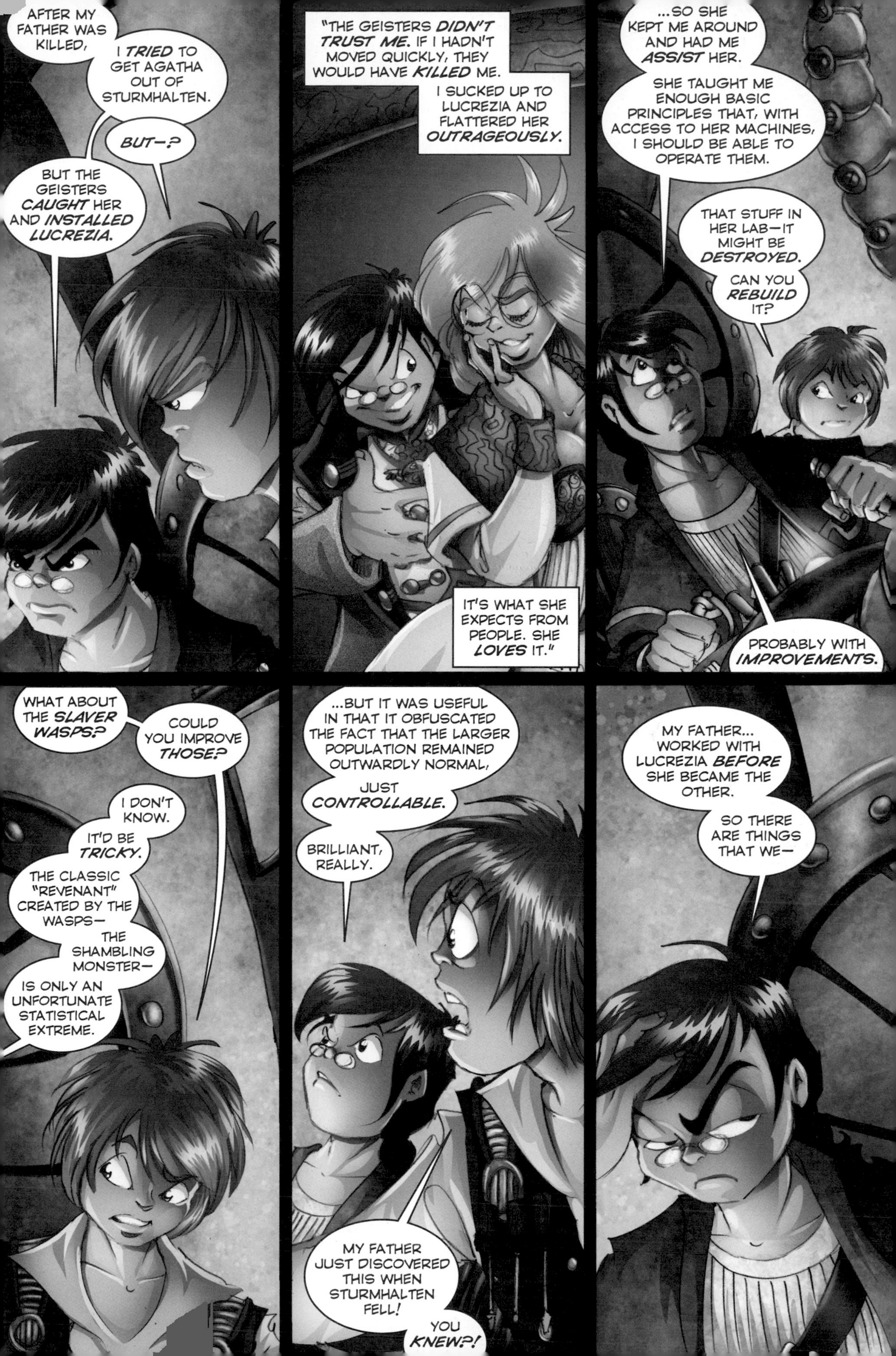
AFTER MY FATHER WAS KILLED,
I TRIED TO GET AGATHA OUT OF STURMHALTEN.
BUT—?
BUT THE GEISTERS CAUGHT HER AND INSTALLED LUCREZIA.
"THE GEISTERS DIDN'T TRUST ME. IF I HADN'T MOVED QUICKLY, THEY WOULD HAVE KILLED ME.
I SUCKED UP TO LUCREZIA AND FLATTERED HER OUTRAGEOUSLY.
IT'S WHAT SHE EXPECTS FROM PEOPLE. SHE LOVES IT."
...SO SHE KEPT ME AROUND AND HAD ME ASSIST HER.
SHE TAUGHT ME ENOUGH BASIC PRINCIPLES THAT, WITH ACCESS TO HER MACHINES, I SHOULD BE ABLE TO OPERATE THEM.
THAT STUFF IN HER LAB—IT MIGHT BE DESTROYED.
CAN YOU REBUILD IT?
PROBABLY WITH IMPROVEMENTS.
WHAT ABOUT THE SLAVER WASPS?
COULD YOU IMPROVE THOSE?
I DON'T KNOW.
IT'D BE TRICKY.
THE CLASSIC "REVENANT" CREATED BY THE WASPS—
THE SHAMBLING MONSTER—
IS ONLY AN UNFORTUNATE STATISTICAL EXTREME.
...BUT IT WAS USEFUL IN THAT IT OBFUSCATED THE FACT THAT THE LARGER POPULATION REMAINED OUTWARDLY NORMAL,
JUST CONTROLLABLE.
BRILLIANT, REALLY.
MY FATHER JUST DISCOVERED THIS WHEN STURMHALTEN FELL!
YOU KNEW?!
MY FATHER... WORKED WITH LUCREZIA BEFORE SHE BECAME THE OTHER.
SO THERE ARE THINGS THAT WE—

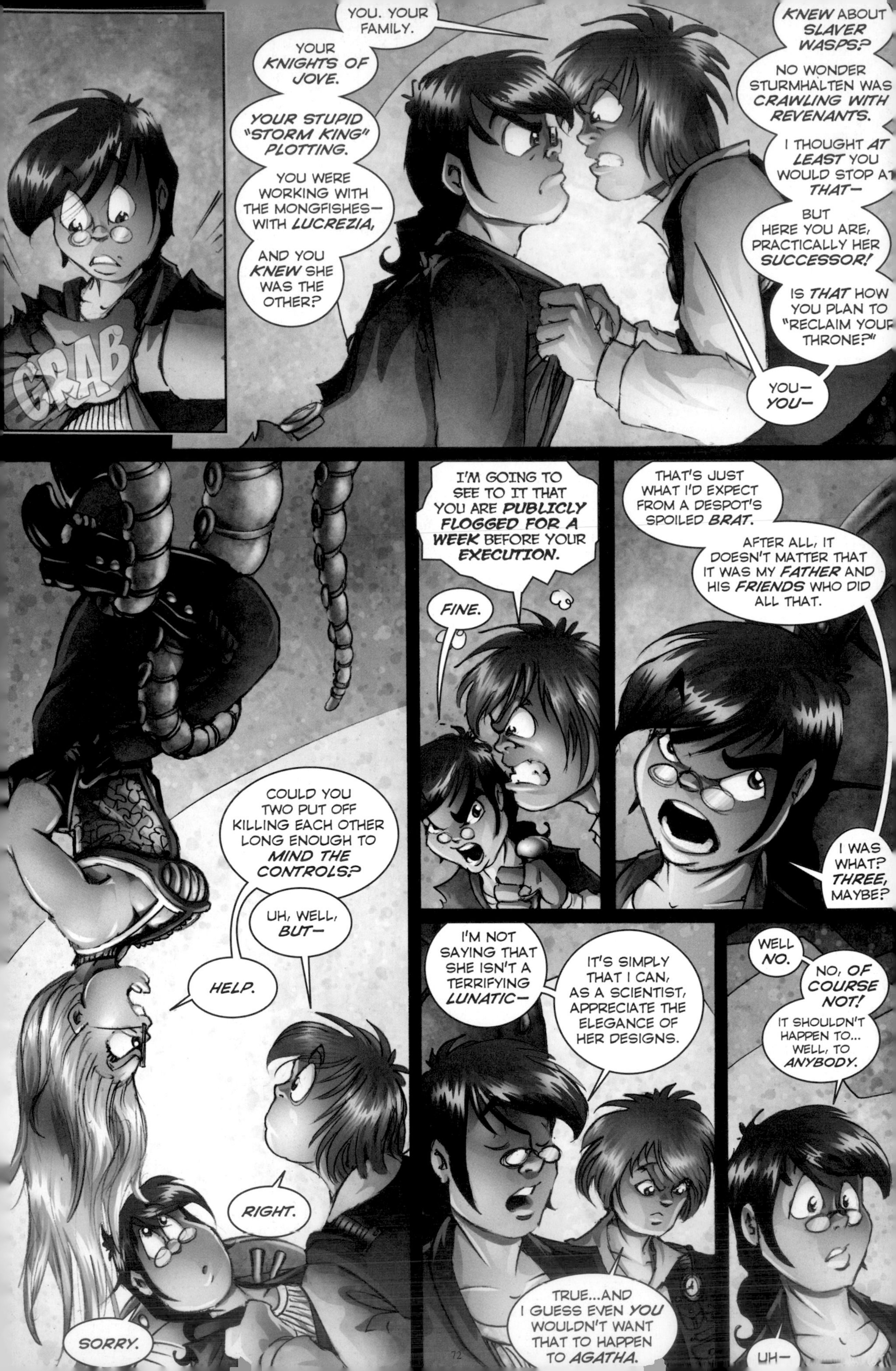
GRAB
YOU. YOUR FAMILY.
YOUR KNIGHTS OF JOVE.
YOUR STUPID "STORM KING" PLOTTING.
YOU WERE WORKING WITH THE MONGFISHES— WITH LUCREZIA,
AND YOU KNEW SHE WAS THE OTHER?
KNEW ABOUT SLAVER WASPS?
NO WONDER STURMHALTEN WAS CRAWLING WITH REVENANTS.
I THOUGHT AT LEAST YOU WOULD STOP AT THAT—
BUT HERE YOU ARE, PRACTICALLY HER SUCCESSOR!
IS THAT HOW YOU PLAN TO "RECLAIM YOUR THRONE?"
YOU— YOU—
I'M GOING TO SEE TO IT THAT YOU ARE PUBLICLY FLOGGED FOR A WEEK BEFORE YOUR EXECUTION.
FINE.
THAT'S JUST WHAT I'D EXPECT FROM A DESPOT'S SPOILED BRAT.
AFTER ALL, IT DOESN'T MATTER THAT IT WAS MY FATHER AND HIS FRIENDS WHO DID ALL THAT.
I WAS WHAT? THREE, MAYBE?
COULD YOU TWO PUT OFF KILLING EACH OTHER LONG ENOUGH TO MIND THE CONTROLS?
UH, WELL, BUT—
HELP.
RIGHT.
SORRY.
I'M NOT SAYING THAT SHE ISN'T A TERRIFYING LUNATIC—
IT'S SIMPLY THAT I CAN, AS A SCIENTIST, APPRECIATE THE ELEGANCE OF HER DESIGNS.
TRUE...AND I GUESS EVEN YOU WOULDN'T WANT THAT TO HAPPEN TO AGATHA.
WELL NO.
NO, OF COURSE NOT!
IT SHOULDN'T HAPPEN TO... WELL, TO ANYBODY.
UH—

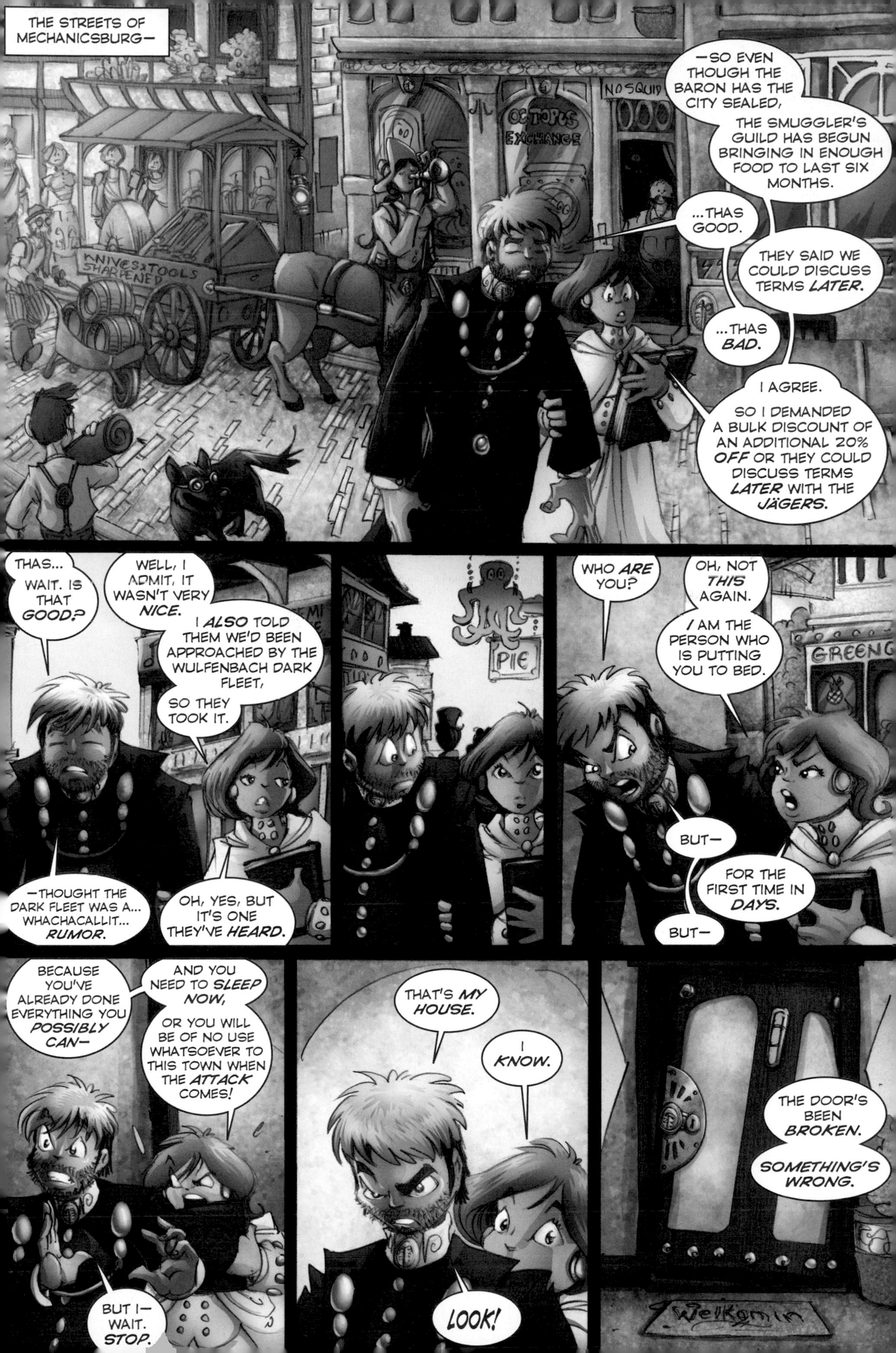
THE STREETS OF MECHANICSBURG—
—SO EVEN THOUGH THE BARON HAS THE CITY SEALED,
THE SMUGGLER'S GUILD HAS BEGUN BRINGING IN ENOUGH FOOD TO LAST SIX MONTHS.
...THAS GOOD.
THEY SAID WE COULD DISCUSS TERMS LATER.
...THAS BAD.
I AGREE.
SO I DEMANDED A BULK DISCOUNT OF AN ADDITIONAL 20% OFF OR THEY COULD DISCUSS TERMS LATER WITH THE JÄGERS.
KNIVES & TOOLS SHARPENED
OCTOPUS EXCHANGE
NO SQUID
THAS... WAIT. IS THAT GOOD?
WELL, I ADMIT, IT WASN'T VERY NICE.
I ALSO TOLD THEM WE'D BEEN APPROACHED BY THE WULFENBACH DARK FLEET,
SO THEY TOOK IT.
—THOUGHT THE DARK FLEET WAS A... WHACHACALLIT... RUMOR.
OH, YES, BUT IT'S ONE THEY'VE HEARD.
PIE
WHO ARE YOU?
OH, NOT THIS AGAIN.
I AM THE PERSON WHO IS PUTTING YOU TO BED.
BUT—
FOR THE FIRST TIME IN DAYS.
BUT—
BECAUSE YOU'VE ALREADY DONE EVERYTHING YOU POSSIBLY CAN—
AND YOU NEED TO SLEEP NOW,
OR YOU WILL BE OF NO USE WHATSOEVER TO THIS TOWN WHEN THE ATTACK COMES!
BUT I— WAIT. STOP.
THAT'S MY HOUSE.
I KNOW.
LOOK!
THE DOOR'S BEEN BROKEN.
SOMETHING'S WRONG.
Welkomin

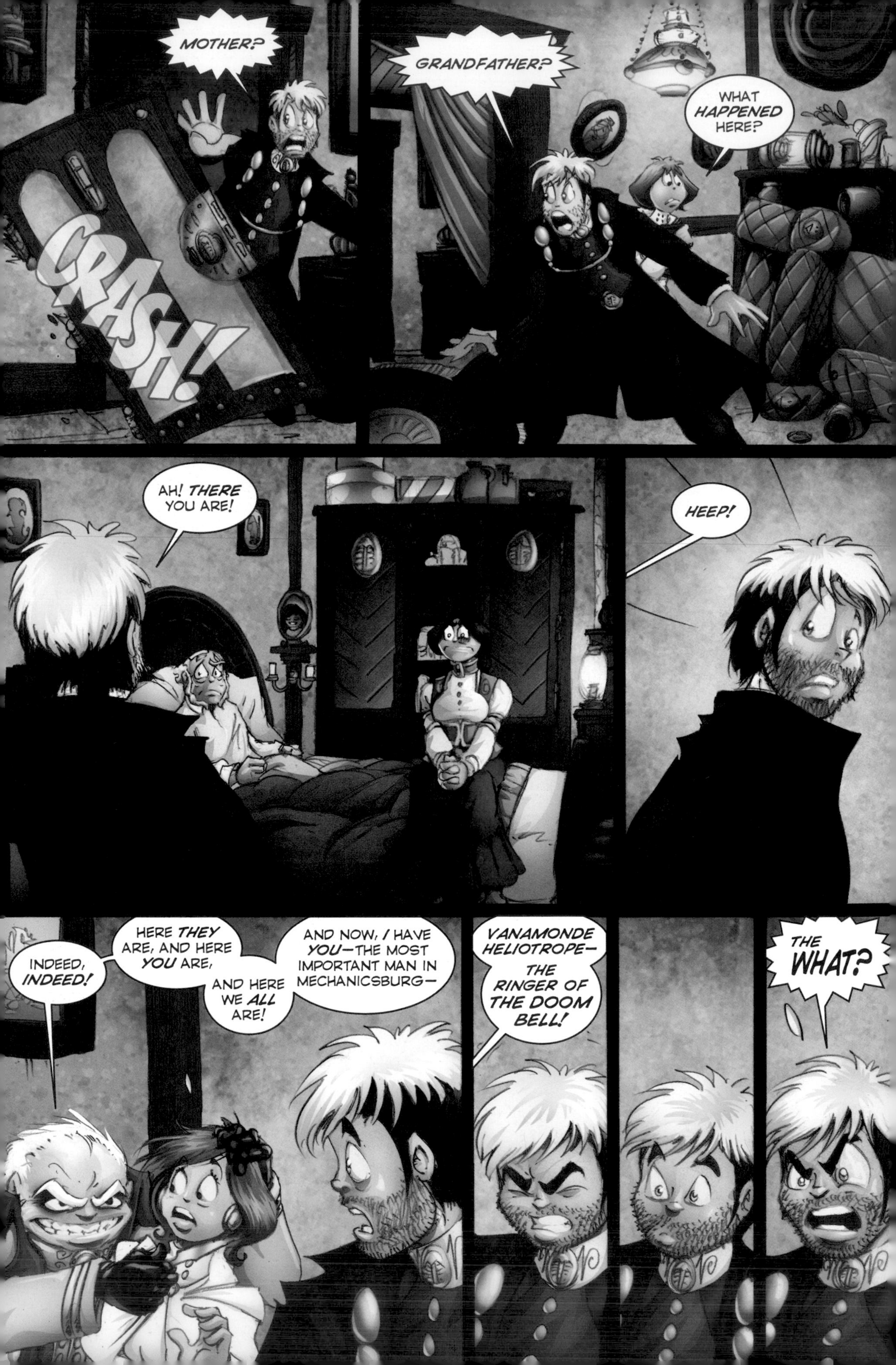

MOTHER?
CRASH!
GRANDFATHER?
WHAT HAPPENED HERE?
AH! THERE YOU ARE!
HEEP!
INDEED, INDEED!
HERE THEY ARE, AND HERE YOU ARE,
AND HERE WE ALL ARE!
AND NOW, I HAVE YOU—THE MOST IMPORTANT MAN IN MECHANICSBURG—
VANAMONDE HELIOTROPE—
THE RINGER OF THE DOOM BELL!
THE WHAT?

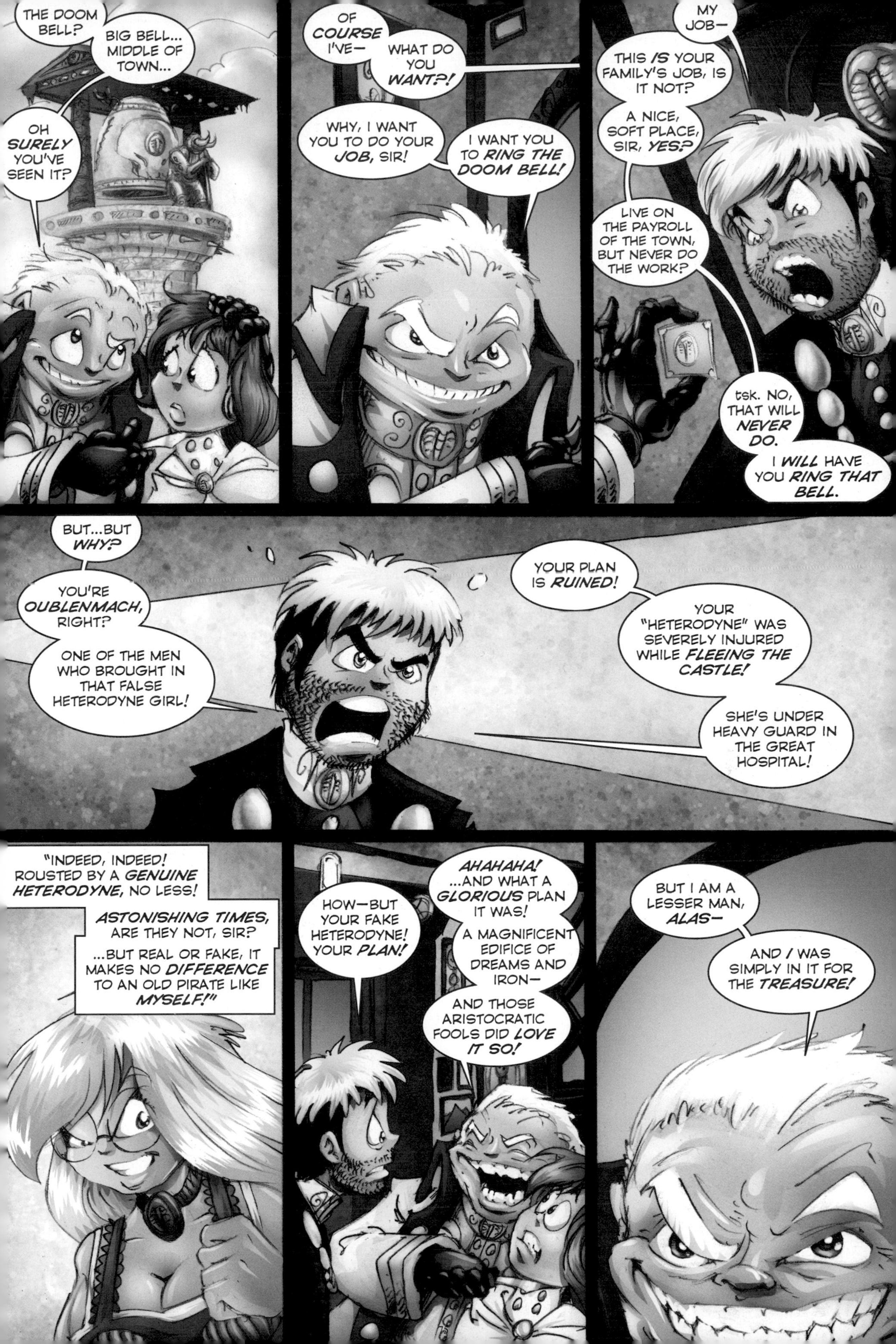
THE DOOM BELL?
BIG BELL... MIDDLE OF TOWN...
OH SURELY YOU'VE SEEN IT?
OF COURSE I'VE—
WHAT DO YOU WANT?!
WHY, I WANT YOU TO DO YOUR JOB, SIR!
I WANT YOU TO RING THE DOOM BELL!
MY JOB—
THIS IS YOUR FAMILY'S JOB, IS IT NOT?
A NICE, SOFT PLACE, SIR, YES?
LIVE ON THE PAYROLL OF THE TOWN, BUT NEVER DO THE WORK?
tsk. NO, THAT WILL NEVER DO.
I WILL HAVE YOU RING THAT BELL.
BUT...BUT WHY?
YOU'RE OUBLENMACH, RIGHT?
ONE OF THE MEN WHO BROUGHT IN THAT FALSE HETERODYNE GIRL!
YOUR PLAN IS RUINED!
YOUR "HETERODYNE" WAS SEVERELY INJURED WHILE FLEEING THE CASTLE!
SHE'S UNDER HEAVY GUARD IN THE GREAT HOSPITAL!
"INDEED, INDEED! ROUSTED BY A GENUINE HETERODYNE, NO LESS!
ASTONISHING TIMES, ARE THEY NOT, SIR?
...BUT REAL OR FAKE, IT MAKES NO DIFFERENCE TO AN OLD PIRATE LIKE MYSELF!"
HOW—BUT YOUR FAKE HETERODYNE! YOUR PLAN!
AHAHAHA! ...AND WHAT A GLORIOUS PLAN IT WAS!
A MAGNIFICENT EDIFICE OF DREAMS AND IRON—
AND THOSE ARISTOCRATIC FOOLS DID LOVE IT SO!
BUT I AM A LESSER MAN, ALAS—
AND I WAS SIMPLY IN IT FOR THE TREASURE!

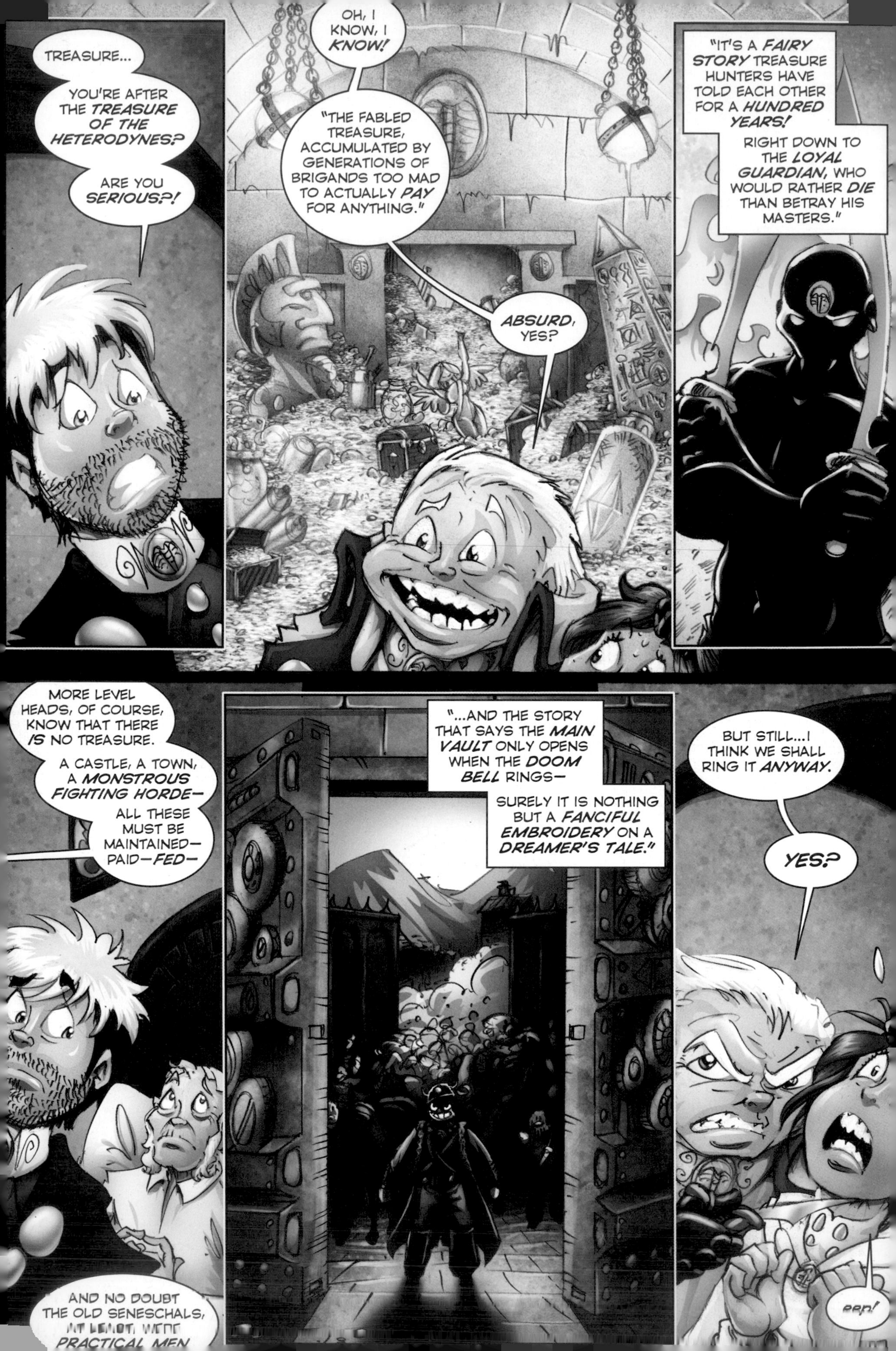

TREASURE...
YOU'RE AFTER THE *TREASURE OF THE HETERODYNES?*
ARE YOU *SERIOUS?!*
OH, I KNOW, I *KNOW!*
"THE FABLED TREASURE, ACCUMULATED BY GENERATIONS OF BRIGANDS TOO MAD TO ACTUALLY *PAY* FOR ANYTHING."
ABSURD, YES?
"IT'S A *FAIRY STORY* TREASURE HUNTERS HAVE TOLD EACH OTHER FOR A *HUNDRED YEARS!*
RIGHT DOWN TO THE *LOYAL GUARDIAN*, WHO WOULD RATHER *DIE* THAN BETRAY HIS MASTERS."
MORE LEVEL HEADS, OF COURSE, KNOW THAT THERE *IS* NO TREASURE.
A CASTLE, A TOWN, A *MONSTROUS FIGHTING HORDE*—
ALL THESE MUST BE MAINTAINED—PAID—*FED*—
AND NO DOUBT THE OLD SENESCHALS, AT LEAST, WERE *PRACTICAL MEN*
"...AND THE STORY THAT SAYS THE *MAIN VAULT* ONLY OPENS WHEN THE *DOOM BELL* RINGS—
SURELY IT IS NOTHING BUT A *FANCIFUL EMBROIDERY* ON A *DREAMER'S TALE*."
BUT STILL...I THINK WE SHALL RING IT *ANYWAY*.
YES?
eep!

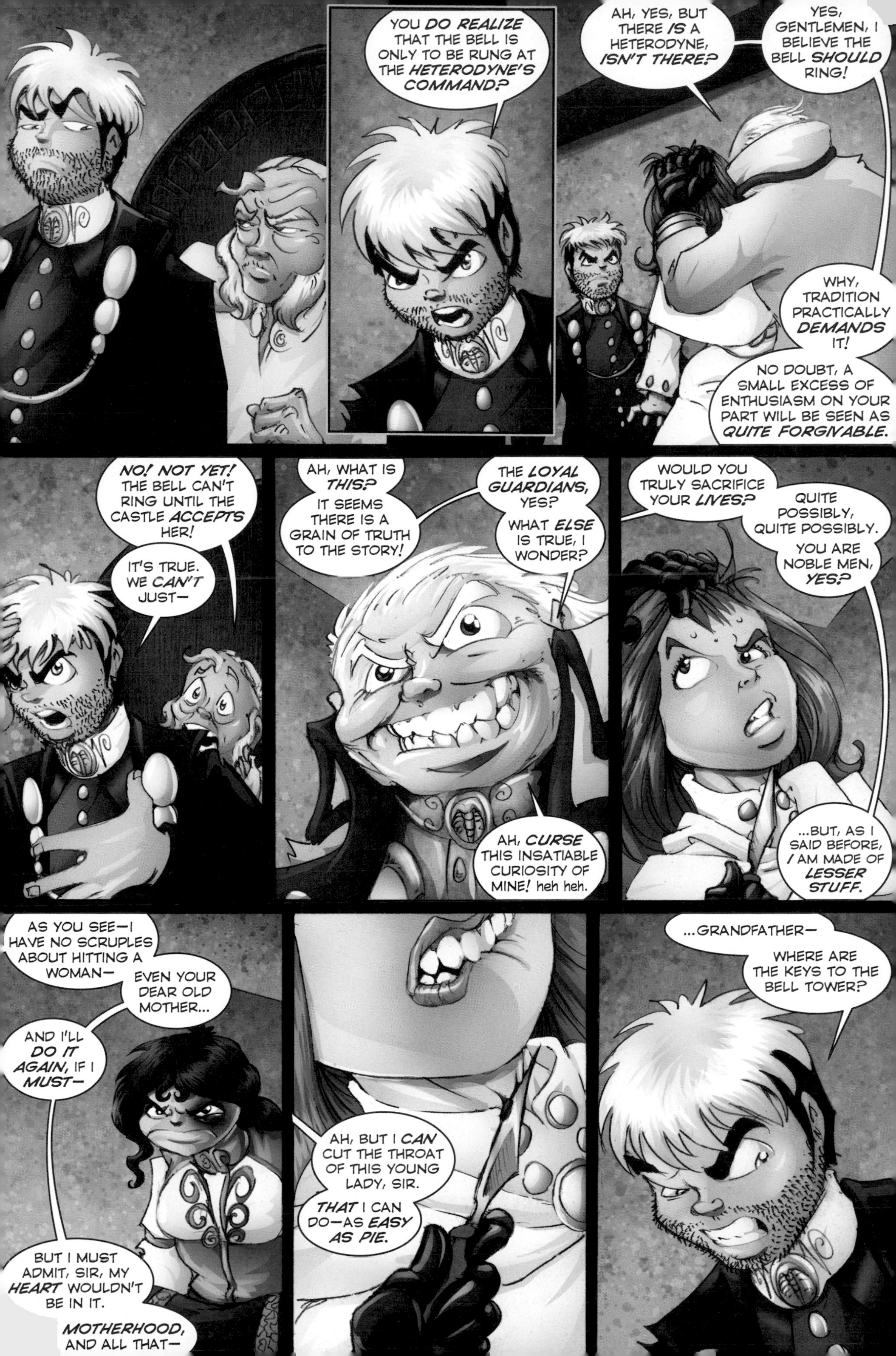
YOU DO REALIZE THAT THE BELL IS ONLY TO BE RUNG AT THE HETERODYNE'S COMMAND?
AH, YES, BUT THERE IS A HETERODYNE, ISN'T THERE?
YES, GENTLEMEN, I BELIEVE THE BELL SHOULD RING!
WHY, TRADITION PRACTICALLY DEMANDS IT!
NO DOUBT, A SMALL EXCESS OF ENTHUSIASM ON YOUR PART WILL BE SEEN AS QUITE FORGIVABLE.
NO! NOT YET! THE BELL CAN'T RING UNTIL THE CASTLE ACCEPTS HER!
IT'S TRUE. WE CAN'T JUST—
AH, WHAT IS THIS?
IT SEEMS THERE IS A GRAIN OF TRUTH TO THE STORY!
THE LOYAL GUARDIANS, YES?
WHAT ELSE IS TRUE, I WONDER?
AH, CURSE THIS INSATIABLE CURIOSITY OF MINE! heh heh.
WOULD YOU TRULY SACRIFICE YOUR LIVES?
QUITE POSSIBLY, QUITE POSSIBLY.
YOU ARE NOBLE MEN, YES?
...BUT, AS I SAID BEFORE, I AM MADE OF LESSER STUFF.
AS YOU SEE—I HAVE NO SCRUPLES ABOUT HITTING A WOMAN—
EVEN YOUR DEAR OLD MOTHER...
AND I'LL DO IT AGAIN, IF I MUST—
BUT I MUST ADMIT, SIR, MY HEART WOULDN'T BE IN IT.
MOTHERHOOD, AND ALL THAT—
AH, BUT I CAN CUT THE THROAT OF THIS YOUNG LADY, SIR.
THAT I CAN DO—AS EASY AS PIE.
...GRANDFATHER—
WHERE ARE THE KEYS TO THE BELL TOWER?

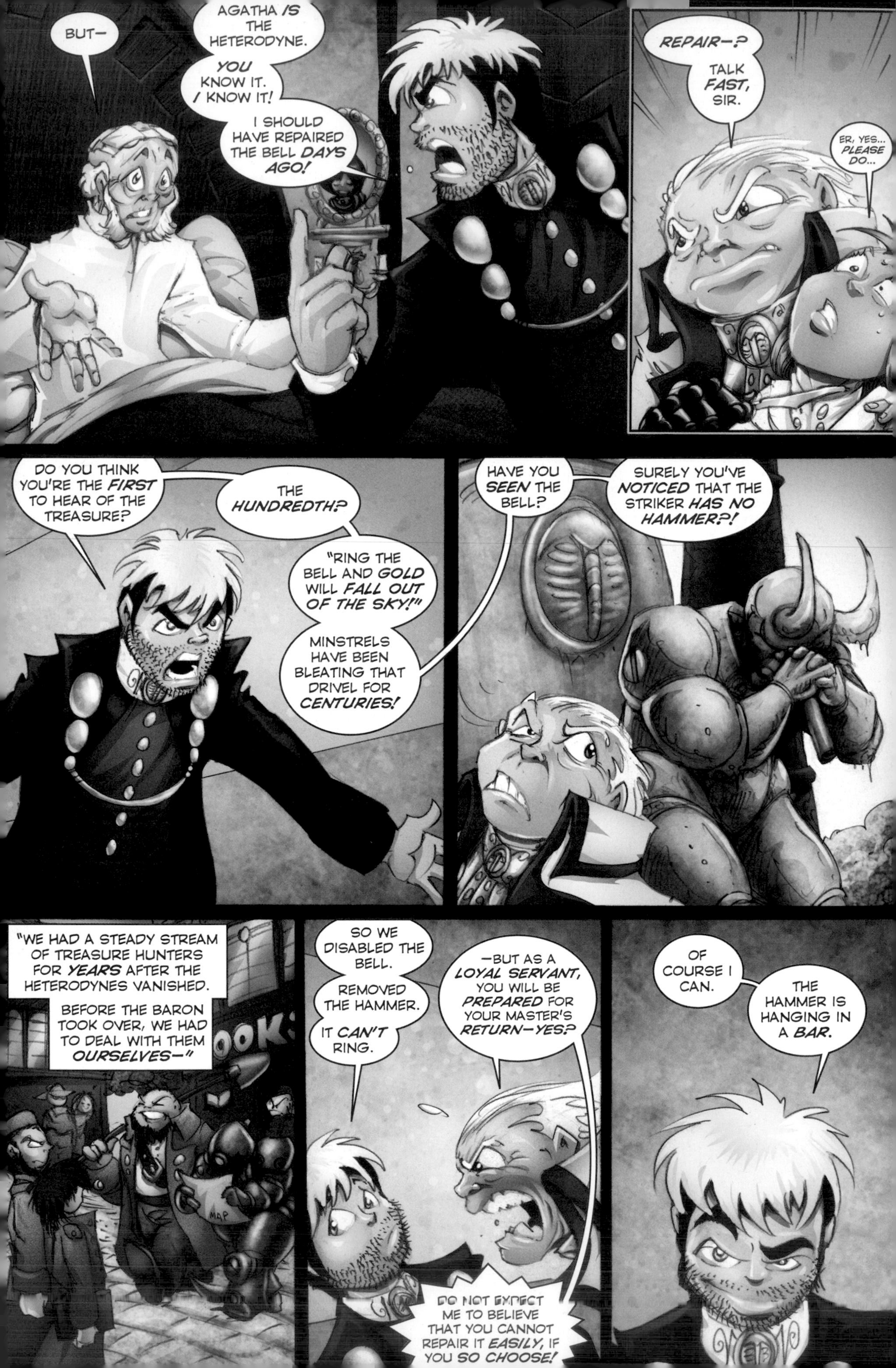
BUT—
AGATHA IS THE HETERODYNE.
YOU KNOW IT. I KNOW IT!
I SHOULD HAVE REPAIRED THE BELL DAYS AGO!
REPAIR—?
TALK FAST, SIR.
ER, YES... PLEASE DO...
DO YOU THINK YOU'RE THE FIRST TO HEAR OF THE TREASURE?
THE HUNDREDTH?
"RING THE BELL AND GOLD WILL FALL OUT OF THE SKY!"
MINSTRELS HAVE BEEN BLEATING THAT DRIVEL FOR CENTURIES!
HAVE YOU SEEN THE BELL?
SURELY YOU'VE NOTICED THAT THE STRIKER HAS NO HAMMER?!
"WE HAD A STEADY STREAM OF TREASURE HUNTERS FOR YEARS AFTER THE HETERODYNES VANISHED.
BEFORE THE BARON TOOK OVER, WE HAD TO DEAL WITH THEM OURSELVES—"
MAP
SO WE DISABLED THE BELL.
REMOVED THE HAMMER.
IT CAN'T RING.
—BUT AS A LOYAL SERVANT, YOU WILL BE PREPARED FOR YOUR MASTER'S RETURN—YES?
DO NOT EXPECT ME TO BELIEVE THAT YOU CANNOT REPAIR IT EASILY, IF YOU SO CHOOSE!
OF COURSE I CAN.
THE HAMMER IS HANGING IN A BAR.

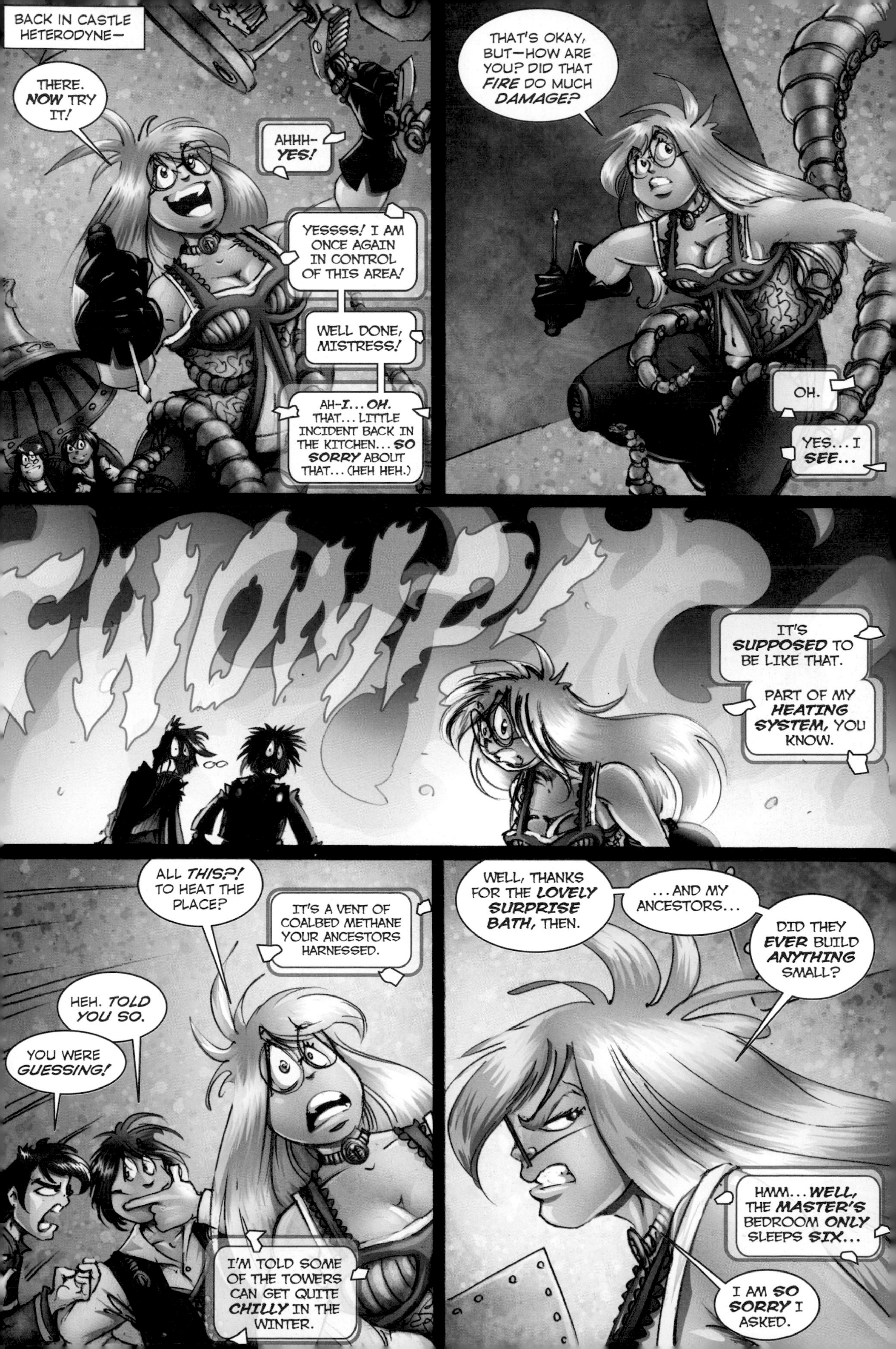
BACK IN CASTLE HETERODYNE—
THERE. NOW TRY IT!
AHHH- YES!
YESSSS! I AM ONCE AGAIN IN CONTROL OF THIS AREA!
WELL DONE, MISTRESS!
AH-I...OH. THAT...LITTLE INCIDENT BACK IN THE KITCHEN...SO SORRY ABOUT THAT...(HEH HEH.)
THAT'S OKAY, BUT—HOW ARE YOU? DID THAT FIRE DO MUCH DAMAGE?
OH.
YES...I SEE...
FWOMP!
IT'S SUPPOSED TO BE LIKE THAT.
PART OF MY HEATING SYSTEM, YOU KNOW.
ALL THIS?! TO HEAT THE PLACE?
IT'S A VENT OF COALBED METHANE YOUR ANCESTORS HARNESSED.
HEH. TOLD YOU SO.
YOU WERE GUESSING!
I'M TOLD SOME OF THE TOWERS CAN GET QUITE CHILLY IN THE WINTER.
WELL, THANKS FOR THE LOVELY SURPRISE BATH, THEN.
...AND MY ANCESTORS...
DID THEY EVER BUILD ANYTHING SMALL?
HMM...WELL, THE MASTER'S BEDROOM ONLY SLEEPS SIX...
I AM SO SORRY I ASKED.

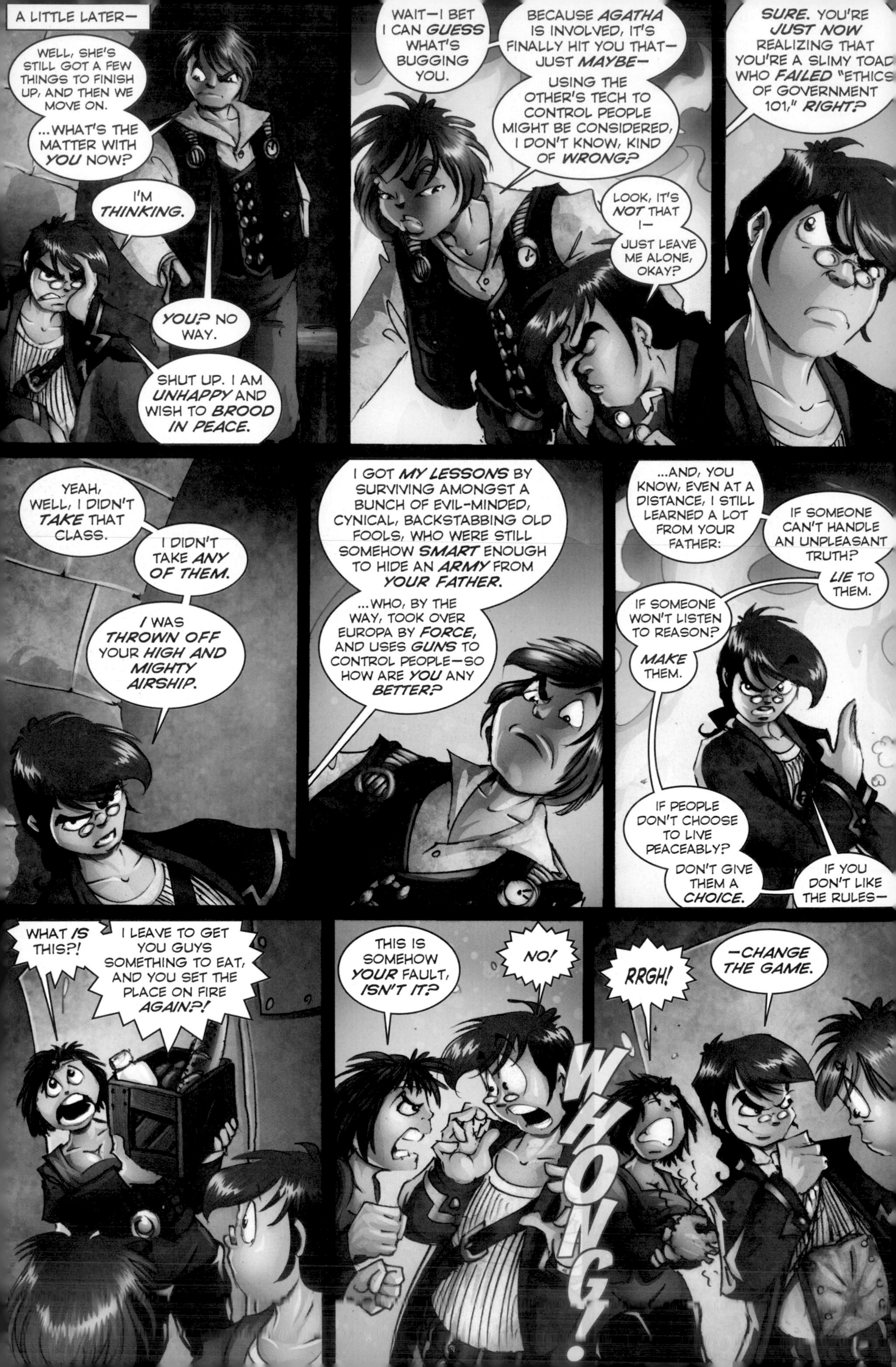
A LITTLE LATER—
WELL, SHE'S STILL GOT A FEW THINGS TO FINISH UP, AND THEN WE MOVE ON.
...WHAT'S THE MATTER WITH YOU NOW?
I'M THINKING.
YOU? NO WAY.
SHUT UP. I AM UNHAPPY AND WISH TO BROOD IN PEACE.
WAIT—I BET I CAN GUESS WHAT'S BUGGING YOU.
BECAUSE AGATHA IS INVOLVED, IT'S FINALLY HIT YOU THAT—JUST MAYBE—
USING THE OTHER'S TECH TO CONTROL PEOPLE MIGHT BE CONSIDERED, I DON'T KNOW, KIND OF WRONG?
LOOK, IT'S NOT THAT I—
JUST LEAVE ME ALONE, OKAY?
SURE. YOU'RE JUST NOW REALIZING THAT YOU'RE A SLIMY TOAD WHO FAILED "ETHICS OF GOVERNMENT 101," RIGHT?
YEAH, WELL, I DIDN'T TAKE THAT CLASS.
I DIDN'T TAKE ANY OF THEM.
I WAS THROWN OFF YOUR HIGH AND MIGHTY AIRSHIP.
I GOT MY LESSONS BY SURVIVING AMONGST A BUNCH OF EVIL-MINDED, CYNICAL, BACKSTABBING OLD FOOLS, WHO WERE STILL SOMEHOW SMART ENOUGH TO HIDE AN ARMY FROM YOUR FATHER.
...WHO, BY THE WAY, TOOK OVER EUROPA BY FORCE, AND USES GUNS TO CONTROL PEOPLE—SO HOW ARE YOU ANY BETTER?
...AND, YOU KNOW, EVEN AT A DISTANCE, I STILL LEARNED A LOT FROM YOUR FATHER:
IF SOMEONE CAN'T HANDLE AN UNPLEASANT TRUTH?
LIE TO THEM.
IF SOMEONE WON'T LISTEN TO REASON?
MAKE THEM.
IF PEOPLE DON'T CHOOSE TO LIVE PEACEABLY?
DON'T GIVE THEM A CHOICE.
IF YOU DON'T LIKE THE RULES—
WHAT IS THIS?!
I LEAVE TO GET YOU GUYS SOMETHING TO EAT, AND YOU SET THE PLACE ON FIRE AGAIN?!
THIS IS SOMEHOW YOUR FAULT, ISN'T IT?
NO!
RRGH!
—CHANGE THE GAME.
WHONG!

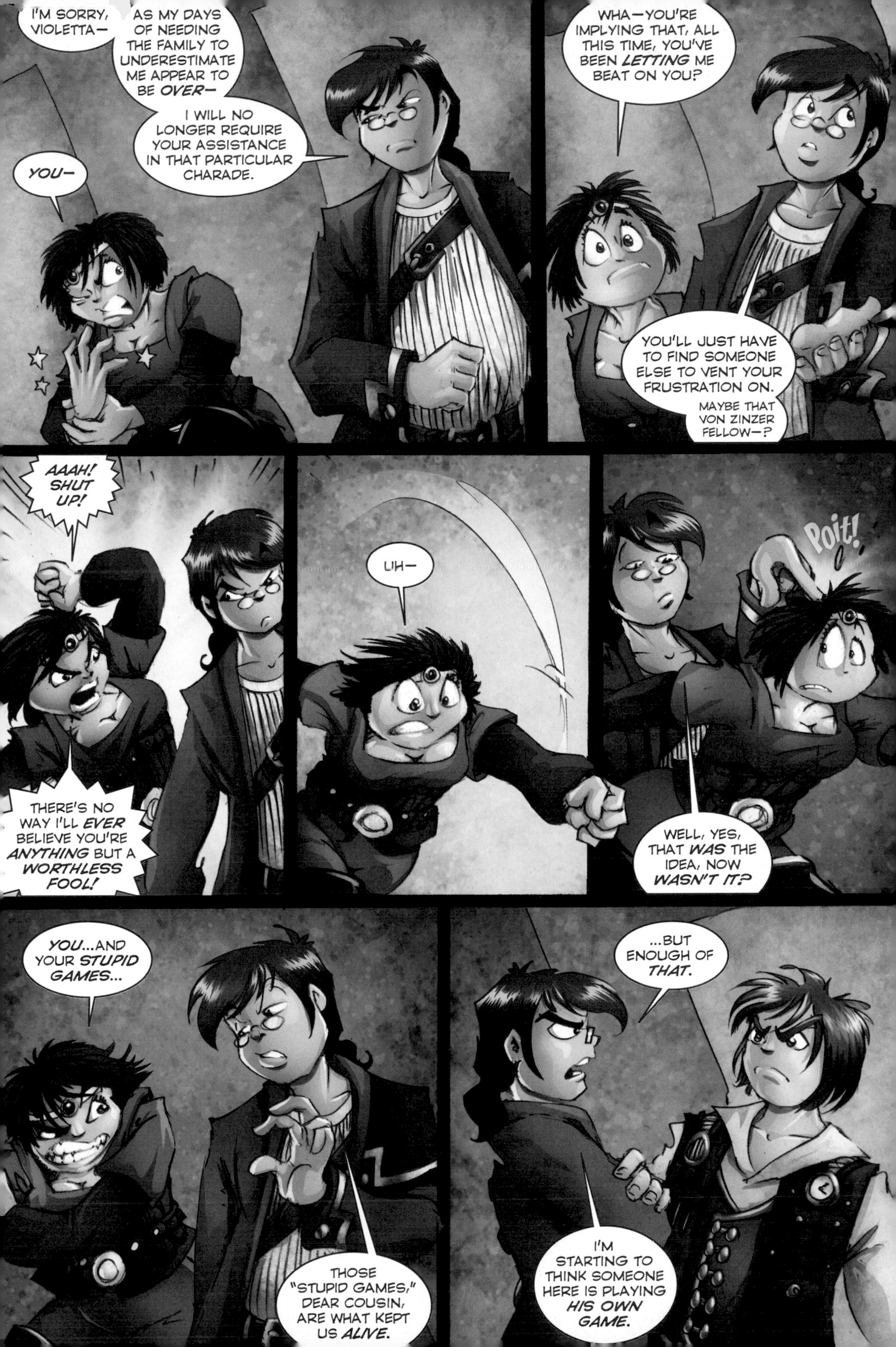

I'M SORRY, VIOLETTA—
AS MY DAYS OF NEEDING THE FAMILY TO UNDERESTIMATE ME APPEAR TO BE OVER—
I WILL NO LONGER REQUIRE YOUR ASSISTANCE IN THAT PARTICULAR CHARADE.
YOU—
WHA—YOU'RE IMPLYING THAT, ALL THIS TIME, YOU'VE BEEN LETTING ME BEAT ON YOU?
YOU'LL JUST HAVE TO FIND SOMEONE ELSE TO VENT YOUR FRUSTRATION ON.
MAYBE THAT VON ZINZER FELLOW—?
AAAH! SHUT UP!
THERE'S NO WAY I'LL EVER BELIEVE YOU'RE ANYTHING BUT A WORTHLESS FOOL!
UH—
Poit!
WELL, YES, THAT WAS THE IDEA, NOW WASN'T IT?
YOU...AND YOUR STUPID GAMES...
THOSE "STUPID GAMES," DEAR COUSIN, ARE WHAT KEPT US ALIVE.
...BUT ENOUGH OF THAT.
I'M STARTING TO THINK SOMEONE HERE IS PLAYING HIS OWN GAME.

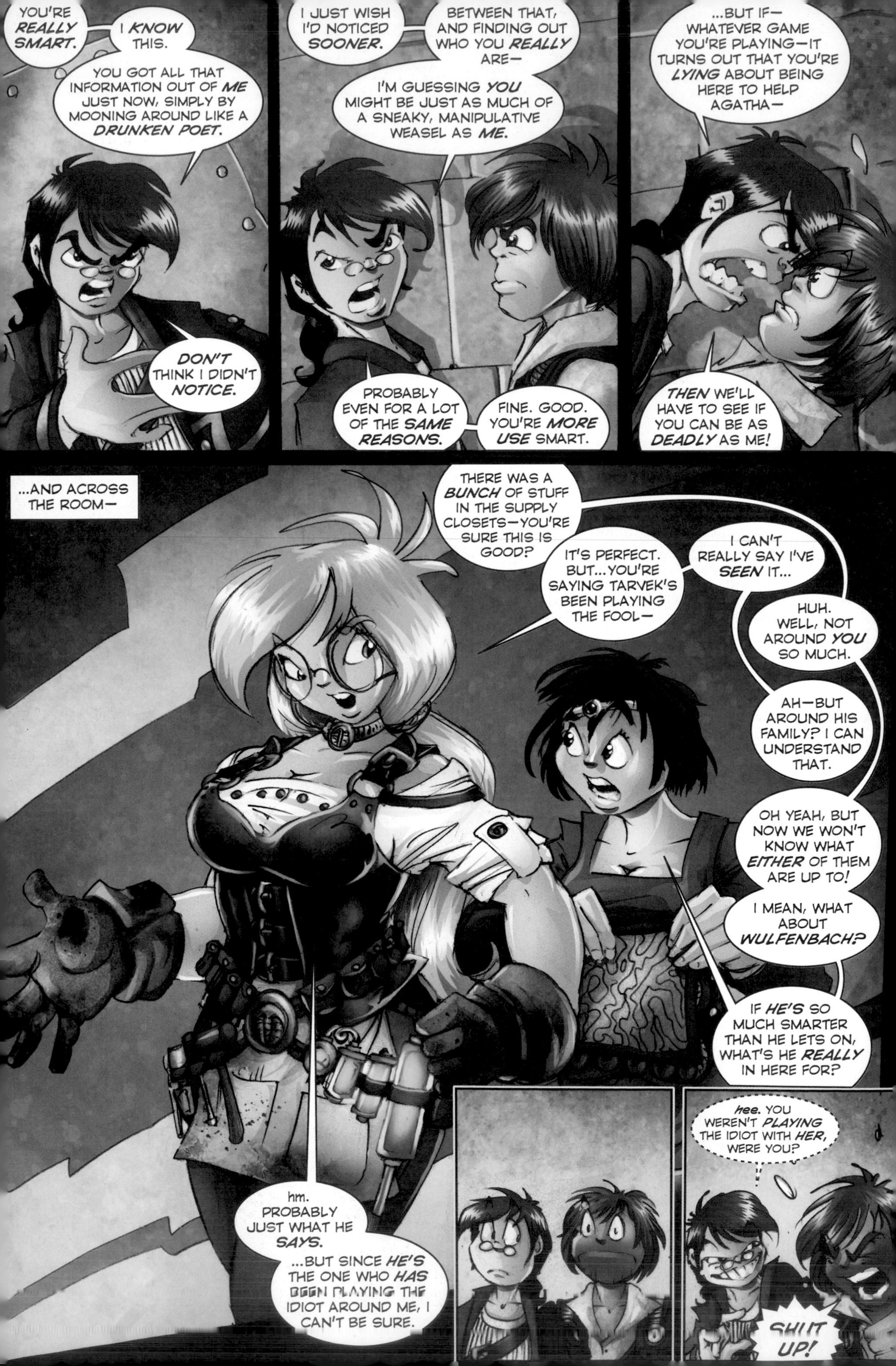
YOU'RE REALLY SMART.
I KNOW THIS.
YOU GOT ALL THAT INFORMATION OUT OF ME JUST NOW, SIMPLY BY MOONING AROUND LIKE A DRUNKEN POET.
DON'T THINK I DIDN'T NOTICE.
I JUST WISH I'D NOTICED SOONER.
BETWEEN THAT, AND FINDING OUT WHO YOU REALLY ARE—
I'M GUESSING YOU MIGHT BE JUST AS MUCH OF A SNEAKY, MANIPULATIVE WEASEL AS ME.
PROBABLY EVEN FOR A LOT OF THE SAME REASONS.
FINE. GOOD. YOU'RE MORE USE SMART.
...BUT IF—WHATEVER GAME YOU'RE PLAYING—IT TURNS OUT THAT YOU'RE LYING ABOUT BEING HERE TO HELP AGATHA—
THEN WE'LL HAVE TO SEE IF YOU CAN BE AS DEADLY AS ME!
...AND ACROSS THE ROOM—
THERE WAS A BUNCH OF STUFF IN THE SUPPLY CLOSETS—YOU'RE SURE THIS IS GOOD?
IT'S PERFECT. BUT...YOU'RE SAYING TARVEK'S BEEN PLAYING THE FOOL—
I CAN'T REALLY SAY I'VE SEEN IT...
HUH. WELL, NOT AROUND YOU SO MUCH.
AH—BUT AROUND HIS FAMILY? I CAN UNDERSTAND THAT.
OH YEAH, BUT NOW WE WON'T KNOW WHAT EITHER OF THEM ARE UP TO!
I MEAN, WHAT ABOUT WULFENBACH?
IF HE'S SO MUCH SMARTER THAN HE LETS ON, WHAT'S HE REALLY IN HERE FOR?
hm. PROBABLY JUST WHAT HE SAYS.
...BUT SINCE HE'S THE ONE WHO HAS BEEN PLAYING THE IDIOT AROUND ME, I CAN'T BE SURE.
hee. YOU WEREN'T PLAYING THE IDIOT WITH HER, WERE YOU?
SHUT UP!

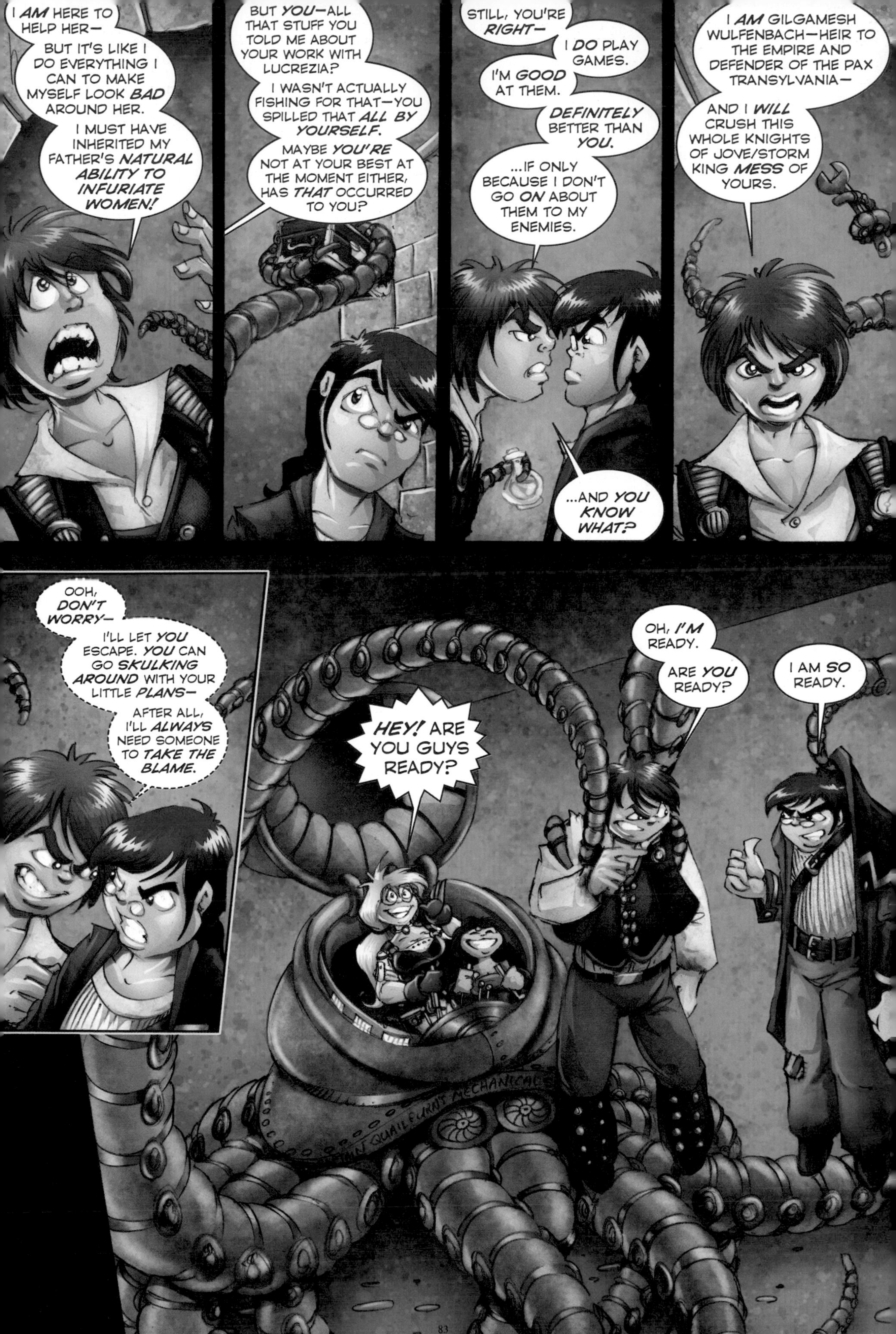
I AM HERE TO HELP HER—
BUT IT'S LIKE I DO EVERYTHING I CAN TO MAKE MYSELF LOOK BAD AROUND HER.
I MUST HAVE INHERITED MY FATHER'S NATURAL ABILITY TO INFURIATE WOMEN!
BUT YOU—ALL THAT STUFF YOU TOLD ME ABOUT YOUR WORK WITH LUCREZIA?
I WASN'T ACTUALLY FISHING FOR THAT—YOU SPILLED THAT ALL BY YOURSELF.
MAYBE YOU'RE NOT AT YOUR BEST AT THE MOMENT EITHER, HAS THAT OCCURRED TO YOU?
STILL, YOU'RE RIGHT—
I DO PLAY GAMES.
I'M GOOD AT THEM.
DEFINITELY BETTER THAN YOU.
...IF ONLY BECAUSE I DON'T GO ON ABOUT THEM TO MY ENEMIES.
...AND YOU KNOW WHAT?
I AM GILGAMESH WULFENBACH—HEIR TO THE EMPIRE AND DEFENDER OF THE PAX TRANSYLVANIA—
AND I WILL CRUSH THIS WHOLE KNIGHTS OF JOVE/STORM KING MESS OF YOURS.
OOH, DON'T WORRY—
I'LL LET YOU ESCAPE. YOU CAN GO SKULKING AROUND WITH YOUR LITTLE PLANS—
AFTER ALL, I'LL ALWAYS NEED SOMEONE TO TAKE THE BLAME.
HEY! ARE YOU GUYS READY?
OH, I'M READY.
ARE YOU READY?
I AM SO READY.

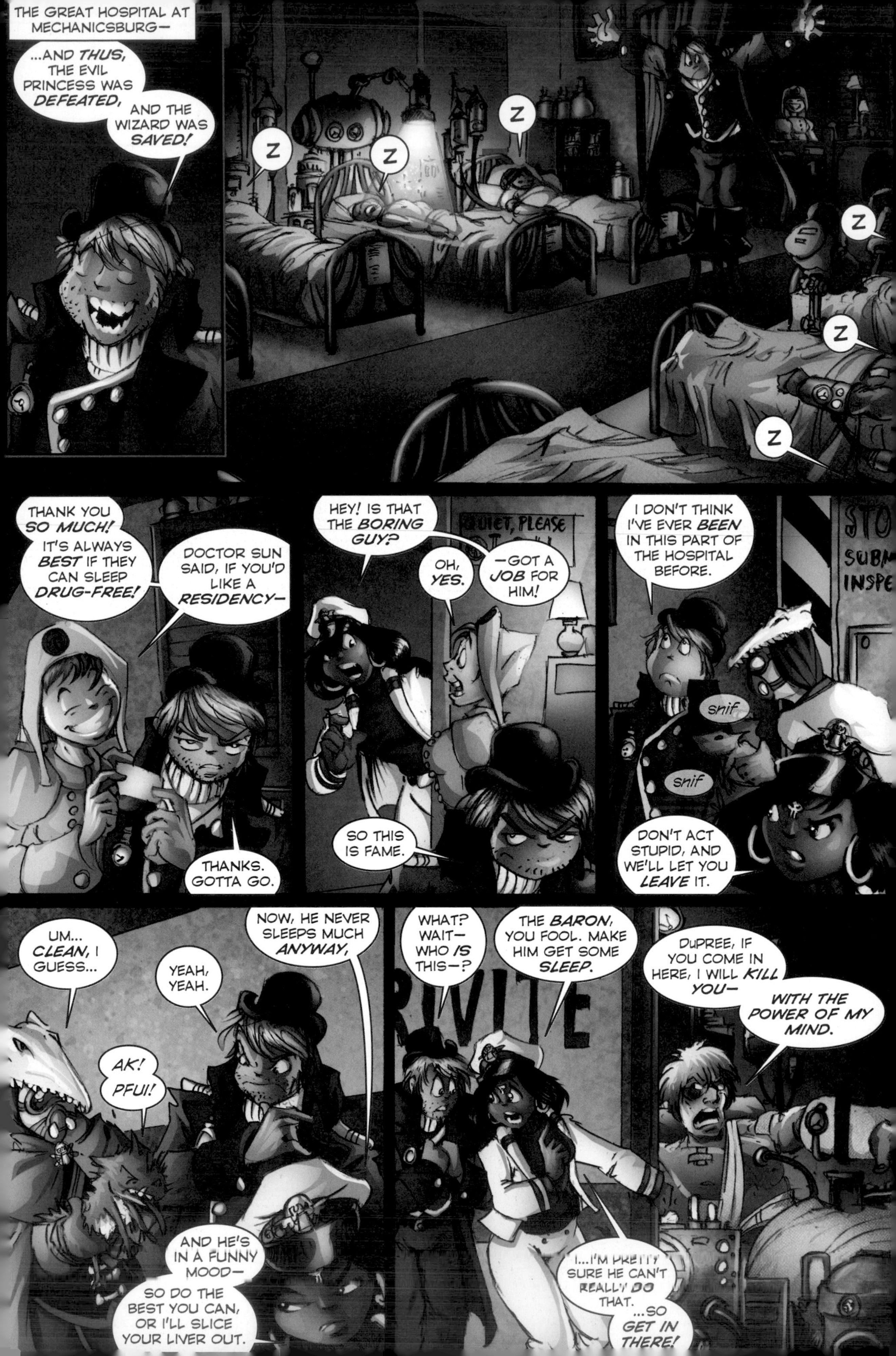
THE GREAT HOSPITAL AT MECHANICSBURG—
...AND *THUS*, THE EVIL PRINCESS WAS *DEFEATED*,
AND THE WIZARD WAS *SAVED!*
Z
Z
Z
Z
Z
Z
THANK YOU *SO MUCH!*
IT'S ALWAYS *BEST* IF THEY CAN SLEEP *DRUG-FREE!*
DOCTOR SUN SAID, IF YOU'D LIKE A *RESIDENCY*—
THANKS. GOTTA GO.
QUIET, PLEASE
HEY! IS THAT THE *BORING GUY?*
—GOT A *JOB* FOR HIM!
OH, *YES.*
SO THIS IS FAME.
I DON'T THINK I'VE EVER *BEEN* IN THIS PART OF THE HOSPITAL BEFORE.
snif
snif
DON'T ACT STUPID, AND WE'LL LET YOU *LEAVE* IT.
UM... *CLEAN*, I GUESS...
NOW, HE NEVER SLEEPS MUCH *ANYWAY*,
YEAH, YEAH.
AK!
PFUI!
AND HE'S IN A FUNNY MOOD—
SO DO THE BEST YOU CAN, OR I'LL SLICE YOUR LIVER OUT.
WHAT? WAIT— WHO *IS* THIS—?
THE *BARON*, YOU FOOL. MAKE HIM GET SOME *SLEEP*.
I...I'M PRETTY SURE HE CAN'T *REALLY DO* THAT. ...SO *GET IN THERE!*
DuPREE, IF YOU COME IN HERE, I WILL *KILL YOU*—
WITH THE POWER OF MY MIND.

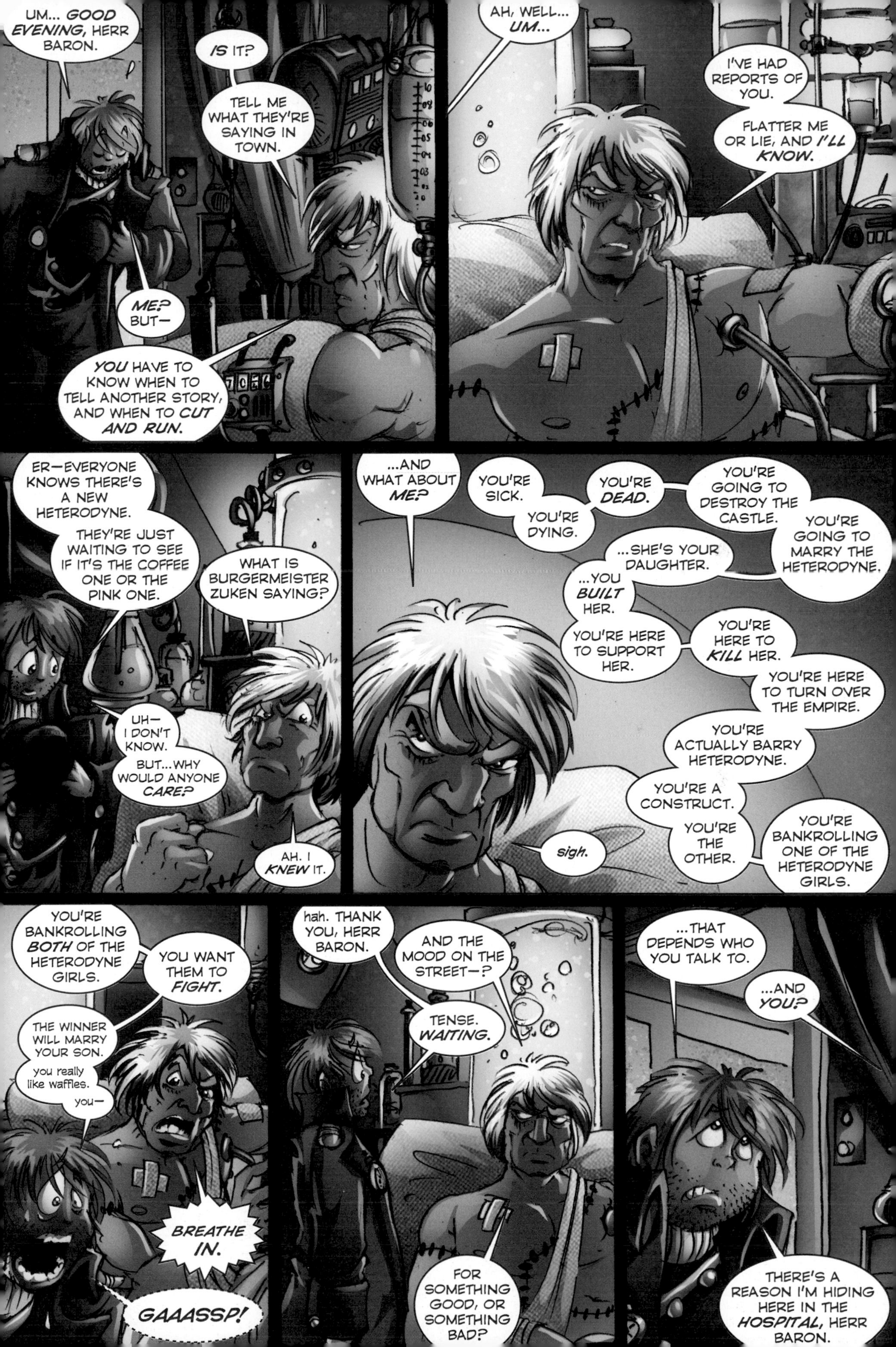
UM... GOOD EVENING, HERR BARON.
IS IT?
TELL ME WHAT THEY'RE SAYING IN TOWN.
ME? BUT—
YOU HAVE TO KNOW WHEN TO TELL ANOTHER STORY, AND WHEN TO CUT AND RUN.
AH, WELL... UM...
I'VE HAD REPORTS OF YOU.
FLATTER ME OR LIE, AND I'LL KNOW.
ER—EVERYONE KNOWS THERE'S A NEW HETERODYNE.
THEY'RE JUST WAITING TO SEE IF IT'S THE COFFEE ONE OR THE PINK ONE.
WHAT IS BURGERMEISTER ZUKEN SAYING?
UH— I DON'T KNOW.
BUT... WHY WOULD ANYONE CARE?
AH. I KNEW IT.
...AND WHAT ABOUT ME?
YOU'RE SICK.
YOU'RE DYING.
YOU'RE DEAD.
YOU'RE GOING TO DESTROY THE CASTLE.
YOU'RE GOING TO MARRY THE HETERODYNE.
...SHE'S YOUR DAUGHTER.
...YOU BUILT HER.
YOU'RE HERE TO SUPPORT HER.
YOU'RE HERE TO KILL HER.
YOU'RE HERE TO TURN OVER THE EMPIRE.
YOU'RE ACTUALLY BARRY HETERODYNE.
YOU'RE A CONSTRUCT.
YOU'RE THE OTHER.
YOU'RE BANKROLLING ONE OF THE HETERODYNE GIRLS.
sigh.
YOU'RE BANKROLLING BOTH OF THE HETERODYNE GIRLS.
YOU WANT THEM TO FIGHT.
THE WINNER WILL MARRY YOUR SON.
you really like waffles.
you—
BREATHE IN.
GAAASSP!
hah. THANK YOU, HERR BARON.
AND THE MOOD ON THE STREET—?
TENSE. WAITING.
FOR SOMETHING GOOD, OR SOMETHING BAD?
...THAT DEPENDS WHO YOU TALK TO.
...AND YOU?
THERE'S A REASON I'M HIDING HERE IN THE HOSPITAL, HERR BARON.

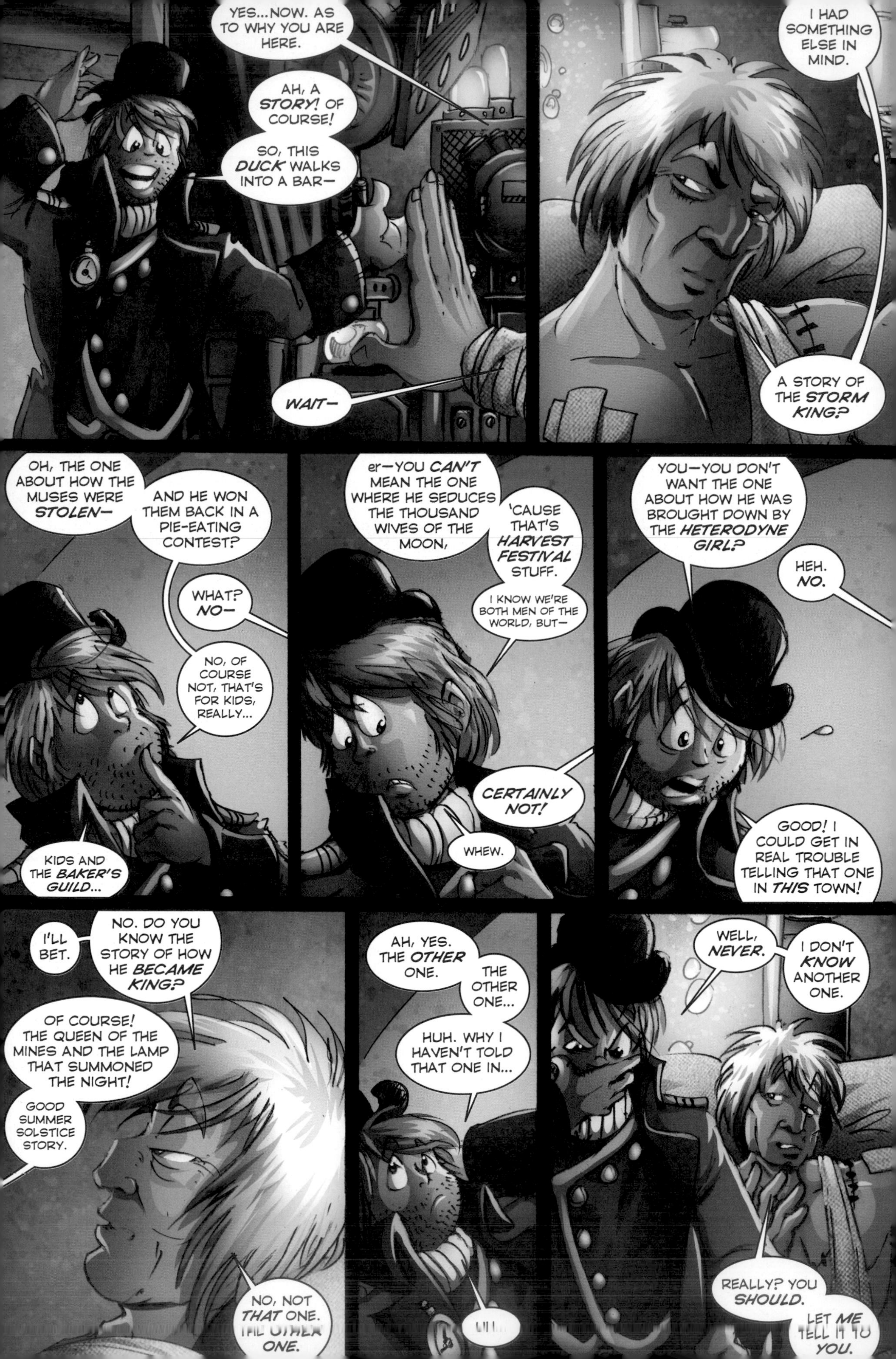
YES...NOW. AS TO WHY YOU ARE HERE.
AH, A STORY! OF COURSE!
SO, THIS DUCK WALKS INTO A BAR—
WAIT—
I HAD SOMETHING ELSE IN MIND.
A STORY OF THE STORM KING?
OH, THE ONE ABOUT HOW THE MUSES WERE STOLEN—
AND HE WON THEM BACK IN A PIE-EATING CONTEST?
WHAT? NO—
NO, OF COURSE NOT, THAT'S FOR KIDS, REALLY...
KIDS AND THE BAKER'S GUILD...
er—YOU CAN'T MEAN THE ONE WHERE HE SEDUCES THE THOUSAND WIVES OF THE MOON,
'CAUSE THAT'S HARVEST FESTIVAL STUFF.
I KNOW WE'RE BOTH MEN OF THE WORLD, BUT—
CERTAINLY NOT!
WHEW.
YOU—YOU DON'T WANT THE ONE ABOUT HOW HE WAS BROUGHT DOWN BY THE HETERODYNE GIRL?
HEH. NO.
GOOD! I COULD GET IN REAL TROUBLE TELLING THAT ONE IN THIS TOWN!
I'LL BET.
NO. DO YOU KNOW THE STORY OF HOW HE BECAME KING?
OF COURSE! THE QUEEN OF THE MINES AND THE LAMP THAT SUMMONED THE NIGHT!
GOOD SUMMER SOLSTICE STORY.
NO, NOT THAT ONE. THE OTHER ONE.
AH, YES. THE OTHER ONE.
THE OTHER ONE...
HUH. WHY I HAVEN'T TOLD THAT ONE IN...
WELL, NEVER.
I DON'T KNOW ANOTHER ONE.
REALLY? YOU SHOULD.
LET ME TELL IT TO YOU.

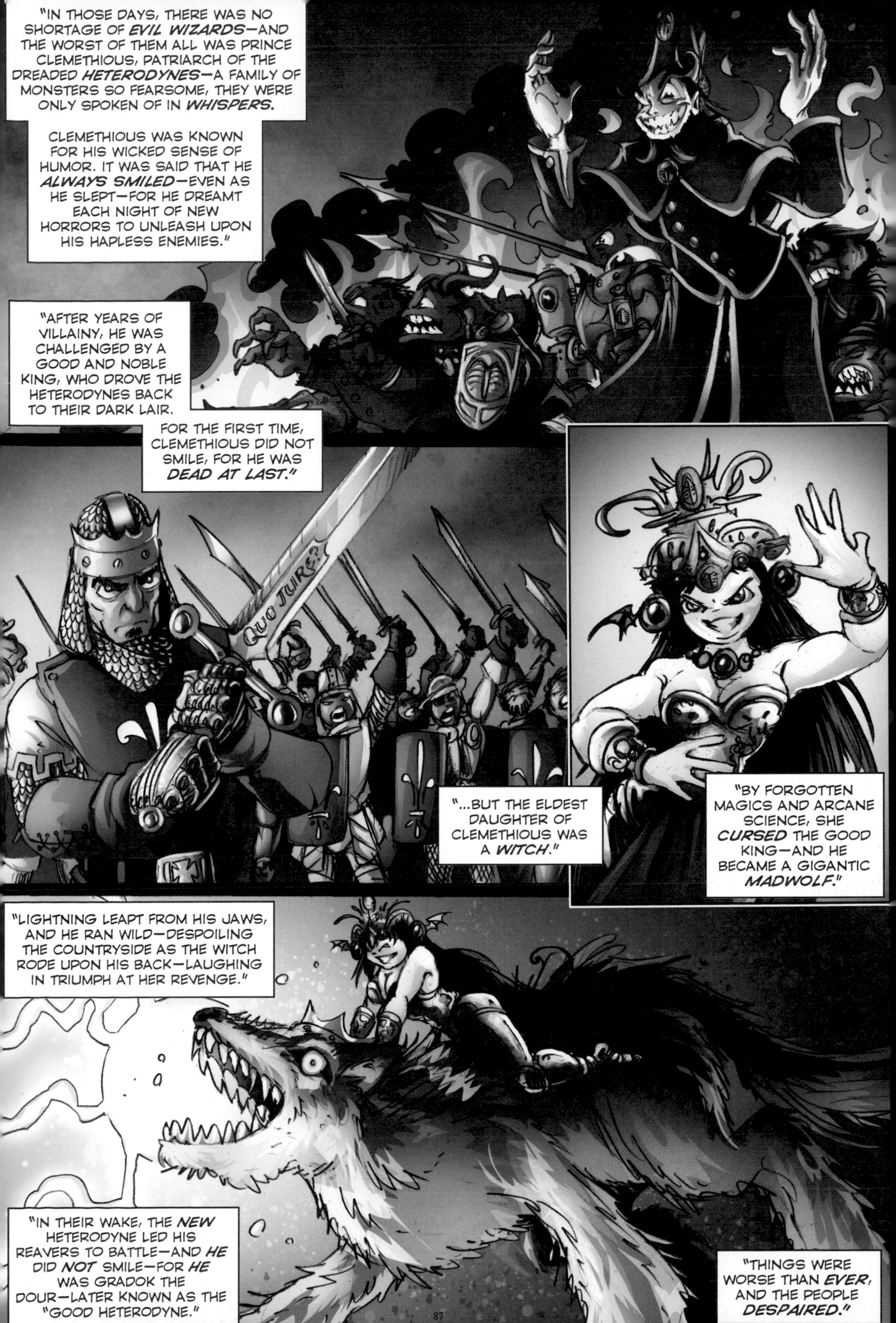
"IN THOSE DAYS, THERE WAS NO SHORTAGE OF EVIL WIZARDS—AND THE WORST OF THEM ALL WAS PRINCE CLEMETHIOUS, PATRIARCH OF THE DREADED HETERODYNES—A FAMILY OF MONSTERS SO FEARSOME, THEY WERE ONLY SPOKEN OF IN WHISPERS.
CLEMETHIOUS WAS KNOWN FOR HIS WICKED SENSE OF HUMOR. IT WAS SAID THAT HE ALWAYS SMILED—EVEN AS HE SLEPT—FOR HE DREAMT EACH NIGHT OF NEW HORRORS TO UNLEASH UPON HIS HAPLESS ENEMIES."
"AFTER YEARS OF VILLAINY, HE WAS CHALLENGED BY A GOOD AND NOBLE KING, WHO DROVE THE HETERODYNES BACK TO THEIR DARK LAIR.
FOR THE FIRST TIME, CLEMETHIOUS DID NOT SMILE, FOR HE WAS DEAD AT LAST."
QUO IURE?
"...BUT THE ELDEST DAUGHTER OF CLEMETHIOUS WAS A WITCH."
"BY FORGOTTEN MAGICS AND ARCANE SCIENCE, SHE CURSED THE GOOD KING—AND HE BECAME A GIGANTIC MADWOLF."
"LIGHTNING LEAPT FROM HIS JAWS, AND HE RAN WILD—DESPOILING THE COUNTRYSIDE AS THE WITCH RODE UPON HIS BACK—LAUGHING IN TRIUMPH AT HER REVENGE."
"IN THEIR WAKE, THE NEW HETERODYNE LED HIS REAVERS TO BATTLE—AND HE DID NOT SMILE—FOR HE WAS GRADOK THE DOUR—LATER KNOWN AS THE "GOOD HETERODYNE."
"THINGS WERE WORSE THAN EVER, AND THE PEOPLE DESPAIRED."

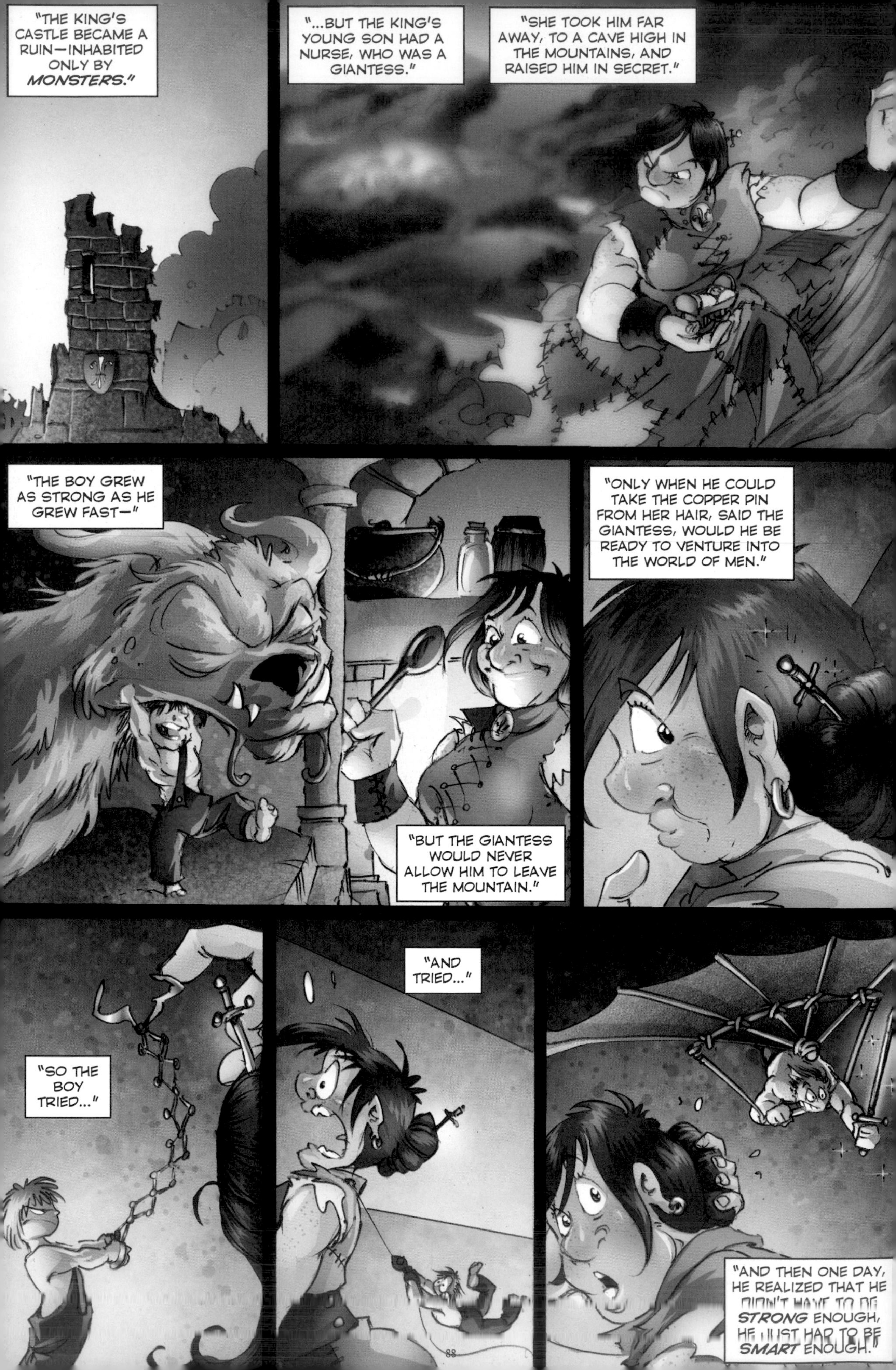
"THE KING'S CASTLE BECAME A RUIN—INHABITED ONLY BY *MONSTERS.*"
"...BUT THE KING'S YOUNG SON HAD A NURSE, WHO WAS A GIANTESS."
"SHE TOOK HIM FAR AWAY, TO A CAVE HIGH IN THE MOUNTAINS, AND RAISED HIM IN SECRET."
"THE BOY GREW AS STRONG AS HE GREW FAST—"
"BUT THE GIANTESS WOULD NEVER ALLOW HIM TO LEAVE THE MOUNTAIN."
"ONLY WHEN HE COULD TAKE THE COPPER PIN FROM HER HAIR, SAID THE GIANTESS, WOULD HE BE READY TO VENTURE INTO THE WORLD OF MEN."
"SO THE BOY TRIED..."
"AND TRIED..."
"AND THEN ONE DAY, HE REALIZED THAT HE DIDN'T HAVE TO BE *STRONG* ENOUGH, HE JUST HAD TO BE *SMART* ENOUGH."

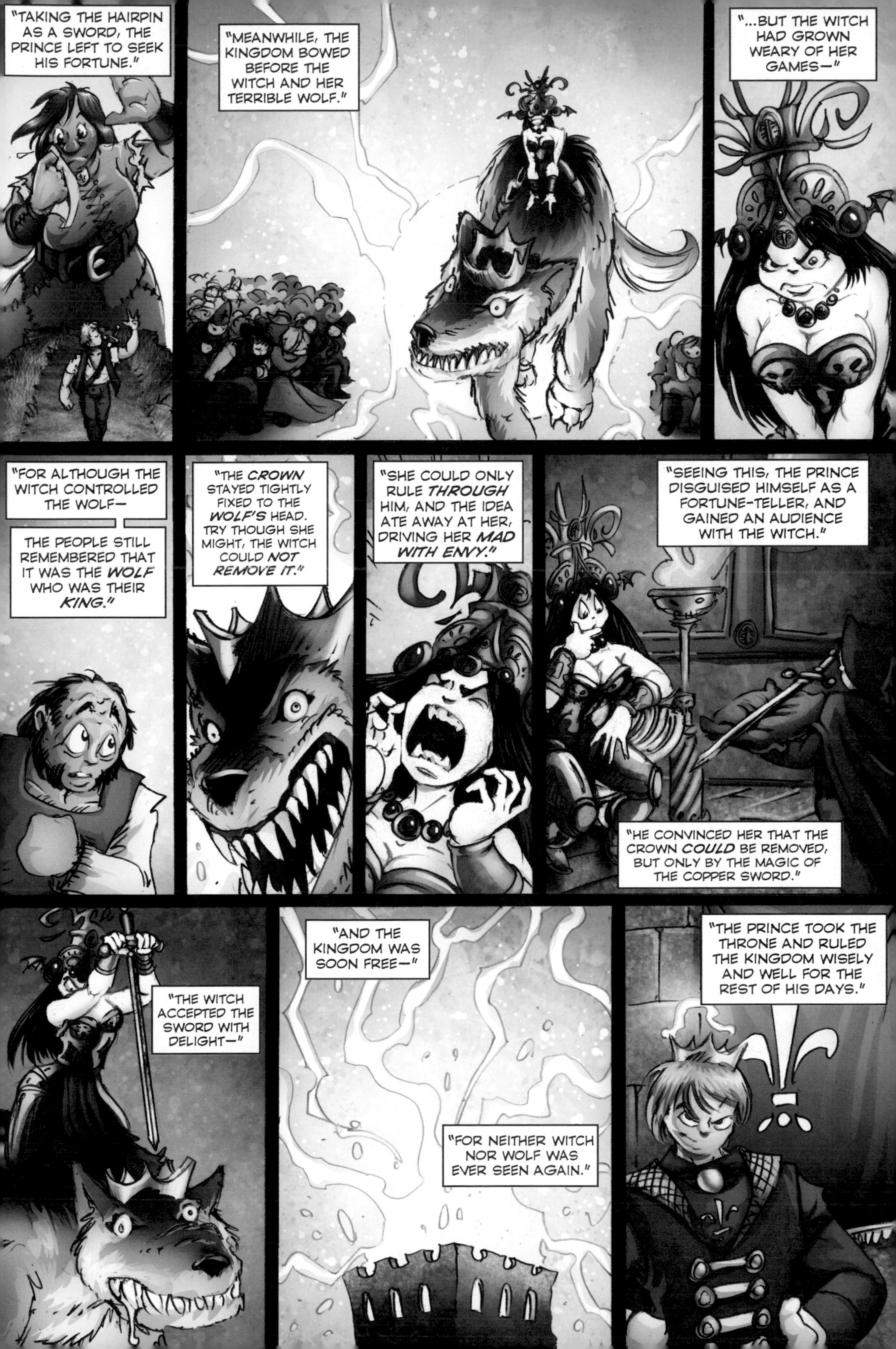
"TAKING THE HAIRPIN AS A SWORD, THE PRINCE LEFT TO SEEK HIS FORTUNE."
"MEANWHILE, THE KINGDOM BOWED BEFORE THE WITCH AND HER TERRIBLE WOLF."
"...BUT THE WITCH HAD GROWN WEARY OF HER GAMES—"
"FOR ALTHOUGH THE WITCH CONTROLLED THE WOLF—
THE PEOPLE STILL REMEMBERED THAT IT WAS THE WOLF WHO WAS THEIR KING."
"THE CROWN STAYED TIGHTLY FIXED TO THE WOLF'S HEAD. TRY THOUGH SHE MIGHT, THE WITCH COULD NOT REMOVE IT."
"SHE COULD ONLY RULE THROUGH HIM, AND THE IDEA ATE AWAY AT HER, DRIVING HER MAD WITH ENVY."
"SEEING THIS, THE PRINCE DISGUISED HIMSELF AS A FORTUNE-TELLER, AND GAINED AN AUDIENCE WITH THE WITCH."
"HE CONVINCED HER THAT THE CROWN COULD BE REMOVED, BUT ONLY BY THE MAGIC OF THE COPPER SWORD."
"THE WITCH ACCEPTED THE SWORD WITH DELIGHT—"
"AND THE KINGDOM WAS SOON FREE—"
"FOR NEITHER WITCH NOR WOLF WAS EVER SEEN AGAIN."
"THE PRINCE TOOK THE THRONE AND RULED THE KINGDOM WISELY AND WELL FOR THE REST OF HIS DAYS."

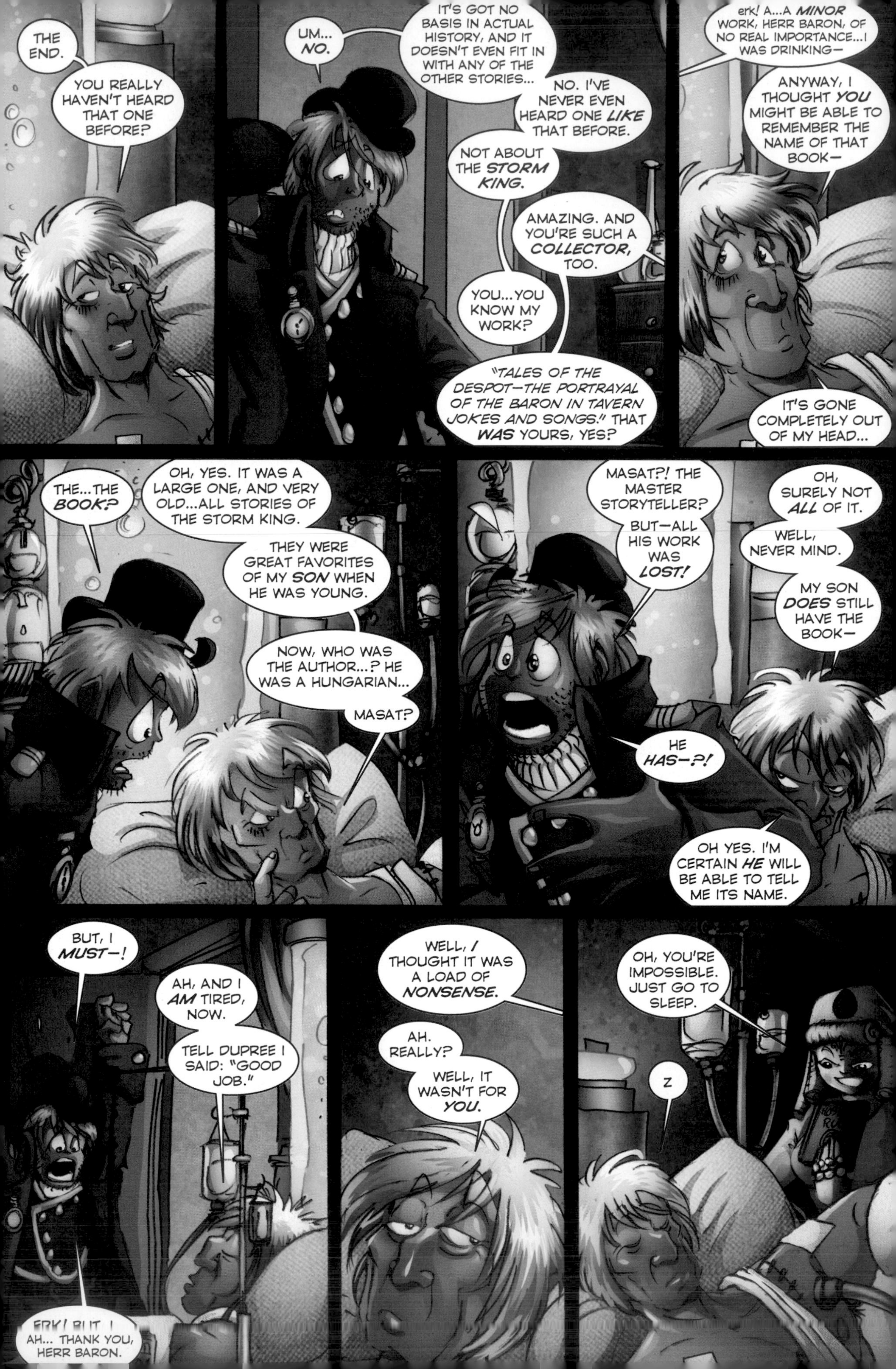
THE END.
YOU REALLY HAVEN'T HEARD THAT ONE BEFORE?
UM... NO.
IT'S GOT NO BASIS IN ACTUAL HISTORY, AND IT DOESN'T EVEN FIT IN WITH ANY OF THE OTHER STORIES...
NO. I'VE NEVER EVEN HEARD ONE LIKE THAT BEFORE.
NOT ABOUT THE STORM KING.
AMAZING. AND YOU'RE SUCH A COLLECTOR, TOO.
YOU...YOU KNOW MY WORK?
"TALES OF THE DESPOT—THE PORTRAYAL OF THE BARON IN TAVERN JOKES AND SONGS." THAT WAS YOURS, YES?
erk! A...A MINOR WORK, HERR BARON, OF NO REAL IMPORTANCE...I WAS DRINKING—
ANYWAY, I THOUGHT YOU MIGHT BE ABLE TO REMEMBER THE NAME OF THAT BOOK—
IT'S GONE COMPLETELY OUT OF MY HEAD...
THE...THE BOOK?
OH, YES. IT WAS A LARGE ONE, AND VERY OLD...ALL STORIES OF THE STORM KING.
THEY WERE GREAT FAVORITES OF MY SON WHEN HE WAS YOUNG.
NOW, WHO WAS THE AUTHOR...? HE WAS A HUNGARIAN...
MASAT?
MASAT?! THE MASTER STORYTELLER?
BUT—ALL HIS WORK WAS LOST!
OH, SURELY NOT ALL OF IT.
WELL, NEVER MIND.
MY SON DOES STILL HAVE THE BOOK—
HE HAS—?!
OH YES. I'M CERTAIN HE WILL BE ABLE TO TELL ME ITS NAME.
BUT, I MUST—!
AH, AND I AM TIRED, NOW.
TELL DUPREE I SAID: "GOOD JOB."
ERK! BUT I AH... THANK YOU, HERR BARON.
WELL, I THOUGHT IT WAS A LOAD OF NONSENSE.
AH. REALLY?
WELL, IT WASN'T FOR YOU.
OH, YOU'RE IMPOSSIBLE. JUST GO TO SLEEP.
Z

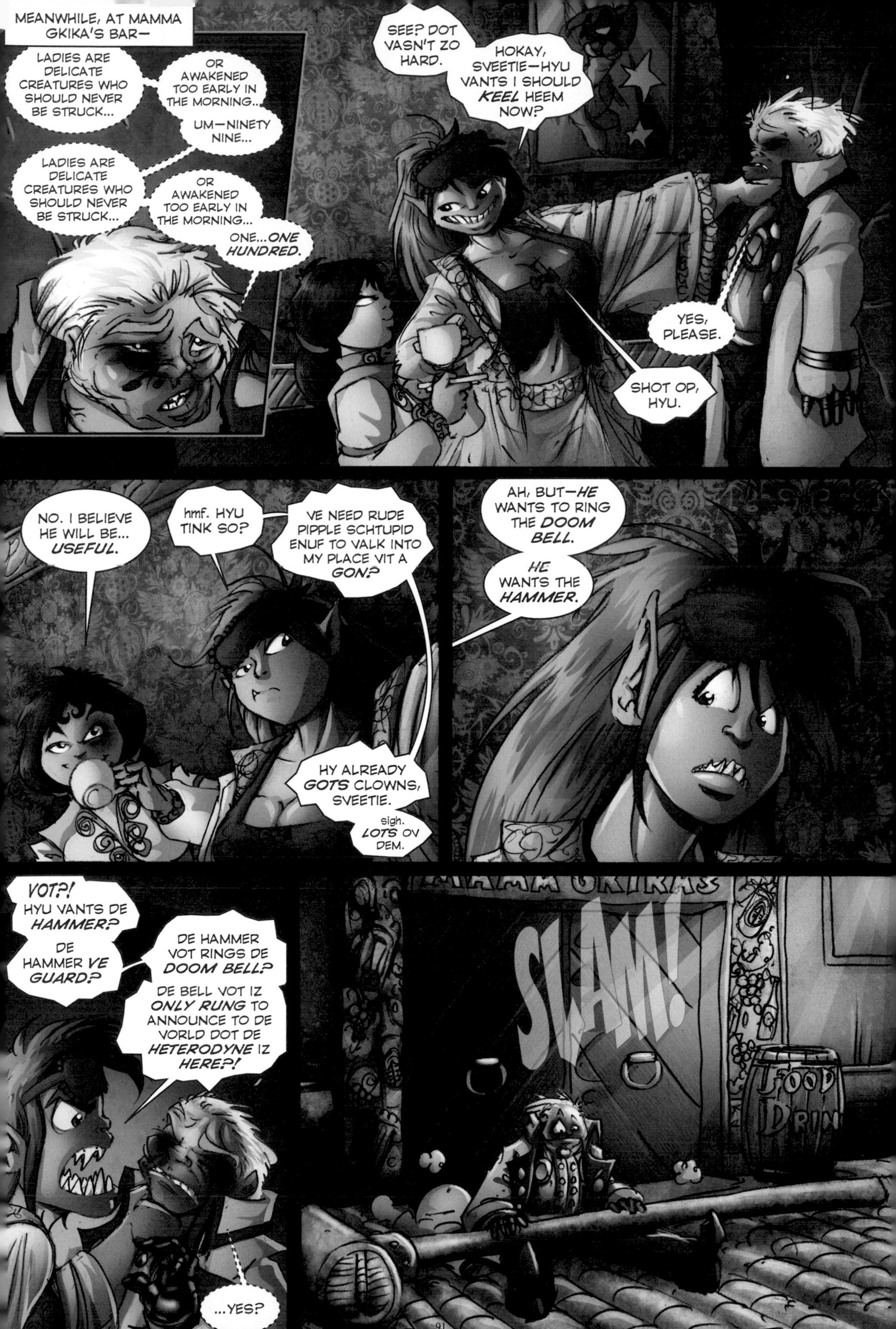
MEANWHILE, AT MAMMA GKIKA'S BAR—
LADIES ARE DELICATE CREATURES WHO SHOULD NEVER BE STRUCK...
OR AWAKENED TOO EARLY IN THE MORNING...
UM—NINETY NINE...
LADIES ARE DELICATE CREATURES WHO SHOULD NEVER BE STRUCK...
OR AWAKENED TOO EARLY IN THE MORNING...
ONE...ONE HUNDRED.
SEE? DOT VASN'T ZO HARD.
HOKAY, SVEETIE—HYU VANTS I SHOULD KEEL HEEM NOW?
YES, PLEASE.
SHOT OP, HYU.
NO. I BELIEVE HE WILL BE... USEFUL.
hmf. HYU TINK SO?
VE NEED RUDE PIPPLE SCHTUPID ENUF TO VALK INTO MY PLACE VIT A GON?
HY ALREADY GOTS CLOWNS, SVEETIE.
sigh. LOTS OV DEM.
AH, BUT—HE WANTS TO RING THE DOOM BELL.
HE WANTS THE HAMMER.
VOT?! HYU VANTS DE HAMMER?
DE HAMMER VE GUARD?
DE HAMMER VOT RINGS DE DOOM BELL?
DE BELL VOT IZ ONLY RUNG TO ANNOUNCE TO DE VORLD DOT DE HETERODYNE IZ HERE?!
...YES?
SLAM!
FOOD DRIN

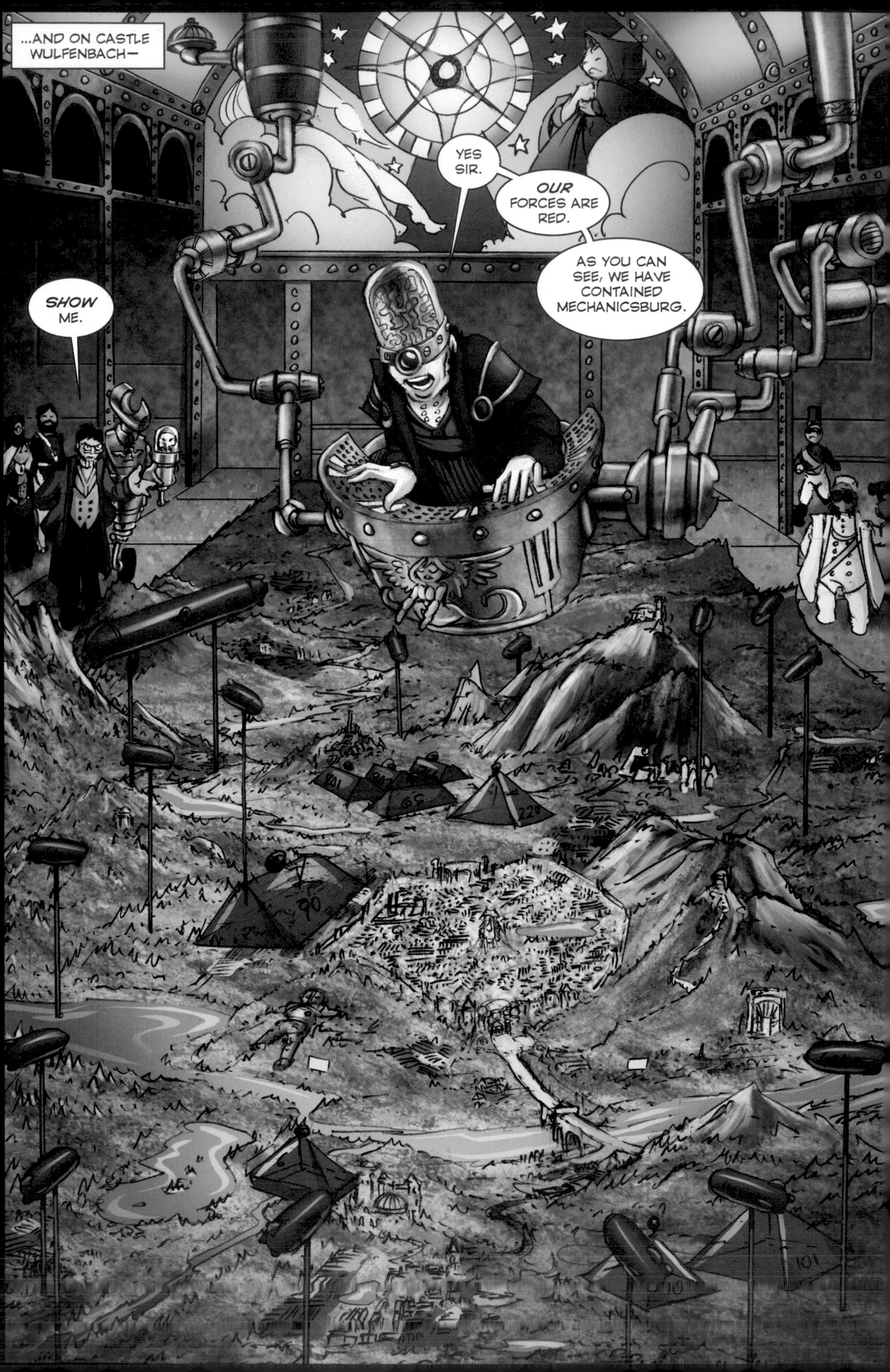
...AND ON CASTLE WULFENBACH—
SHOW ME.
YES SIR.
OUR FORCES ARE RED.
AS YOU CAN SEE, WE HAVE CONTAINED MECHANICSBURG.

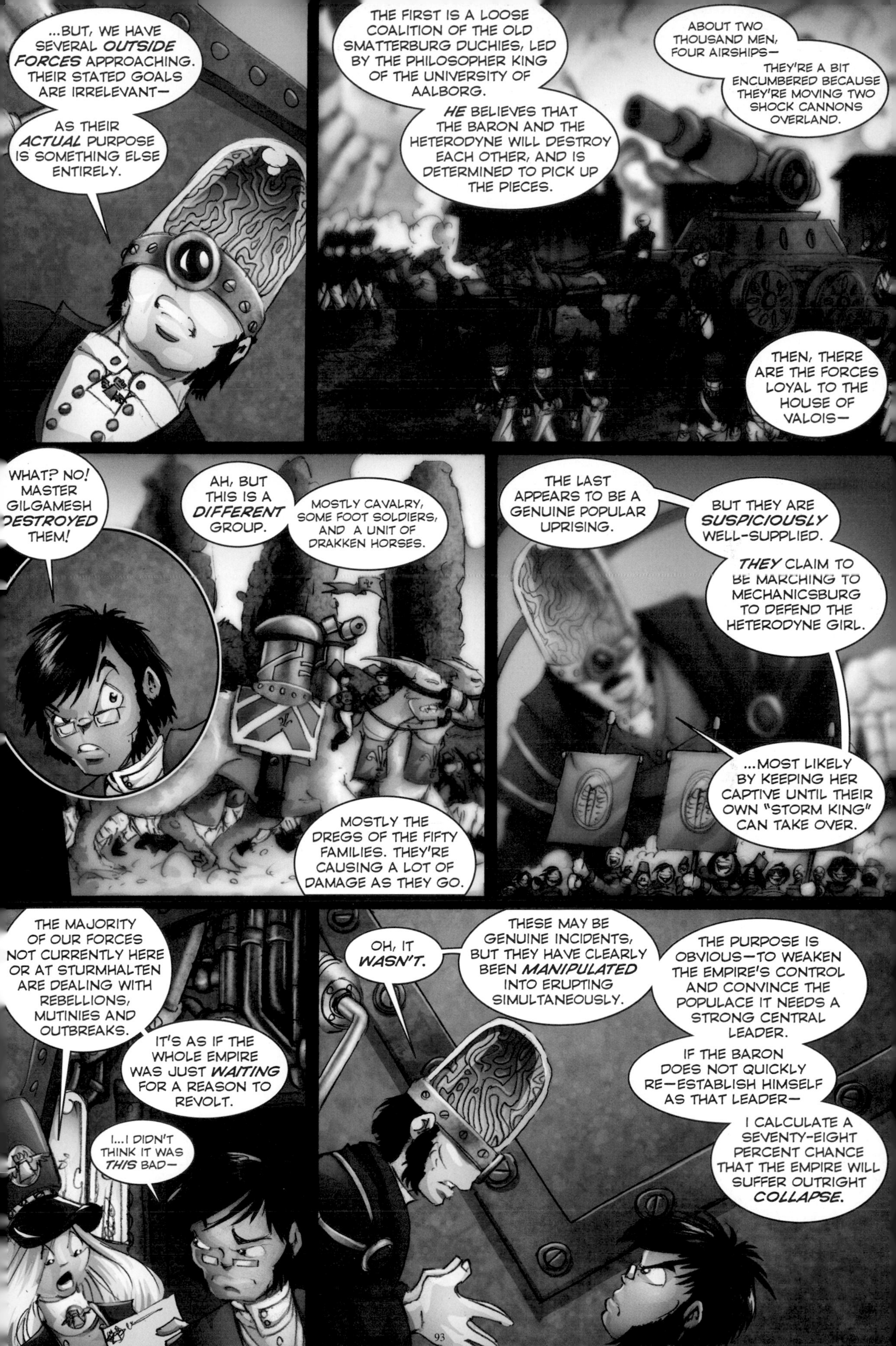
...BUT, WE HAVE SEVERAL OUTSIDE FORCES APPROACHING. THEIR STATED GOALS ARE IRRELEVANT—
AS THEIR ACTUAL PURPOSE IS SOMETHING ELSE ENTIRELY.
THE FIRST IS A LOOSE COALITION OF THE OLD SMATTERBURG DUCHIES, LED BY THE PHILOSOPHER KING OF THE UNIVERSITY OF AALBORG.
HE BELIEVES THAT THE BARON AND THE HETERODYNE WILL DESTROY EACH OTHER, AND IS DETERMINED TO PICK UP THE PIECES.
ABOUT TWO THOUSAND MEN, FOUR AIRSHIPS—
THEY'RE A BIT ENCUMBERED BECAUSE THEY'RE MOVING TWO SHOCK CANNONS OVERLAND.
THEN, THERE ARE THE FORCES LOYAL TO THE HOUSE OF VALOIS—
WHAT? NO! MASTER GILGAMESH DESTROYED THEM!
AH, BUT THIS IS A DIFFERENT GROUP.
MOSTLY CAVALRY, SOME FOOT SOLDIERS, AND A UNIT OF DRAKKEN HORSES.
MOSTLY THE DREGS OF THE FIFTY FAMILIES. THEY'RE CAUSING A LOT OF DAMAGE AS THEY GO.
THE LAST APPEARS TO BE A GENUINE POPULAR UPRISING.
BUT THEY ARE SUSPICIOUSLY WELL-SUPPLIED.
THEY CLAIM TO BE MARCHING TO MECHANICSBURG TO DEFEND THE HETERODYNE GIRL.
...MOST LIKELY BY KEEPING HER CAPTIVE UNTIL THEIR OWN "STORM KING" CAN TAKE OVER.
THE MAJORITY OF OUR FORCES NOT CURRENTLY HERE OR AT STURMHALTEN ARE DEALING WITH REBELLIONS, MUTINIES AND OUTBREAKS.
IT'S AS IF THE WHOLE EMPIRE WAS JUST WAITING FOR A REASON TO REVOLT.
I...I DIDN'T THINK IT WAS THIS BAD—
OH, IT WASN'T.
THESE MAY BE GENUINE INCIDENTS, BUT THEY HAVE CLEARLY BEEN MANIPULATED INTO ERUPTING SIMULTANEOUSLY.
THE PURPOSE IS OBVIOUS—TO WEAKEN THE EMPIRE'S CONTROL AND CONVINCE THE POPULACE IT NEEDS A STRONG CENTRAL LEADER.
IF THE BARON DOES NOT QUICKLY RE—ESTABLISH HIMSELF AS THAT LEADER—
I CALCULATE A SEVENTY-EIGHT PERCENT CHANCE THAT THE EMPIRE WILL SUFFER OUTRIGHT COLLAPSE.

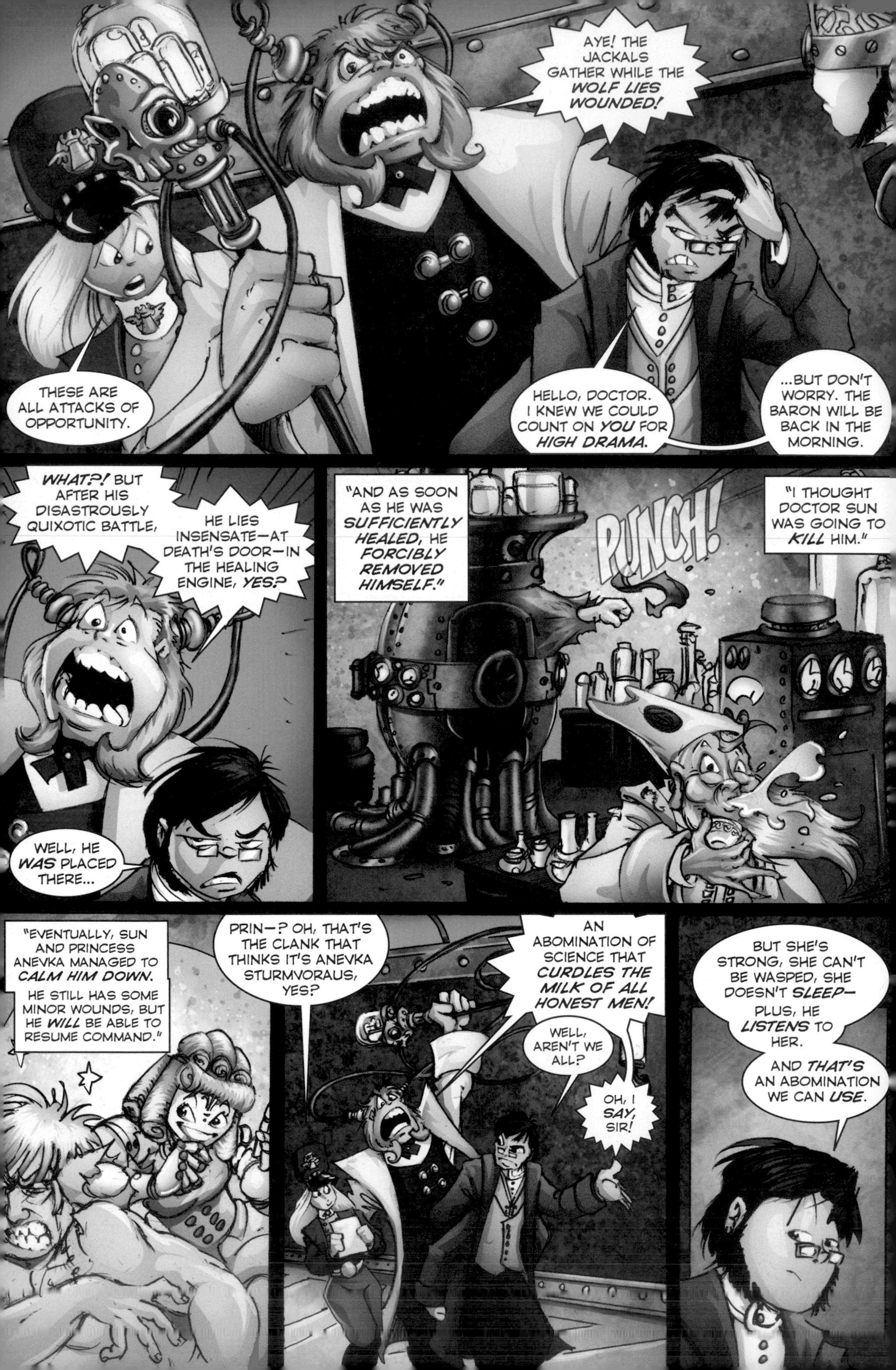
AYE! THE JACKALS GATHER WHILE THE WOLF LIES WOUNDED!
THESE ARE ALL ATTACKS OF OPPORTUNITY.
HELLO, DOCTOR. I KNEW WE COULD COUNT ON YOU FOR HIGH DRAMA.
...BUT DON'T WORRY. THE BARON WILL BE BACK IN THE MORNING.
WHAT?! BUT AFTER HIS DISASTROUSLY QUIXOTIC BATTLE,
HE LIES INSENSATE—AT DEATH'S DOOR—IN THE HEALING ENGINE, YES?
WELL, HE WAS PLACED THERE...
"AND AS SOON AS HE WAS SUFFICIENTLY HEALED, HE FORCIBLY REMOVED HIMSELF."
PUNCH!
"I THOUGHT DOCTOR SUN WAS GOING TO KILL HIM."
"EVENTUALLY, SUN AND PRINCESS ANEVKA MANAGED TO CALM HIM DOWN.
HE STILL HAS SOME MINOR WOUNDS, BUT HE WILL BE ABLE TO RESUME COMMAND."
PRIN—? OH, THAT'S THE CLANK THAT THINKS IT'S ANEVKA STURMVORAUS, YES?
AN ABOMINATION OF SCIENCE THAT CURDLES THE MILK OF ALL HONEST MEN!
WELL, AREN'T WE ALL?
OH, I SAY, SIR!
BUT SHE'S STRONG, SHE CAN'T BE WASPED, SHE DOESN'T SLEEP—
PLUS, HE LISTENS TO HER.
AND THAT'S AN ABOMINATION WE CAN USE.

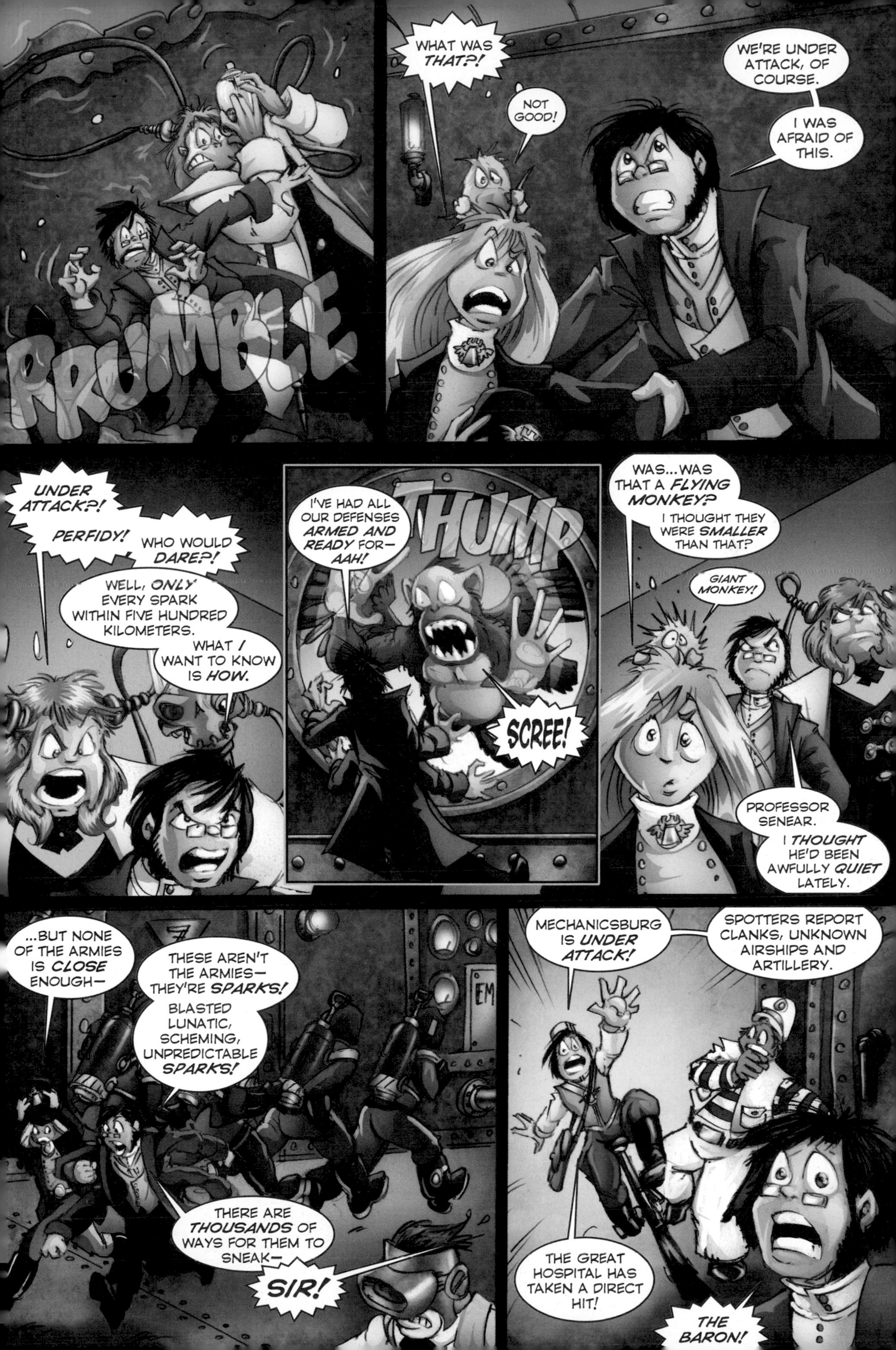
RRUMBLE
WHAT WAS THAT?!
NOT GOOD!
WE'RE UNDER ATTACK, OF COURSE.
I WAS AFRAID OF THIS.
UNDER ATTACK?!
PERFIDY!
WHO WOULD DARE?!
WELL, ONLY EVERY SPARK WITHIN FIVE HUNDRED KILOMETERS.
WHAT I WANT TO KNOW IS HOW.
THUMP
I'VE HAD ALL OUR DEFENSES ARMED AND READY FOR—AAH!
SCREE!
WAS...WAS THAT A FLYING MONKEY?
I THOUGHT THEY WERE SMALLER THAN THAT?
GIANT MONKEY!
PROFESSOR SENEAR.
I THOUGHT HE'D BEEN AWFULLY QUIET LATELY.
...BUT NONE OF THE ARMIES IS CLOSE ENOUGH—
THESE AREN'T THE ARMIES—THEY'RE SPARKS!
BLASTED LUNATIC, SCHEMING, UNPREDICTABLE SPARKS!
THERE ARE THOUSANDS OF WAYS FOR THEM TO SNEAK—
SIR!
MECHANICSBURG IS UNDER ATTACK!
SPOTTERS REPORT CLANKS, UNKNOWN AIRSHIPS AND ARTILLERY.
THE GREAT HOSPITAL HAS TAKEN A DIRECT HIT!
THE BARON!

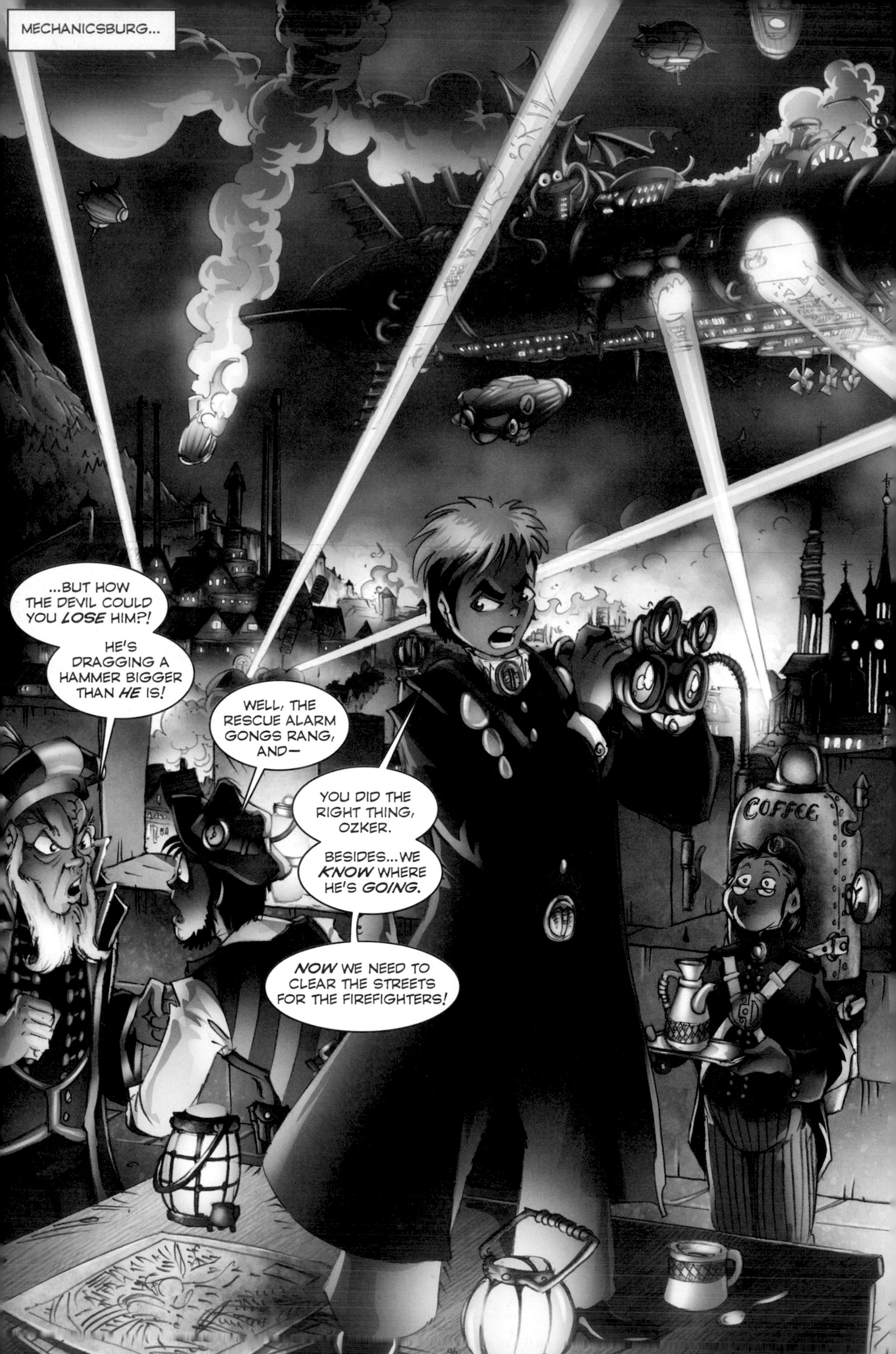
MECHANICSBURG...
...BUT HOW THE DEVIL COULD YOU LOSE HIM?!
HE'S DRAGGING A HAMMER BIGGER THAN HE IS!
WELL, THE RESCUE ALARM GONGS RANG, AND—
YOU DID THE RIGHT THING, OZKER.
BESIDES...WE KNOW WHERE HE'S GOING.
NOW WE NEED TO CLEAR THE STREETS FOR THE FIREFIGHTERS!
COFFEE

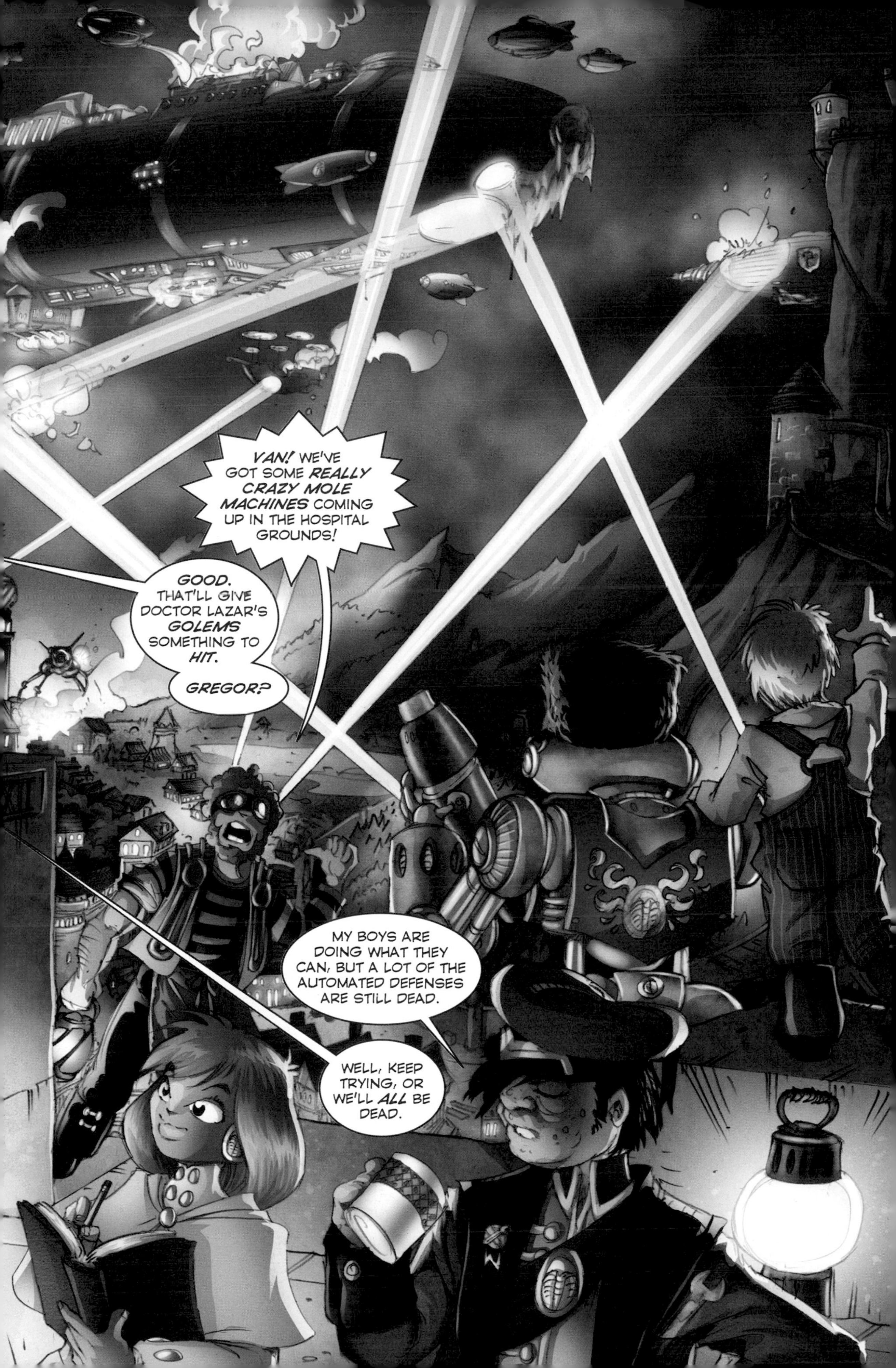

VAN! WE'VE GOT SOME REALLY CRAZY MOLE MACHINES COMING UP IN THE HOSPITAL GROUNDS!
GOOD. THAT'LL GIVE DOCTOR LAZAR'S GOLEMS SOMETHING TO HIT.
GREGOR?
MY BOYS ARE DOING WHAT THEY CAN, BUT A LOT OF THE AUTOMATED DEFENSES ARE STILL DEAD.
WELL, KEEP TRYING, OR WE'LL ALL BE DEAD.

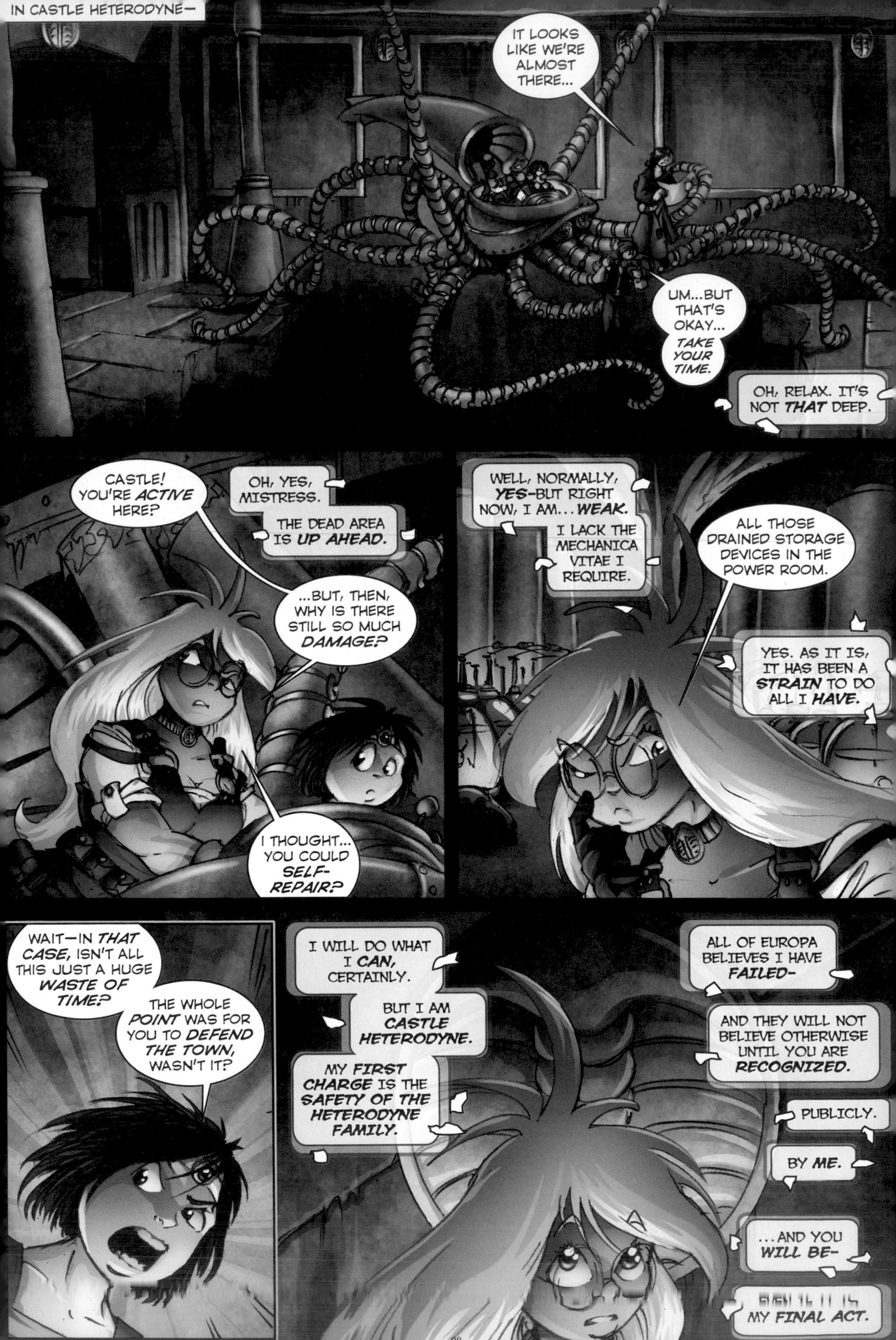
IN CASTLE HETERODYNE—
IT LOOKS LIKE WE'RE ALMOST THERE...
UM...BUT THAT'S OKAY... TAKE YOUR TIME.
OH, RELAX. IT'S NOT THAT DEEP.
CASTLE! YOU'RE ACTIVE HERE?
OH, YES, MISTRESS.
THE DEAD AREA IS UP AHEAD.
...BUT, THEN, WHY IS THERE STILL SO MUCH DAMAGE?
I THOUGHT... YOU COULD SELF-REPAIR?
WELL, NORMALLY, YES—BUT RIGHT NOW, I AM... WEAK.
I LACK THE MECHANICA VITAE I REQUIRE.
ALL THOSE DRAINED STORAGE DEVICES IN THE POWER ROOM.
YES. AS IT IS, IT HAS BEEN A STRAIN TO DO ALL I HAVE.
WAIT—IN THAT CASE, ISN'T ALL THIS JUST A HUGE WASTE OF TIME?
THE WHOLE POINT WAS FOR YOU TO DEFEND THE TOWN, WASN'T IT?
I WILL DO WHAT I CAN, CERTAINLY.
BUT I AM CASTLE HETERODYNE.
MY FIRST CHARGE IS THE SAFETY OF THE HETERODYNE FAMILY.
ALL OF EUROPA BELIEVES I HAVE FAILED-
AND THEY WILL NOT BELIEVE OTHERWISE UNTIL YOU ARE RECOGNIZED.
PUBLICLY.
BY ME.
...AND YOU WILL BE-
MY FINAL ACT.

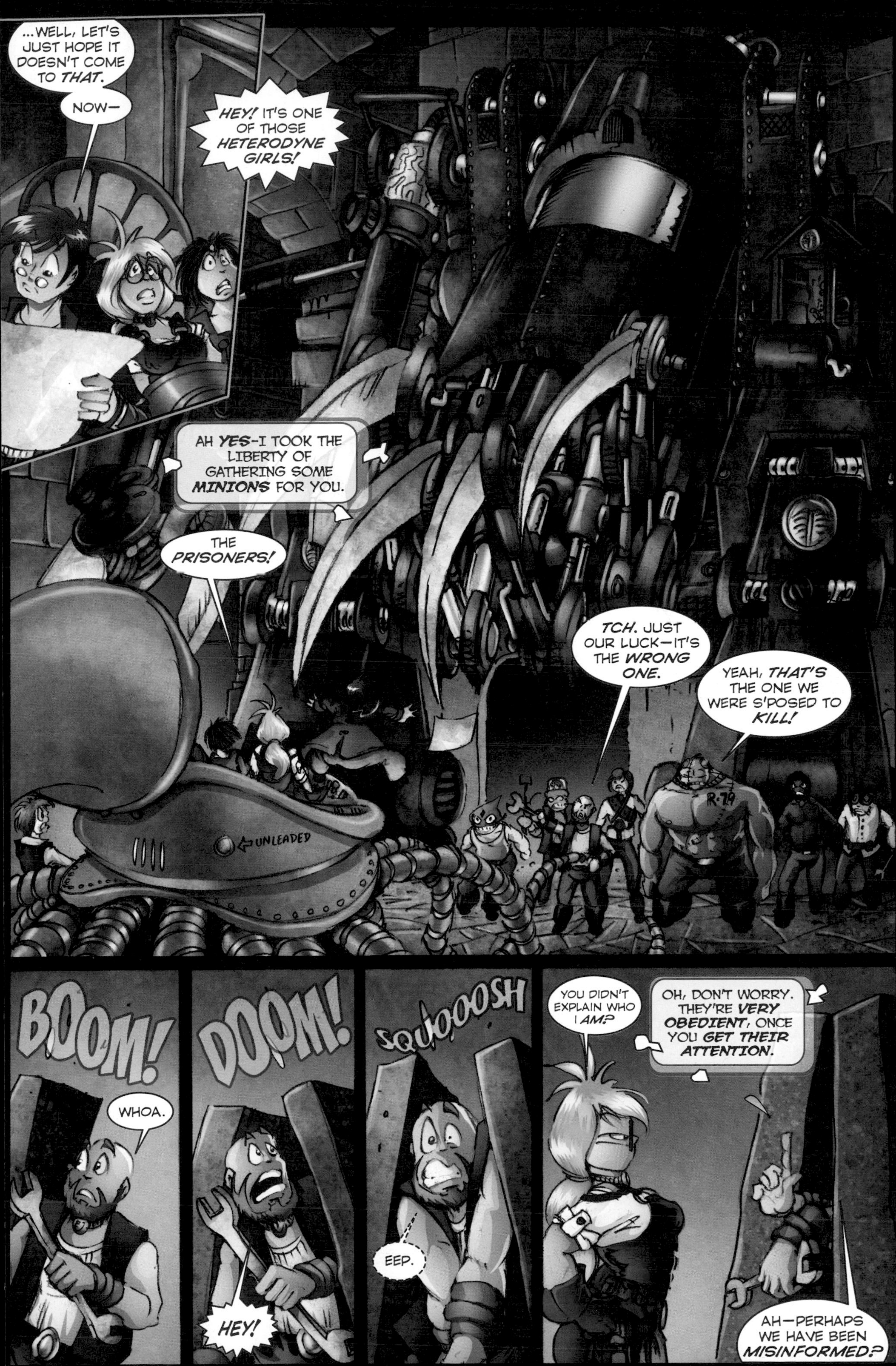
...WELL, LET'S JUST HOPE IT DOESN'T COME TO THAT.
NOW—
HEY! IT'S ONE OF THOSE HETERODYNE GIRLS!
AH YES–I TOOK THE LIBERTY OF GATHERING SOME MINIONS FOR YOU.
THE PRISONERS!
TCH. JUST OUR LUCK—IT'S THE WRONG ONE.
YEAH, THAT'S THE ONE WE WERE S'POSED TO KILL!
UNLEADED
R-79
BOOM!
WHOA.
DOOM!
HEY!
SQUOOOSH
EEP.
YOU DIDN'T EXPLAIN WHO I AM?
OH, DON'T WORRY. THEY'RE VERY OBEDIENT, ONCE YOU GET THEIR ATTENTION.
AH—PERHAPS WE HAVE BEEN MISINFORMED?

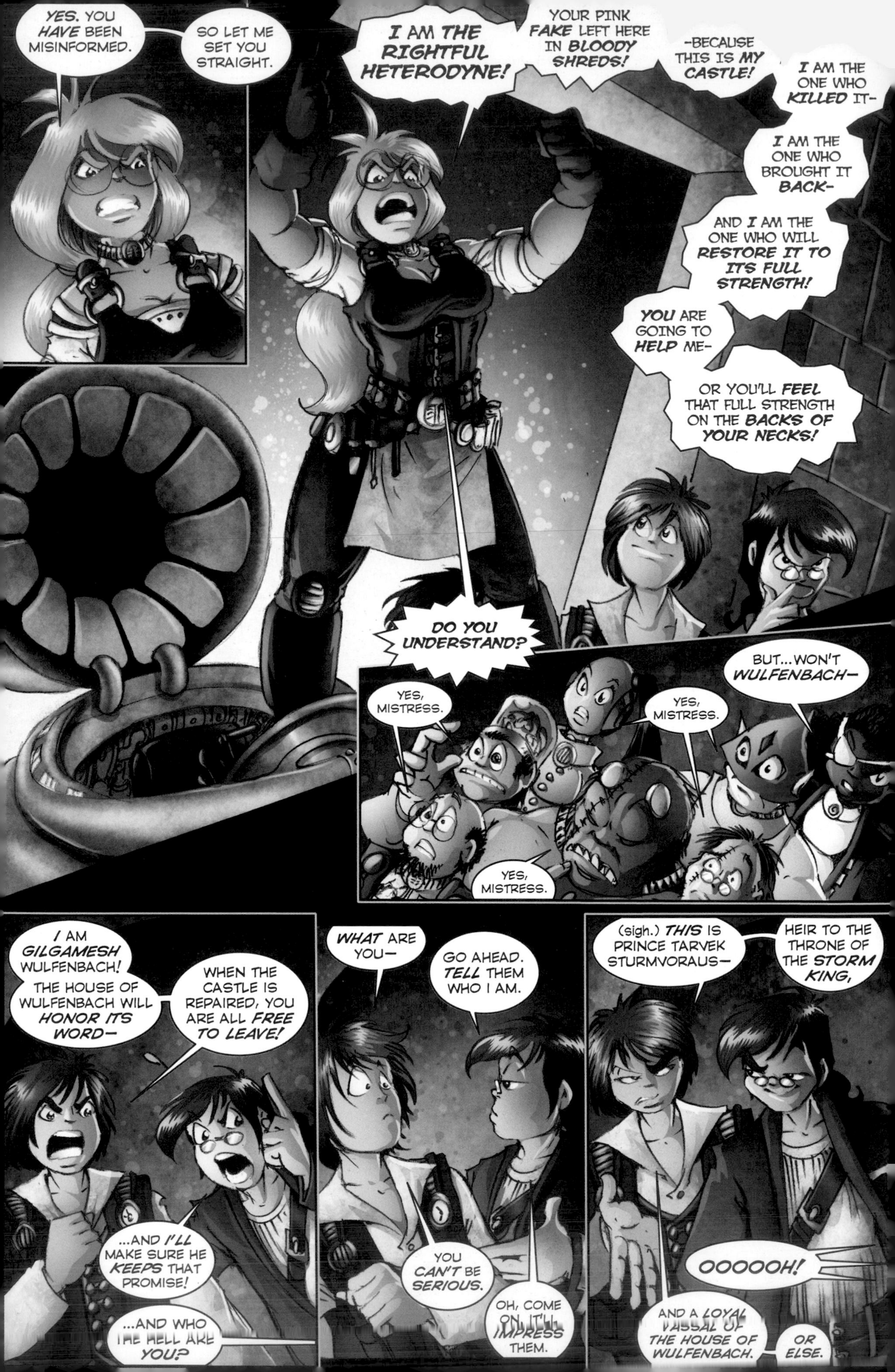
YES. YOU HAVE BEEN MISINFORMED.
SO LET ME SET YOU STRAIGHT.
I AM THE RIGHTFUL HETERODYNE!
YOUR PINK FAKE LEFT HERE IN BLOODY SHREDS!
-BECAUSE THIS IS MY CASTLE!
I AM THE ONE WHO KILLED IT-
I AM THE ONE WHO BROUGHT IT BACK-
AND I AM THE ONE WHO WILL RESTORE IT TO ITS FULL STRENGTH!
YOU ARE GOING TO HELP ME-
OR YOU'LL FEEL THAT FULL STRENGTH ON THE BACKS OF YOUR NECKS!
DO YOU UNDERSTAND?
YES, MISTRESS.
YES, MISTRESS.
BUT...WON'T WULFENBACH—
YES, MISTRESS.
I AM GILGAMESH WULFENBACH!
THE HOUSE OF WULFENBACH WILL HONOR ITS WORD—
WHEN THE CASTLE IS REPAIRED, YOU ARE ALL FREE TO LEAVE!
...AND I'LL MAKE SURE HE KEEPS THAT PROMISE!
...AND WHO THE HELL ARE YOU?
WHAT ARE YOU—
GO AHEAD. TELL THEM WHO I AM.
YOU CAN'T BE SERIOUS.
OH, COME ON, IT'LL IMPRESS THEM.
(sigh.) THIS IS PRINCE TARVEK STURMVORAUS—
HEIR TO THE THRONE OF THE STORM KING,
OOOOOH!
AND A LOYAL VASSAL OF THE HOUSE OF WULFENBACH.
OR ELSE.

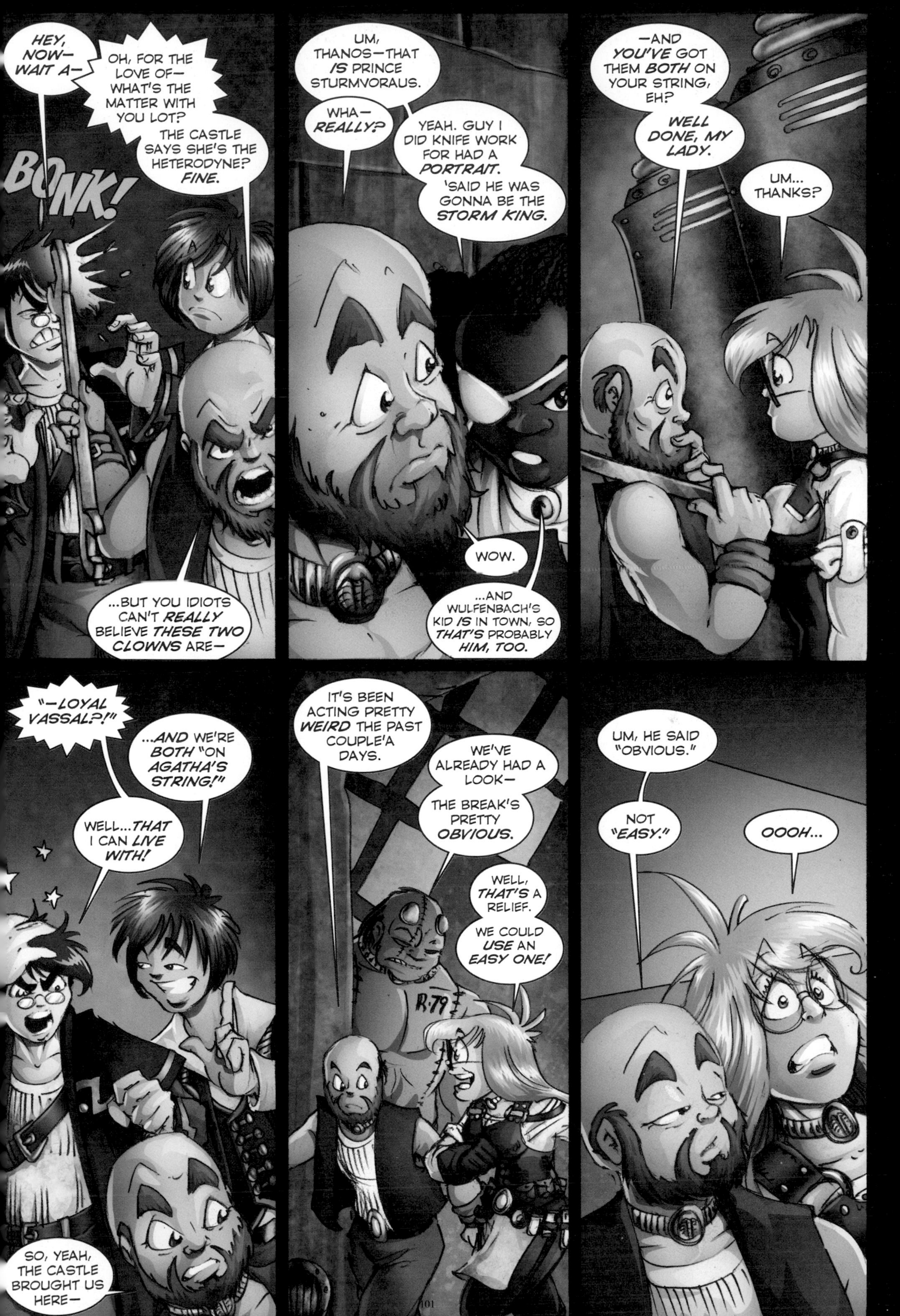
HEY, NOW— WAIT A—
OH, FOR THE LOVE OF— WHAT'S THE MATTER WITH YOU LOT?
THE CASTLE SAYS SHE'S THE HETERODYNE? FINE.
BONK!
...BUT YOU IDIOTS CAN'T REALLY BELIEVE THESE TWO CLOWNS ARE—
UM, THANOS—THAT IS PRINCE STURMVORAUS.
WHA— REALLY?
YEAH. GUY I DID KNIFE WORK FOR HAD A PORTRAIT.
'SAID HE WAS GONNA BE THE STORM KING.
WOW.
...AND WULFENBACH'S KID IS IN TOWN, SO THAT'S PROBABLY HIM, TOO.
—AND YOU'VE GOT THEM BOTH ON YOUR STRING, EH?
WELL DONE, MY LADY.
UM... THANKS?
"—LOYAL VASSAL?!"
...AND WE'RE BOTH "ON AGATHA'S STRING!"
WELL...THAT I CAN LIVE WITH!
SO, YEAH, THE CASTLE BROUGHT US HERE—
IT'S BEEN ACTING PRETTY WEIRD THE PAST COUPLE'A DAYS.
WE'VE ALREADY HAD A LOOK—
THE BREAK'S PRETTY OBVIOUS.
WELL, THAT'S A RELIEF.
WE COULD USE AN EASY ONE!
R:79
UM, HE SAID "OBVIOUS."
NOT "EASY."
OOOH...

THEY'RE NOT *ATTACKING?*
WELL, *NO,* BUT...
YOU'RE *COMPLAINING?*
THEY'RE JUST AS HAYWIRE AS THE REST OF THIS PLACE, I GUESS.
...BUT THEY'LL STILL GET YOU QUICK ENOUGH IF YOU'RE IN THE WRONG AREA.
WHICH IS—?
SEE THAT DARK SMEAR AT THE BOTTOM OF THE LADDER?
DR. OTT FIGURED *THAT* WAS WHERE IT STARTED.
DID HE SAY WHY?
NOPE. ALL HE SAID WAS:

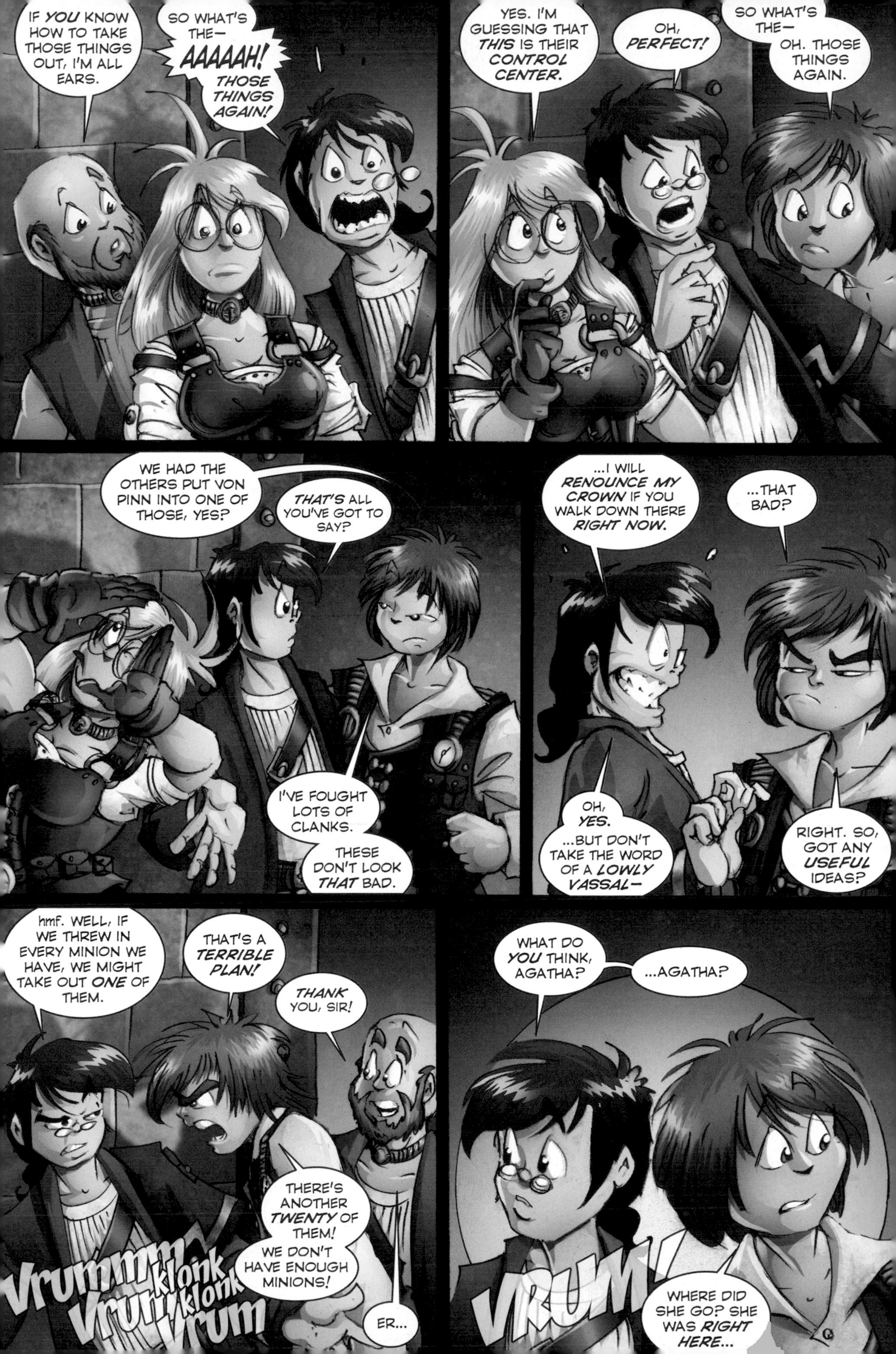
IF YOU KNOW HOW TO TAKE THOSE THINGS OUT, I'M ALL EARS.
SO WHAT'S THE—
AAAAAH! THOSE THINGS AGAIN!
YES. I'M GUESSING THAT THIS IS THEIR CONTROL CENTER.
OH, PERFECT!
SO WHAT'S THE— OH. THOSE THINGS AGAIN.
WE HAD THE OTHERS PUT VON PINN INTO ONE OF THOSE, YES?
THAT'S ALL YOU'VE GOT TO SAY?
I'VE FOUGHT LOTS OF CLANKS.
THESE DON'T LOOK THAT BAD.
...I WILL RENOUNCE MY CROWN IF YOU WALK DOWN THERE RIGHT NOW.
...THAT BAD?
OH, YES.
...BUT DON'T TAKE THE WORD OF A LOWLY VASSAL—
RIGHT. SO, GOT ANY USEFUL IDEAS?
hmf. WELL, IF WE THREW IN EVERY MINION WE HAVE, WE MIGHT TAKE OUT ONE OF THEM.
THAT'S A TERRIBLE PLAN!
THANK YOU, SIR!
THERE'S ANOTHER TWENTY OF THEM!
WE DON'T HAVE ENOUGH MINIONS!
Vrummm klonk Vrum klonk Vrum
ER...
WHAT DO YOU THINK, AGATHA?
...AGATHA?
VRUM!
WHERE DID SHE GO? SHE WAS RIGHT HERE...

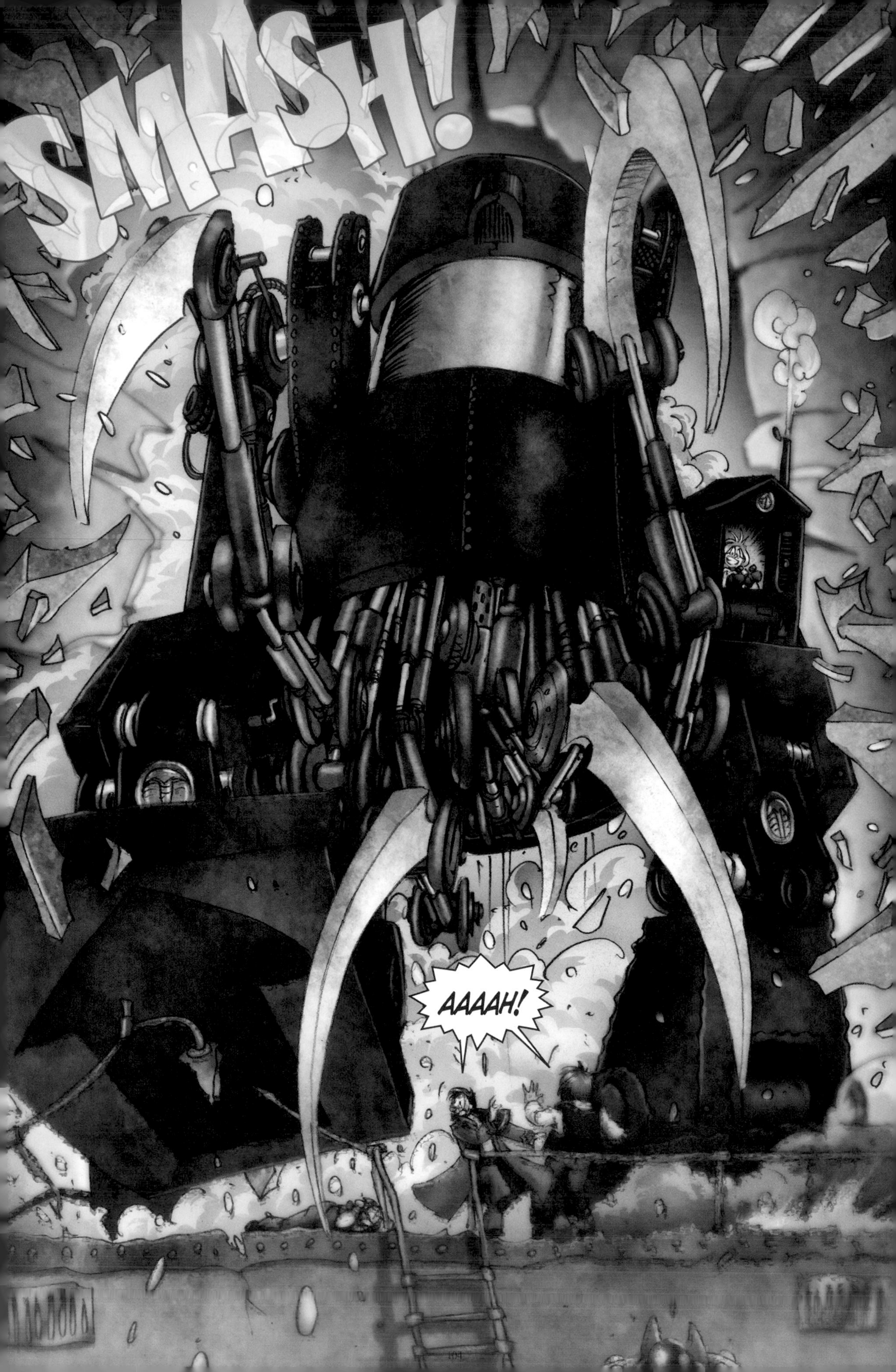
SMASH!
AAAAH!

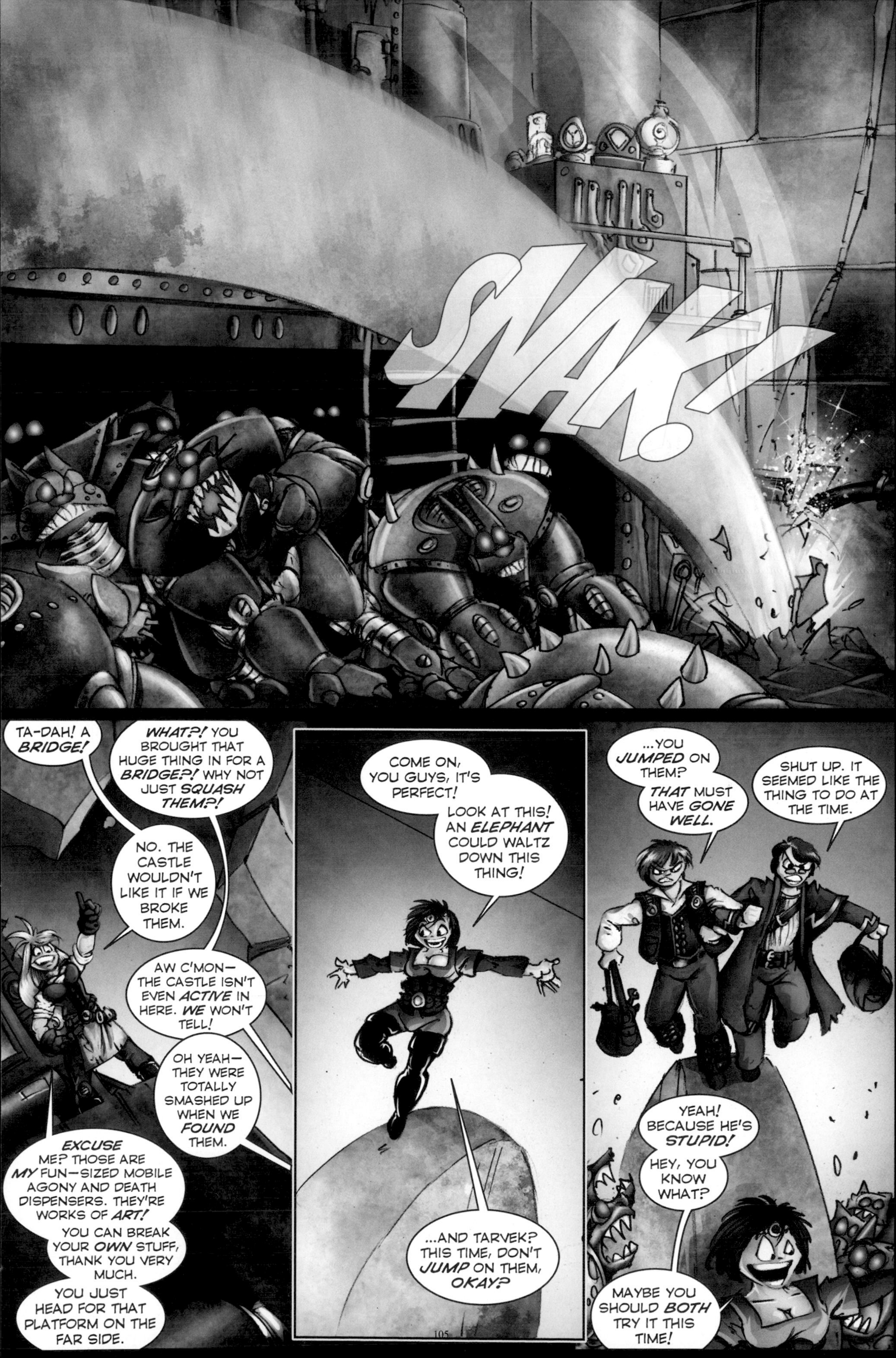

SNAK!
TA-DAH! A BRIDGE!
WHAT?! YOU BROUGHT THAT HUGE THING IN FOR A BRIDGE?! WHY NOT JUST SQUASH THEM?!
NO. THE CASTLE WOULDN'T LIKE IT IF WE BROKE THEM.
AW C'MON— THE CASTLE ISN'T EVEN ACTIVE IN HERE. WE WON'T TELL!
OH YEAH— THEY WERE TOTALLY SMASHED UP WHEN WE FOUND THEM.
EXCUSE ME? THOSE ARE MY FUN—SIZED MOBILE AGONY AND DEATH DISPENSERS. THEY'RE WORKS OF ART!
YOU CAN BREAK YOUR OWN STUFF, THANK YOU VERY MUCH.
YOU JUST HEAD FOR THAT PLATFORM ON THE FAR SIDE.
COME ON, YOU GUYS, IT'S PERFECT!
LOOK AT THIS! AN ELEPHANT COULD WALTZ DOWN THIS THING!
...AND TARVEK? THIS TIME, DON'T JUMP ON THEM, OKAY?
...YOU JUMPED ON THEM?
THAT MUST HAVE GONE WELL.
SHUT UP. IT SEEMED LIKE THE THING TO DO AT THE TIME.
YEAH! BECAUSE HE'S STUPID!
HEY, YOU KNOW WHAT?
MAYBE YOU SHOULD BOTH TRY IT THIS TIME!

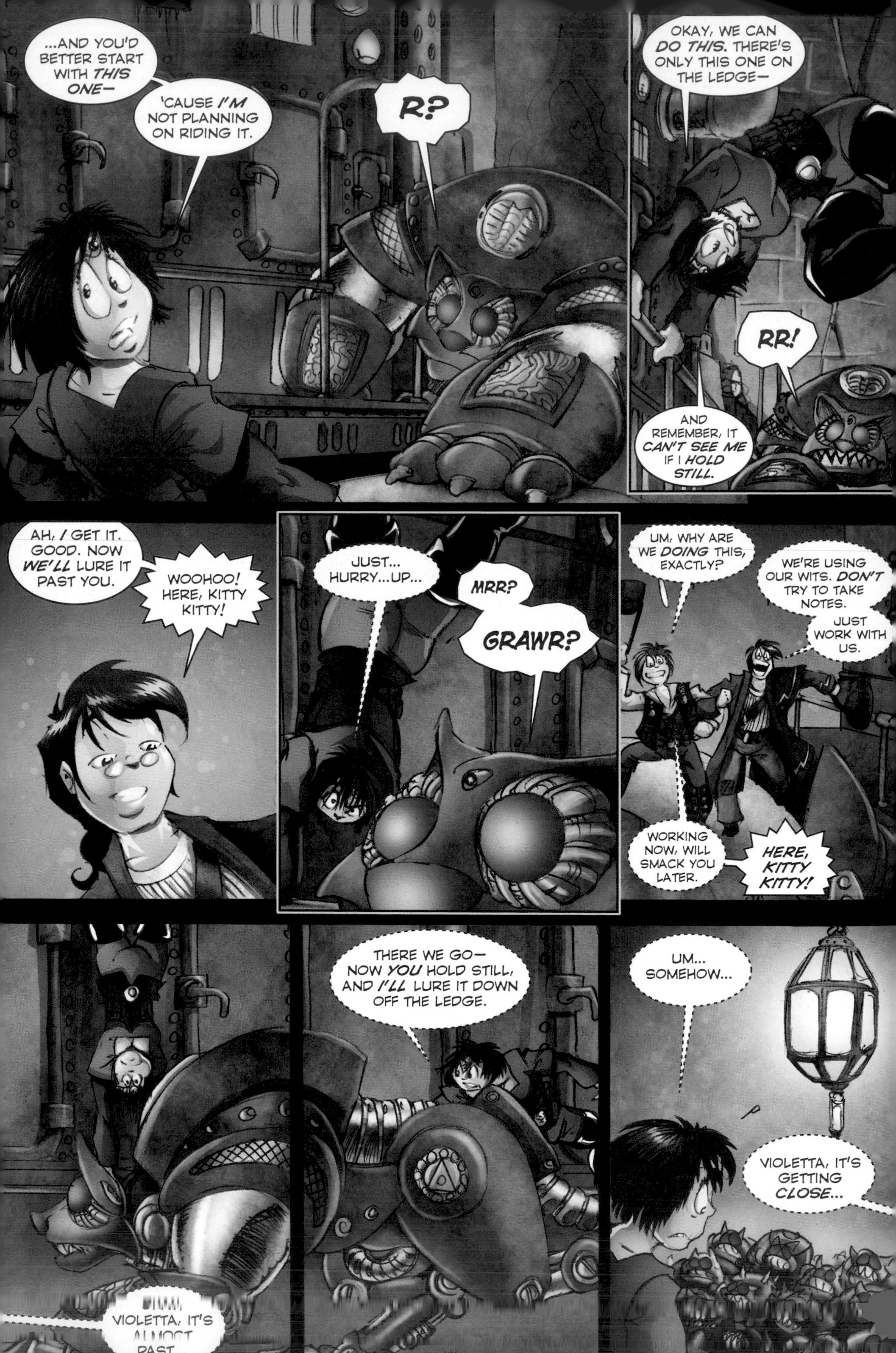
...AND YOU'D BETTER START WITH *THIS ONE*—
'CAUSE *I'M* NOT PLANNING ON RIDING IT.
R?
OKAY, WE CAN *DO THIS*. THERE'S ONLY THIS ONE ON THE LEDGE—
RR!
AND REMEMBER, IT *CAN'T SEE ME* IF I *HOLD STILL*.
AH, *I* GET IT. GOOD. NOW *WE'LL* LURE IT PAST YOU.
WOOHOO! HERE, KITTY KITTY!
JUST... HURRY...UP...
MRR?
GRAWR?
UM, WHY ARE WE *DOING* THIS, EXACTLY?
WE'RE USING OUR WITS. *DON'T* TRY TO TAKE NOTES.
JUST WORK WITH US.
WORKING NOW, WILL SMACK YOU LATER.
HERE, KITTY KITTY!
VIOLETTA, IT'S ALMOST PAST...
THERE WE GO— NOW *YOU* HOLD STILL, AND *I'LL* LURE IT DOWN OFF THE LEDGE.
UM... SOMEHOW...
VIOLETTA, IT'S GETTING *CLOSE*...

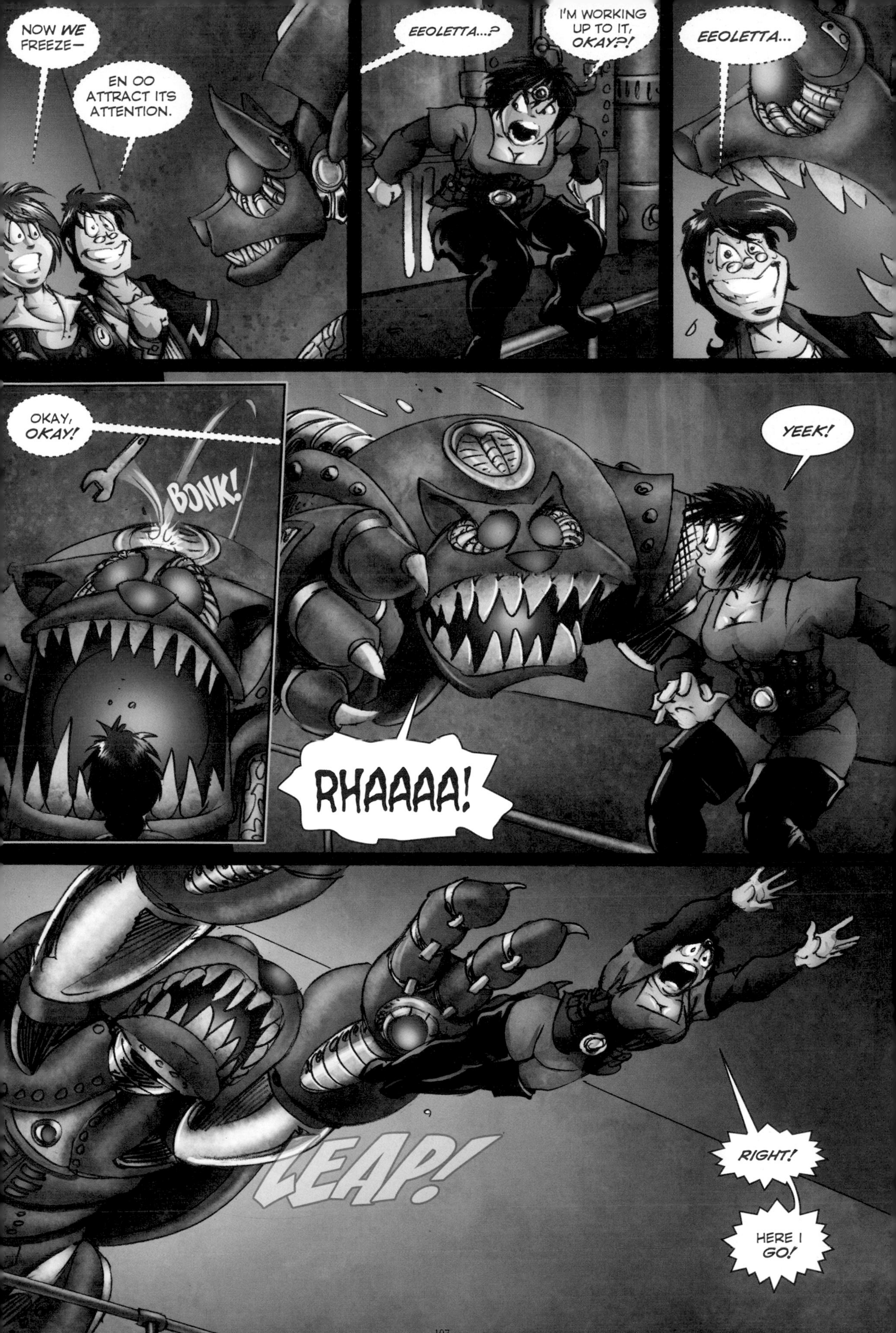

NOW WE FREEZE—
EN OO ATTRACT ITS ATTENTION.
EEOLETTA...?
I'M WORKING UP TO IT, OKAY?!
EEOLETTA...
OKAY, OKAY!
BONK!
YEEK!
RHAAAA!
LEAP!
RIGHT!
HERE I GO!

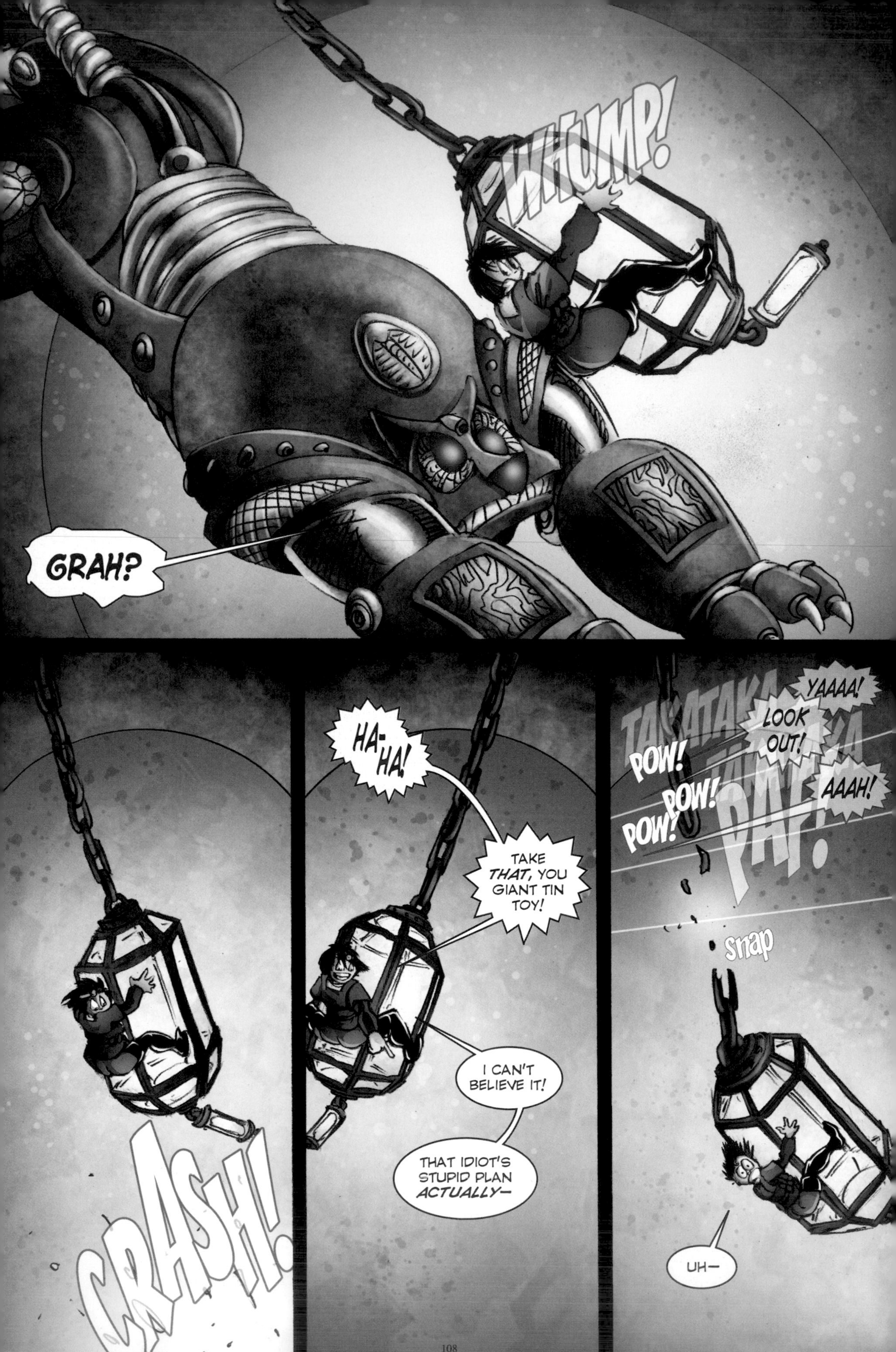
WHUMP!
GRAH?
CRASH!!
HA-HA!
TAKE THAT, YOU GIANT TIN TOY!
I CAN'T BELIEVE IT!
THAT IDIOT'S STUPID PLAN ACTUALLY—
YAAAA!
LOOK OUT!
POW!
POW!
POW!
PAF!
AAAH!
snap
UH—

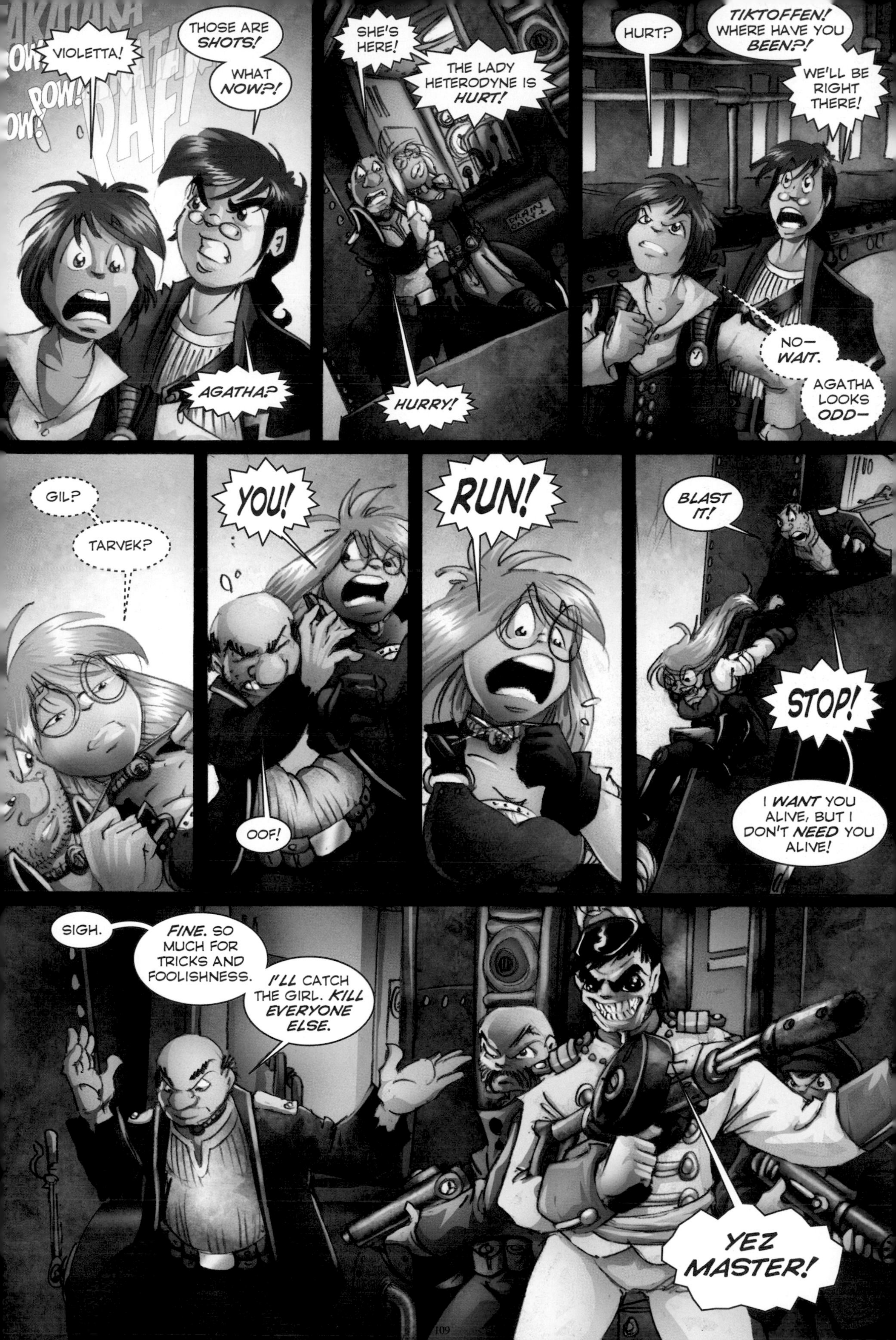
POW!
VIOLETTA!
THOSE ARE SHOTS!
WHAT NOW?!
AGATHA?
SHE'S HERE!
THE LADY HETERODYNE IS HURT!
HURRY!
HURT?
TIKTOFFEN! WHERE HAVE YOU BEEN?!
WE'LL BE RIGHT THERE!
NO— WAIT.
AGATHA LOOKS ODD—
GIL?
TARVEK?
YOU!
OOF!
RUN!
BLAST IT!
STOP!
I WANT YOU ALIVE, BUT I DON'T NEED YOU ALIVE!
SIGH.
FINE. SO MUCH FOR TRICKS AND FOOLISHNESS.
I'LL CATCH THE GIRL. KILL EVERYONE ELSE.
YEZ MASTER!

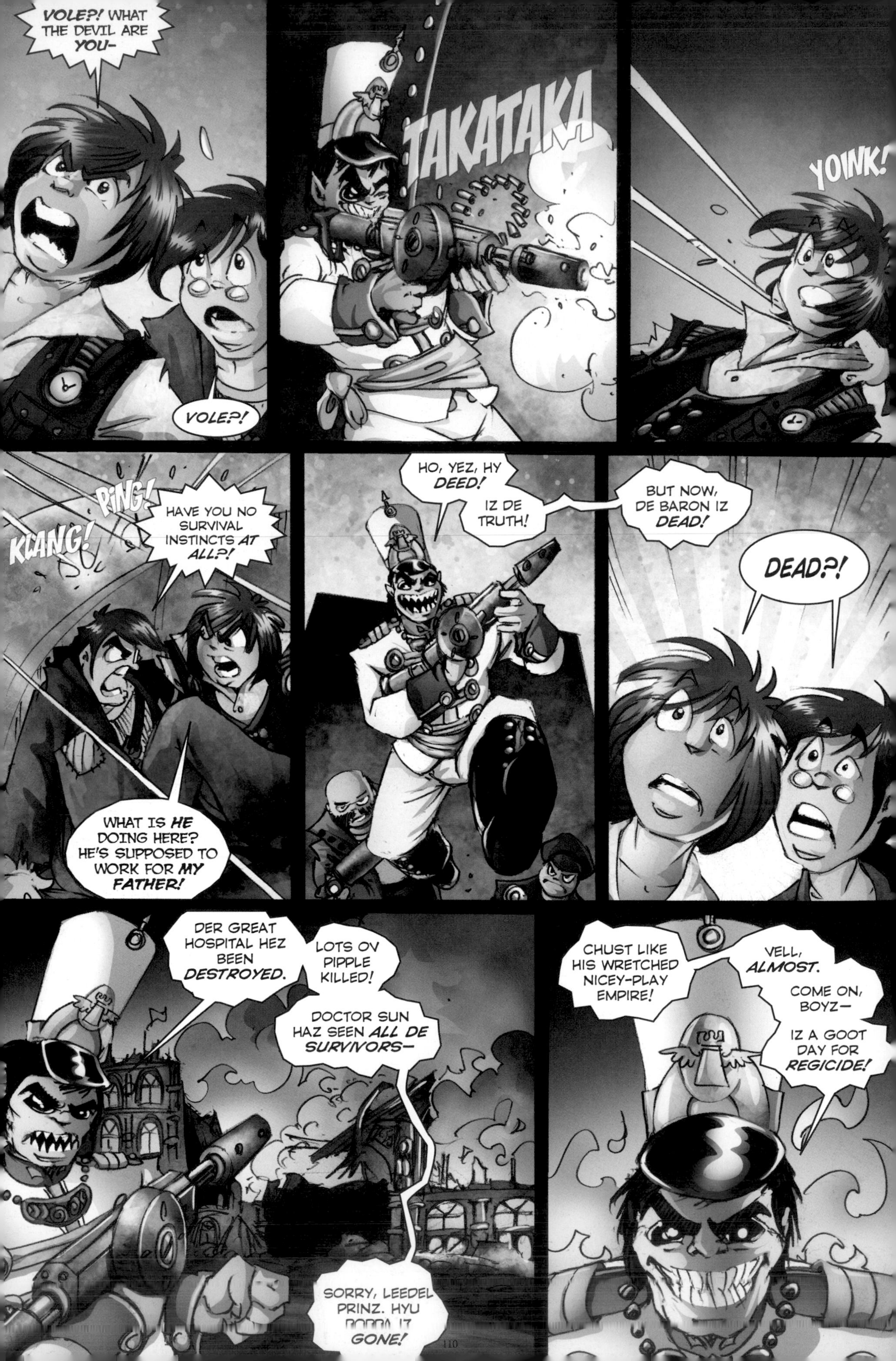
VOLE?! WHAT THE DEVIL ARE YOU–
VOLE?!
TAKATAKA
YOINK!
PING!
KLANG!
HAVE YOU NO SURVIVAL INSTINCTS AT ALL?!
WHAT IS HE DOING HERE? HE'S SUPPOSED TO WORK FOR MY FATHER!
HO, YEZ, HY DEED!
IZ DE TRUTH!
BUT NOW, DE BARON IZ DEAD!
DEAD?!
DER GREAT HOSPITAL HEZ BEEN DESTROYED.
LOTS OV PIPPLE KILLED!
DOCTOR SUN HAZ SEEN ALL DE SURVIVORS–
SORRY, LEEDEL PRINZ. HYU
GONE!
CHUST LIKE HIS WRETCHED NICEY-PLAY EMPIRE!
VELL, ALMOST.
COME ON, BOYZ–
IZ A GOOT DAY FOR REGICIDE!

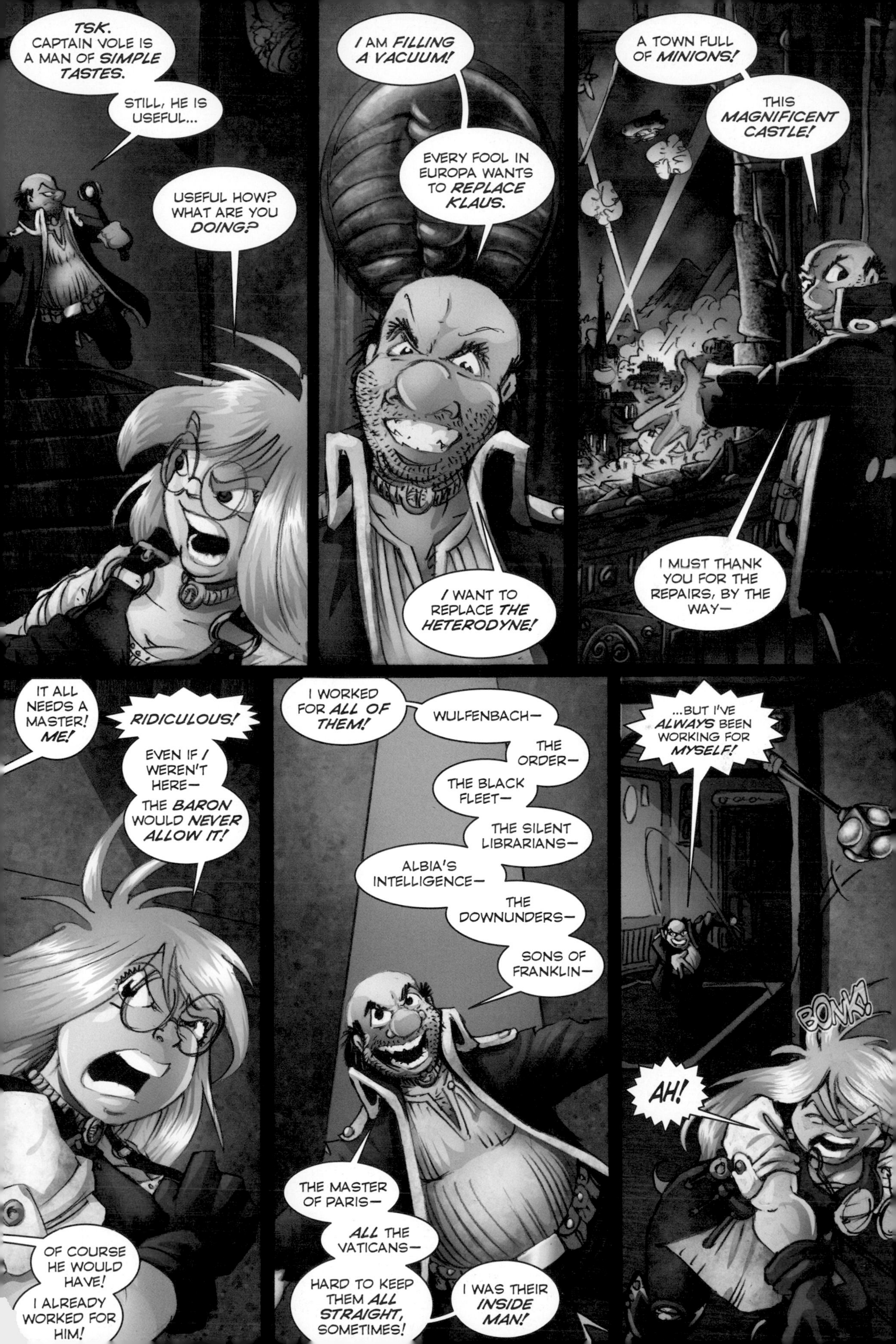
TSK. CAPTAIN VOLE IS A MAN OF SIMPLE TASTES.
STILL, HE IS USEFUL...
USEFUL HOW? WHAT ARE YOU DOING?
I AM FILLING A VACUUM!
EVERY FOOL IN EUROPA WANTS TO REPLACE KLAUS.
I WANT TO REPLACE THE HETERODYNE!
A TOWN FULL OF MINIONS!
THIS MAGNIFICENT CASTLE!
I MUST THANK YOU FOR THE REPAIRS, BY THE WAY—
IT ALL NEEDS A MASTER! ME!
RIDICULOUS!
EVEN IF I WEREN'T HERE—
THE BARON WOULD NEVER ALLOW IT!
OF COURSE HE WOULD HAVE!
I ALREADY WORKED FOR HIM!
I WORKED FOR ALL OF THEM!
WULFENBACH—
THE ORDER—
THE BLACK FLEET—
THE SILENT LIBRARIANS—
ALBIA'S INTELLIGENCE—
THE DOWNUNDERS—
SONS OF FRANKLIN—
THE MASTER OF PARIS—
ALL THE VATICANS—
HARD TO KEEP THEM ALL STRAIGHT, SOMETIMES!
I WAS THEIR INSIDE MAN!
...BUT I'VE ALWAYS BEEN WORKING FOR MYSELF!
BONK!
AH!

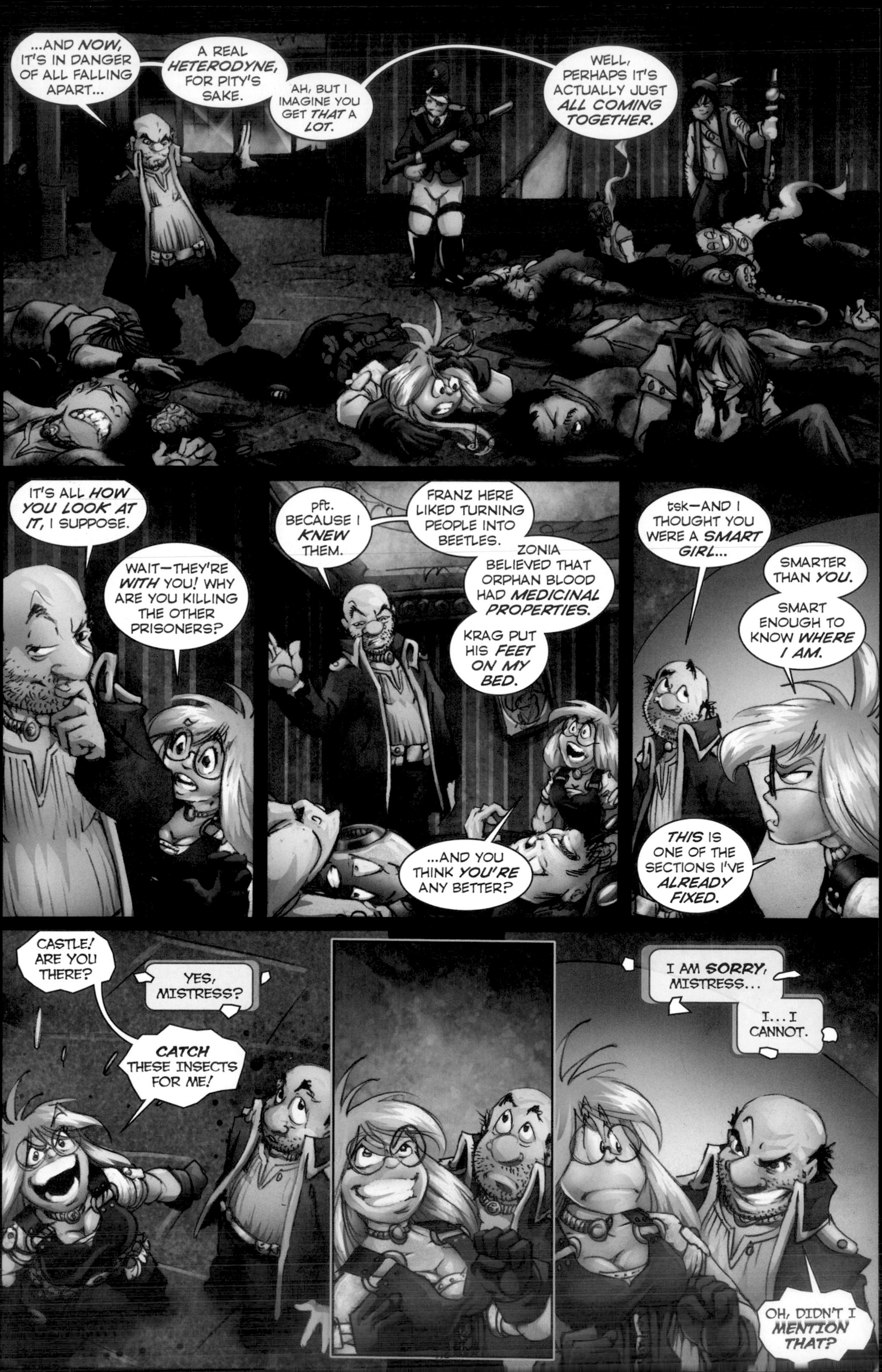
...AND NOW, IT'S IN DANGER OF ALL FALLING APART...
A REAL HETERODYNE, FOR PITY'S SAKE.
AH, BUT I IMAGINE YOU GET THAT A LOT.
WELL, PERHAPS IT'S ACTUALLY JUST ALL COMING TOGETHER.
IT'S ALL HOW YOU LOOK AT IT, I SUPPOSE.
WAIT—THEY'RE WITH YOU! WHY ARE YOU KILLING THE OTHER PRISONERS?
pft. BECAUSE I KNEW THEM.
FRANZ HERE LIKED TURNING PEOPLE INTO BEETLES.
ZONIA BELIEVED THAT ORPHAN BLOOD HAD MEDICINAL PROPERTIES.
KRAG PUT HIS FEET ON MY BED.
...AND YOU THINK YOU'RE ANY BETTER?
tsk—AND I THOUGHT YOU WERE A SMART GIRL...
SMARTER THAN YOU.
SMART ENOUGH TO KNOW WHERE I AM.
THIS IS ONE OF THE SECTIONS I'VE ALREADY FIXED.
CASTLE! ARE YOU THERE?
YES, MISTRESS?
CATCH THESE INSECTS FOR ME!
I AM SORRY, MISTRESS...
I... I CANNOT.
OH, DIDN'T I MENTION THAT?

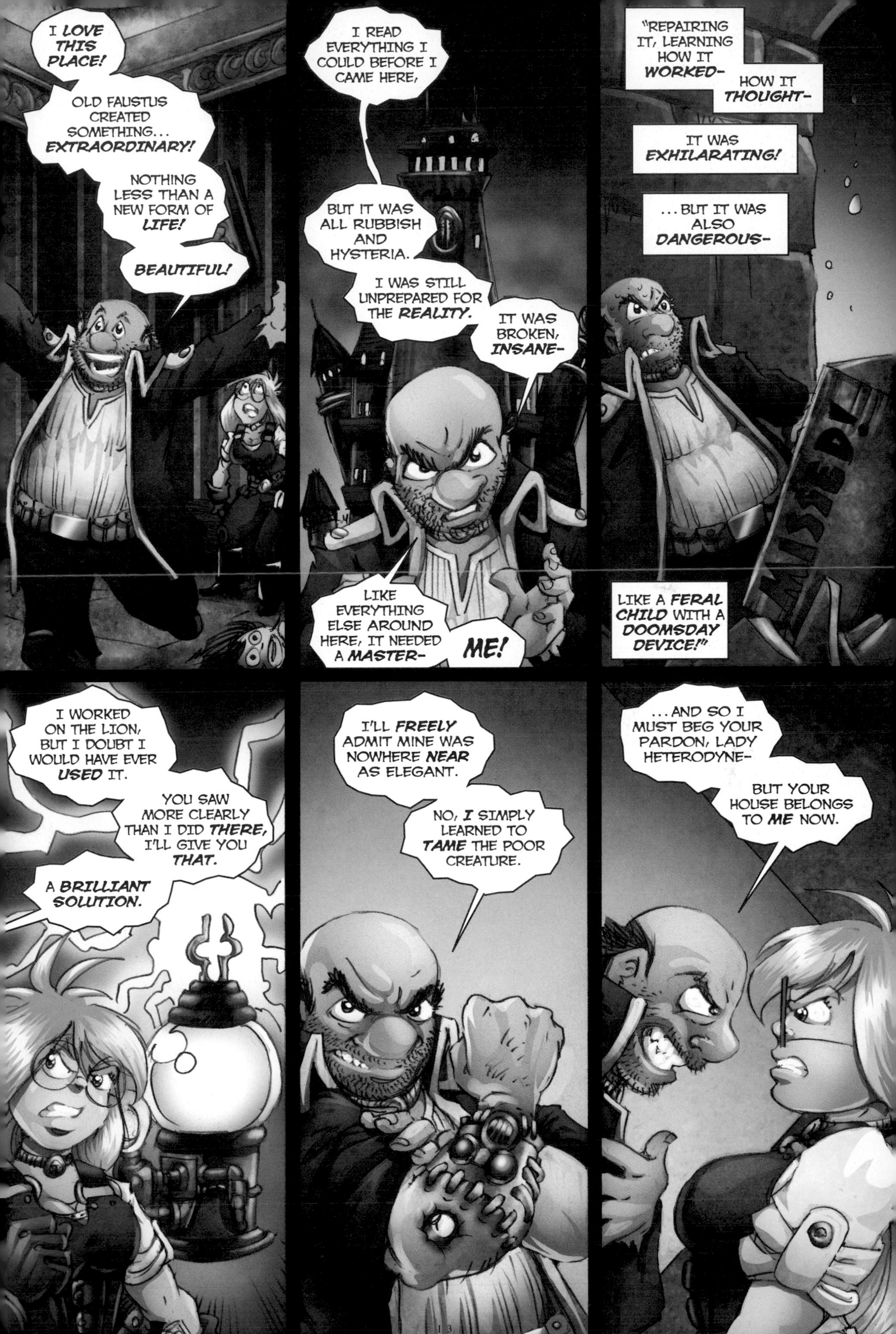
I LOVE THIS PLACE!
OLD FAUSTUS CREATED SOMETHING... EXTRAORDINARY!
NOTHING LESS THAN A NEW FORM OF LIFE!
BEAUTIFUL!
I READ EVERYTHING I COULD BEFORE I CAME HERE,
BUT IT WAS ALL RUBBISH AND HYSTERIA.
I WAS STILL UNPREPARED FOR THE REALITY.
IT WAS BROKEN, INSANE-
LIKE EVERYTHING ELSE AROUND HERE, IT NEEDED A MASTER-
ME!
"REPAIRING IT, LEARNING HOW IT WORKED-
HOW IT THOUGHT-
IT WAS EXHILARATING!
...BUT IT WAS ALSO DANGEROUS-
LIKE A FERAL CHILD WITH A DOOMSDAY DEVICE!"
I WORKED ON THE LION, BUT I DOUBT I WOULD HAVE EVER USED IT.
YOU SAW MORE CLEARLY THAN I DID THERE, I'LL GIVE YOU THAT.
A BRILLIANT SOLUTION.
I'LL FREELY ADMIT MINE WAS NOWHERE NEAR AS ELEGANT.
NO, I SIMPLY LEARNED TO TAME THE POOR CREATURE.
...AND SO I MUST BEG YOUR PARDON, LADY HETERODYNE-
BUT YOUR HOUSE BELONGS TO ME NOW.

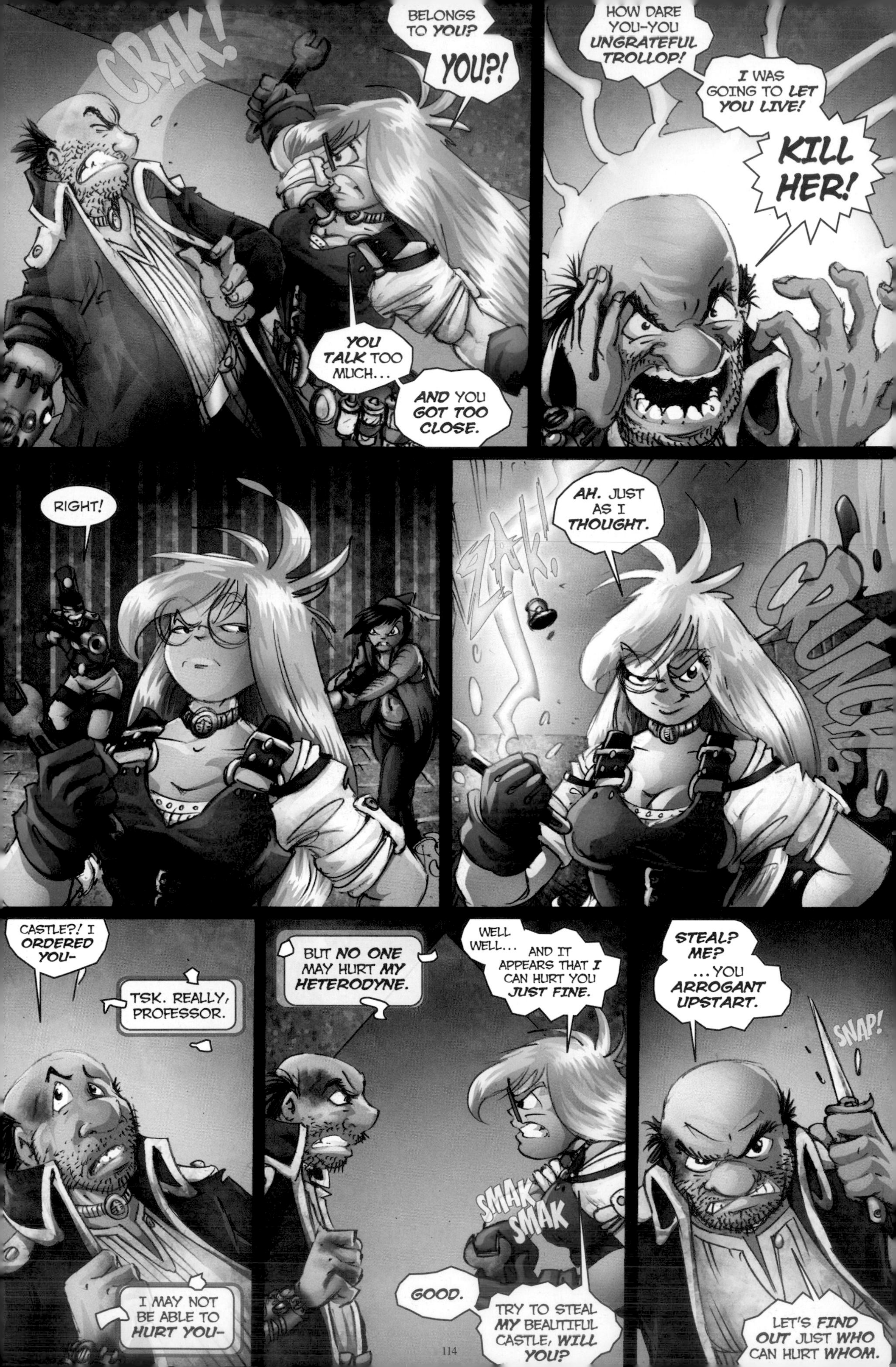
CRAK!
BELONGS TO YOU? YOU?!
YOU TALK TOO MUCH...
AND YOU GOT TOO CLOSE.
HOW DARE YOU-YOU UNGRATEFUL TROLLOP!
I WAS GOING TO LET YOU LIVE!
KILL HER!
RIGHT!
ZAK!
AH. JUST AS I THOUGHT.
CRUNCH!
CASTLE?! I ORDERED YOU-
TSK. REALLY, PROFESSOR.
I MAY NOT BE ABLE TO HURT YOU-
BUT NO ONE MAY HURT MY HETERODYNE.
WELL WELL...
AND IT APPEARS THAT I CAN HURT YOU JUST FINE.
SMAK SMAK
GOOD.
TRY TO STEAL MY BEAUTIFUL CASTLE, WILL YOU?
STEAL? ME? ...YOU ARROGANT UPSTART.
SNAP!
LET'S FIND OUT JUST WHO CAN HURT WHOM.

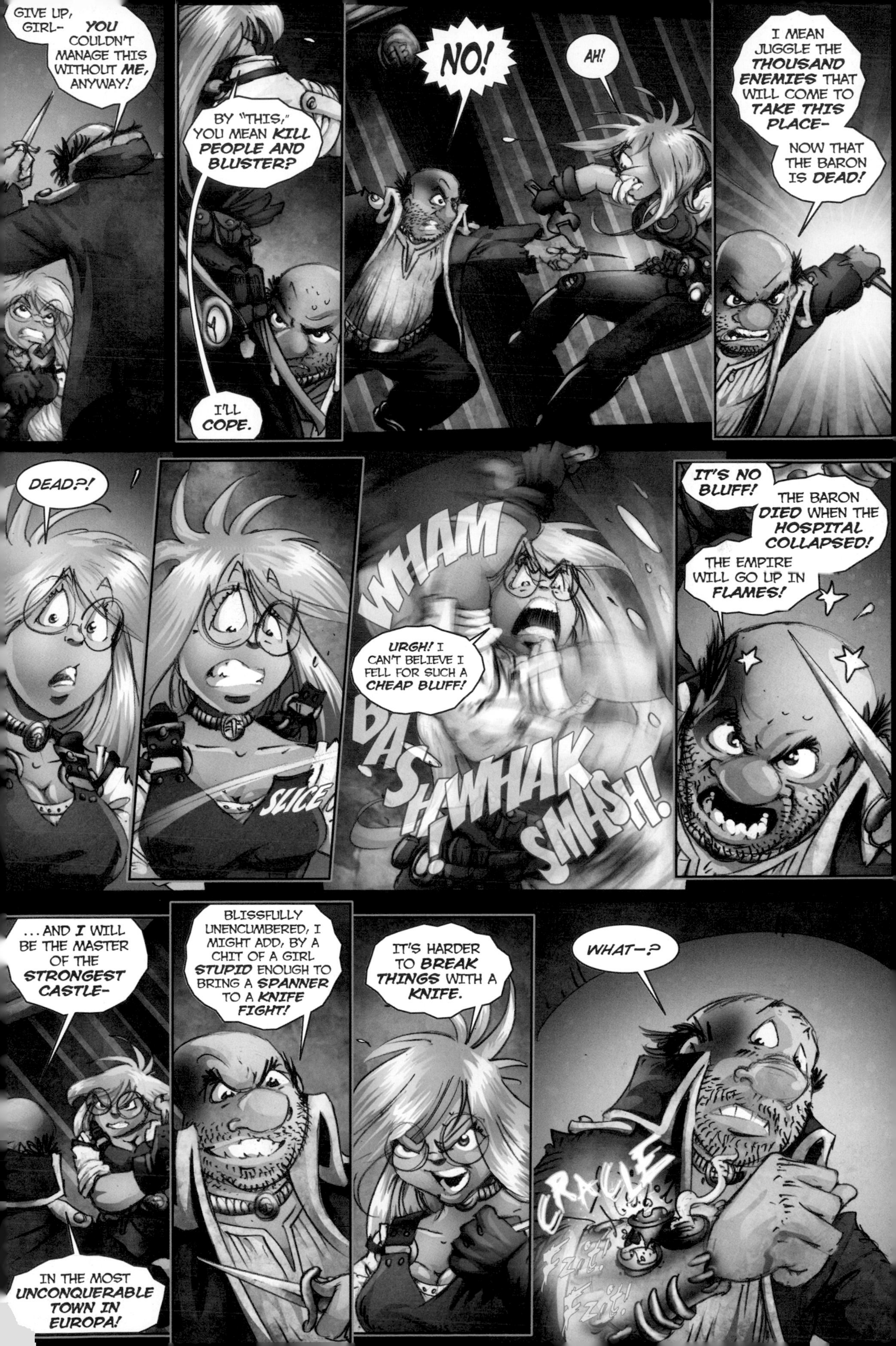
GIVE UP, GIRL- YOU COULDN'T MANAGE THIS WITHOUT ME, ANYWAY!
BY "THIS," YOU MEAN KILL PEOPLE AND BLUSTER?
I'LL COPE.
NO!
AH!
I MEAN JUGGLE THE THOUSAND ENEMIES THAT WILL COME TO TAKE THIS PLACE-
NOW THAT THE BARON IS DEAD!
DEAD?!
SLICE
WHAM
URGH! I CAN'T BELIEVE I FELL FOR SUCH A CHEAP BLUFF!
BASH!
WHAK
SMASH!
IT'S NO BLUFF!
THE BARON DIED WHEN THE HOSPITAL COLLAPSED!
THE EMPIRE WILL GO UP IN FLAMES!
...AND I WILL BE THE MASTER OF THE STRONGEST CASTLE-
IN THE MOST UNCONQUERABLE TOWN IN EUROPA!
BLISSFULLY UNENCUMBERED, I MIGHT ADD, BY A CHIT OF A GIRL STUPID ENOUGH TO BRING A SPANNER TO A KNIFE FIGHT!
IT'S HARDER TO BREAK THINGS WITH A KNIFE.
WHAT-?
CRACKLE

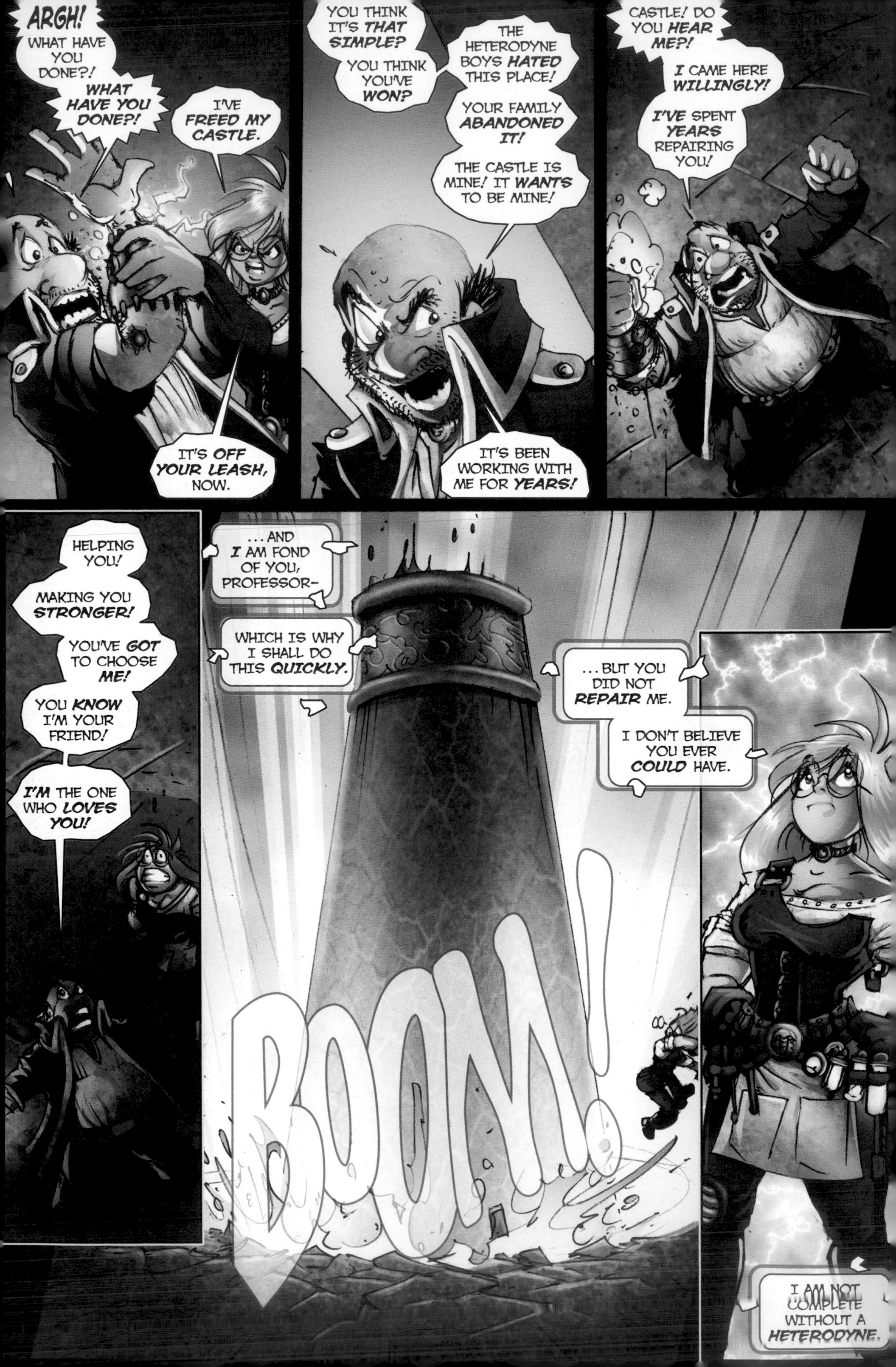

ARGH! WHAT HAVE YOU DONE?! WHAT HAVE YOU DONE?!
I'VE FREED MY CASTLE.
IT'S OFF YOUR LEASH, NOW.
YOU THINK IT'S THAT SIMPLE?
YOU THINK YOU'VE WON?
THE HETERODYNE BOYS HATED THIS PLACE!
YOUR FAMILY ABANDONED IT!
THE CASTLE IS MINE! IT WANTS TO BE MINE!
IT'S BEEN WORKING WITH ME FOR YEARS!
CASTLE! DO YOU HEAR ME?!
I CAME HERE WILLINGLY!
I'VE SPENT YEARS REPAIRING YOU!
HELPING YOU!
MAKING YOU STRONGER!
YOU'VE GOT TO CHOOSE ME!
YOU KNOW I'M YOUR FRIEND!
I'M THE ONE WHO LOVES YOU!
...AND I AM FOND OF YOU, PROFESSOR-
WHICH IS WHY I SHALL DO THIS QUICKLY.
BOOM!
...BUT YOU DID NOT REPAIR ME.
I DON'T BELIEVE YOU EVER COULD HAVE.
I AM NOT COMPLETE WITHOUT A HETERODYNE.

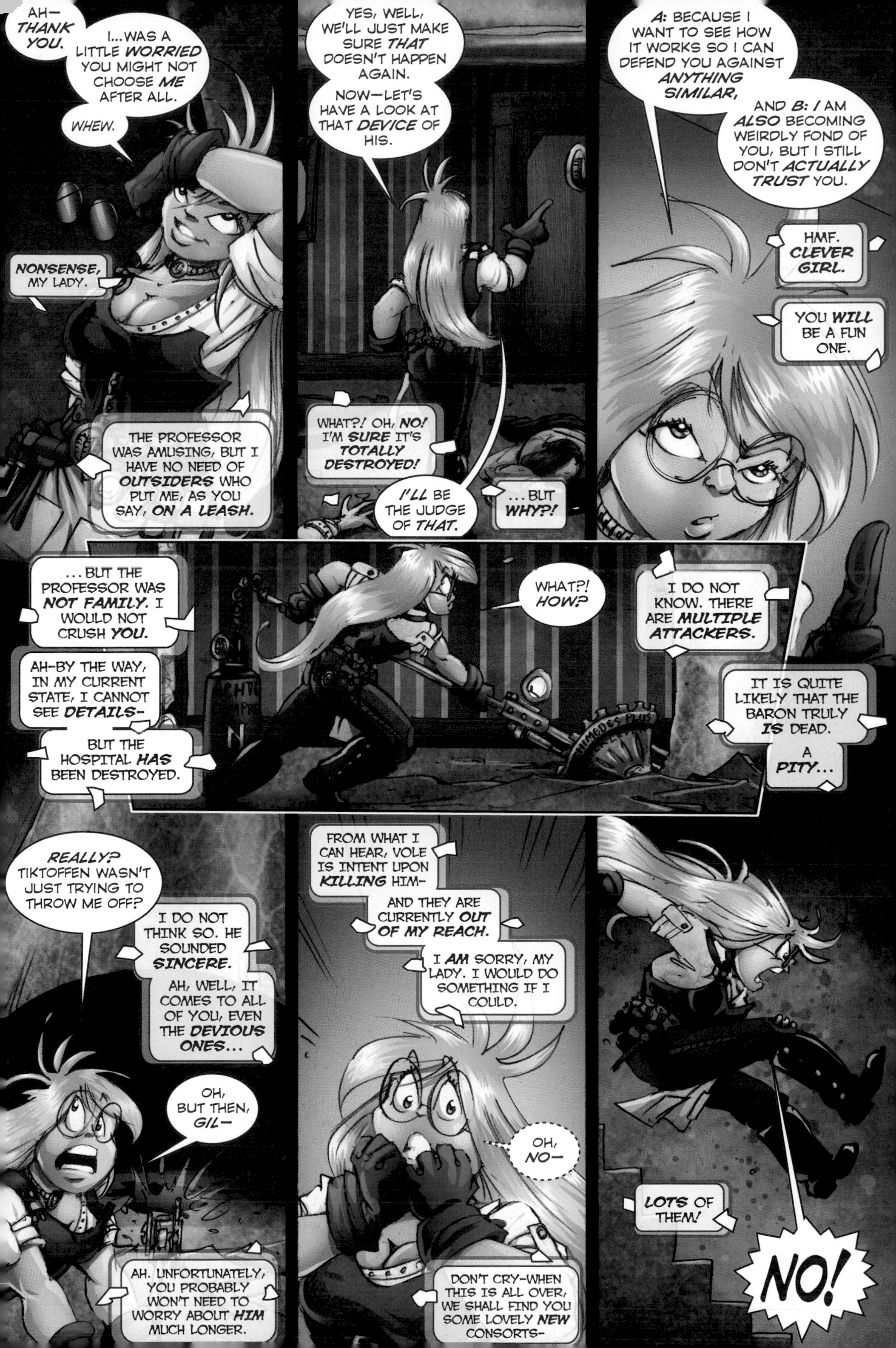
AH—THANK YOU.
I...WAS A LITTLE WORRIED YOU MIGHT NOT CHOOSE ME AFTER ALL.
WHEW.
NONSENSE, MY LADY.
THE PROFESSOR WAS AMUSING, BUT I HAVE NO NEED OF OUTSIDERS WHO PUT ME, AS YOU SAY, ON A LEASH.
YES, WELL, WE'LL JUST MAKE SURE THAT DOESN'T HAPPEN AGAIN.
NOW—LET'S HAVE A LOOK AT THAT DEVICE OF HIS.
WHAT?! OH, NO! I'M SURE IT'S TOTALLY DESTROYED!
I'LL BE THE JUDGE OF THAT.
...BUT WHY?!
A: BECAUSE I WANT TO SEE HOW IT WORKS SO I CAN DEFEND YOU AGAINST ANYTHING SIMILAR,
AND B: I AM ALSO BECOMING WEIRDLY FOND OF YOU, BUT I STILL DON'T ACTUALLY TRUST YOU.
HMF. CLEVER GIRL.
YOU WILL BE A FUN ONE.
...BUT THE PROFESSOR WAS NOT FAMILY. I WOULD NOT CRUSH YOU.
AH-BY THE WAY, IN MY CURRENT STATE, I CANNOT SEE DETAILS-
BUT THE HOSPITAL HAS BEEN DESTROYED.
WHAT?! HOW?
I DO NOT KNOW. THERE ARE MULTIPLE ATTACKERS.
IT IS QUITE LIKELY THAT THE BARON TRULY IS DEAD.
A PITY...
REALLY? TIKTOFFEN WASN'T JUST TRYING TO THROW ME OFF?
I DO NOT THINK SO. HE SOUNDED SINCERE.
AH, WELL, IT COMES TO ALL OF YOU, EVEN THE DEVIOUS ONES...
OH, BUT THEN, GIL—
AH. UNFORTUNATELY, YOU PROBABLY WON'T NEED TO WORRY ABOUT HIM MUCH LONGER.
FROM WHAT I CAN HEAR, VOLE IS INTENT UPON KILLING HIM-
AND THEY ARE CURRENTLY OUT OF MY REACH.
I AM SORRY, MY LADY. I WOULD DO SOMETHING IF I COULD.
OH, NO—
DON'T CRY-WHEN THIS IS ALL OVER, WE SHALL FIND YOU SOME LOVELY NEW CONSORTS-
LOTS OF THEM!
NO!

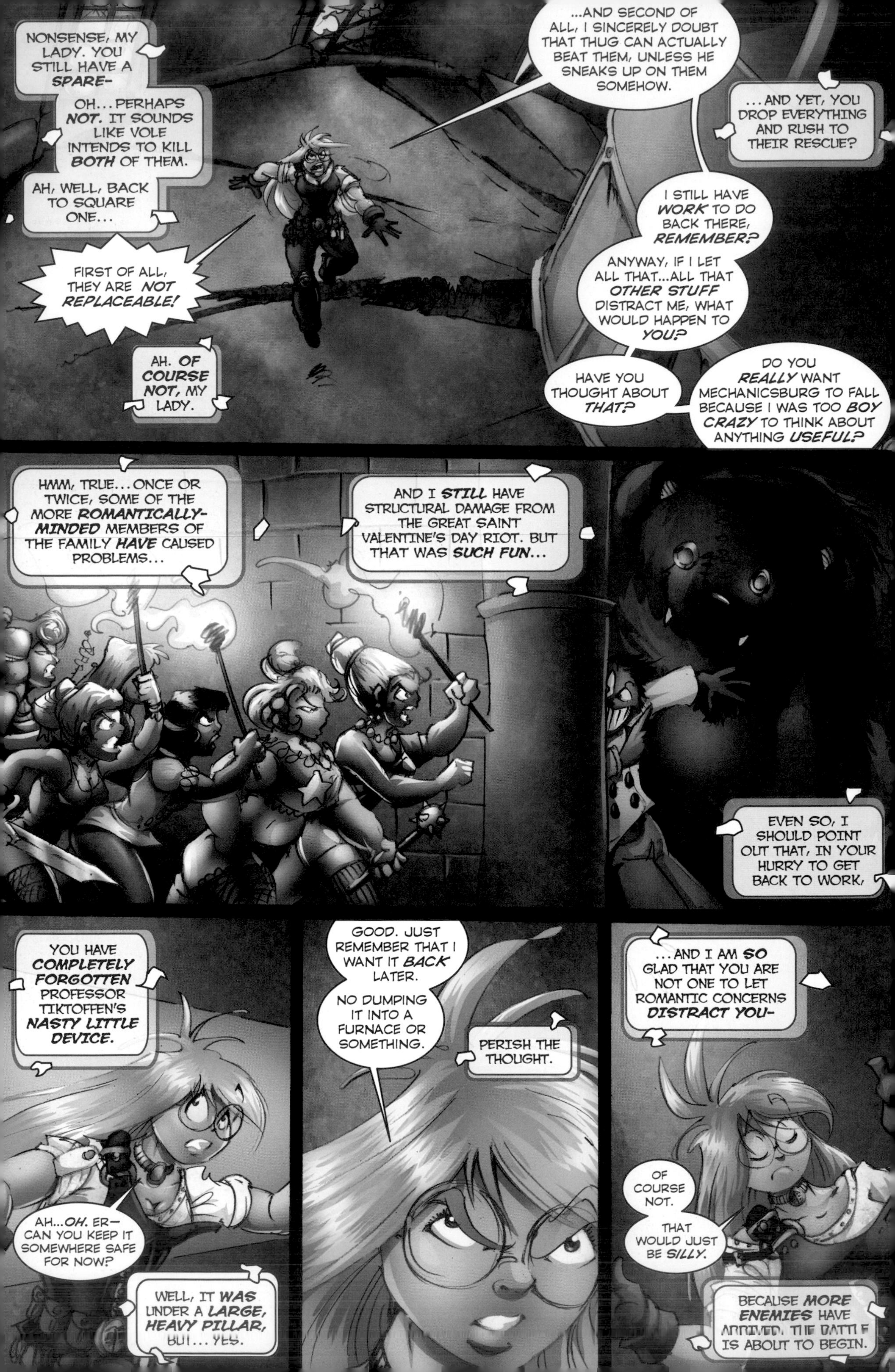
NONSENSE, MY LADY. YOU STILL HAVE A SPARE-
OH... PERHAPS NOT. IT SOUNDS LIKE VOLE INTENDS TO KILL BOTH OF THEM.
AH, WELL, BACK TO SQUARE ONE...
FIRST OF ALL, THEY ARE NOT REPLACEABLE!
...AND SECOND OF ALL, I SINCERELY DOUBT THAT THUG CAN ACTUALLY BEAT THEM, UNLESS HE SNEAKS UP ON THEM SOMEHOW.
AH. OF COURSE NOT, MY LADY.
...AND YET, YOU DROP EVERYTHING AND RUSH TO THEIR RESCUE?
I STILL HAVE WORK TO DO BACK THERE, REMEMBER?
ANYWAY, IF I LET ALL THAT...ALL THAT OTHER STUFF DISTRACT ME, WHAT WOULD HAPPEN TO YOU?
HAVE YOU THOUGHT ABOUT THAT?
DO YOU REALLY WANT MECHANICSBURG TO FALL BECAUSE I WAS TOO BOY CRAZY TO THINK ABOUT ANYTHING USEFUL?
HMM, TRUE... ONCE OR TWICE, SOME OF THE MORE ROMANTICALLY-MINDED MEMBERS OF THE FAMILY HAVE CAUSED PROBLEMS...
AND I STILL HAVE STRUCTURAL DAMAGE FROM THE GREAT SAINT VALENTINE'S DAY RIOT. BUT THAT WAS SUCH FUN...
EVEN SO, I SHOULD POINT OUT THAT, IN YOUR HURRY TO GET BACK TO WORK,
YOU HAVE COMPLETELY FORGOTTEN PROFESSOR TIKTOFFEN'S NASTY LITTLE DEVICE.
AH...OH. ER— CAN YOU KEEP IT SOMEWHERE SAFE FOR NOW?
WELL, IT WAS UNDER A LARGE, HEAVY PILLAR, BUT... YES.
GOOD. JUST REMEMBER THAT I WANT IT BACK LATER.
NO DUMPING IT INTO A FURNACE OR SOMETHING.
PERISH THE THOUGHT.
...AND I AM SO GLAD THAT YOU ARE NOT ONE TO LET ROMANTIC CONCERNS DISTRACT YOU-
OF COURSE NOT.
THAT WOULD JUST BE SILLY.
BECAUSE MORE ENEMIES HAVE ARRIVED. THE BATTLE IS ABOUT TO BEGIN.

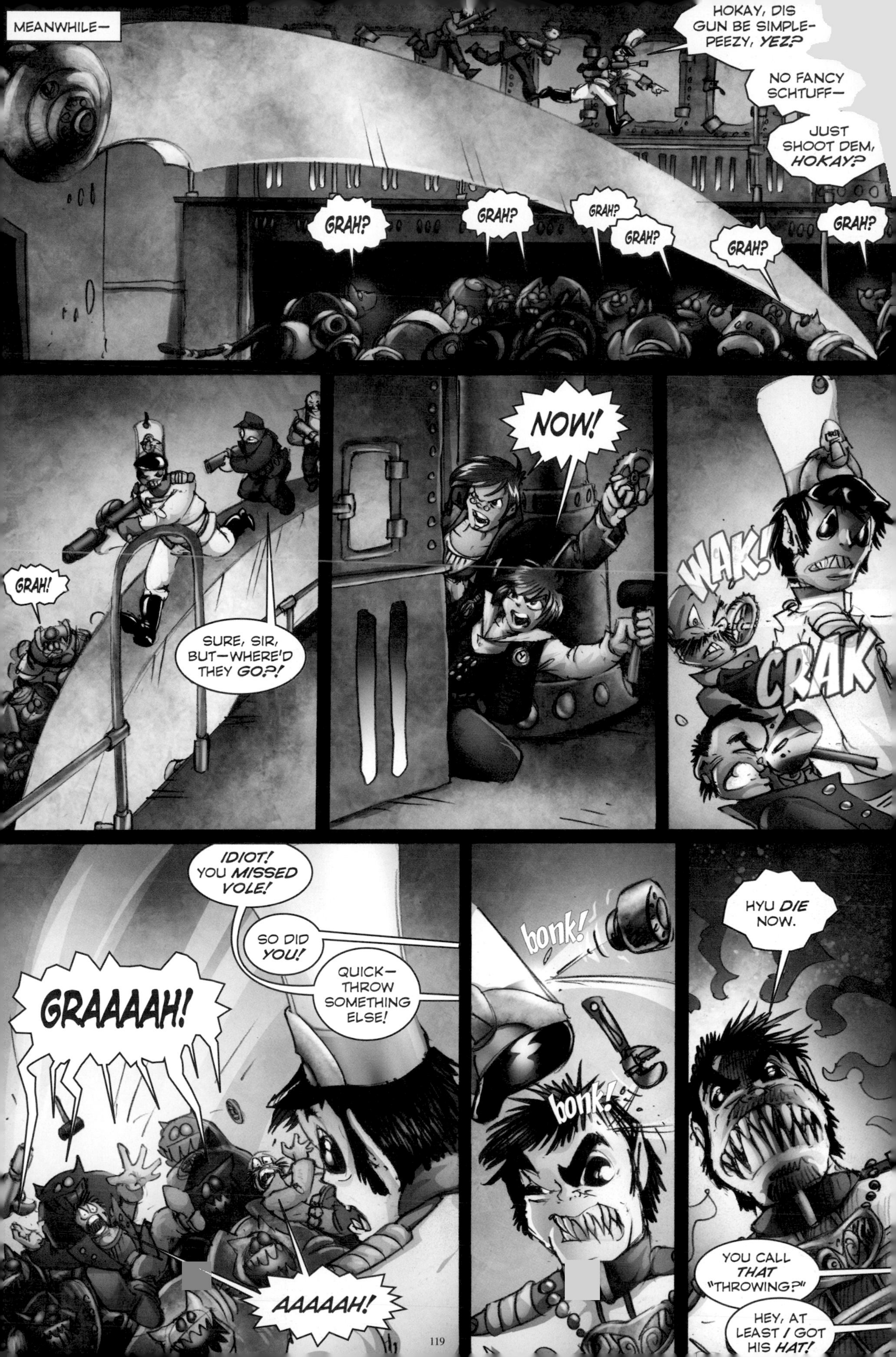
MEANWHILE—
HOKAY, DIS GUN BE SIMPLE-PEEZY, YEZ?
NO FANCY SCHTUFF—
JUST SHOOT DEM, HOKAY?
GRAH?
GRAH?
GRAH?
GRAH?
GRAH?
GRAH?
GRAH!
SURE, SIR, BUT—WHERE'D THEY GO?!
NOW!
WAK!
CRAK
IDIOT! YOU MISSED VOLE!
SO DID YOU!
QUICK—THROW SOMETHING ELSE!
GRAAAAH!
AAAAAH!
bonk!
bonk!
HYU DIE NOW.
YOU CALL THAT "THROWING?"
HEY, AT LEAST I GOT HIS HAT!

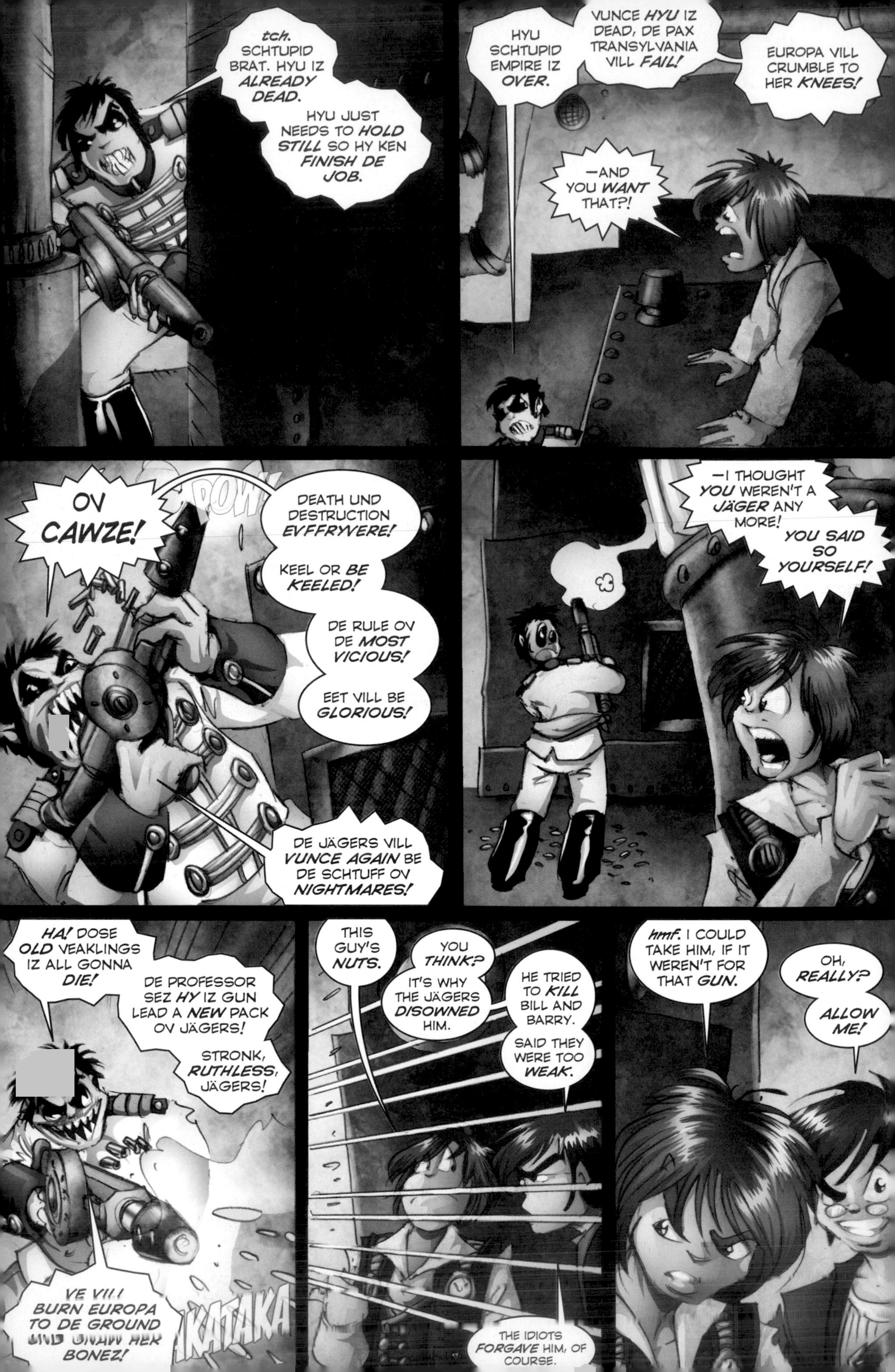
tch. SCHTUPID BRAT. HYU IZ ALREADY DEAD.
HYU JUST NEEDS TO HOLD STILL SO HY KEN FINISH DE JOB.
HYU SCHTUPID EMPIRE IZ OVER.
VUNCE HYU IZ DEAD, DE PAX TRANSYLVANIA VILL FAIL!
EUROPA VILL CRUMBLE TO HER KNEES!
—AND YOU WANT THAT?!
OV CAWZE!
POW!
DEATH UND DESTRUCTION EVFFRYVERE!
KEEL OR BE KEELED!
DE RULE OV DE MOST VICIOUS!
EET VILL BE GLORIOUS!
DE JÄGERS VILL VUNCE AGAIN BE DE SCHTUFF OV NIGHTMARES!
—I THOUGHT YOU WEREN'T A JÄGER ANY MORE!
YOU SAID SO YOURSELF!
HA! DOSE OLD VEAKLINGS IZ ALL GONNA DIE!
DE PROFESSOR SEZ HY IZ GUN LEAD A NEW PACK OV JÄGERS!
STRONK, RUTHLESS, JÄGERS!
VE VILL BURN EUROPA TO DE GROUND UND GNAW HER BONEZ!
KATAKA
THIS GUY'S NUTS.
YOU THINK?
IT'S WHY THE JÄGERS DISOWNED HIM.
HE TRIED TO KILL BILL AND BARRY.
SAID THEY WERE TOO WEAK.
THE IDIOTS FORGAVE HIM, OF COURSE.
hmf. I COULD TAKE HIM, IF IT WEREN'T FOR THAT GUN.
OH, REALLY?
ALLOW ME!

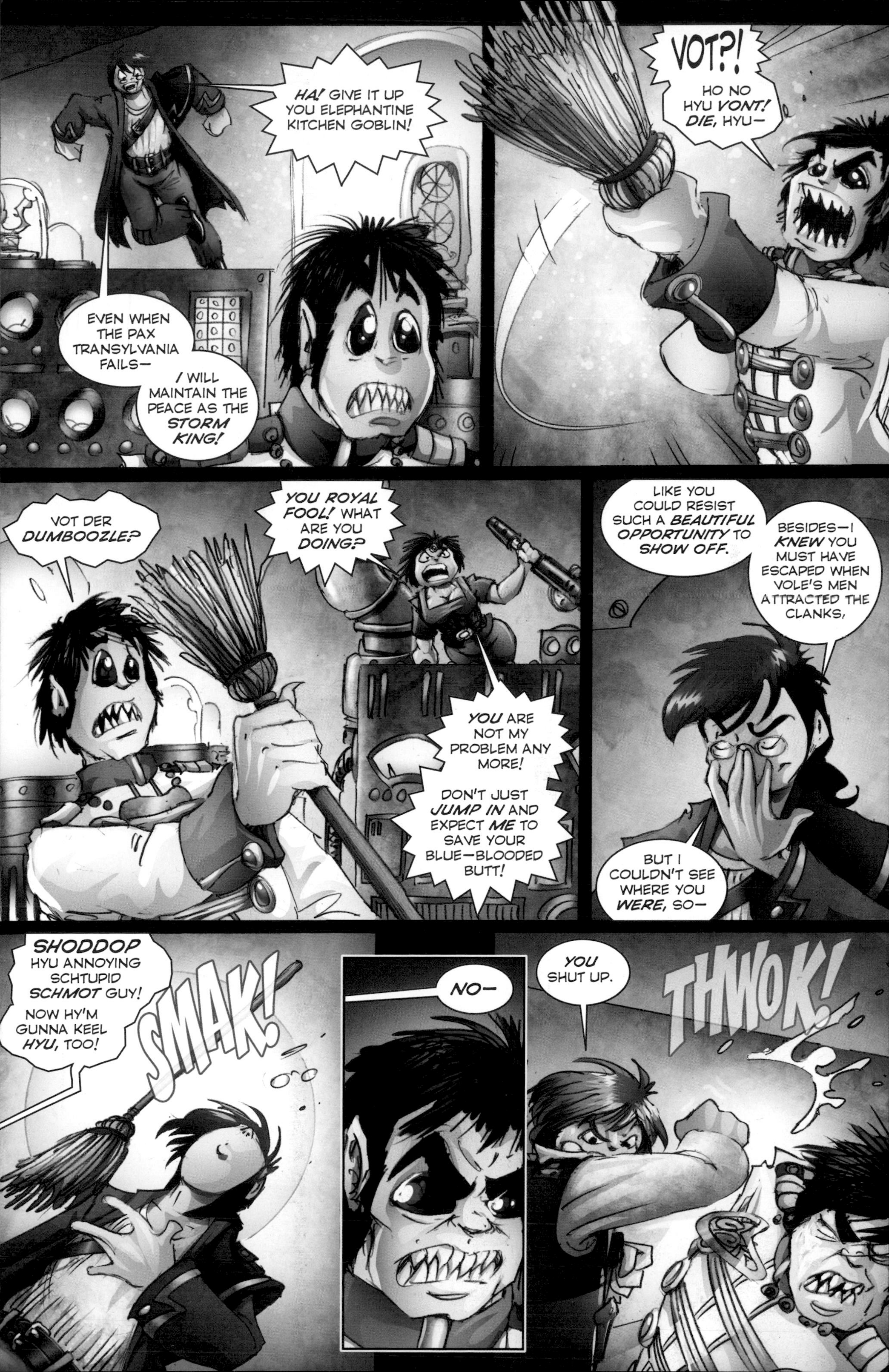
HA! GIVE IT UP YOU ELEPHANTINE KITCHEN GOBLIN!
EVEN WHEN THE PAX TRANSYLVANIA FAILS—
I WILL MAINTAIN THE PEACE AS THE STORM KING!
VOT?!
HO NO HYU VONT! DIE, HYU—
VOT DER DUMBOOZLE?
YOU ROYAL FOOL! WHAT ARE YOU DOING?
YOU ARE NOT MY PROBLEM ANY MORE!
DON'T JUST JUMP IN AND EXPECT ME TO SAVE YOUR BLUE-BLOODED BUTT!
LIKE YOU COULD RESIST SUCH A BEAUTIFUL OPPORTUNITY TO SHOW OFF.
BESIDES—I KNEW YOU MUST HAVE ESCAPED WHEN VOLE'S MEN ATTRACTED THE CLANKS,
BUT I COULDN'T SEE WHERE YOU WERE, SO—
SHODDOP HYU ANNOYING SCHTUPID SCHMOT GUY!
NOW HY'M GUNNA KEEL HYU, TOO!
SMAK!
NO—
YOU SHUT UP.
THWOK!

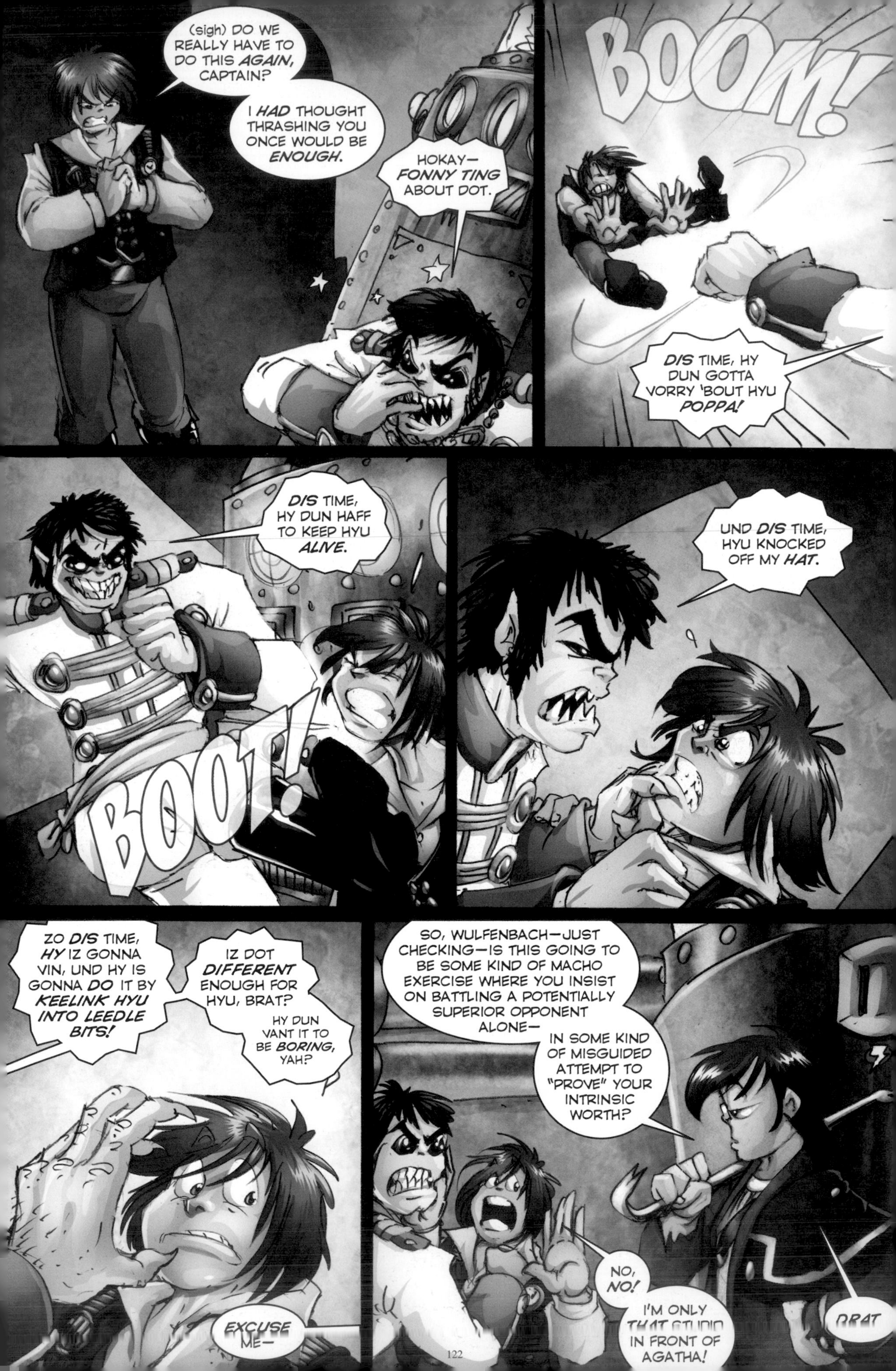
(sigh) DO WE REALLY HAVE TO DO THIS *AGAIN*, CAPTAIN?
I *HAD* THOUGHT THRASHING YOU ONCE WOULD BE *ENOUGH*.
HOKAY— *FONNY TING* ABOUT DOT.
BOOM!
DIS TIME, HY DUN GOTTA VORRY 'BOUT HYU *POPPA!*
DIS TIME, HY DUN HAFF TO KEEP HYU *ALIVE*.
BOOT!
UND *DIS* TIME, HYU KNOCKED OFF MY *HAT*.
ZO *DIS* TIME, *HY* IZ GONNA VIN, UND HY IS GONNA *DO* IT BY *KEELINK HYU INTO LEEDLE BITS!*
IZ DOT *DIFFERENT* ENOUGH FOR HYU, BRAT?
HY DUN VANT IT TO BE *BORING*, YAH?
EXCUSE ME—
SO, WULFENBACH—JUST CHECKING—IS THIS GOING TO BE SOME KIND OF MACHO EXERCISE WHERE YOU INSIST ON BATTLING A POTENTIALLY SUPERIOR OPPONENT ALONE—
IN SOME KIND OF MISGUIDED ATTEMPT TO "PROVE" YOUR INTRINSIC WORTH?
NO, *NO!*
I'M ONLY *THAT* STUPID IN FRONT OF AGATHA!
DRAT

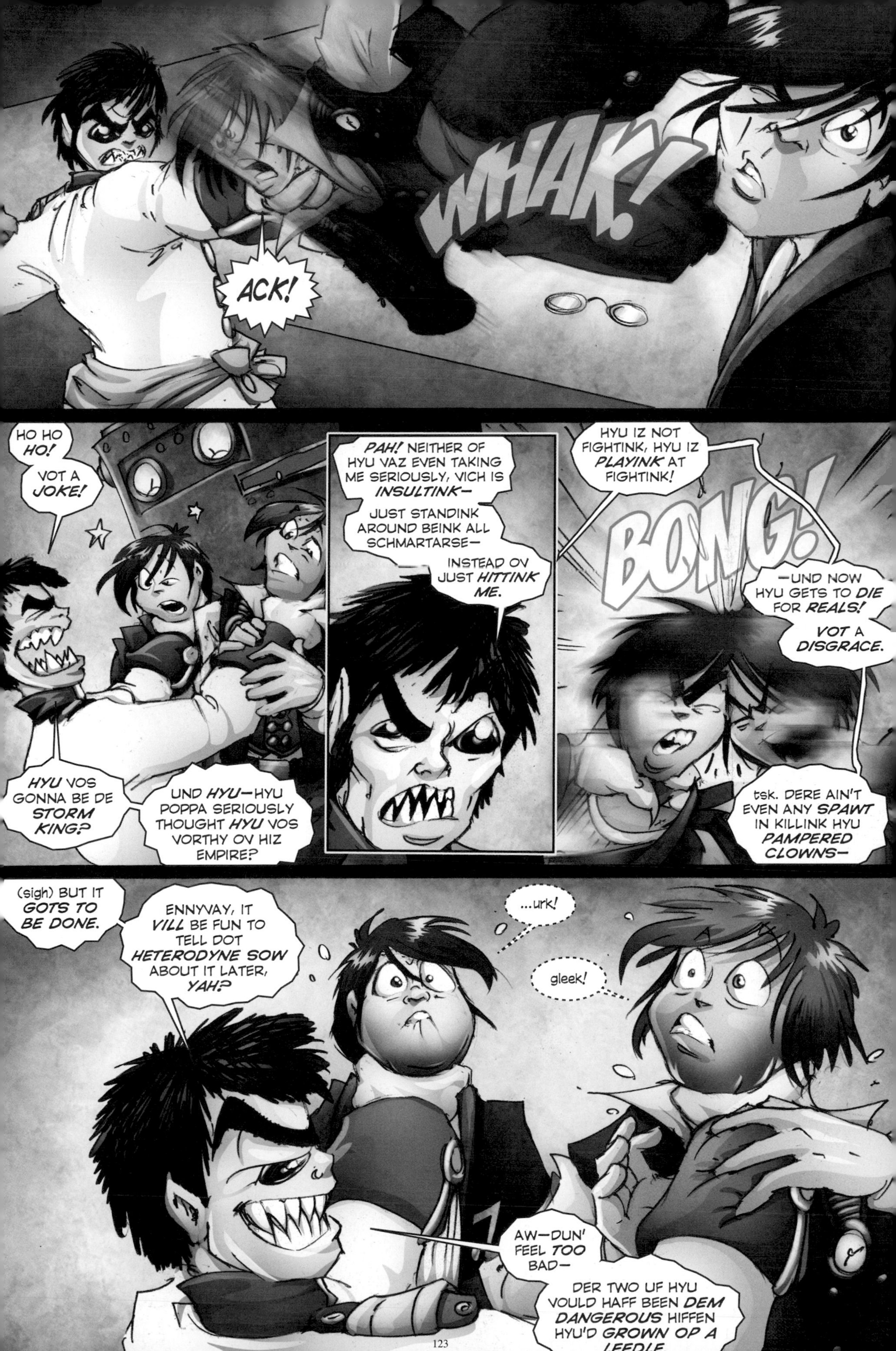
WHAK!
ACK!
HO HO HO!
VOT A JOKE!
HYU VOS GONNA BE DE STORM KING?
UND HYU—HYU POPPA SERIOUSLY THOUGHT HYU VOS VORTHY OV HIZ EMPIRE?
PAH! NEITHER OF HYU VAZ EVEN TAKING ME SERIOUSLY, VICH IS INSULTINK—
JUST STANDINK AROUND BEINK ALL SCHMARTARSE—
INSTEAD OV JUST HITTINK ME.
HYU IZ NOT FIGHTINK, HYU IZ PLAYINK AT FIGHTINK!
BONG!
—UND NOW HYU GETS TO DIE FOR REALS!
VOT A DISGRACE.
tsk. DERE AIN'T EVEN ANY SPAWT IN KILLINK HYU PAMPERED CLOWNS—
(sigh) BUT IT GOTS TO BE DONE.
ENNYVAY, IT VILL BE FUN TO TELL DOT HETERODYNE SOW ABOUT IT LATER, YAH?
...urk!
gleek!
AW—DUN' FEEL TOO BAD—
DER TWO UF HYU VOULD HAFF BEEN DEM DANGEROUS HIFFEN HYU'D GROWN OP A LEEDLE.

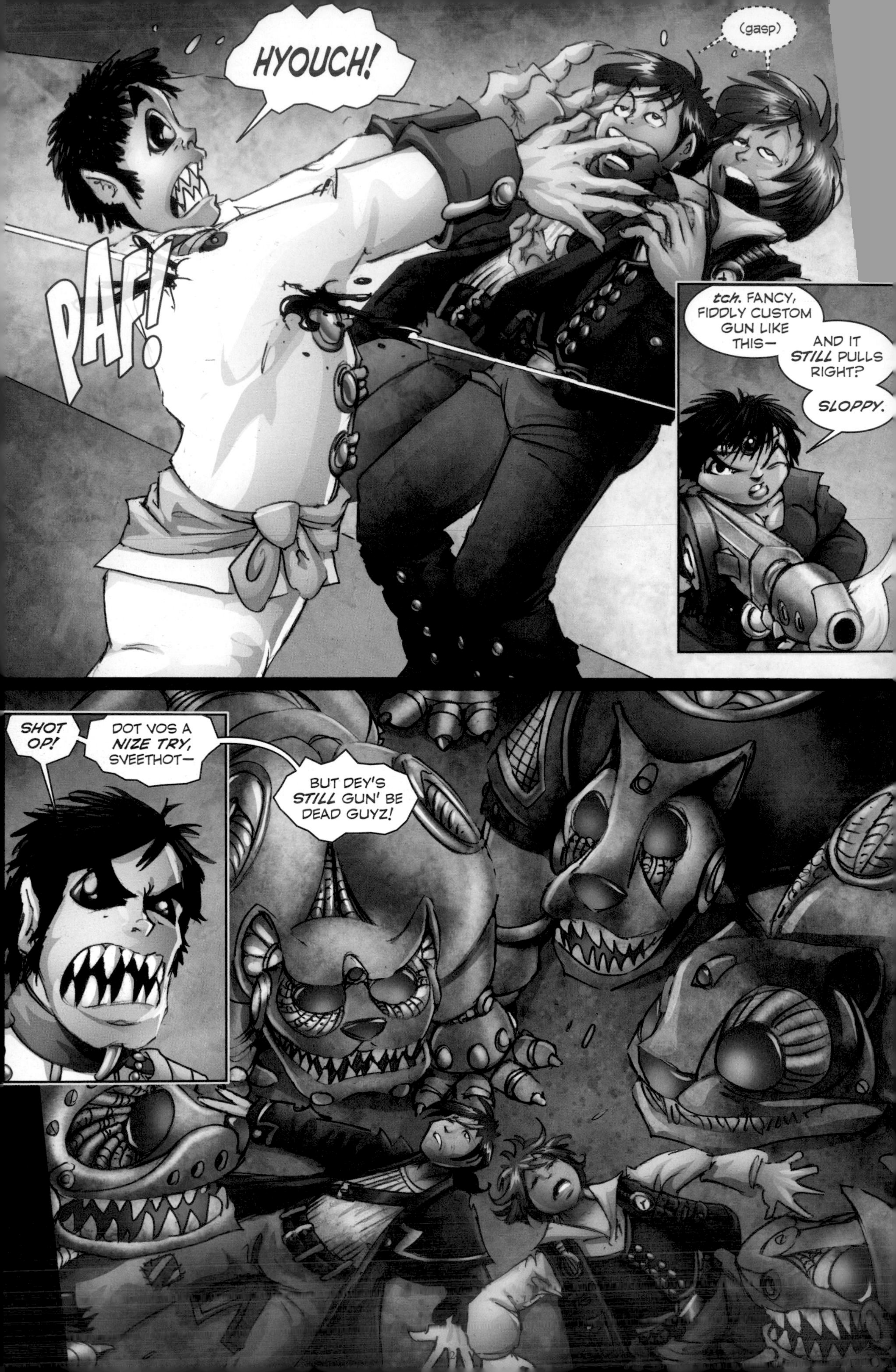
HYOUCH!
(gasp)
PAF!
tch. FANCY, FIDDLY CUSTOM GUN LIKE THIS—
AND IT STILL PULLS RIGHT?
SLOPPY.
SHOT OP!
DOT VOS A NIZE TRY, SVEETHOT—
BUT DEY'S STILL GUN' BE DEAD GUYZ!

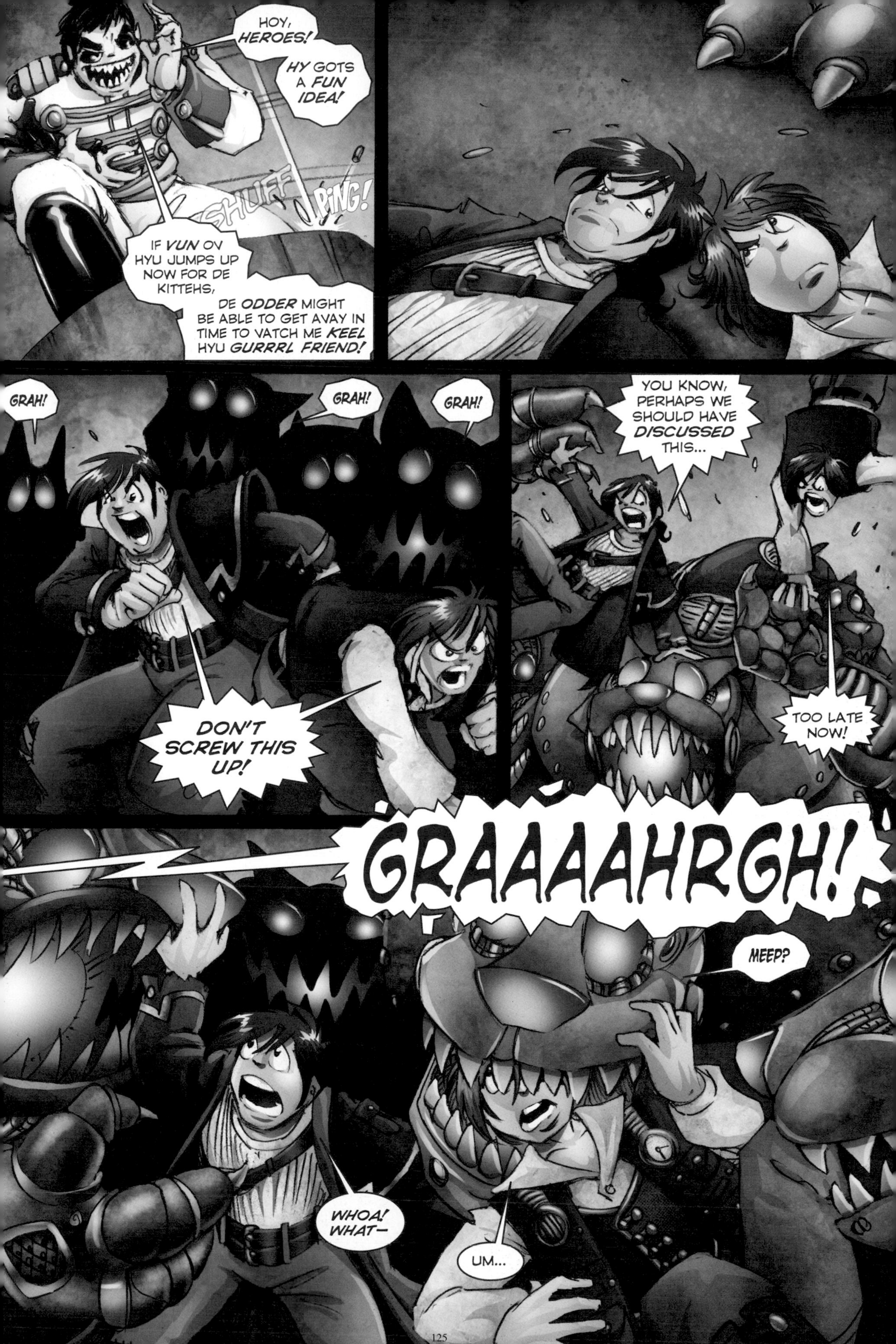
HOY, HEROES!
HY GOTS A FUN IDEA!
SHUFF
PING!
IF VUN OV HYU JUMPS UP NOW FOR DE KITTEHS,
DE ODDER MIGHT BE ABLE TO GET AVAY IN TIME TO VATCH ME KEEL HYU GURRRL FRIEND!
GRAH!
GRAH!
GRAH!
DON'T SCREW THIS UP!
YOU KNOW, PERHAPS WE SHOULD HAVE DISCUSSED THIS...
TOO LATE NOW!
GRAAAAHRGH!
MEEP?
WHOA! WHAT—
UM...

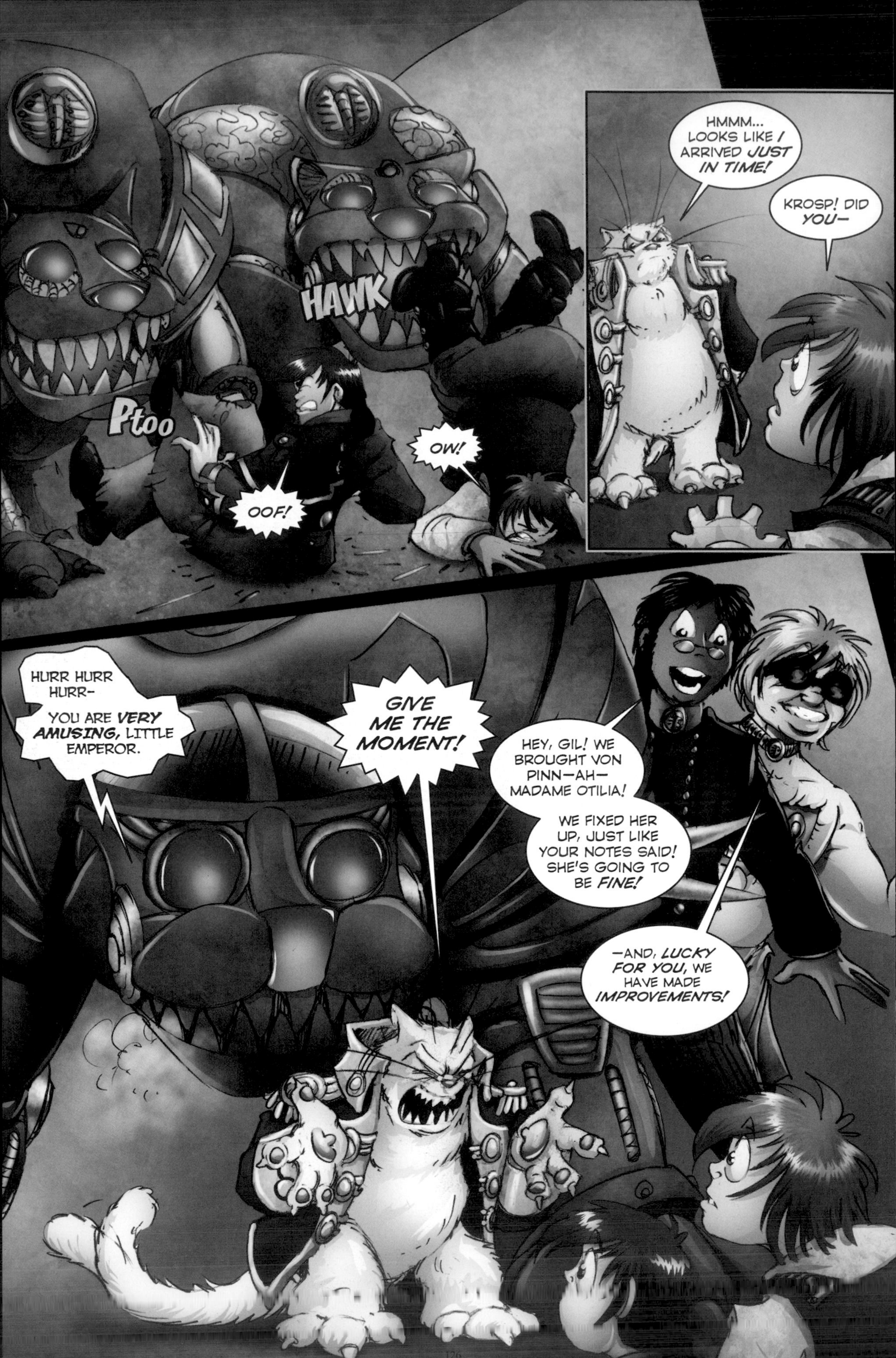

HAWK
Ptoo
OOF!
OW!
HMMM... LOOKS LIKE I ARRIVED JUST IN TIME!
KROSP! DID YOU—
HURR HURR HURR-
YOU ARE VERY AMUSING, LITTLE EMPEROR.
GIVE ME THE MOMENT!
HEY, GIL! WE BROUGHT VON PINN—AH—MADAME OTILIA!
WE FIXED HER UP, JUST LIKE YOUR NOTES SAID! SHE'S GOING TO BE FINE!
—AND, LUCKY FOR YOU, WE HAVE MADE IMPROVEMENTS!

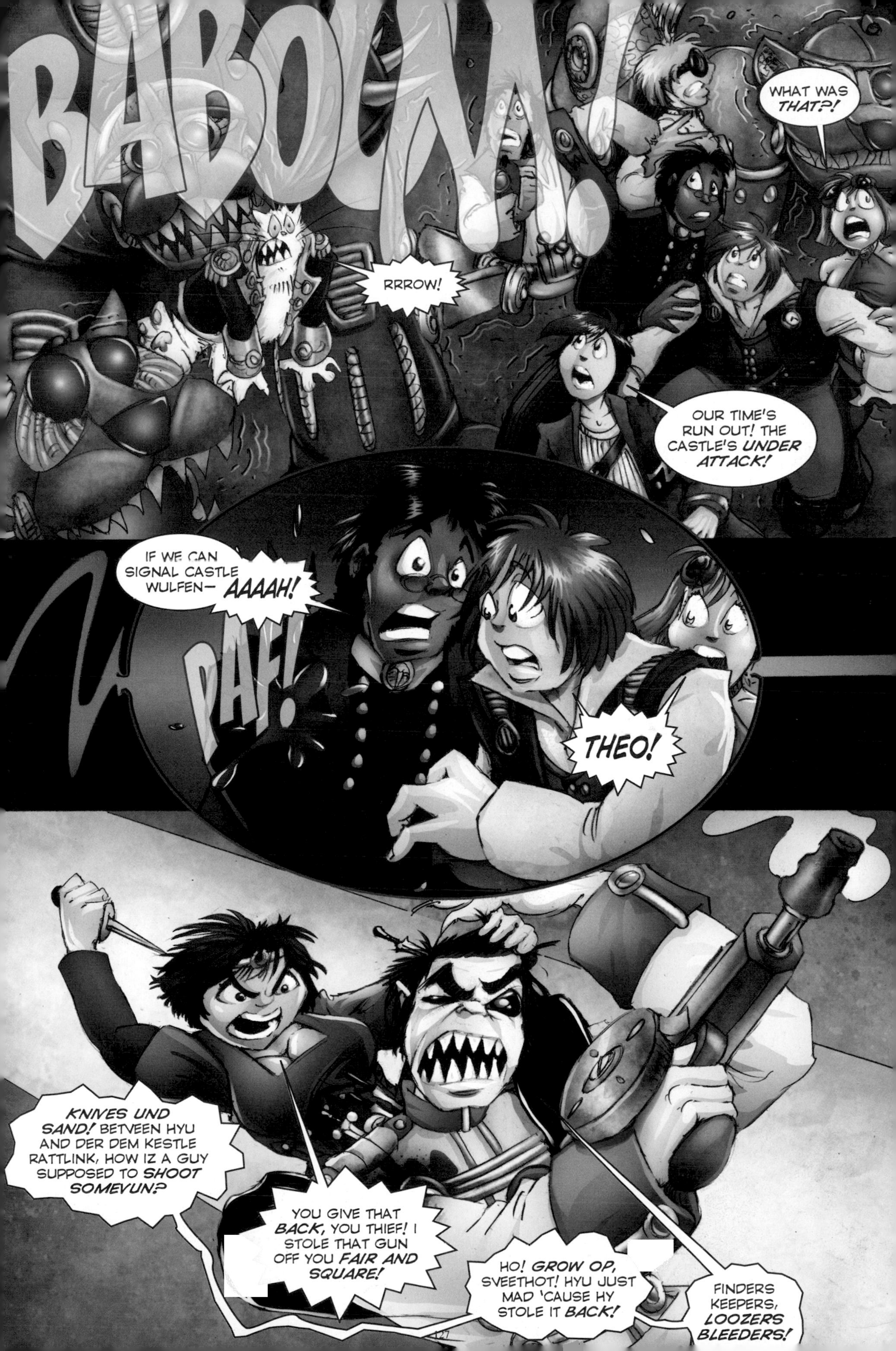
BABOOM!
WHAT WAS THAT?!
RRROW!
OUR TIME'S RUN OUT! THE CASTLE'S UNDER ATTACK!
IF WE CAN SIGNAL CASTLE WULFEN—
AAAAH!
PAF!
THEO!
KNIVES UND SAND! BETVEEN HYU AND DER DEM KESTLE RATTLINK, HOW IZ A GUY SUPPOSED TO SHOOT SOMEVUN?
YOU GIVE THAT BACK, YOU THIEF! I STOLE THAT GUN OFF YOU FAIR AND SQUARE!
HO! GROW OP, SVEETHOT! HYU JUST MAD 'CAUSE HY STOLE IT BACK!
FINDERS KEEPERS, LOOZERS BLEEDERS!

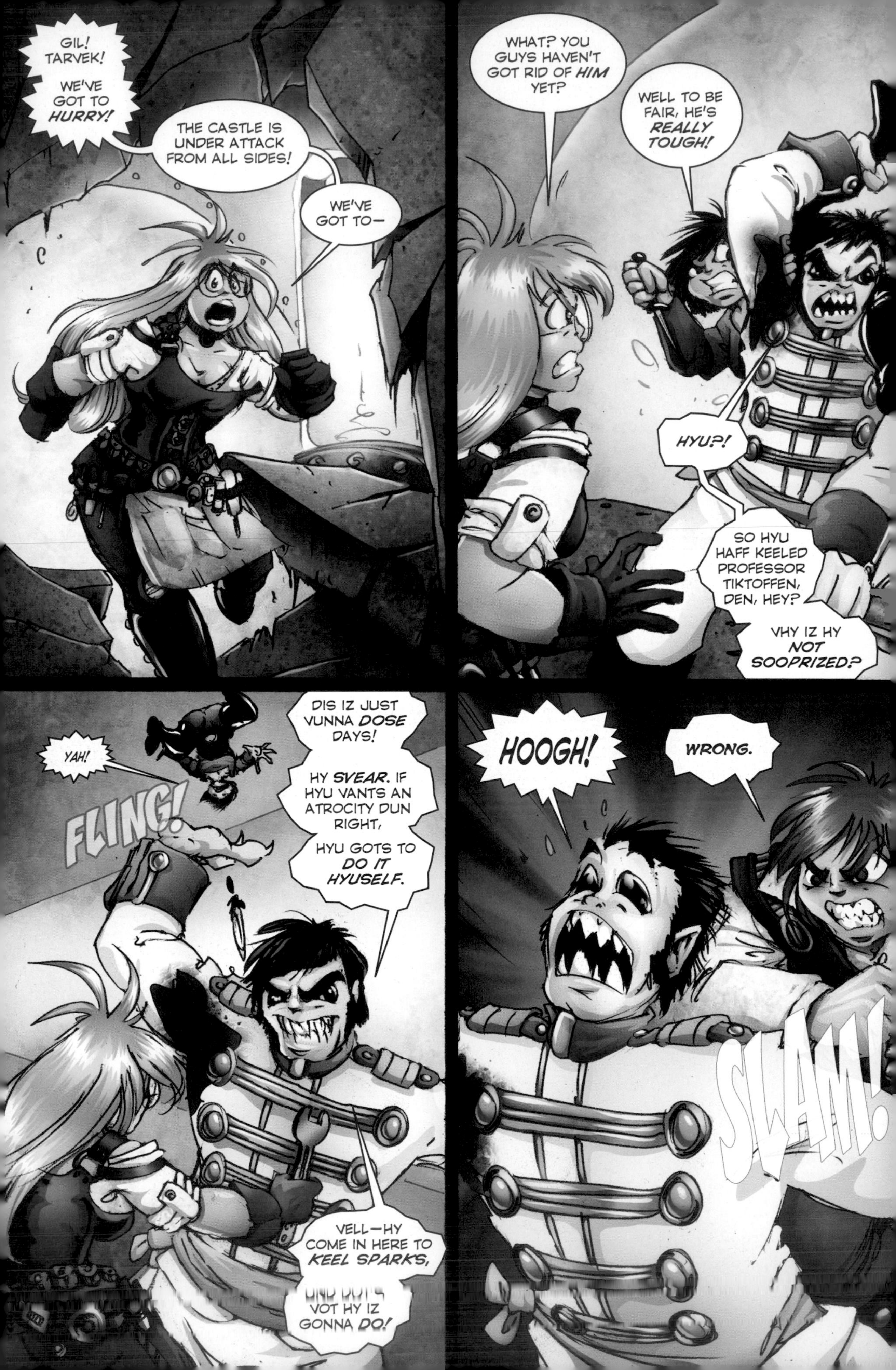
GIL! TARVEK!
WE'VE GOT TO HURRY!
THE CASTLE IS UNDER ATTACK FROM ALL SIDES!
WE'VE GOT TO—
WHAT? YOU GUYS HAVEN'T GOT RID OF HIM YET?
WELL TO BE FAIR, HE'S REALLY TOUGH!
HYU?!
SO HYU HAFF KEELED PROFESSOR TIKTOFFEN, DEN, HEY?
VHY IZ HY NOT SOOPRIZED?
YAH!
FLING!
DIS IZ JUST VUNNA DOSE DAYS!
HY SVEAR. IF HYU VANTS AN ATROCITY DUN RIGHT,
HYU GOTS TO DO IT HYUSELF.
VELL—HY COME IN HERE TO KEEL SPARKS,
VOT HY IZ GONNA DO!
HOOGH!
WRONG.
SLAM!

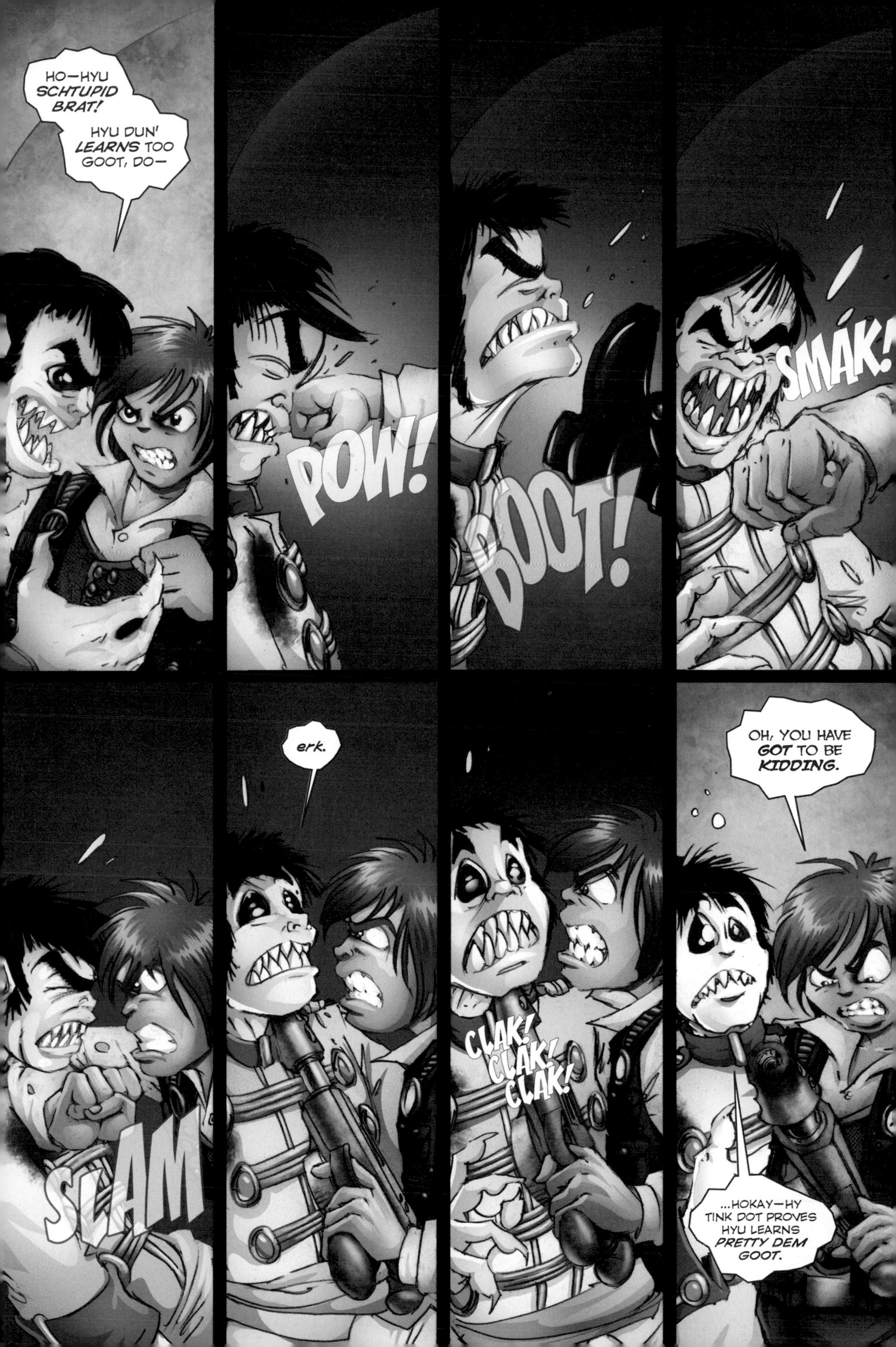
HO–HYU SCHTUPID BRAT!
HYU DUN' LEARNS TOO GOOT, DO—
POW!
BOOT!
SMAK!
SLAM
erk.
CLAK! CLAK! CLAK!
OH, YOU HAVE GOT TO BE KIDDING.
...HOKAY—HY TINK DOT PROVES HYU LEARNS PRETTY DEM GOOT.

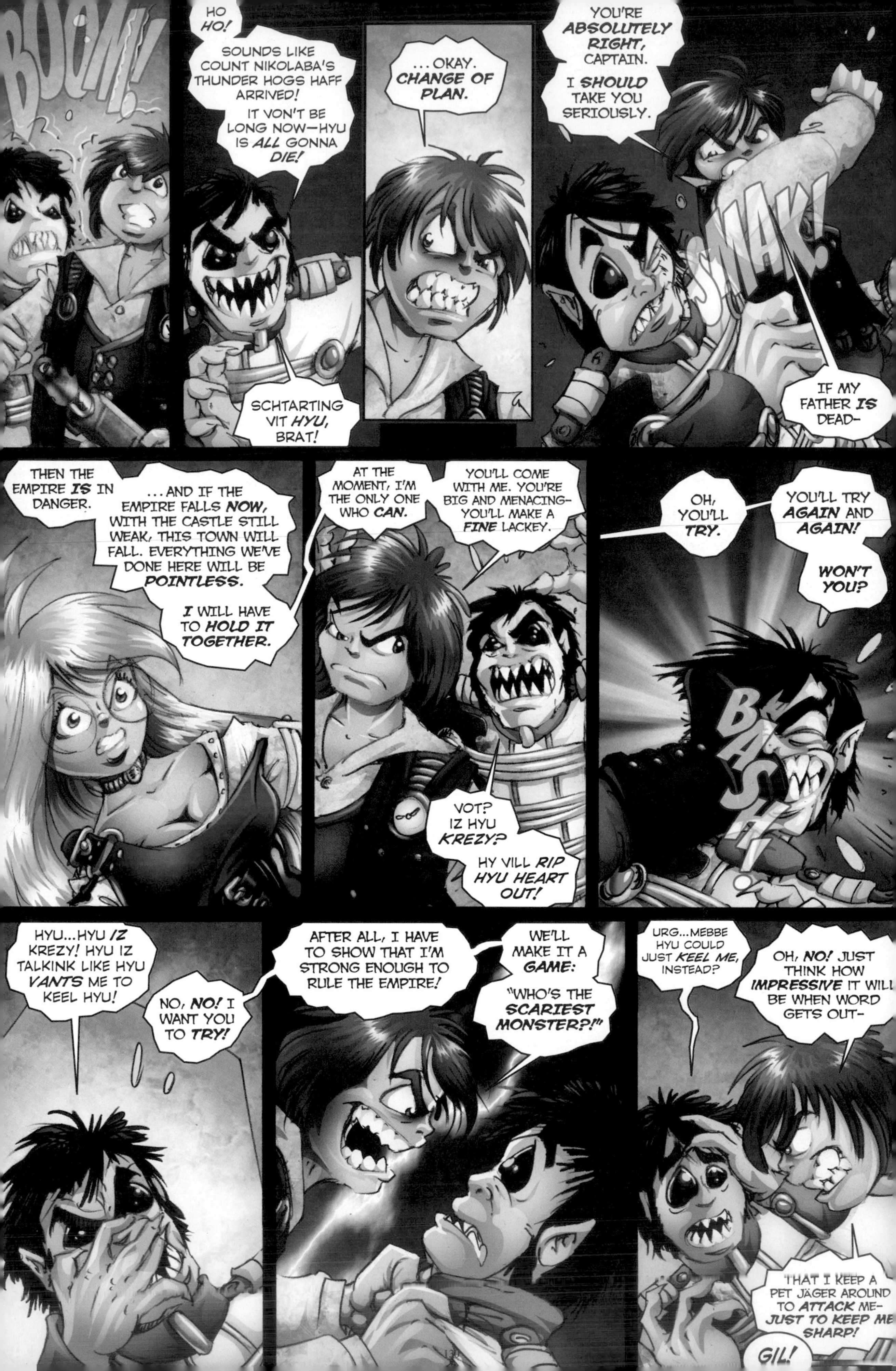
BOOM!
HO HO!
SOUNDS LIKE COUNT NIKOLABA'S THUNDER HOGS HAFF ARRIVED!
IT VON'T BE LONG NOW—HYU IS ALL GONNA DIE!
SCHTARTING VIT HYU, BRAT!
...OKAY. CHANGE OF PLAN.
YOU'RE ABSOLUTELY RIGHT, CAPTAIN.
I SHOULD TAKE YOU SERIOUSLY.
SMAK!
IF MY FATHER IS DEAD-
THEN THE EMPIRE IS IN DANGER.
...AND IF THE EMPIRE FALLS NOW, WITH THE CASTLE STILL WEAK, THIS TOWN WILL FALL. EVERYTHING WE'VE DONE HERE WILL BE POINTLESS.
I WILL HAVE TO HOLD IT TOGETHER.
AT THE MOMENT, I'M THE ONLY ONE WHO CAN.
YOU'LL COME WITH ME. YOU'RE BIG AND MENACING- YOU'LL MAKE A FINE LACKEY.
VOT? IZ HYU KREZY?
HY VILL RIP HYU HEART OUT!
OH, YOU'LL TRY.
YOU'LL TRY AGAIN AND AGAIN!
WON'T YOU?
BASH!
HYU...HYU IZ KREZY! HYU IZ TALKINK LIKE HYU VANTS ME TO KEEL HYU!
NO, NO! I WANT YOU TO TRY!
AFTER ALL, I HAVE TO SHOW THAT I'M STRONG ENOUGH TO RULE THE EMPIRE!
WE'LL MAKE IT A GAME:
"WHO'S THE SCARIEST MONSTER?!"
URG...MEBBE HYU COULD JUST KEEL ME, INSTEAD?
OH, NO! JUST THINK HOW IMPRESSIVE IT WILL BE WHEN WORD GETS OUT-
THAT I KEEP A PET JÄGER AROUND TO ATTACK ME- JUST TO KEEP ME SHARP!
GIL!

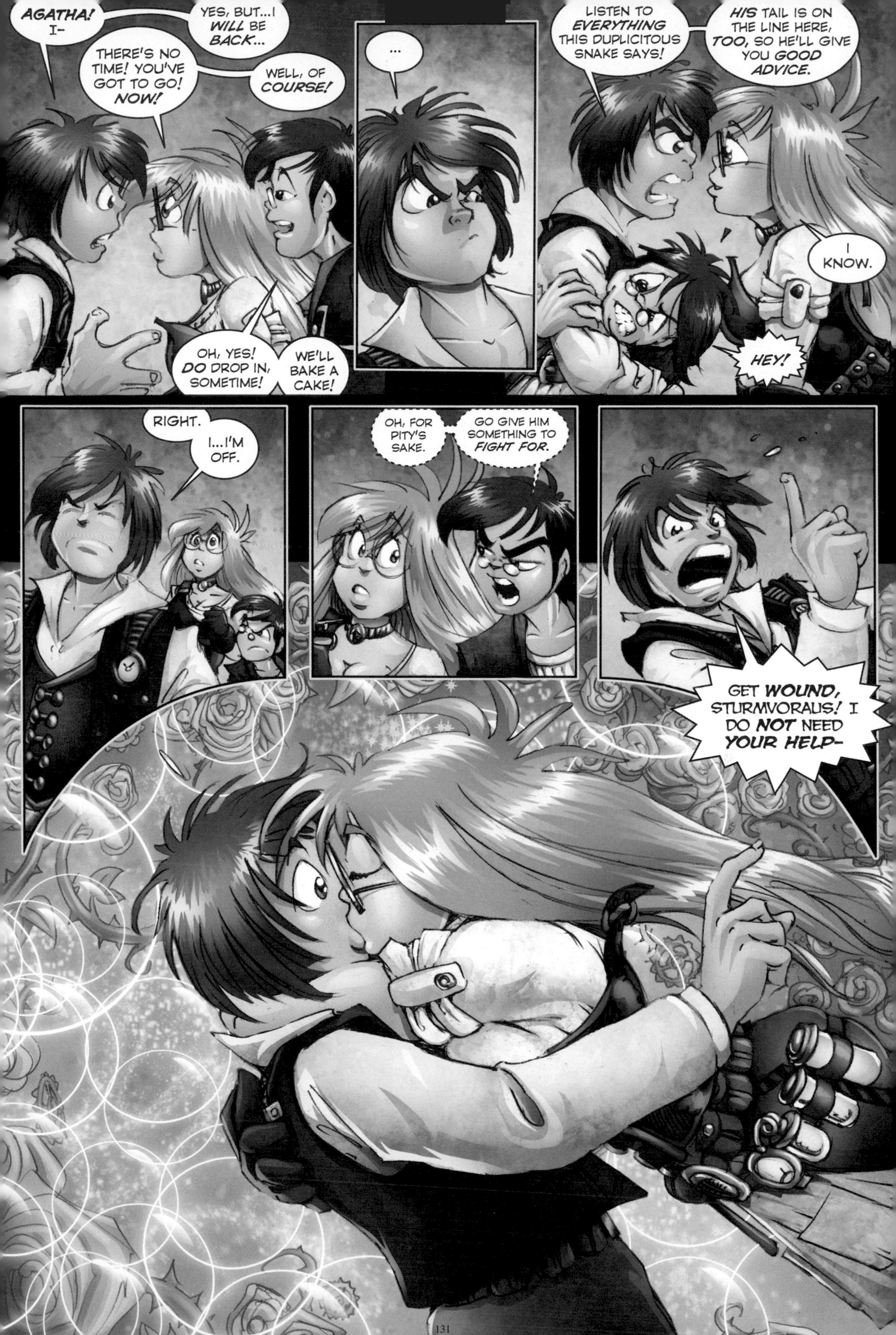
AGATHA! I-
YES, BUT...I WILL BE BACK...
THERE'S NO TIME! YOU'VE GOT TO GO! NOW!
WELL, OF COURSE!
OH, YES! DO DROP IN, SOMETIME!
WE'LL BAKE A CAKE!
...
LISTEN TO EVERYTHING THIS DUPLICITOUS SNAKE SAYS!
HIS TAIL IS ON THE LINE HERE, TOO, SO HE'LL GIVE YOU GOOD ADVICE.
I KNOW.
HEY!
RIGHT.
I...I'M OFF.
OH, FOR PITY'S SAKE.
GO GIVE HIM SOMETHING TO FIGHT FOR.
GET WOUND, STURMVORAUS! I DO NOT NEED YOUR HELP-

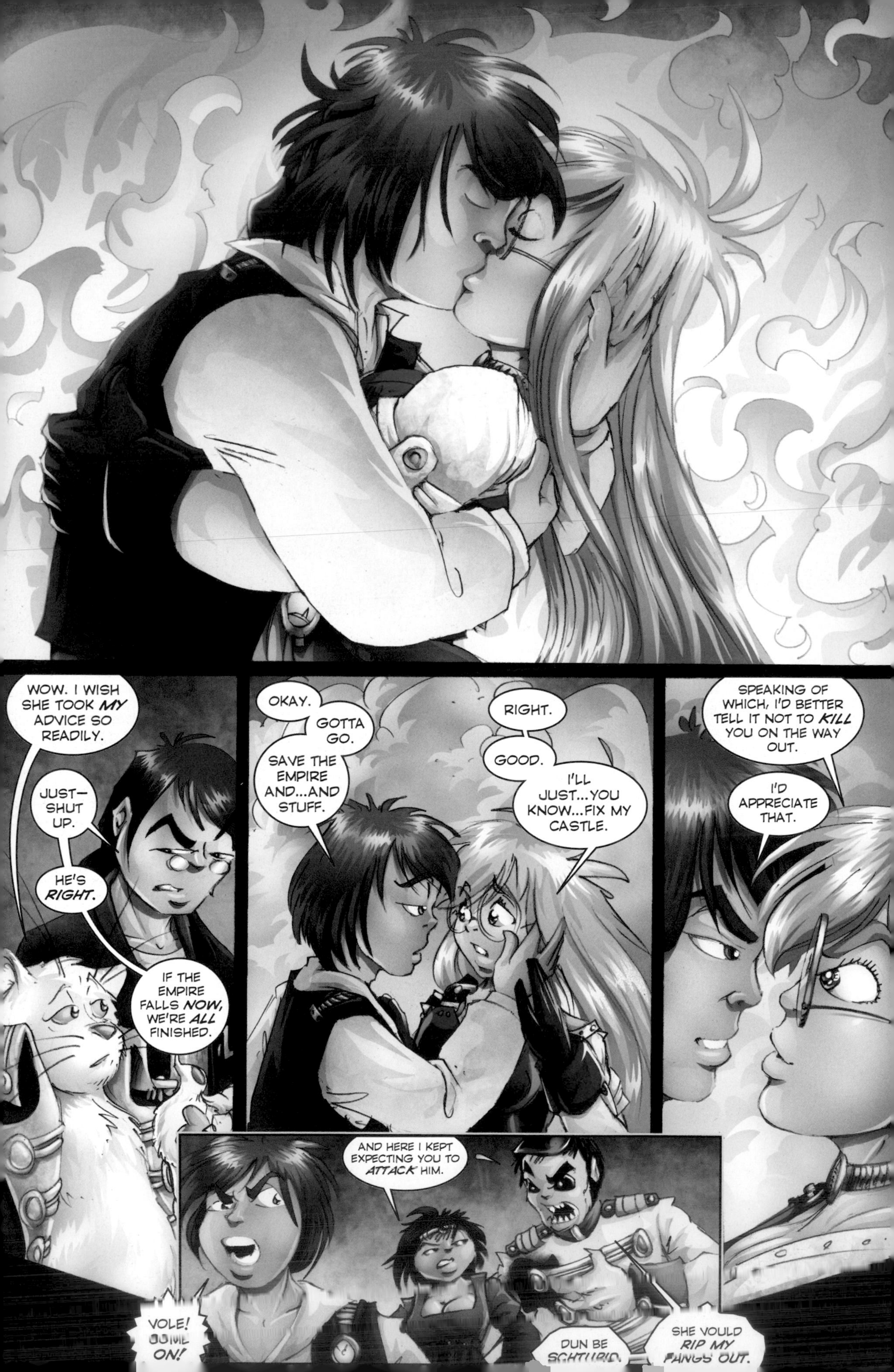
WOW. I WISH SHE TOOK *MY* ADVICE SO READILY.
JUST— SHUT UP.
HE'S *RIGHT*.
IF THE EMPIRE FALLS *NOW*, WE'RE *ALL* FINISHED.
OKAY.
GOTTA GO.
SAVE THE EMPIRE AND...AND STUFF.
RIGHT.
GOOD.
I'LL JUST...YOU KNOW...FIX MY CASTLE.
SPEAKING OF WHICH, I'D BETTER TELL IT NOT TO *KILL* YOU ON THE WAY OUT.
I'D APPRECIATE THAT.
AND HERE I KEPT EXPECTING YOU TO *ATTACK* HIM.
VOLE!
ON!
DUN BE SCHTUPID.
SHE VOULD *RIP MY FANGS OUT.*

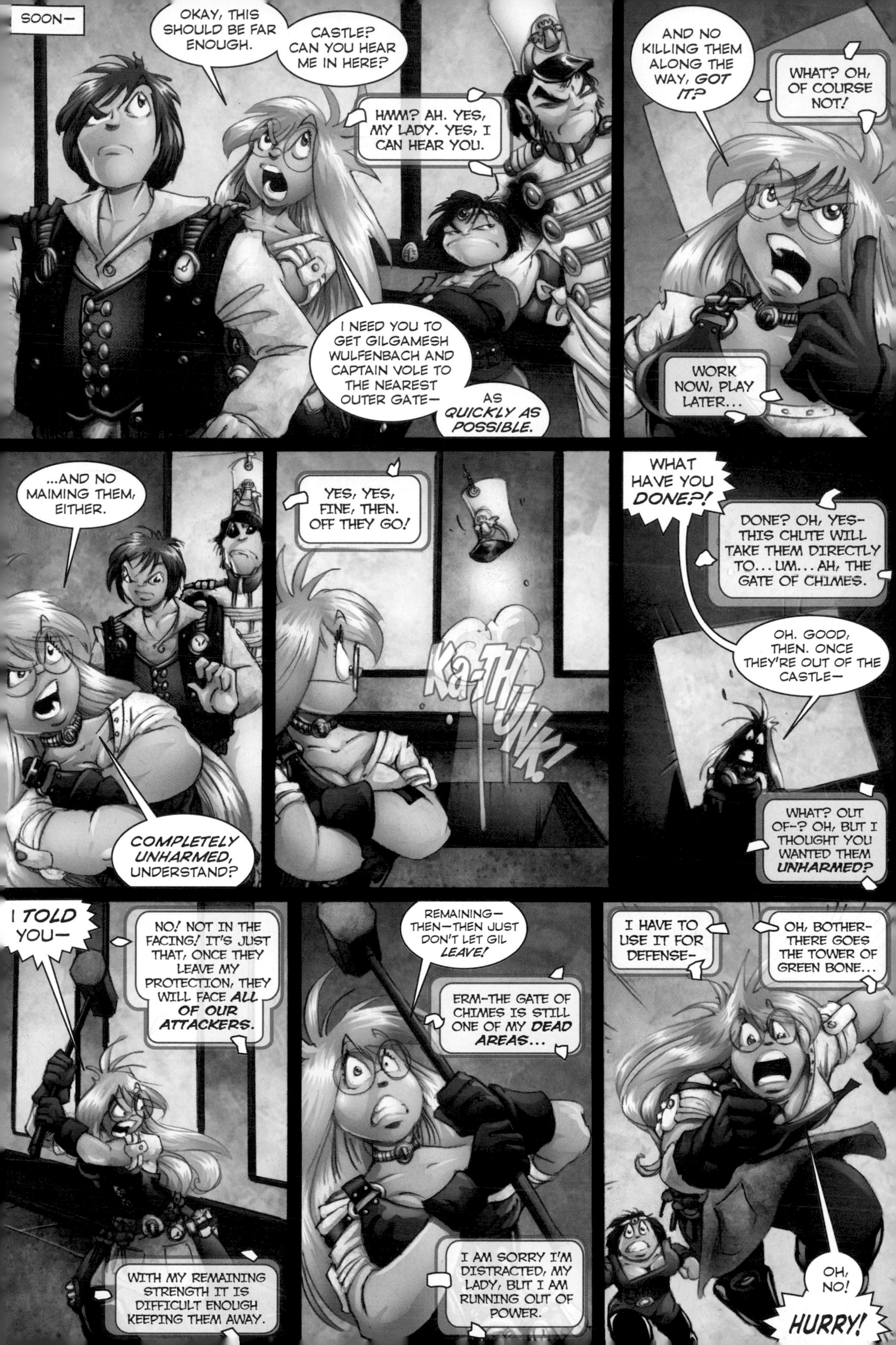
SOON—
OKAY, THIS SHOULD BE FAR ENOUGH.
CASTLE? CAN YOU HEAR ME IN HERE?
HMM? AH. YES, MY LADY. YES, I CAN HEAR YOU.
I NEED YOU TO GET GILGAMESH WULFENBACH AND CAPTAIN VOLE TO THE NEAREST OUTER GATE—
AS QUICKLY AS POSSIBLE.
AND NO KILLING THEM ALONG THE WAY, GOT IT?
WHAT? OH, OF COURSE NOT!
WORK NOW, PLAY LATER...
...AND NO MAIMING THEM, EITHER.
COMPLETELY UNHARMED, UNDERSTAND?
YES, YES, FINE, THEN. OFF THEY GO!
KA-THUNK!
WHAT HAVE YOU DONE?!
DONE? OH, YES—THIS CHUTE WILL TAKE THEM DIRECTLY TO... UM... AH, THE GATE OF CHIMES.
OH. GOOD, THEN. ONCE THEY'RE OUT OF THE CASTLE—
WHAT? OUT OF—? OH, BUT I THOUGHT YOU WANTED THEM UNHARMED?
I TOLD YOU—
NO! NOT IN THE FACING! IT'S JUST THAT, ONCE THEY LEAVE MY PROTECTION, THEY WILL FACE ALL OF OUR ATTACKERS.
WITH MY REMAINING STRENGTH IT IS DIFFICULT ENOUGH KEEPING THEM AWAY.
REMAINING—THEN—THEN JUST DON'T LET GIL LEAVE!
ERM—THE GATE OF CHIMES IS STILL ONE OF MY DEAD AREAS...
I AM SORRY I'M DISTRACTED, MY LADY, BUT I AM RUNNING OUT OF POWER.
I HAVE TO USE IT FOR DEFENSE—
OH, BOTHER—THERE GOES THE TOWER OF GREEN BONE...
OH, NO!
HURRY!

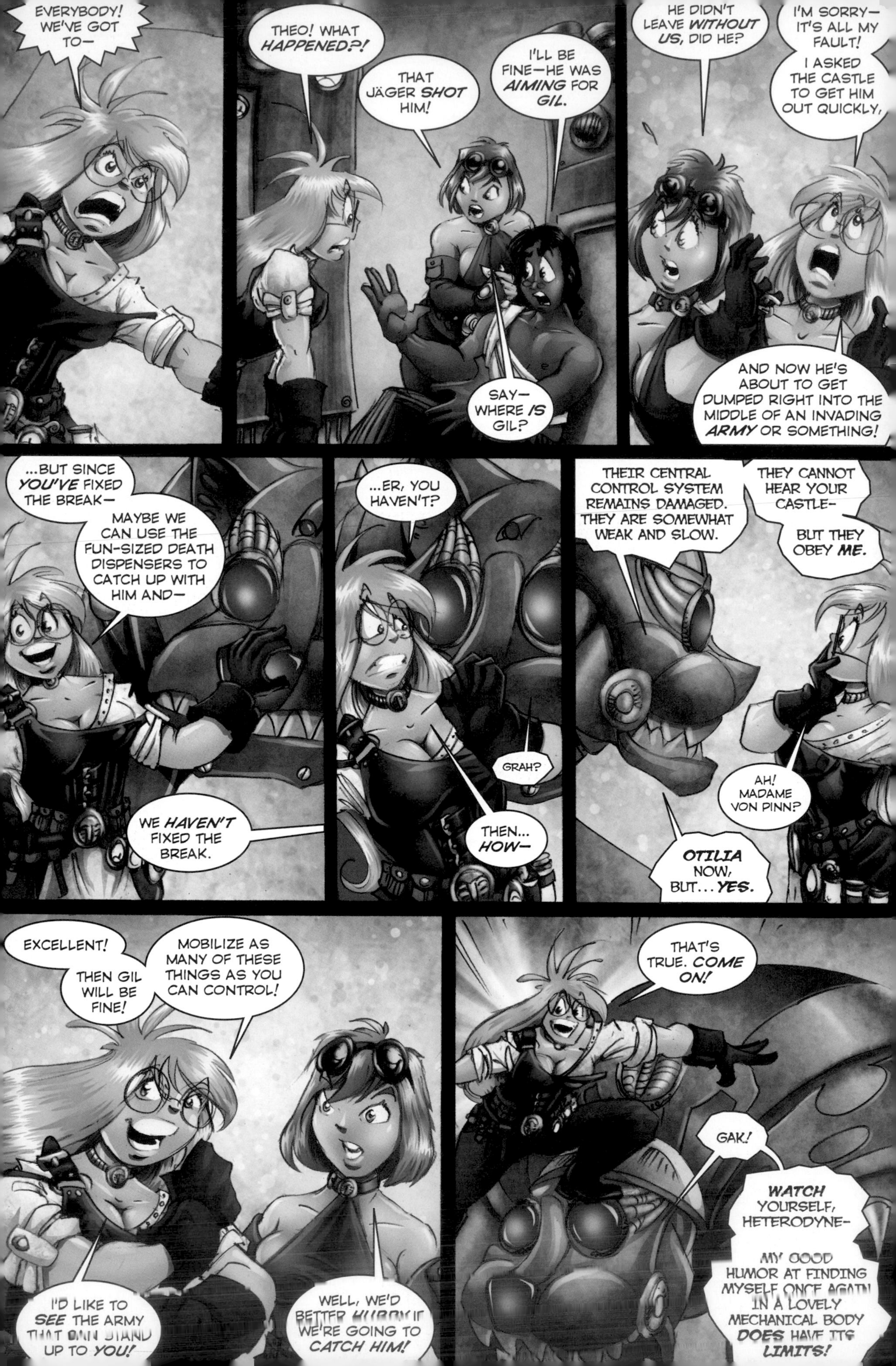
EVERYBODY! WE'VE GOT TO—
THEO! WHAT HAPPENED?!
THAT JÄGER SHOT HIM!
I'LL BE FINE—HE WAS AIMING FOR GIL.
SAY—WHERE IS GIL?
HE DIDN'T LEAVE WITHOUT US, DID HE?
I'M SORRY—IT'S ALL MY FAULT!
I ASKED THE CASTLE TO GET HIM OUT QUICKLY,
AND NOW HE'S ABOUT TO GET DUMPED RIGHT INTO THE MIDDLE OF AN INVADING ARMY OR SOMETHING!
...BUT SINCE YOU'VE FIXED THE BREAK—
MAYBE WE CAN USE THE FUN-SIZED DEATH DISPENSERS TO CATCH UP WITH HIM AND—
WE HAVEN'T FIXED THE BREAK.
...ER, YOU HAVEN'T?
GRAH?
THEN... HOW—
THEIR CENTRAL CONTROL SYSTEM REMAINS DAMAGED. THEY ARE SOMEWHAT WEAK AND SLOW.
THEY CANNOT HEAR YOUR CASTLE—
BUT THEY OBEY ME.
AH! MADAME VON PINN?
OTILIA NOW, BUT... YES.
EXCELLENT!
THEN GIL WILL BE FINE!
MOBILIZE AS MANY OF THESE THINGS AS YOU CAN CONTROL!
I'D LIKE TO SEE THE ARMY THAT CAN STAND UP TO YOU!
WELL, WE'D BETTER HURRY IF WE'RE GOING TO CATCH HIM!
THAT'S TRUE. COME ON!
GAK!
WATCH YOURSELF, HETERODYNE—
MY GOOD HUMOR AT FINDING MYSELF ONCE AGAIN IN A LOVELY MECHANICAL BODY DOES HAVE ITS LIMITS!

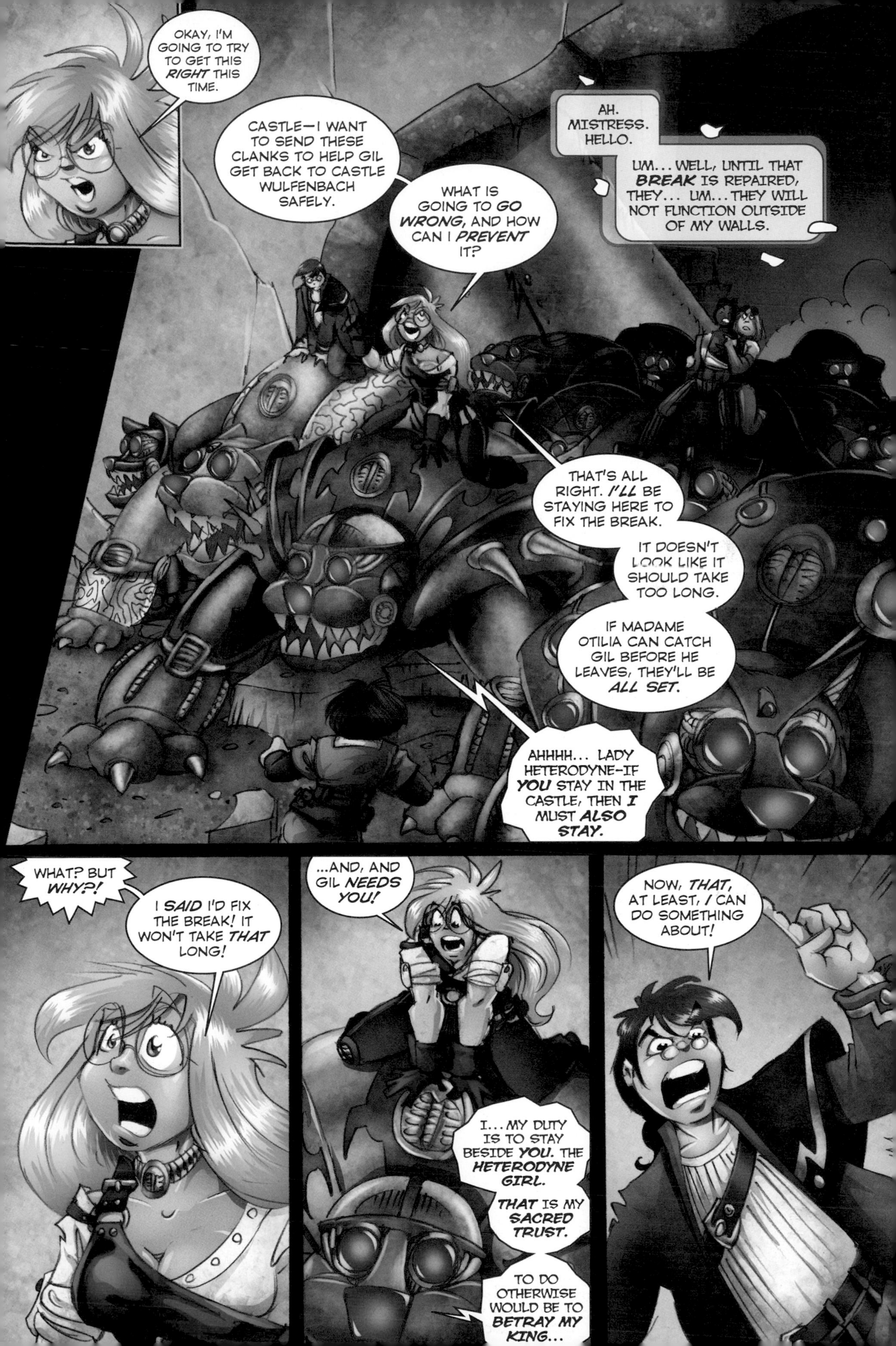

OKAY, I'M GOING TO TRY TO GET THIS RIGHT THIS TIME.
CASTLE—I WANT TO SEND THESE CLANKS TO HELP GIL GET BACK TO CASTLE WULFENBACH SAFELY.
WHAT IS GOING TO GO WRONG, AND HOW CAN I PREVENT IT?
AH. MISTRESS. HELLO.
UM... WELL, UNTIL THAT BREAK IS REPAIRED, THEY... UM... THEY WILL NOT FUNCTION OUTSIDE OF MY WALLS.
THAT'S ALL RIGHT. I'LL BE STAYING HERE TO FIX THE BREAK.
IT DOESN'T LOOK LIKE IT SHOULD TAKE TOO LONG.
IF MADAME OTILIA CAN CATCH GIL BEFORE HE LEAVES, THEY'LL BE ALL SET.
AHHHH... LADY HETERODYNE-IF YOU STAY IN THE CASTLE, THEN I MUST ALSO STAY.
WHAT? BUT WHY?!
I SAID I'D FIX THE BREAK! IT WON'T TAKE THAT LONG!
...AND, AND GIL NEEDS YOU!
I... MY DUTY IS TO STAY BESIDE YOU. THE HETERODYNE GIRL.
THAT IS MY SACRED TRUST.
TO DO OTHERWISE WOULD BE TO BETRAY MY KING...
NOW, THAT, AT LEAST, I CAN DO SOMETHING ABOUT!

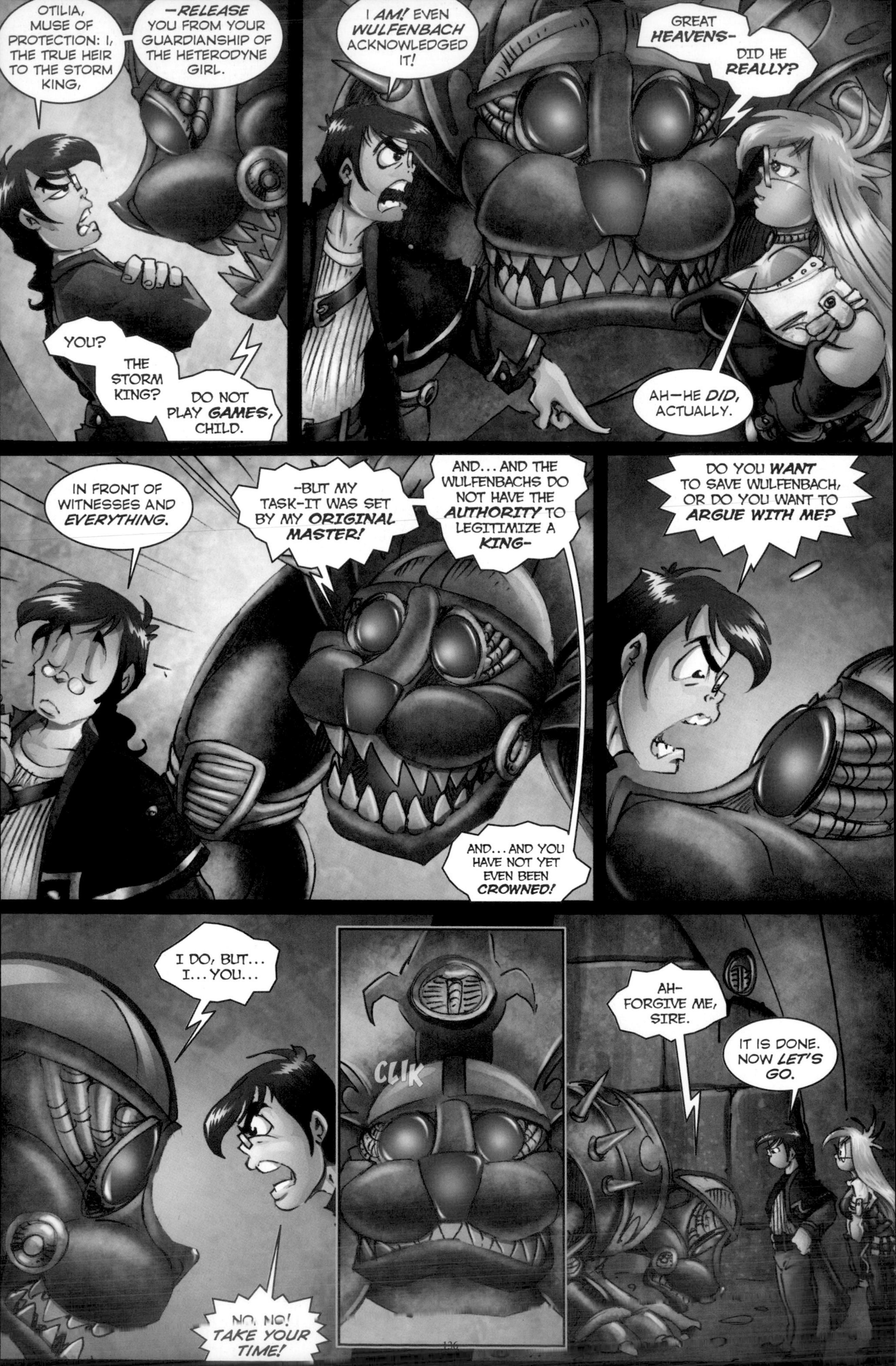
OTILIA, MUSE OF PROTECTION: I, THE TRUE HEIR TO THE STORM KING,
—RELEASE YOU FROM YOUR GUARDIANSHIP OF THE HETERODYNE GIRL.
YOU?
THE STORM KING?
DO NOT PLAY GAMES, CHILD.
I AM! EVEN WULFENBACH ACKNOWLEDGED IT!
GREAT HEAVENS-
DID HE REALLY?
AH—HE DID, ACTUALLY.
IN FRONT OF WITNESSES AND EVERYTHING.
-BUT MY TASK-IT WAS SET BY MY ORIGINAL MASTER!
AND... AND THE WULFENBACHS DO NOT HAVE THE AUTHORITY TO LEGITIMIZE A KING-
AND... AND YOU HAVE NOT YET EVEN BEEN CROWNED!
DO YOU WANT TO SAVE WULFENBACH, OR DO YOU WANT TO ARGUE WITH ME?
I DO, BUT... I... YOU...
NO, NO! TAKE YOUR TIME!
CLIK
AH- FORGIVE ME, SIRE.
IT IS DONE. NOW LET'S GO.

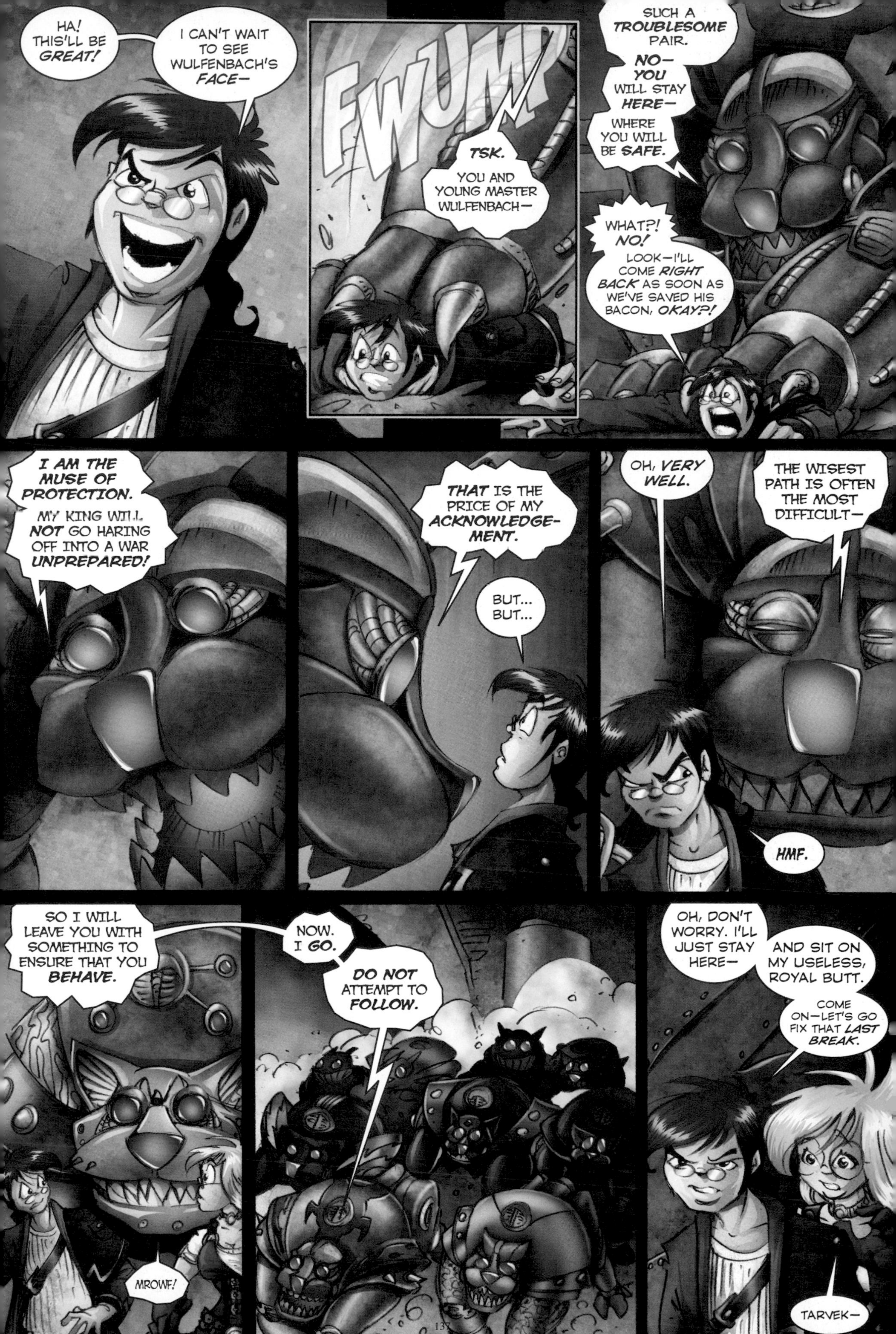
HA! THIS'LL BE GREAT!
I CAN'T WAIT TO SEE WULFENBACH'S FACE—
FWUMP
TSK.
YOU AND YOUNG MASTER WULFENBACH—
SUCH A TROUBLESOME PAIR.
NO— YOU WILL STAY HERE—
WHERE YOU WILL BE SAFE.
WHAT?! NO!
LOOK—I'LL COME RIGHT BACK AS SOON AS WE'VE SAVED HIS BACON, OKAY?!
I AM THE MUSE OF PROTECTION.
MY KING WILL NOT GO HARING OFF INTO A WAR UNPREPARED!
THAT IS THE PRICE OF MY ACKNOWLEDGE-MENT.
BUT... BUT...
OH, VERY WELL.
THE WISEST PATH IS OFTEN THE MOST DIFFICULT—
HMF.
SO I WILL LEAVE YOU WITH SOMETHING TO ENSURE THAT YOU BEHAVE.
MROWF!
NOW. I GO.
DO NOT ATTEMPT TO FOLLOW.
OH, DON'T WORRY. I'LL JUST STAY HERE—
AND SIT ON MY USELESS, ROYAL BUTT.
COME ON—LET'S GO FIX THAT LAST BREAK.
TARVEK—

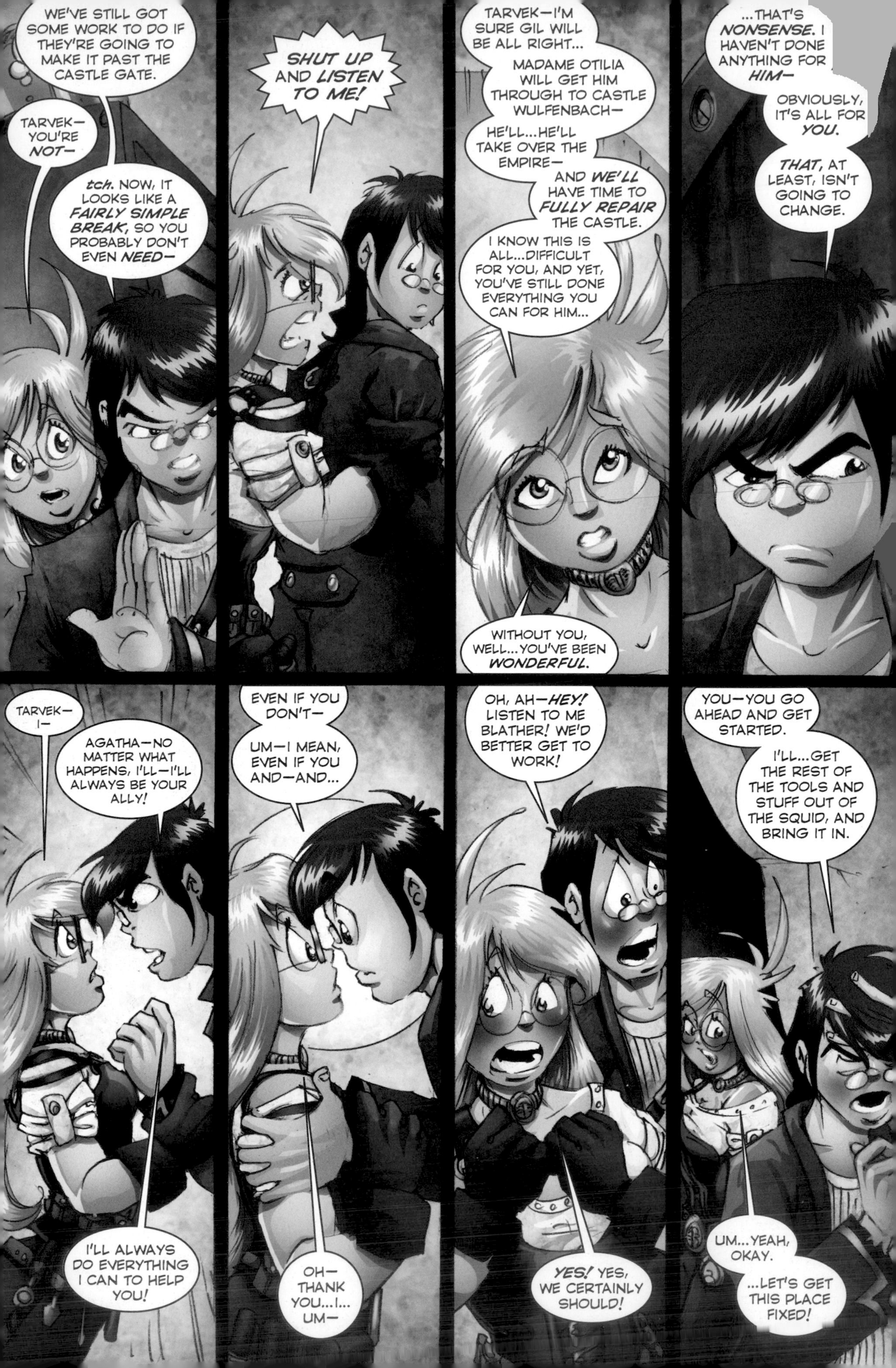
WE'VE STILL GOT SOME WORK TO DO IF THEY'RE GOING TO MAKE IT PAST THE CASTLE GATE.
TARVEK— YOU'RE NOT—
tch. NOW, IT LOOKS LIKE A FAIRLY SIMPLE BREAK, SO YOU PROBABLY DON'T EVEN NEED—
SHUT UP AND LISTEN TO ME!
TARVEK—I'M SURE GIL WILL BE ALL RIGHT...
MADAME OTILIA WILL GET HIM THROUGH TO CASTLE WULFENBACH—
HE'LL...HE'LL TAKE OVER THE EMPIRE—
AND WE'LL HAVE TIME TO FULLY REPAIR THE CASTLE.
I KNOW THIS IS ALL...DIFFICULT FOR YOU, AND YET, YOU'VE STILL DONE EVERYTHING YOU CAN FOR HIM...
WITHOUT YOU, WELL...YOU'VE BEEN WONDERFUL.
...THAT'S NONSENSE. I HAVEN'T DONE ANYTHING FOR HIM—
OBVIOUSLY, IT'S ALL FOR YOU.
THAT, AT LEAST, ISN'T GOING TO CHANGE.
TARVEK— I—
AGATHA—NO MATTER WHAT HAPPENS, I'LL—I'LL ALWAYS BE YOUR ALLY!
I'LL ALWAYS DO EVERYTHING I CAN TO HELP YOU!
EVEN IF YOU DON'T—
UM—I MEAN, EVEN IF YOU AND—AND...
OH— THANK YOU...I... UM—
OH, AH—HEY! LISTEN TO ME BLATHER! WE'D BETTER GET TO WORK!
YES! YES, WE CERTAINLY SHOULD!
YOU—YOU GO AHEAD AND GET STARTED.
I'LL...GET THE REST OF THE TOOLS AND STUFF OUT OF THE SQUID, AND BRING IT IN.
UM...YEAH, OKAY.
...LET'S GET THIS PLACE FIXED!

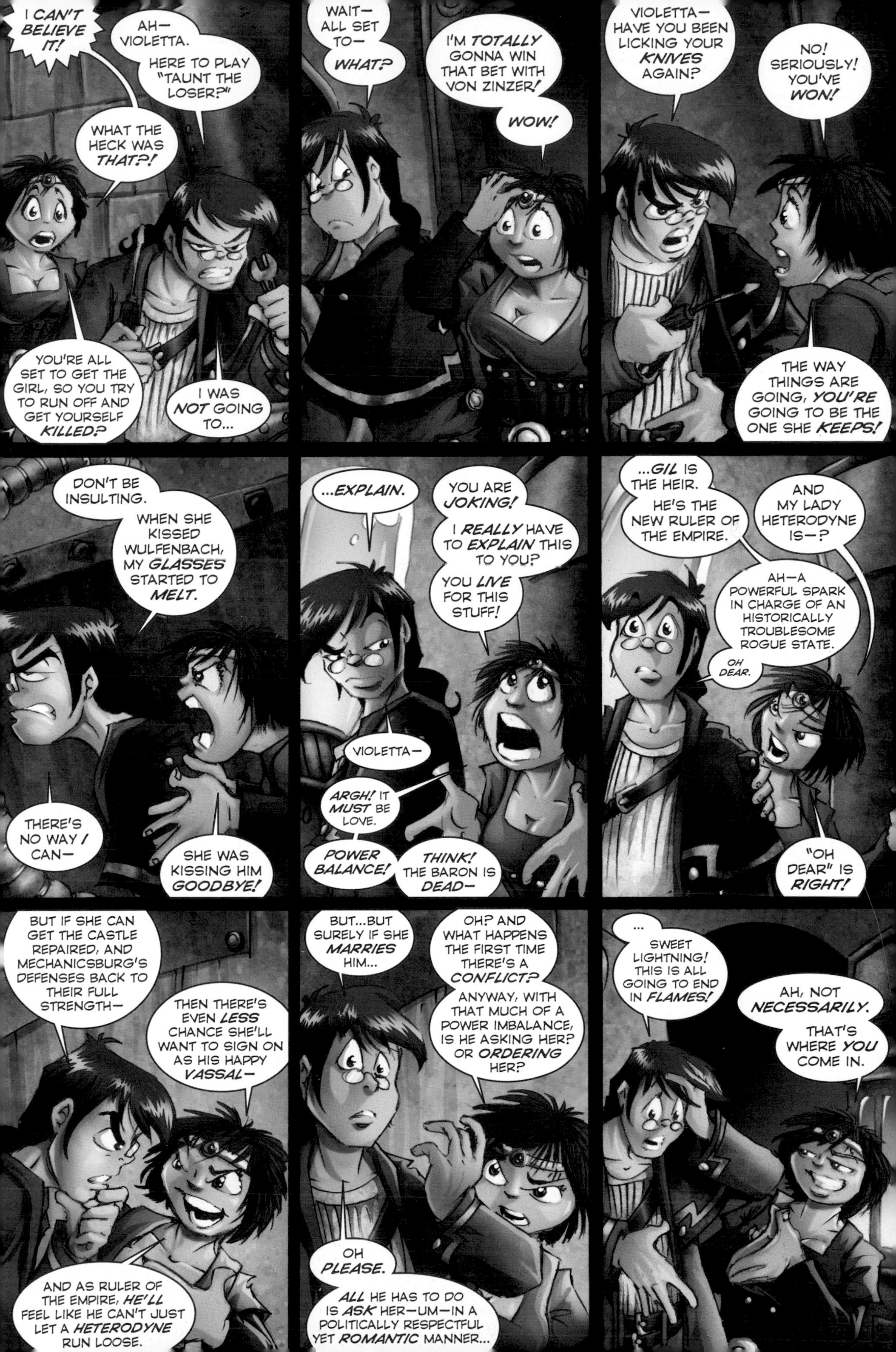
I CAN'T BELIEVE IT!
AH—VIOLETTA.
HERE TO PLAY "TAUNT THE LOSER?"
WHAT THE HECK WAS THAT?!
YOU'RE ALL SET TO GET THE GIRL, SO YOU TRY TO RUN OFF AND GET YOURSELF KILLED?
I WAS NOT GOING TO...
WAIT—ALL SET TO—
WHAT?
I'M TOTALLY GONNA WIN THAT BET WITH VON ZINZER!
WOW!
VIOLETTA—HAVE YOU BEEN LICKING YOUR KNIVES AGAIN?
NO! SERIOUSLY! YOU'VE WON!
THE WAY THINGS ARE GOING, YOU'RE GOING TO BE THE ONE SHE KEEPS!
DON'T BE INSULTING.
WHEN SHE KISSED WULFENBACH, MY GLASSES STARTED TO MELT.
THERE'S NO WAY I CAN—
SHE WAS KISSING HIM GOODBYE!
...EXPLAIN.
YOU ARE JOKING!
I REALLY HAVE TO EXPLAIN THIS TO YOU?
YOU LIVE FOR THIS STUFF!
VIOLETTA—
ARGH! IT MUST BE LOVE.
POWER BALANCE!
THINK! THE BARON IS DEAD—
...GIL IS THE HEIR.
HE'S THE NEW RULER OF THE EMPIRE.
AND MY LADY HETERODYNE IS—?
AH—A POWERFUL SPARK IN CHARGE OF AN HISTORICALLY TROUBLESOME ROGUE STATE.
OH DEAR.
"OH DEAR" IS RIGHT!
BUT IF SHE CAN GET THE CASTLE REPAIRED, AND MECHANICSBURG'S DEFENSES BACK TO THEIR FULL STRENGTH—
THEN THERE'S EVEN LESS CHANCE SHE'LL WANT TO SIGN ON AS HIS HAPPY VASSAL—
AND AS RULER OF THE EMPIRE, HE'LL FEEL LIKE HE CAN'T JUST LET A HETERODYNE RUN LOOSE.
BUT...BUT SURELY IF SHE MARRIES HIM...
OH? AND WHAT HAPPENS THE FIRST TIME THERE'S A CONFLICT?
ANYWAY, WITH THAT MUCH OF A POWER IMBALANCE, IS HE ASKING HER? OR ORDERING HER?
OH PLEASE.
ALL HE HAS TO DO IS ASK HER—UM—IN A POLITICALLY RESPECTFUL YET ROMANTIC MANNER...
...
SWEET LIGHTNING! THIS IS ALL GOING TO END IN FLAMES!
AH, NOT NECESSARILY.
THAT'S WHERE YOU COME IN.

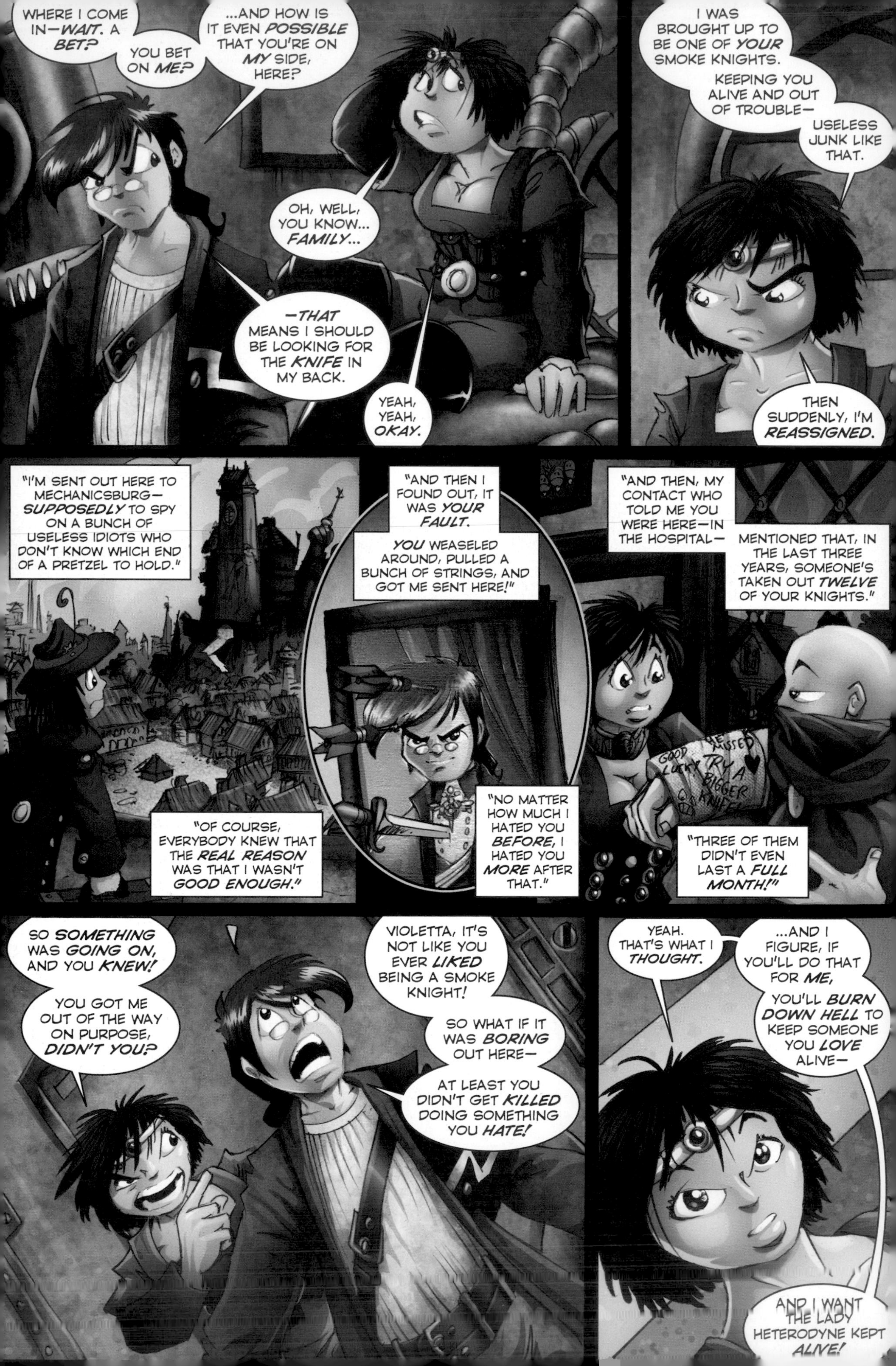

WHERE I COME IN—WAIT. A BET?
YOU BET ON ME?
...AND HOW IS IT EVEN POSSIBLE THAT YOU'RE ON MY SIDE, HERE?
OH, WELL, YOU KNOW... FAMILY...
—THAT MEANS I SHOULD BE LOOKING FOR THE KNIFE IN MY BACK.
YEAH, YEAH, OKAY.
I WAS BROUGHT UP TO BE ONE OF YOUR SMOKE KNIGHTS.
KEEPING YOU ALIVE AND OUT OF TROUBLE—
USELESS JUNK LIKE THAT.
THEN SUDDENLY, I'M REASSIGNED.
"I'M SENT OUT HERE TO MECHANICSBURG—SUPPOSEDLY TO SPY ON A BUNCH OF USELESS IDIOTS WHO DON'T KNOW WHICH END OF A PRETZEL TO HOLD."
"OF COURSE, EVERYBODY KNEW THAT THE REAL REASON WAS THAT I WASN'T GOOD ENOUGH."
"AND THEN I FOUND OUT, IT WAS YOUR FAULT.
YOU WEASELED AROUND, PULLED A BUNCH OF STRINGS, AND GOT ME SENT HERE!"
"NO MATTER HOW MUCH I HATED YOU BEFORE, I HATED YOU MORE AFTER THAT."
"AND THEN, MY CONTACT WHO TOLD ME YOU WERE HERE—IN THE HOSPITAL—
MENTIONED THAT, IN THE LAST THREE YEARS, SOMEONE'S TAKEN OUT TWELVE OF YOUR KNIGHTS."
GOOD LUCK
HE MISSED
TRY A BIGGER KNIFE
"THREE OF THEM DIDN'T EVEN LAST A FULL MONTH!"
SO SOMETHING WAS GOING ON, AND YOU KNEW!
YOU GOT ME OUT OF THE WAY ON PURPOSE, DIDN'T YOU?
VIOLETTA, IT'S NOT LIKE YOU EVER LIKED BEING A SMOKE KNIGHT!
SO WHAT IF IT WAS BORING OUT HERE—
AT LEAST YOU DIDN'T GET KILLED DOING SOMETHING YOU HATE!
YEAH. THAT'S WHAT I THOUGHT.
...AND I FIGURE, IF YOU'LL DO THAT FOR ME,
YOU'LL BURN DOWN HELL TO KEEP SOMEONE YOU LOVE ALIVE—
AND I WANT THE LADY HETERODYNE KEPT ALIVE!

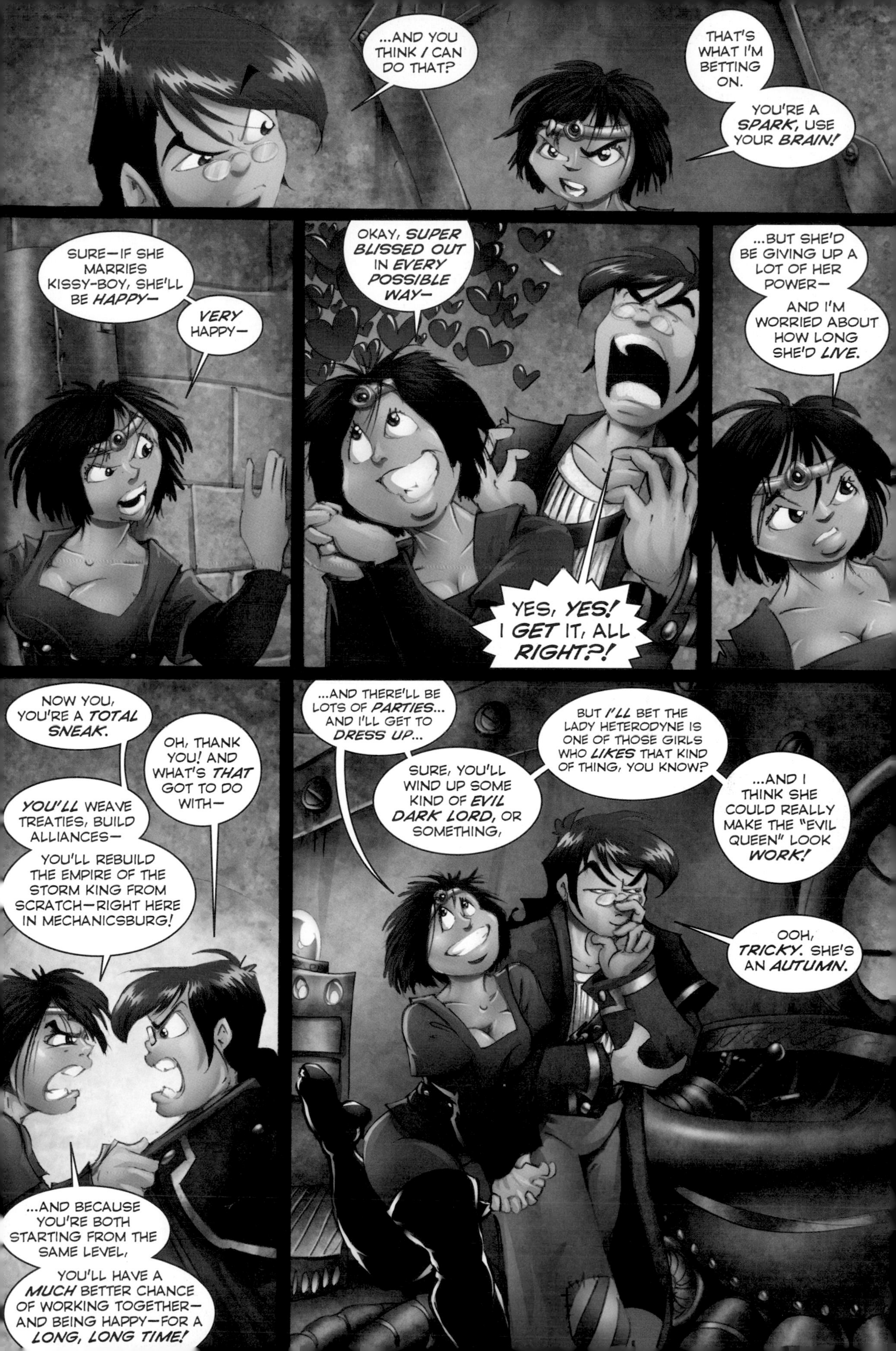
...AND YOU THINK I CAN DO THAT?
THAT'S WHAT I'M BETTING ON.
YOU'RE A SPARK, USE YOUR BRAIN!
SURE—IF SHE MARRIES KISSY-BOY, SHE'LL BE HAPPY—
VERY HAPPY—
OKAY, SUPER BLISSED OUT IN EVERY POSSIBLE WAY—
YES, YES! I GET IT, ALL RIGHT?!
...BUT SHE'D BE GIVING UP A LOT OF HER POWER—
AND I'M WORRIED ABOUT HOW LONG SHE'D LIVE.
NOW YOU, YOU'RE A TOTAL SNEAK.
OH, THANK YOU! AND WHAT'S THAT GOT TO DO WITH—
YOU'LL WEAVE TREATIES, BUILD ALLIANCES—
YOU'LL REBUILD THE EMPIRE OF THE STORM KING FROM SCRATCH—RIGHT HERE IN MECHANICSBURG!
...AND BECAUSE YOU'RE BOTH STARTING FROM THE SAME LEVEL,
YOU'LL HAVE A MUCH BETTER CHANCE OF WORKING TOGETHER—AND BEING HAPPY—FOR A LONG, LONG TIME!
...AND THERE'LL BE LOTS OF PARTIES... AND I'LL GET TO DRESS UP...
SURE, YOU'LL WIND UP SOME KIND OF EVIL DARK LORD, OR SOMETHING,
BUT I'LL BET THE LADY HETERODYNE IS ONE OF THOSE GIRLS WHO LIKES THAT KIND OF THING, YOU KNOW?
...AND I THINK SHE COULD REALLY MAKE THE "EVIL QUEEN" LOOK WORK!
OOH, TRICKY. SHE'S AN AUTUMN.

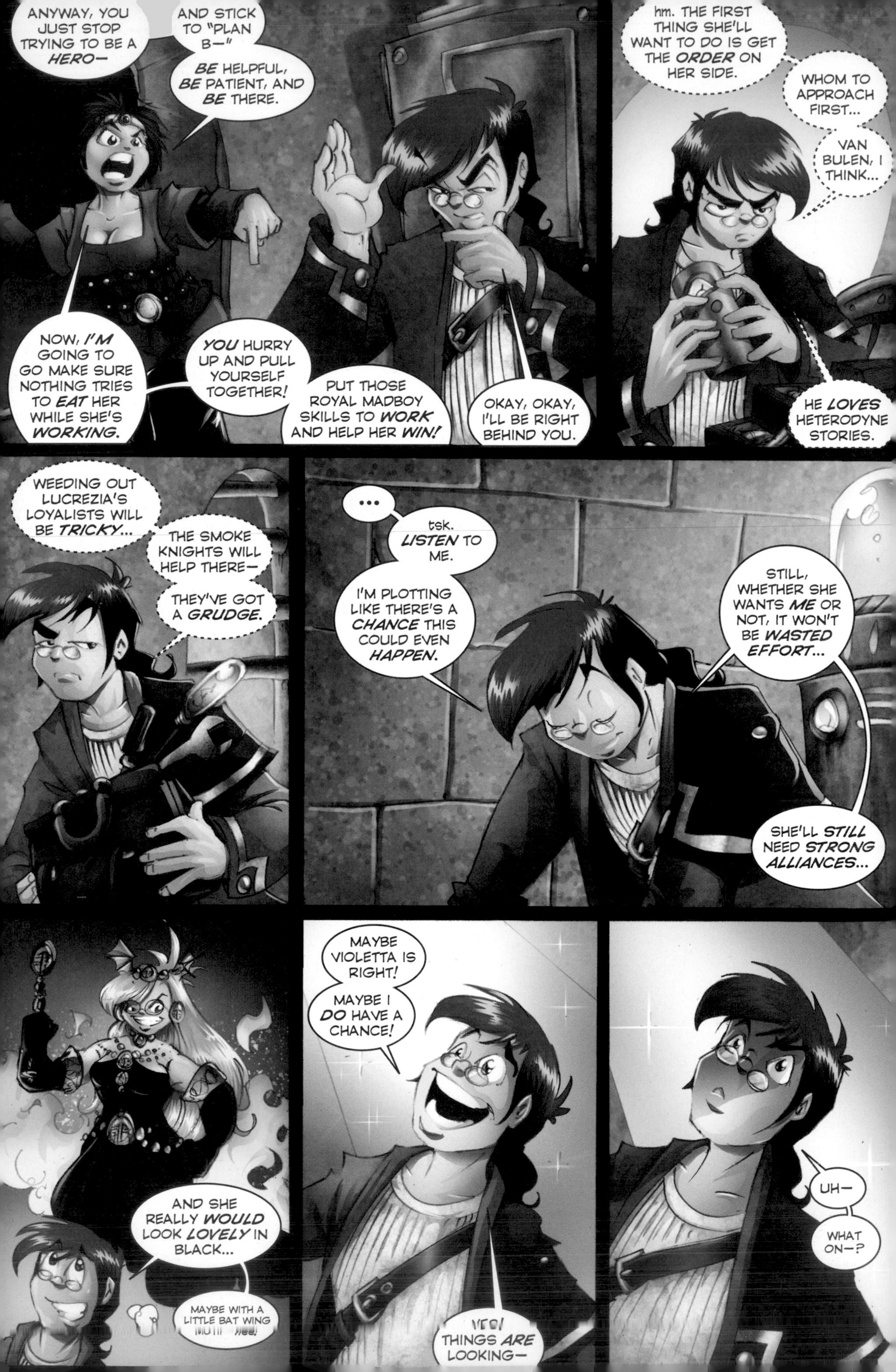
ANYWAY, YOU JUST STOP TRYING TO BE A HERO—
AND STICK TO "PLAN B—"
BE HELPFUL, BE PATIENT, AND BE THERE.
NOW, I'M GOING TO GO MAKE SURE NOTHING TRIES TO EAT HER WHILE SHE'S WORKING.
YOU HURRY UP AND PULL YOURSELF TOGETHER!
PUT THOSE ROYAL MADBOY SKILLS TO WORK AND HELP HER WIN!
OKAY, OKAY, I'LL BE RIGHT BEHIND YOU.
hm. THE FIRST THING SHE'LL WANT TO DO IS GET THE ORDER ON HER SIDE.
WHOM TO APPROACH FIRST...
VAN BULEN, I THINK...
HE LOVES HETERODYNE STORIES.
WEEDING OUT LUCREZIA'S LOYALISTS WILL BE TRICKY...
THE SMOKE KNIGHTS WILL HELP THERE—
THEY'VE GOT A GRUDGE.
...
tsk. LISTEN TO ME.
I'M PLOTTING LIKE THERE'S A CHANCE THIS COULD EVEN HAPPEN.
STILL, WHETHER SHE WANTS ME OR NOT, IT WON'T BE WASTED EFFORT...
SHE'LL STILL NEED STRONG ALLIANCES...
AND SHE REALLY WOULD LOOK LOVELY IN BLACK...
MAYBE WITH A LITTLE BAT WING
MAYBE VIOLETTA IS RIGHT!
MAYBE I DO HAVE A CHANCE!
THINGS ARE LOOKING—
UH—
WHAT ON—?

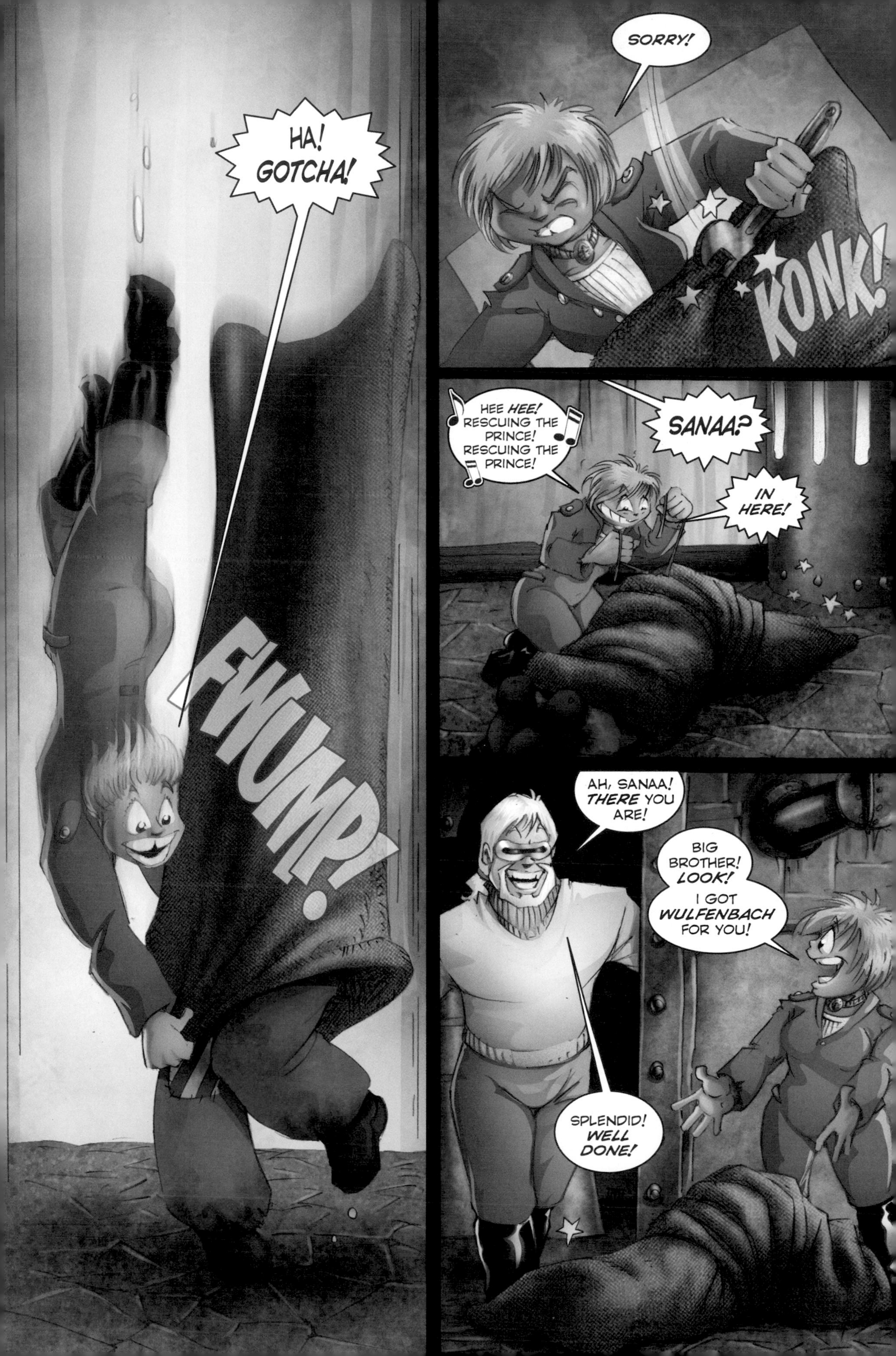
HA! GOTCHA!
FWUMP!
SORRY!
KONK!
SANAA?
IN HERE!
HEE HEE! RESCUING THE PRINCE! RESCUING THE PRINCE!
AH, SANAA! THERE YOU ARE!
BIG BROTHER! LOOK!
I GOT WULFENBACH FOR YOU!
SPLENDID! WELL DONE!

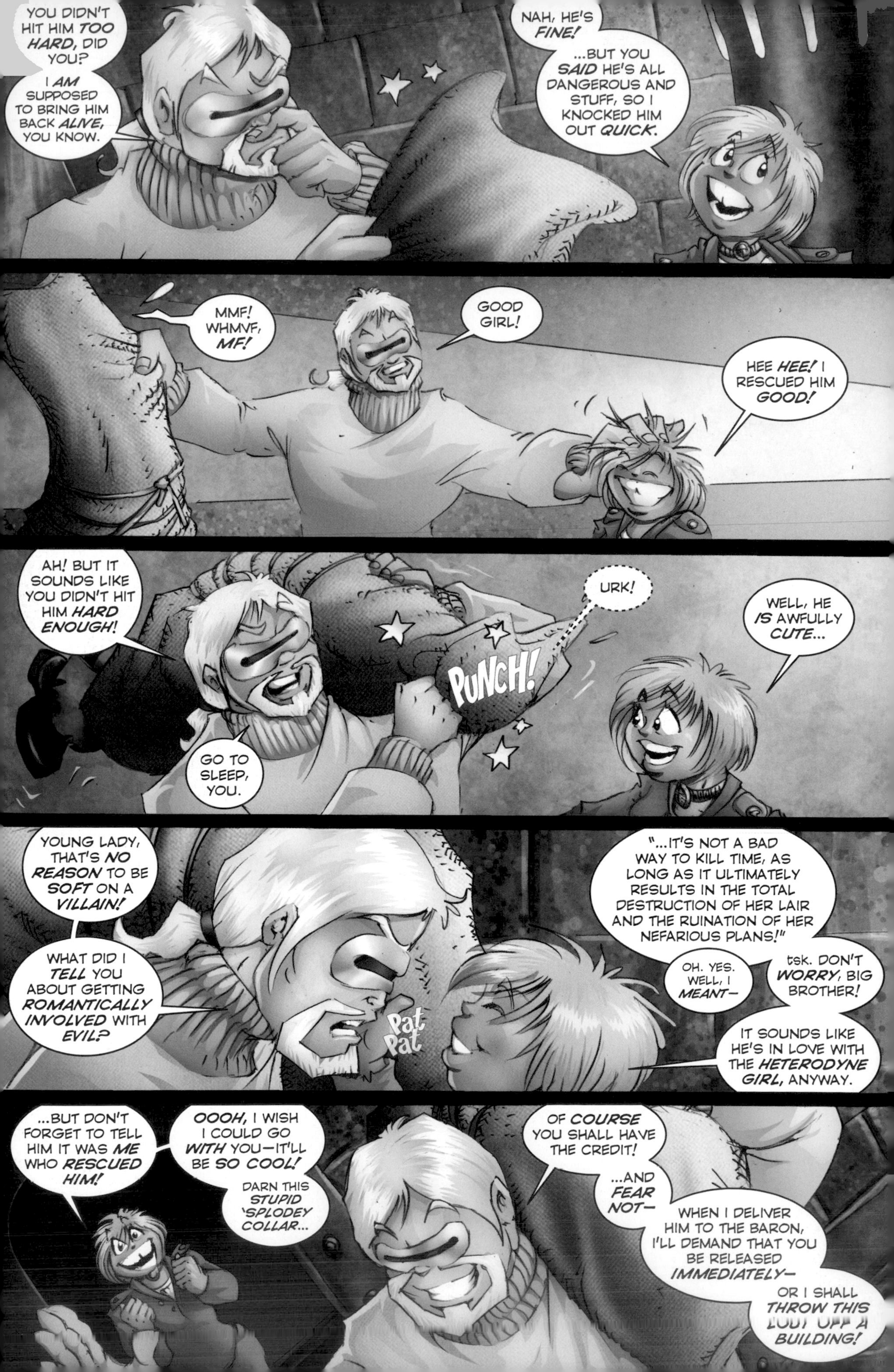
YOU DIDN'T HIT HIM TOO HARD, DID YOU?
I AM SUPPOSED TO BRING HIM BACK ALIVE, YOU KNOW.
NAH, HE'S FINE!
...BUT YOU SAID HE'S ALL DANGEROUS AND STUFF, SO I KNOCKED HIM OUT QUICK.
MMF! WHMVF, MF!
GOOD GIRL!
HEE HEE! I RESCUED HIM GOOD!
AH! BUT IT SOUNDS LIKE YOU DIDN'T HIT HIM HARD ENOUGH!
URK!
PUNCH!
GO TO SLEEP, YOU.
WELL, HE IS AWFULLY CUTE...
YOUNG LADY, THAT'S NO REASON TO BE SOFT ON A VILLAIN!
WHAT DID I TELL YOU ABOUT GETTING ROMANTICALLY INVOLVED WITH EVIL?
PAT PAT
"...IT'S NOT A BAD WAY TO KILL TIME, AS LONG AS IT ULTIMATELY RESULTS IN THE TOTAL DESTRUCTION OF HER LAIR AND THE RUINATION OF HER NEFARIOUS PLANS!"
OH. YES. WELL, I MEANT—
tsk. DON'T WORRY, BIG BROTHER!
IT SOUNDS LIKE HE'S IN LOVE WITH THE HETERODYNE GIRL, ANYWAY.
...BUT DON'T FORGET TO TELL HIM IT WAS ME WHO RESCUED HIM!
OOOH, I WISH I COULD GO WITH YOU—IT'LL BE SO COOL!
DARN THIS STUPID 'SPLODEY COLLAR...
OF COURSE YOU SHALL HAVE THE CREDIT!
...AND FEAR NOT—
WHEN I DELIVER HIM TO THE BARON, I'LL DEMAND THAT YOU BE RELEASED IMMEDIATELY—
OR I SHALL THROW THIS LOUT OFF A BUILDING!

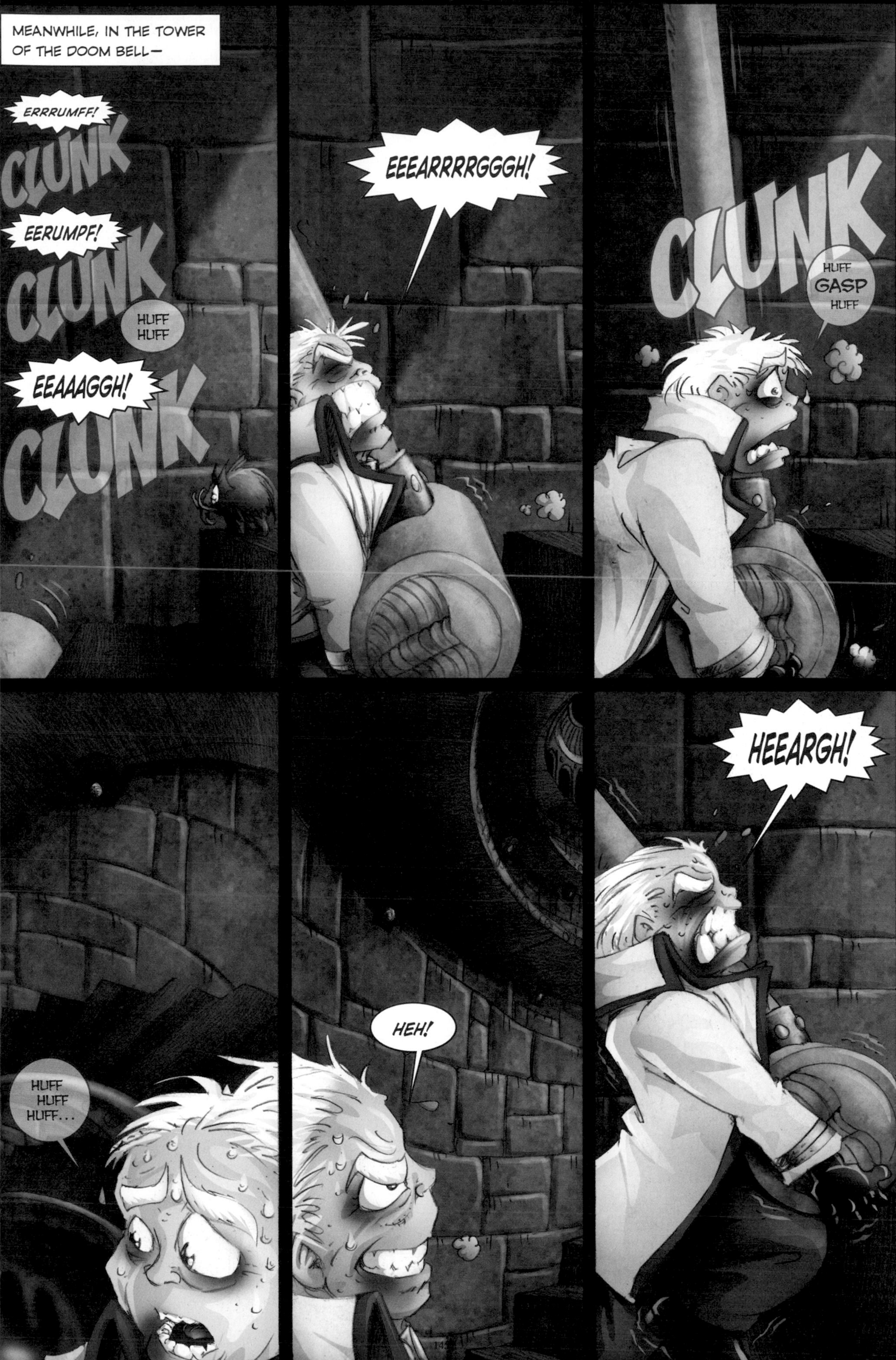
MEANWHILE, IN THE TOWER OF THE DOOM BELL—
ERRRUMFF!
CLUNK
EERUMPF!
CLUNK
HUFF HUFF
EEAAAGGH!
CLUNK
EEEARRRRGGGH!
CLUNK
HUFF GASP HUFF
HUFF HUFF HUFF...
HEH!
HEEARGH!

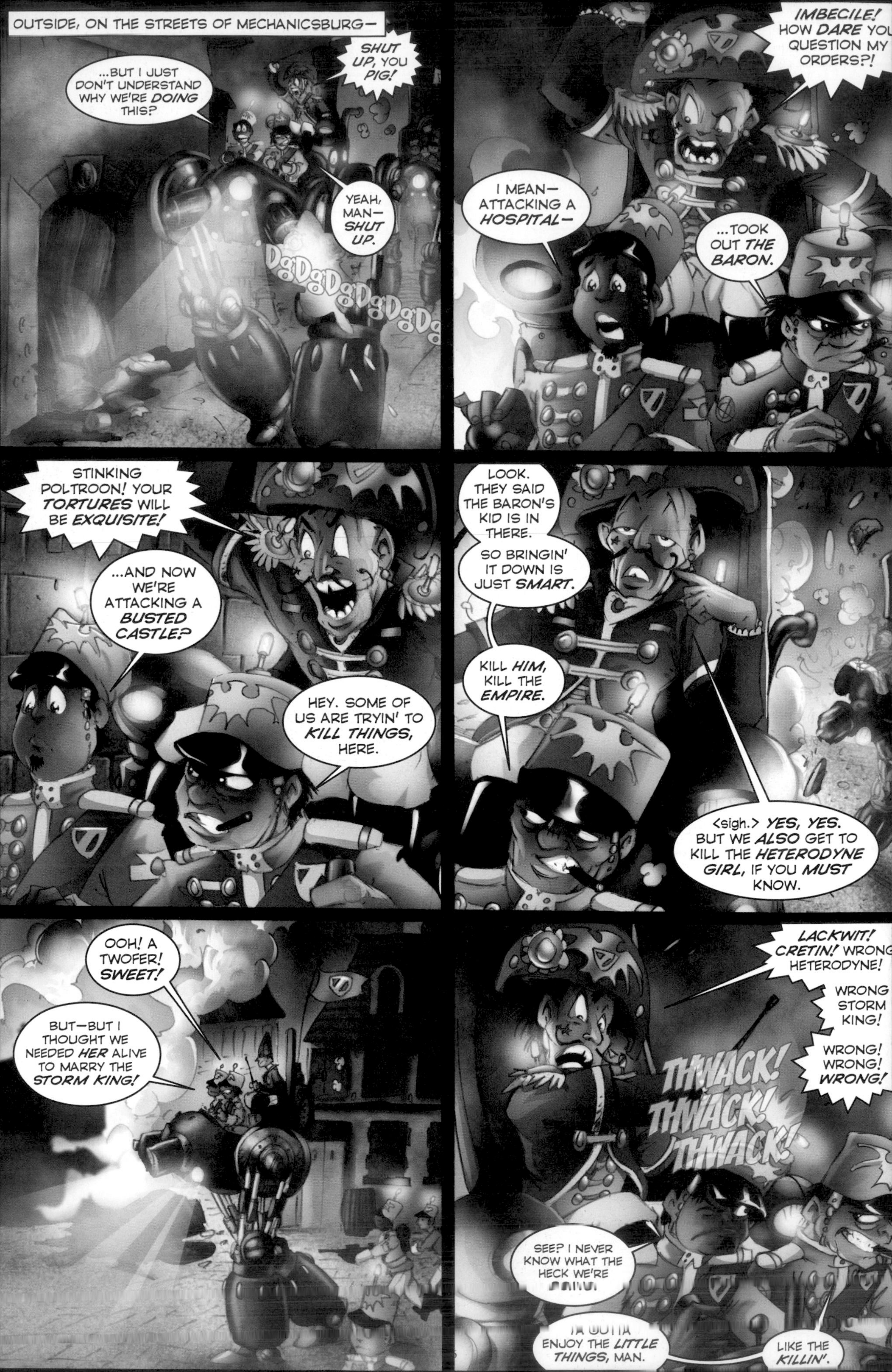
OUTSIDE, ON THE STREETS OF MECHANICSBURG—
...BUT I JUST DON'T UNDERSTAND WHY WE'RE *DOING* THIS?
SHUT UP, YOU *PIG!*
YEAH, MAN— *SHUT UP*.
DgDgDgDgDgDgDg
IMBECILE! HOW *DARE* YOU QUESTION MY ORDERS?!
I MEAN— ATTACKING A *HOSPITAL*—
...TOOK OUT *THE BARON*.
STINKING POLTROON! YOUR *TORTURES* WILL BE *EXQUISITE!*
...AND NOW WE'RE ATTACKING A *BUSTED CASTLE?*
HEY. SOME OF US ARE TRYIN' TO *KILL THINGS*, HERE.
LOOK. THEY SAID THE BARON'S KID IS IN THERE.
SO BRINGIN' IT DOWN IS JUST *SMART*.
KILL *HIM*, KILL THE *EMPIRE*.
<sigh.> *YES, YES.* BUT WE *ALSO* GET TO KILL THE *HETERODYNE GIRL*, IF YOU *MUST* KNOW.
OOH! A TWOFER! *SWEET!*
BUT—BUT I THOUGHT WE NEEDED *HER* ALIVE TO MARRY THE *STORM KING!*
LACKWIT! CRETIN! WRONG HETERODYNE!
WRONG STORM KING!
WRONG! WRONG! *WRONG!*
THWACK! THWACK! THWACK!
SEE? I NEVER KNOW WHAT THE HECK WE'RE
ENJOY THE *LITTLE THINGS*, MAN.
LIKE THE *KILLIN'*.

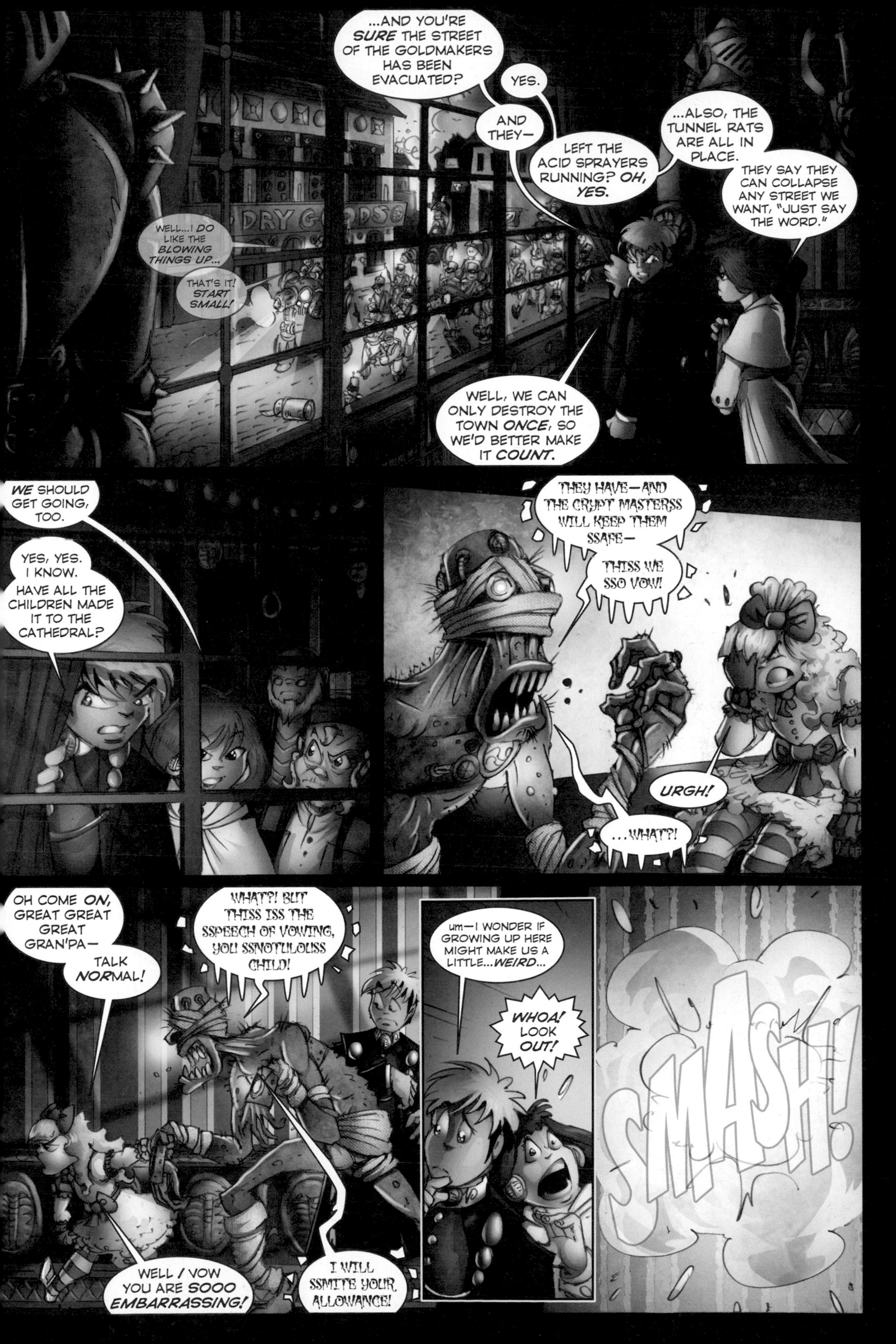
...AND YOU'RE SURE THE STREET OF THE GOLDMAKERS HAS BEEN EVACUATED?
YES.
AND THEY—
LEFT THE ACID SPRAYERS RUNNING? OH, YES.
...ALSO, THE TUNNEL RATS ARE ALL IN PLACE.
THEY SAY THEY CAN COLLAPSE ANY STREET WE WANT, "JUST SAY THE WORD."
DRY GOODS
WELL...I DO LIKE THE BLOWING THINGS UP...
THAT'S IT! START SMALL!
WELL, WE CAN ONLY DESTROY THE TOWN ONCE, SO WE'D BETTER MAKE IT COUNT.
WE SHOULD GET GOING, TOO.
YES, YES. I KNOW. HAVE ALL THE CHILDREN MADE IT TO THE CATHEDRAL?
THEY HAVE—AND THE CRYPT MASTERSS WILL KEEP THEM SSAFE—
THISS WE SSO VOW!
URGH!
...WHAT?!
OH COME ON, GREAT GREAT GREAT GRAN'PA—
TALK NORMAL!
WHAT?! BUT THISS ISS THE SSPEECH OF VOWING, YOU SSNOTULOUSS CHILD!
WELL I VOW YOU ARE SOOO EMBARRASSING!
I WILL SSMITE YOUR ALLOWANCE!
um—I WONDER IF GROWING UP HERE MIGHT MAKE US A LITTLE...WEIRD...
WHOA! LOOK OUT!
SMASH!

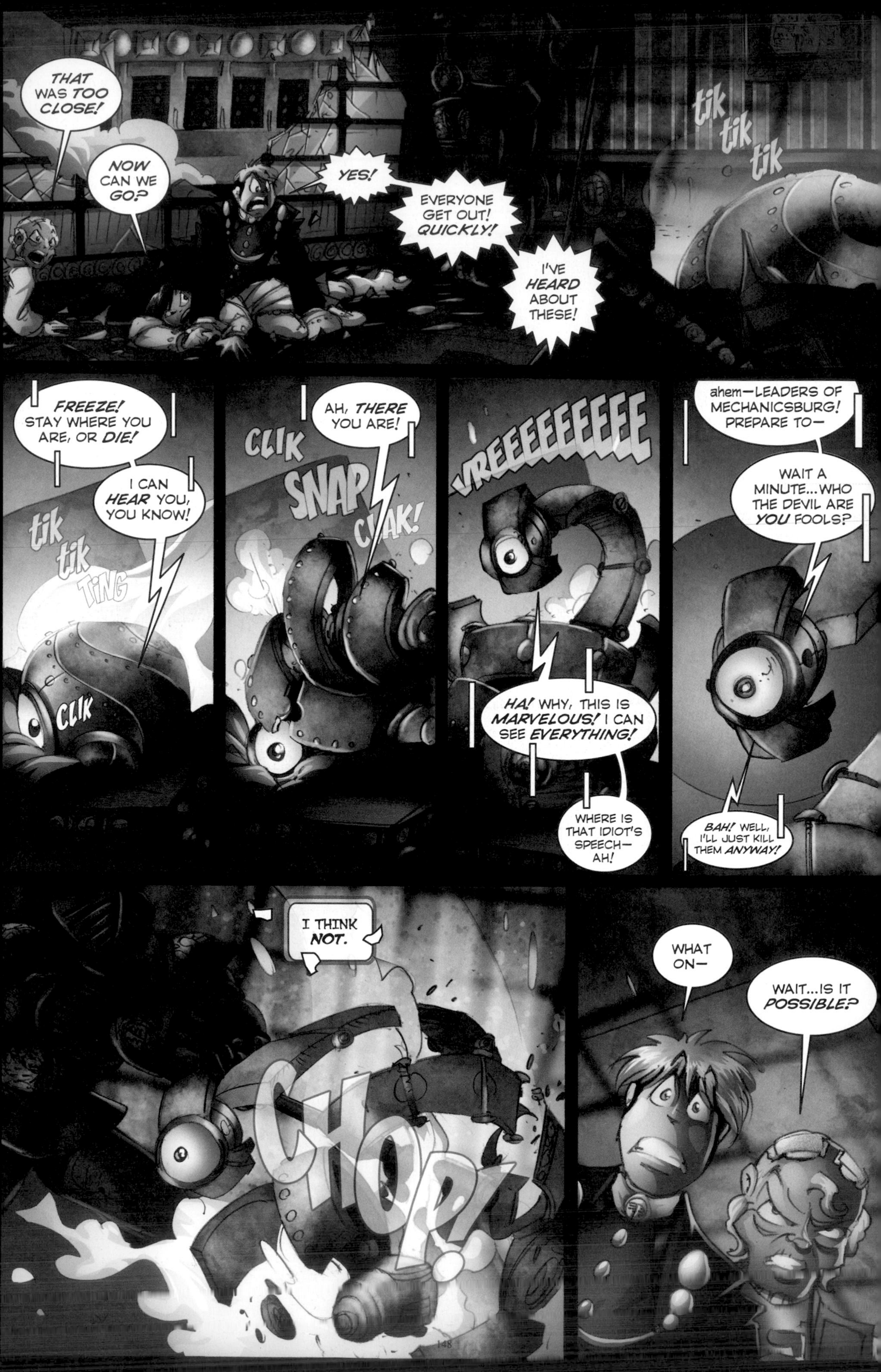
THAT WAS TOO CLOSE!
NOW CAN WE GO?
YES!
EVERYONE GET OUT! QUICKLY!
I'VE HEARD ABOUT THESE!
tik tik tik
FREEZE! STAY WHERE YOU ARE, OR DIE!
I CAN HEAR YOU, YOU KNOW!
tik tik TING
CLIK
AH, THERE YOU ARE!
CLIK
SNAP
CLAK!
VREEEEEEEEEE
HA! WHY, THIS IS MARVELOUS! I CAN SEE EVERYTHING!
WHERE IS THAT IDIOT'S SPEECH— AH!
ahem—LEADERS OF MECHANICSBURG! PREPARE TO—
WAIT A MINUTE...WHO THE DEVIL ARE YOU FOOLS?
BAH! WELL, I'LL JUST KILL THEM ANYWAY!
I THINK NOT.
CHOP!
WHAT ON—
WAIT...IS IT POSSIBLE?

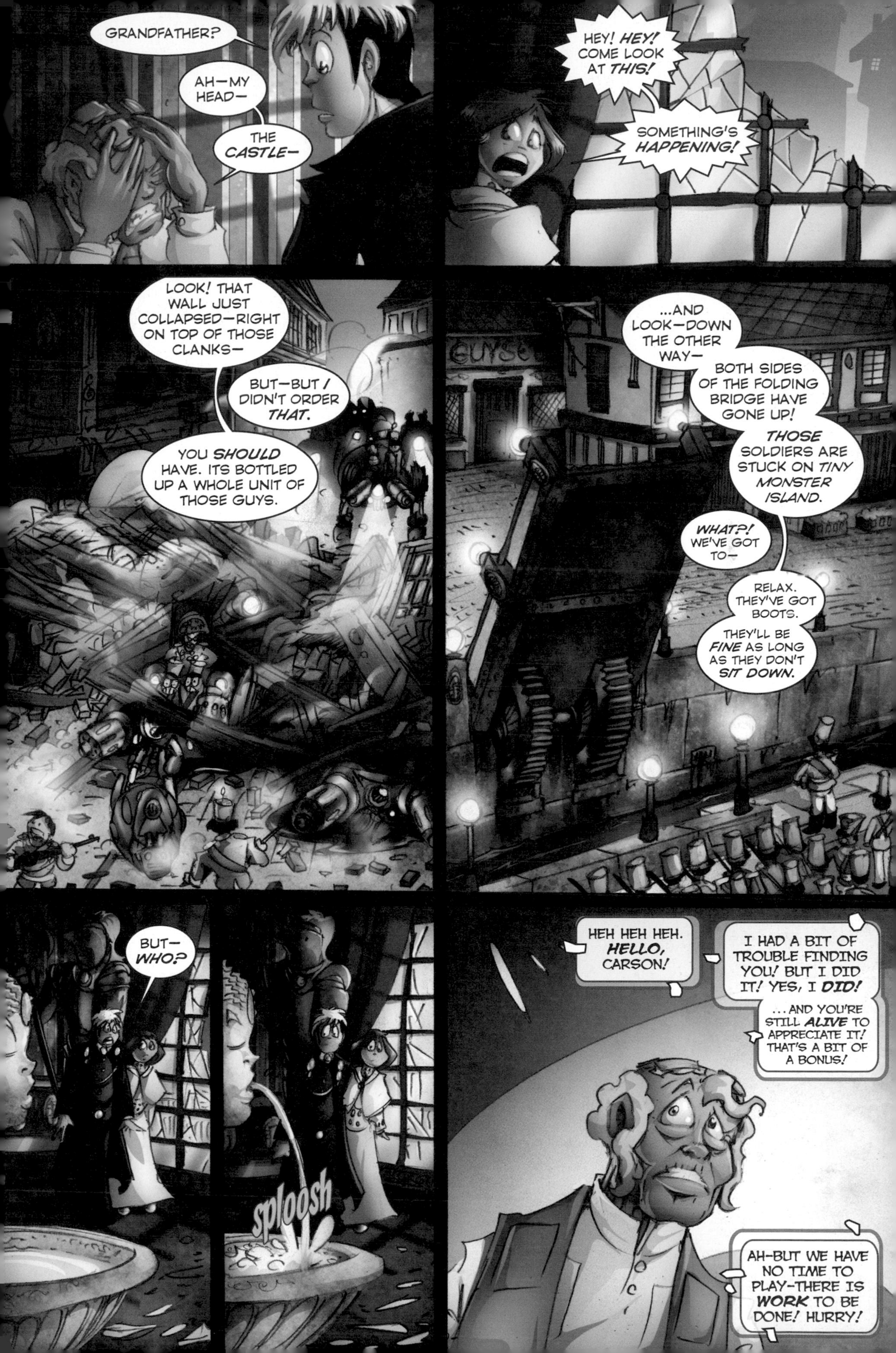
GRANDFATHER?
AH—MY HEAD—
THE CASTLE—
HEY! HEY! COME LOOK AT THIS!
SOMETHING'S HAPPENING!
LOOK! THAT WALL JUST COLLAPSED—RIGHT ON TOP OF THOSE CLANKS—
BUT—BUT I DIDN'T ORDER THAT.
YOU SHOULD HAVE. ITS BOTTLED UP A WHOLE UNIT OF THOSE GUYS.
...AND LOOK—DOWN THE OTHER WAY—
BOTH SIDES OF THE FOLDING BRIDGE HAVE GONE UP!
THOSE SOLDIERS ARE STUCK ON TINY MONSTER ISLAND.
WHAT?! WE'VE GOT TO—
RELAX. THEY'VE GOT BOOTS.
THEY'LL BE FINE AS LONG AS THEY DON'T SIT DOWN.
BUT— WHO?
sploosh
HEH HEH HEH. HELLO, CARSON!
I HAD A BIT OF TROUBLE FINDING YOU! BUT I DID IT! YES, I DID!
...AND YOU'RE STILL ALIVE TO APPRECIATE IT! THAT'S A BIT OF A BONUS!
AH-BUT WE HAVE NO TIME TO PLAY-THERE IS WORK TO BE DONE! HURRY!

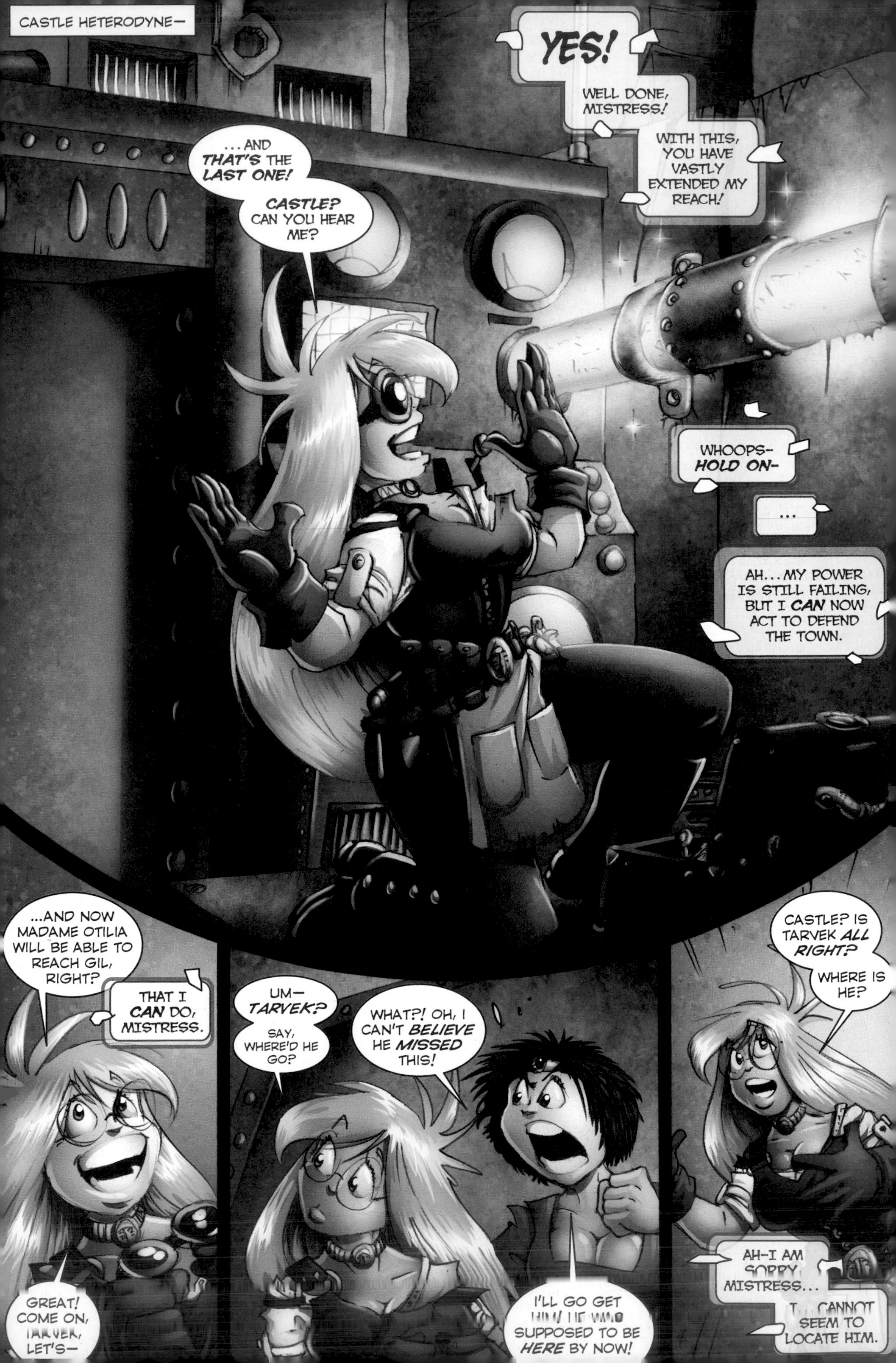
CASTLE HETERODYNE—
...AND THAT'S THE LAST ONE!
CASTLE? CAN YOU HEAR ME?
YES!
WELL DONE, MISTRESS!
WITH THIS, YOU HAVE VASTLY EXTENDED MY REACH!
WHOOPS- HOLD ON-
...
AH...MY POWER IS STILL FAILING, BUT I CAN NOW ACT TO DEFEND THE TOWN.
...AND NOW MADAME OTILIA WILL BE ABLE TO REACH GIL, RIGHT?
THAT I CAN DO, MISTRESS.
GREAT! COME ON,
LET'S—
UM— TARVEK? SAY, WHERE'D HE GO?
WHAT?! OH, I CAN'T BELIEVE HE MISSED THIS!
I'LL GO GET
SUPPOSED TO BE HERE BY NOW!
CASTLE? IS TARVEK ALL RIGHT?
WHERE IS HE?
AH—I AM SORRY, MISTRESS...
CANNOT SEEM TO LOCATE HIM.

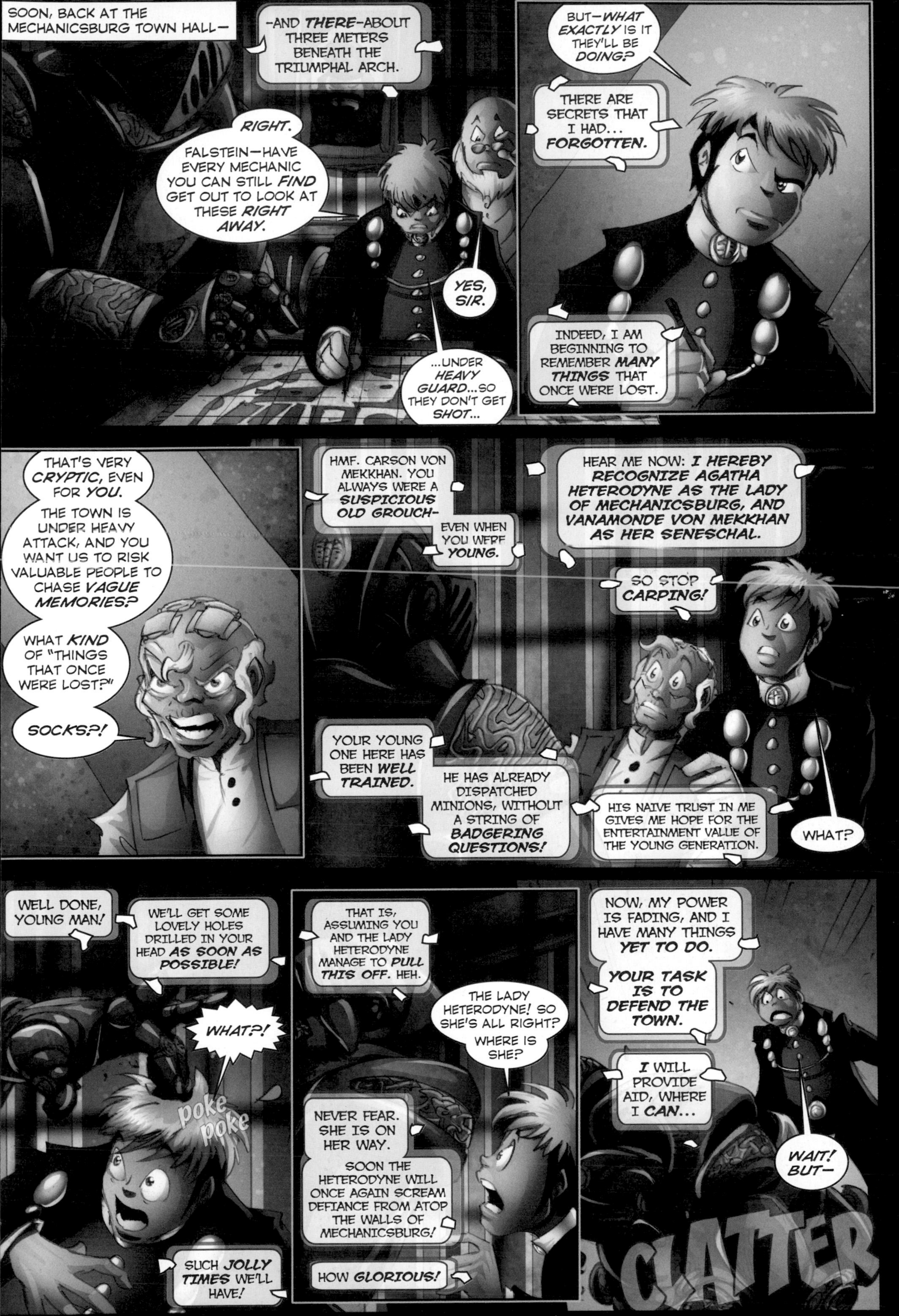
SOON, BACK AT THE MECHANICSBURG TOWN HALL—
—AND THERE—ABOUT THREE METERS BENEATH THE TRIUMPHAL ARCH.
RIGHT.
FALSTEIN—HAVE EVERY MECHANIC YOU CAN STILL FIND GET OUT TO LOOK AT THESE RIGHT AWAY.
YES, SIR.
...UNDER HEAVY GUARD...SO THEY DON'T GET SHOT...
BUT—WHAT EXACTLY IS IT THEY'LL BE DOING?
THERE ARE SECRETS THAT I HAD... FORGOTTEN.
INDEED, I AM BEGINNING TO REMEMBER MANY THINGS THAT ONCE WERE LOST.
THAT'S VERY CRYPTIC, EVEN FOR YOU.
THE TOWN IS UNDER HEAVY ATTACK, AND YOU WANT US TO RISK VALUABLE PEOPLE TO CHASE VAGUE MEMORIES?
WHAT KIND OF "THINGS THAT ONCE WERE LOST?"
SOCKS?!
HMF. CARSON VON MEKKHAN. YOU ALWAYS WERE A SUSPICIOUS OLD GROUCH—
EVEN WHEN YOU WERE YOUNG.
HEAR ME NOW: I HEREBY RECOGNIZE AGATHA HETERODYNE AS THE LADY OF MECHANICSBURG, AND VANAMONDE VON MEKKHAN AS HER SENESCHAL.
SO STOP CARPING!
YOUR YOUNG ONE HERE HAS BEEN WELL TRAINED.
HE HAS ALREADY DISPATCHED MINIONS, WITHOUT A STRING OF BADGERING QUESTIONS!
HIS NAIVE TRUST IN ME GIVES ME HOPE FOR THE ENTERTAINMENT VALUE OF THE YOUNG GENERATION.
WHAT?
WELL DONE, YOUNG MAN!
WE'LL GET SOME LOVELY HOLES DRILLED IN YOUR HEAD AS SOON AS POSSIBLE!
WHAT?!
poke poke
SUCH JOLLY TIMES WE'LL HAVE!
THAT IS, ASSUMING YOU AND THE LADY HETERODYNE MANAGE TO PULL THIS OFF. HEH.
THE LADY HETERODYNE! SO SHE'S ALL RIGHT? WHERE IS SHE?
NEVER FEAR. SHE IS ON HER WAY.
SOON THE HETERODYNE WILL ONCE AGAIN SCREAM DEFIANCE FROM ATOP THE WALLS OF MECHANICSBURG!
HOW GLORIOUS!
NOW, MY POWER IS FADING, AND I HAVE MANY THINGS YET TO DO.
YOUR TASK IS TO DEFEND THE TOWN.
I WILL PROVIDE AID, WHERE I CAN...
WAIT! BUT—
CLATTER

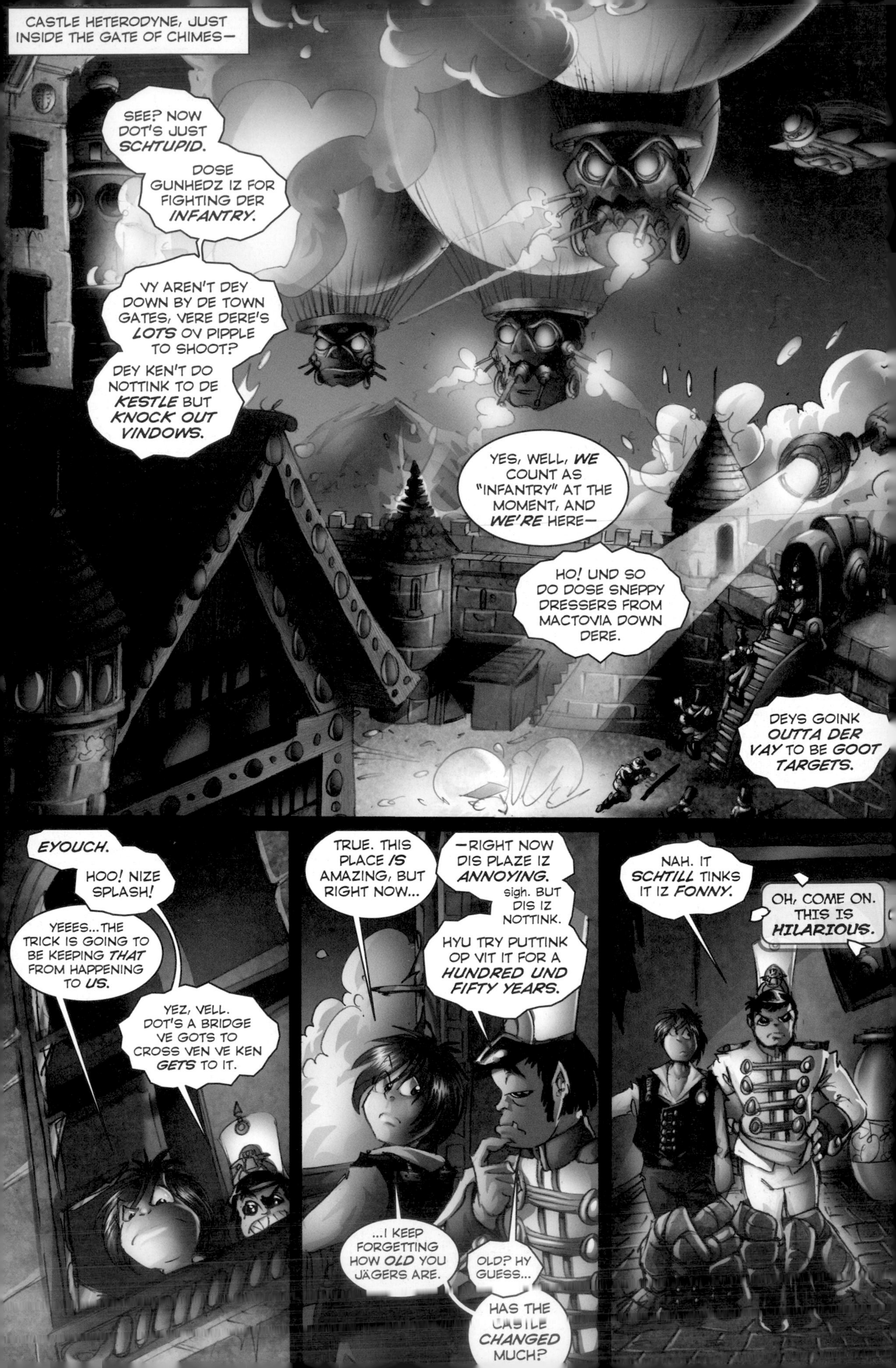

CASTLE HETERODYNE, JUST INSIDE THE GATE OF CHIMES—
SEE? NOW DOT'S JUST *SCHTUPID*.
DOSE GUNHEDZ IZ FOR FIGHTING DER *INFANTRY*.
VY AREN'T DEY DOWN BY DE TOWN GATES, VERE DERE'S *LOTS* OV PIPPLE TO SHOOT?
DEY KEN'T DO NOTTINK TO DE *KESTLE* BUT *KNOCK OUT VINDOWS*.
YES, WELL, *WE* COUNT AS "INFANTRY" AT THE MOMENT, AND *WE'RE* HERE—
HO! UND SO DO DOSE SNEPPY DRESSERS FROM MACTOVIA DOWN DERE.
DEYS GOINK *OUTTA DER VAY* TO BE *GOOT TARGETS*.
EYOUCH.
HOO! NIZE SPLASH!
YEEES... THE TRICK IS GOING TO BE KEEPING *THAT* FROM HAPPENING TO *US*.
YEZ, VELL. DOT'S A BRIDGE VE GOTS TO CROSS VEN VE KEN *GETS* TO IT.
TRUE. THIS PLACE *IS* AMAZING, BUT RIGHT NOW...
—RIGHT NOW DIS PLAZE IZ *ANNOYING*.
sigh. BUT DIS IZ NOTTINK.
HYU TRY PUTTINK OP VIT IT FOR A *HUNDRED UND FIFTY YEARS*.
...I KEEP FORGETTING HOW *OLD* YOU JÄGERS ARE.
OLD? HY GUESS...
HAS THE CASTLE *CHANGED* MUCH?
NAH. IT *SCHTILL* TINKS IT IZ *FONNY*.
OH, COME ON. THIS IS *HILARIOUS*.

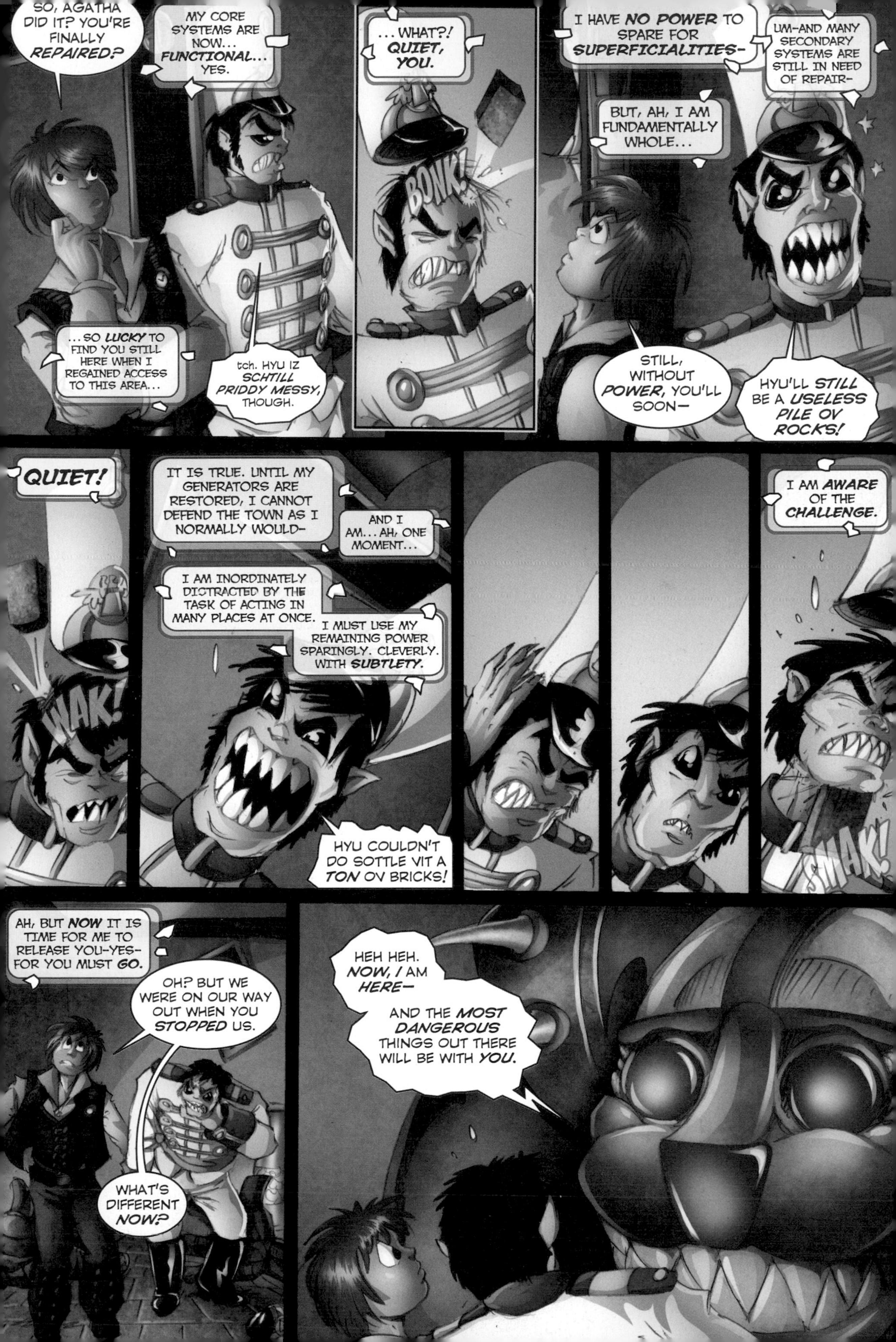
SO, AGATHA DID IT? YOU'RE FINALLY REPAIRED?
MY CORE SYSTEMS ARE NOW... FUNCTIONAL... YES.
...SO LUCKY TO FIND YOU STILL HERE WHEN I REGAINED ACCESS TO THIS AREA...
tch. HYU IZ SCHTILL PRIDDY MESSY, THOUGH.
...WHAT?! QUIET, YOU.
BONK!
I HAVE NO POWER TO SPARE FOR SUPERFICIALITIES-
UM-AND MANY SECONDARY SYSTEMS ARE STILL IN NEED OF REPAIR-
BUT, AH, I AM FUNDAMENTALLY WHOLE...
STILL, WITHOUT POWER, YOU'LL SOON—
HYU'LL STILL BE A USELESS PILE OV ROCKS!
QUIET!
WAK!
IT IS TRUE. UNTIL MY GENERATORS ARE RESTORED, I CANNOT DEFEND THE TOWN AS I NORMALLY WOULD-
AND I AM... AH, ONE MOMENT...
I AM INORDINATELY DISTRACTED BY THE TASK OF ACTING IN MANY PLACES AT ONCE.
I MUST USE MY REMAINING POWER SPARINGLY. CLEVERLY. WITH SUBTLETY.
HYU COULDN'T DO SOTTLE VIT A TON OV BRICKS!
I AM AWARE OF THE CHALLENGE.
SMAK!
AH, BUT NOW IT IS TIME FOR ME TO RELEASE YOU-YES-FOR YOU MUST GO.
OH? BUT WE WERE ON OUR WAY OUT WHEN YOU STOPPED US.
WHAT'S DIFFERENT NOW?
HEH HEH. NOW, I AM HERE—
AND THE MOST DANGEROUS THINGS OUT THERE WILL BE WITH YOU.

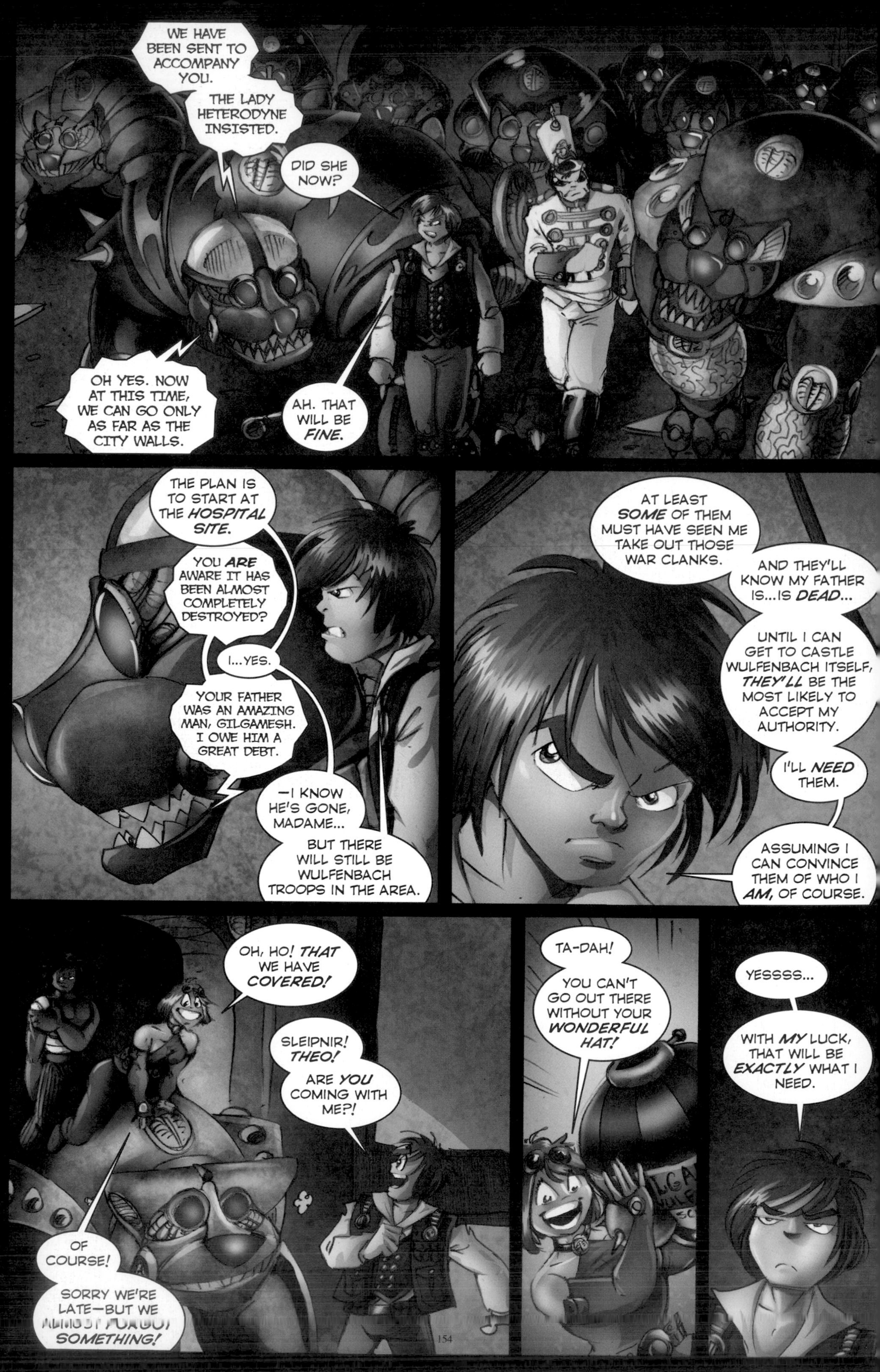
WE HAVE BEEN SENT TO ACCOMPANY YOU.
THE LADY HETERODYNE INSISTED.
DID SHE NOW?
OH YES. NOW AT THIS TIME, WE CAN GO ONLY AS FAR AS THE CITY WALLS.
AH. THAT WILL BE *FINE*.
THE PLAN IS TO START AT THE *HOSPITAL SITE*.
YOU *ARE* AWARE IT HAS BEEN ALMOST COMPLETELY DESTROYED?
I...YES.
YOUR FATHER WAS AN AMAZING MAN, GILGAMESH. I OWE HIM A GREAT DEBT.
—I KNOW HE'S GONE, MADAME...
BUT THERE WILL STILL BE WULFENBACH TROOPS IN THE AREA.
AT LEAST *SOME* OF THEM MUST HAVE SEEN ME TAKE OUT THOSE WAR CLANKS.
AND THEY'LL KNOW MY FATHER IS...IS *DEAD*...
UNTIL I CAN GET TO CASTLE WULFENBACH ITSELF, *THEY'LL* BE THE MOST LIKELY TO ACCEPT MY AUTHORITY.
I'LL *NEED* THEM.
ASSUMING I CAN CONVINCE THEM OF WHO I *AM*, OF COURSE.
OH, HO! *THAT* WE HAVE *COVERED!*
SLEIPNIR! *THEO!*
ARE *YOU* COMING WITH ME?!
OF COURSE!
SORRY WE'RE LATE—BUT WE
SOMETHING!
TA-DAH!
YOU CAN'T GO OUT THERE WITHOUT YOUR *WONDERFUL HAT!*
YESSSS...
WITH *MY* LUCK, THAT WILL BE *EXACTLY* WHAT I NEED.

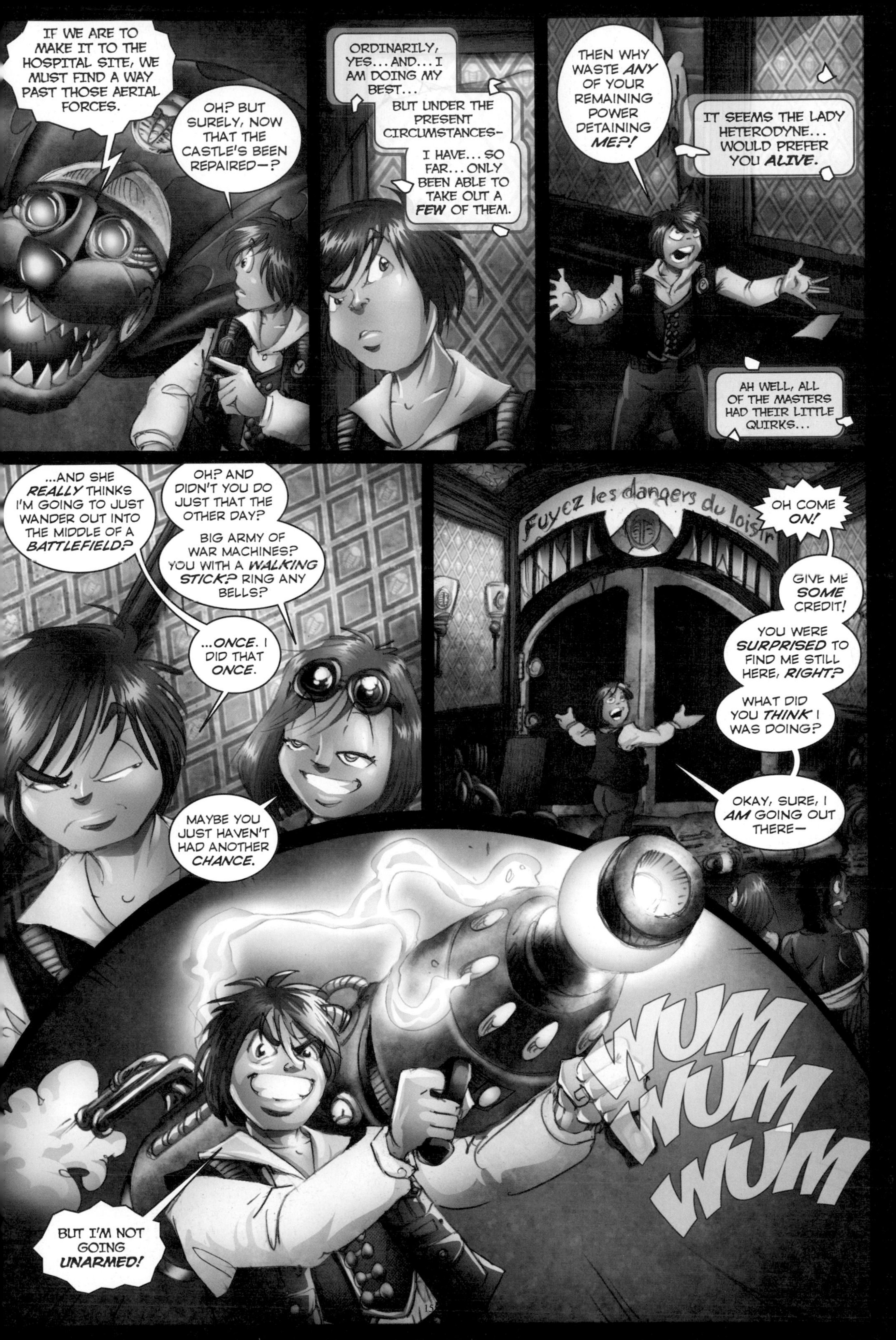
IF WE ARE TO MAKE IT TO THE HOSPITAL SITE, WE MUST FIND A WAY PAST THOSE AERIAL FORCES.
OH? BUT SURELY, NOW THAT THE CASTLE'S BEEN REPAIRED—?
ORDINARILY, YES... AND... I AM DOING MY BEST...
BUT UNDER THE PRESENT CIRCUMSTANCES-
I HAVE... SO FAR... ONLY BEEN ABLE TO TAKE OUT A FEW OF THEM.
THEN WHY WASTE ANY OF YOUR REMAINING POWER DETAINING ME?!
IT SEEMS THE LADY HETERODYNE... WOULD PREFER YOU ALIVE.
AH WELL, ALL OF THE MASTERS HAD THEIR LITTLE QUIRKS...
...AND SHE REALLY THINKS I'M GOING TO JUST WANDER OUT INTO THE MIDDLE OF A BATTLEFIELD?
OH? AND DIDN'T YOU DO JUST THAT THE OTHER DAY?
BIG ARMY OF WAR MACHINES? YOU WITH A WALKING STICK? RING ANY BELLS?
...ONCE. I DID THAT ONCE.
MAYBE YOU JUST HAVEN'T HAD ANOTHER CHANCE.
Fuyez les dangers du loisir
OH COME ON!
GIVE ME SOME CREDIT!
YOU WERE SURPRISED TO FIND ME STILL HERE, RIGHT?
WHAT DID YOU THINK I WAS DOING?
OKAY, SURE, I AM GOING OUT THERE—
BUT I'M NOT GOING UNARMED!
WUM WUM WUM

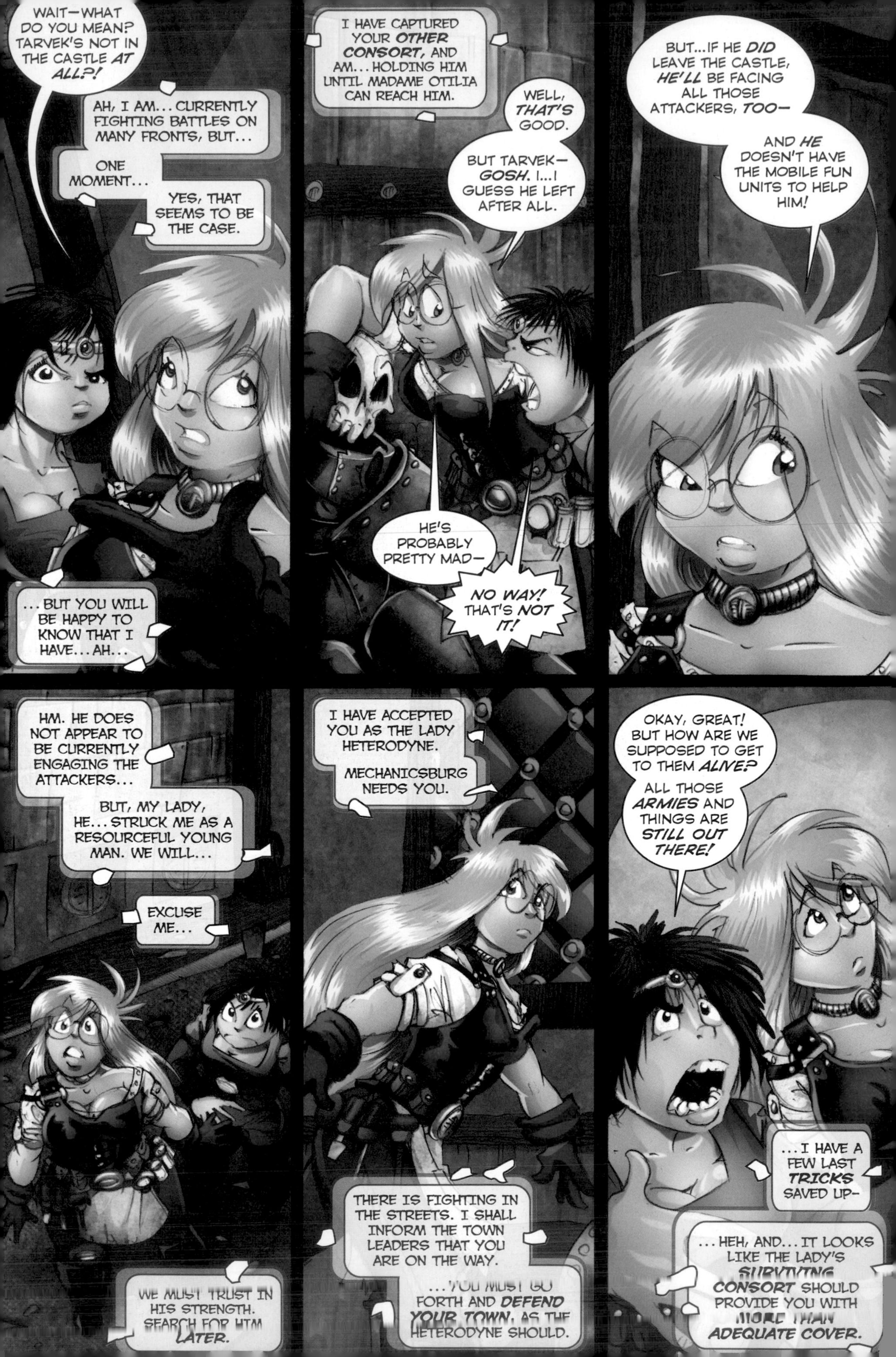
WAIT—WHAT DO YOU MEAN? TARVEK'S NOT IN THE CASTLE AT ALL?!
AH, I AM... CURRENTLY FIGHTING BATTLES ON MANY FRONTS, BUT...
ONE MOMENT...
YES, THAT SEEMS TO BE THE CASE.
...BUT YOU WILL BE HAPPY TO KNOW THAT I HAVE... AH...
I HAVE CAPTURED YOUR OTHER CONSORT, AND AM... HOLDING HIM UNTIL MADAME OTILIA CAN REACH HIM.
WELL, THAT'S GOOD.
BUT TARVEK— GOSH. I...I GUESS HE LEFT AFTER ALL.
HE'S PROBABLY PRETTY MAD—
NO WAY! THAT'S NOT IT!
BUT...IF HE DID LEAVE THE CASTLE, HE'LL BE FACING ALL THOSE ATTACKERS, TOO—
AND HE DOESN'T HAVE THE MOBILE FUN UNITS TO HELP HIM!
HM. HE DOES NOT APPEAR TO BE CURRENTLY ENGAGING THE ATTACKERS...
BUT, MY LADY, HE... STRUCK ME AS A RESOURCEFUL YOUNG MAN. WE WILL...
EXCUSE ME...
WE MUST TRUST IN HIS STRENGTH. SEARCH FOR HIM LATER.
I HAVE ACCEPTED YOU AS THE LADY HETERODYNE.
MECHANICSBURG NEEDS YOU.
THERE IS FIGHTING IN THE STREETS. I SHALL INFORM THE TOWN LEADERS THAT YOU ARE ON THE WAY.
...YOU MUST GO FORTH AND DEFEND YOUR TOWN, AS THE HETERODYNE SHOULD.
OKAY, GREAT! BUT HOW ARE WE SUPPOSED TO GET TO THEM ALIVE?
ALL THOSE ARMIES AND THINGS ARE STILL OUT THERE!
...I HAVE A FEW LAST TRICKS SAVED UP—
...HEH, AND... IT LOOKS LIKE THE LADY'S SURVIVING CONSORT SHOULD PROVIDE YOU WITH MORE THAN ADEQUATE COVER.

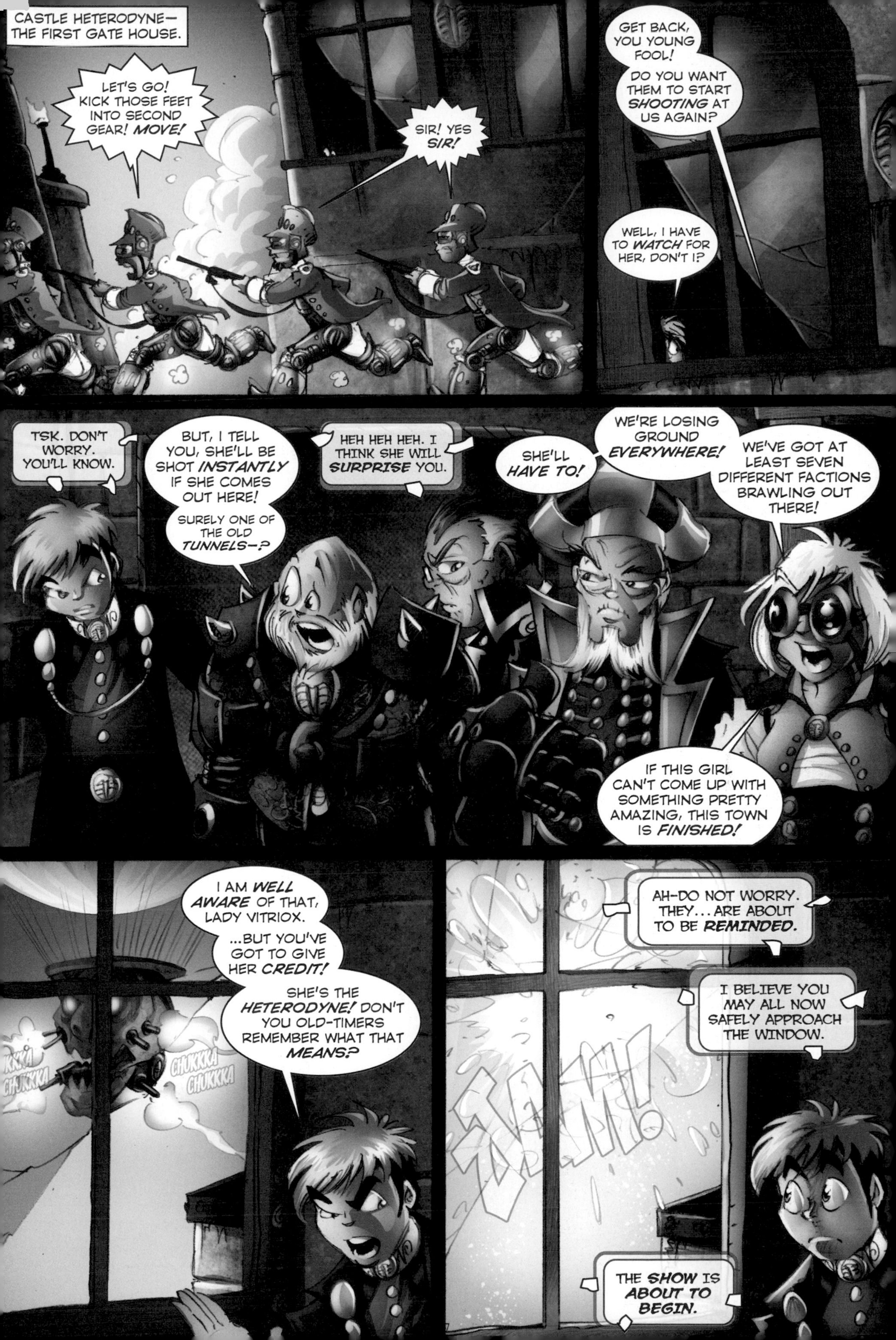
CASTLE HETERODYNE— THE FIRST GATE HOUSE.
LET'S GO! KICK THOSE FEET INTO SECOND GEAR! MOVE!
SIR! YES SIR!
GET BACK, YOU YOUNG FOOL!
DO YOU WANT THEM TO START SHOOTING AT US AGAIN?
WELL, I HAVE TO WATCH FOR HER, DON'T I?
TSK. DON'T WORRY. YOU'LL KNOW.
BUT, I TELL YOU, SHE'LL BE SHOT INSTANTLY IF SHE COMES OUT HERE!
SURELY ONE OF THE OLD TUNNELS—?
HEH HEH HEH. I THINK SHE WILL SURPRISE YOU.
SHE'LL HAVE TO!
WE'RE LOSING GROUND EVERYWHERE!
WE'VE GOT AT LEAST SEVEN DIFFERENT FACTIONS BRAWLING OUT THERE!
IF THIS GIRL CAN'T COME UP WITH SOMETHING PRETTY AMAZING, THIS TOWN IS FINISHED!
I AM WELL AWARE OF THAT, LADY VITRIOX.
...BUT YOU'VE GOT TO GIVE HER CREDIT!
SHE'S THE HETERODYNE! DON'T YOU OLD-TIMERS REMEMBER WHAT THAT MEANS?
CHUKKKA CHUKKKA
CHUKKKA CHUKKKA
AH—DO NOT WORRY. THEY... ARE ABOUT TO BE REMINDED.
I BELIEVE YOU MAY ALL NOW SAFELY APPROACH THE WINDOW.
THE SHOW IS ABOUT TO BEGIN.

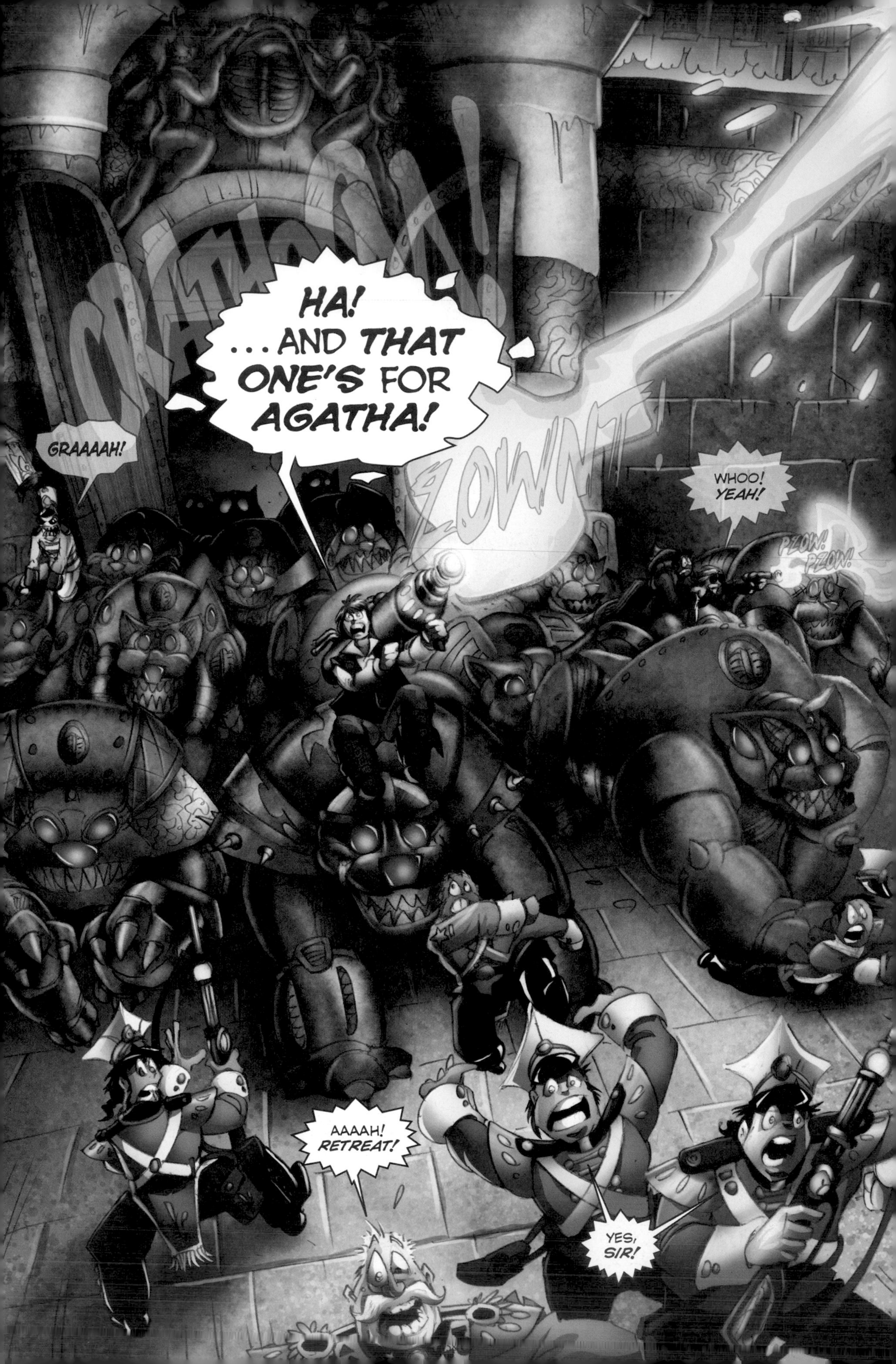
CRATHOOM!
HA! ...AND THAT ONE'S FOR AGATHA!
ZOWNT!
GRAAAAH!
WHOO! YEAH!
PZOW! PZOW!
AAAAH! RETREAT!
YES, SIR!

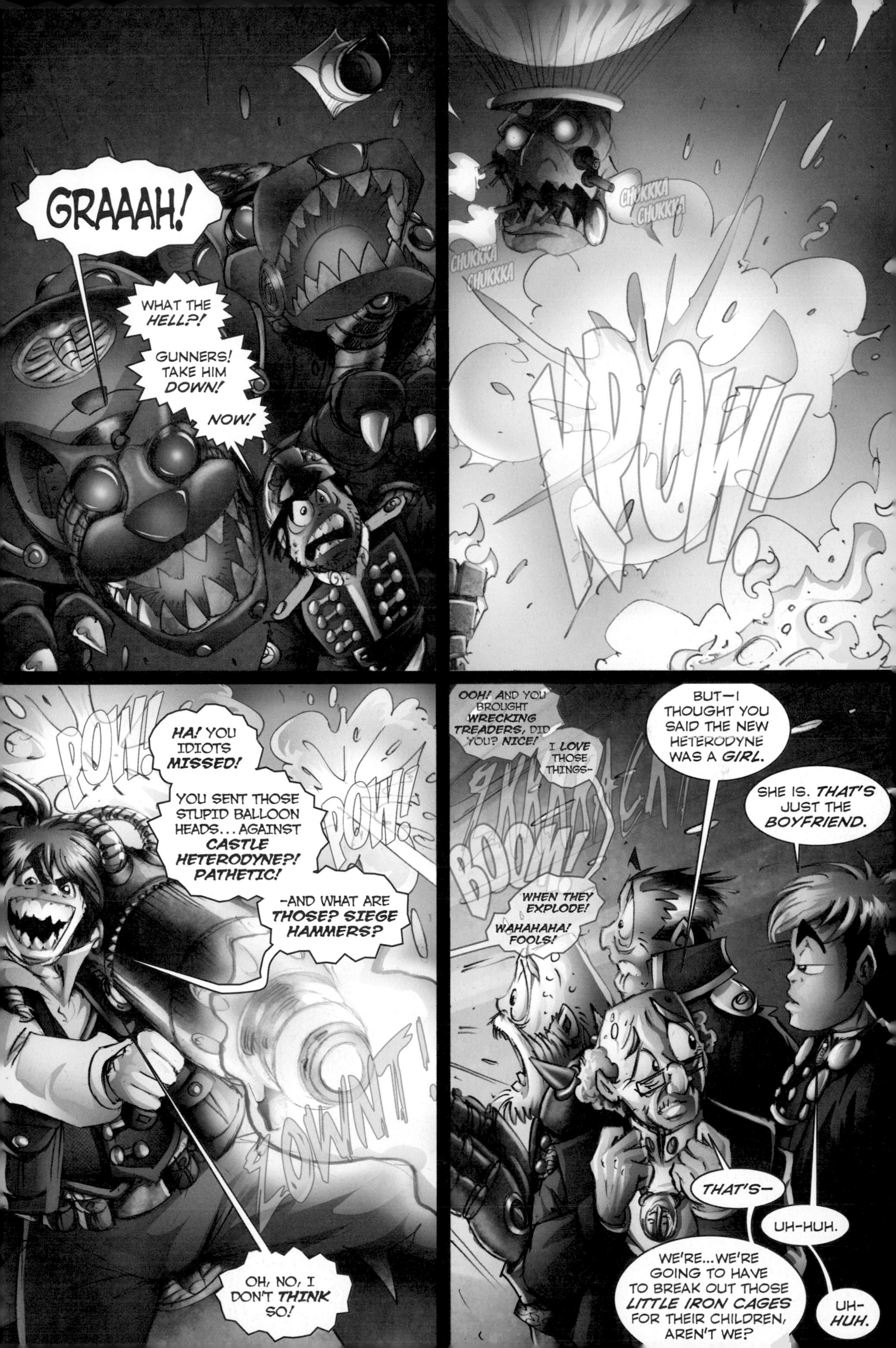
GRAAAH!
WHAT THE HELL?!
GUNNERS! TAKE HIM DOWN!
NOW!
CHUKKKA CHUKKKA
CHUKKKA CHUKKKA
KPOW!
POW!
HA! YOU IDIOTS MISSED!
YOU SENT THOSE STUPID BALLOON HEADS... AGAINST CASTLE HETERODYNE?! PATHETIC!
POW!
-AND WHAT ARE THOSE? SIEGE HAMMERS?
ZOWNT!
OH, NO, I DON'T THINK SO!
OOH! AND YOU BROUGHT WRECKING TREADERS, DID YOU? NICE!
I LOVE THOSE THINGS-
BOOM!
WHEN THEY EXPLODE!
WAHAHAHA! FOOLS!
BUT—I THOUGHT YOU SAID THE NEW HETERODYNE WAS A GIRL.
SHE IS. THAT'S JUST THE BOYFRIEND.
THAT'S—
UH-HUH.
WE'RE...WE'RE GOING TO HAVE TO BREAK OUT THOSE LITTLE IRON CAGES FOR THEIR CHILDREN, AREN'T WE?
UH-HUH.

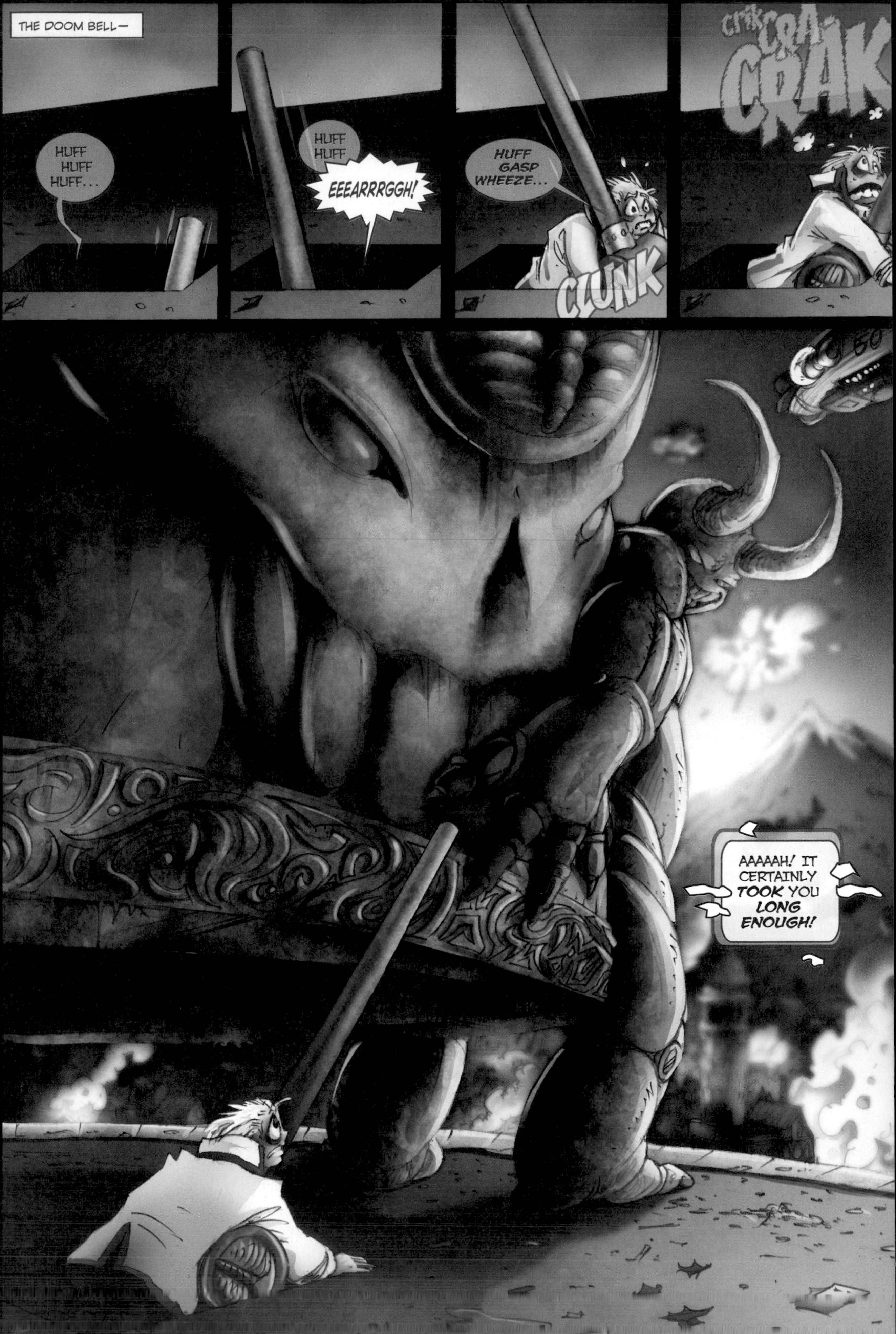
THE DOOM BELL—
HUFF HUFF HUFF...
HUFF HUFF
EEEARRRGGH!
HUFF GASP WHEEZE...
CLUNK
CRIK CRA-CRAK
AAAAAH! IT CERTAINLY TOOK YOU LONG ENOUGH!

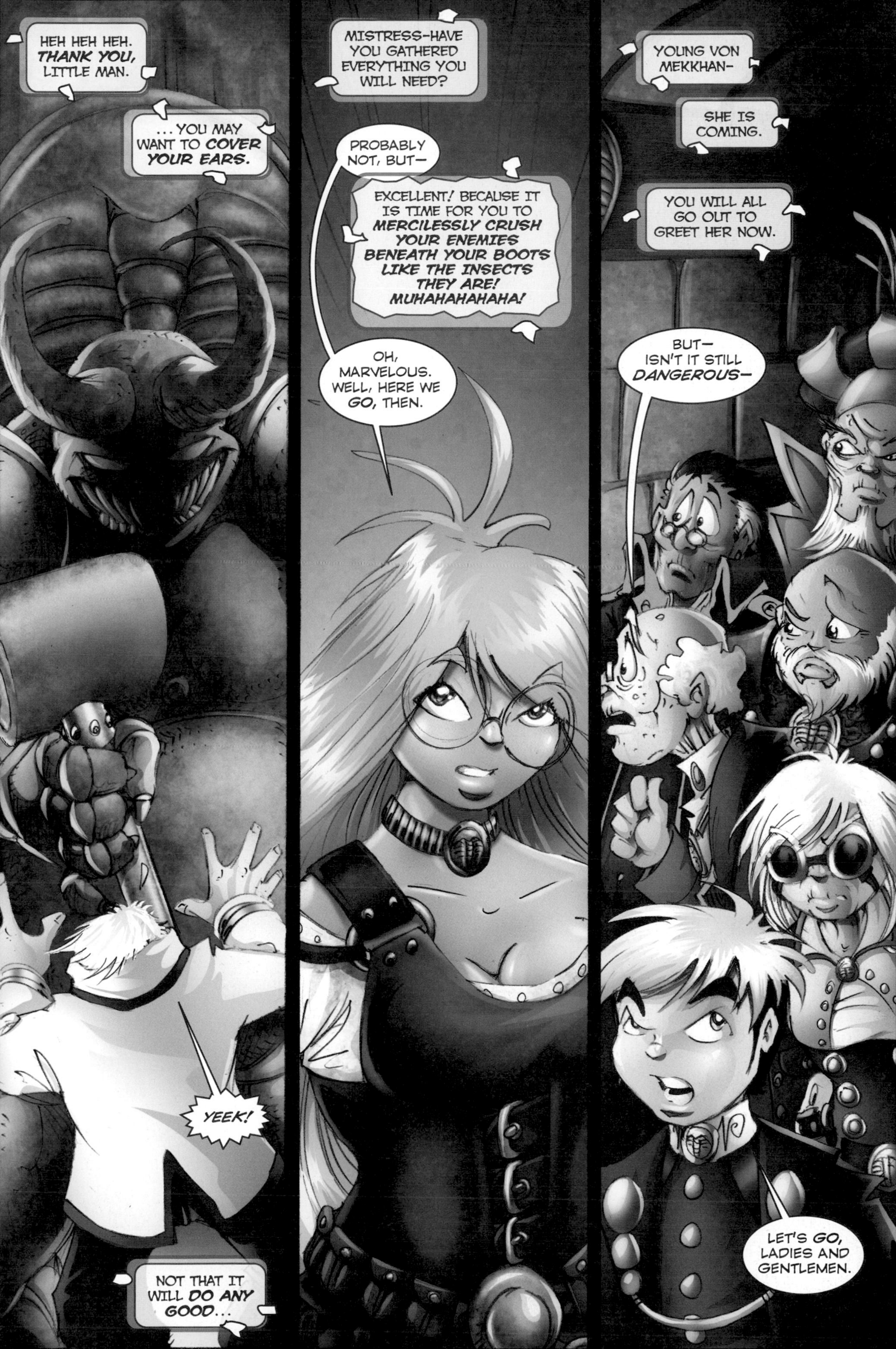
HEH HEH HEH. THANK YOU, LITTLE MAN.
...YOU MAY WANT TO COVER YOUR EARS.
YEEK!
NOT THAT IT WILL DO ANY GOOD...
MISTRESS-HAVE YOU GATHERED EVERYTHING YOU WILL NEED?
PROBABLY NOT, BUT—
EXCELLENT! BECAUSE IT IS TIME FOR YOU TO MERCILESSLY CRUSH YOUR ENEMIES BENEATH YOUR BOOTS LIKE THE INSECTS THEY ARE! MUHAHAHAHAHA!
OH, MARVELOUS. WELL, HERE WE GO, THEN.
YOUNG VON MEKKHAN-
SHE IS COMING.
YOU WILL ALL GO OUT TO GREET HER NOW.
BUT— ISN'T IT STILL DANGEROUS—
LET'S GO, LADIES AND GENTLEMEN.

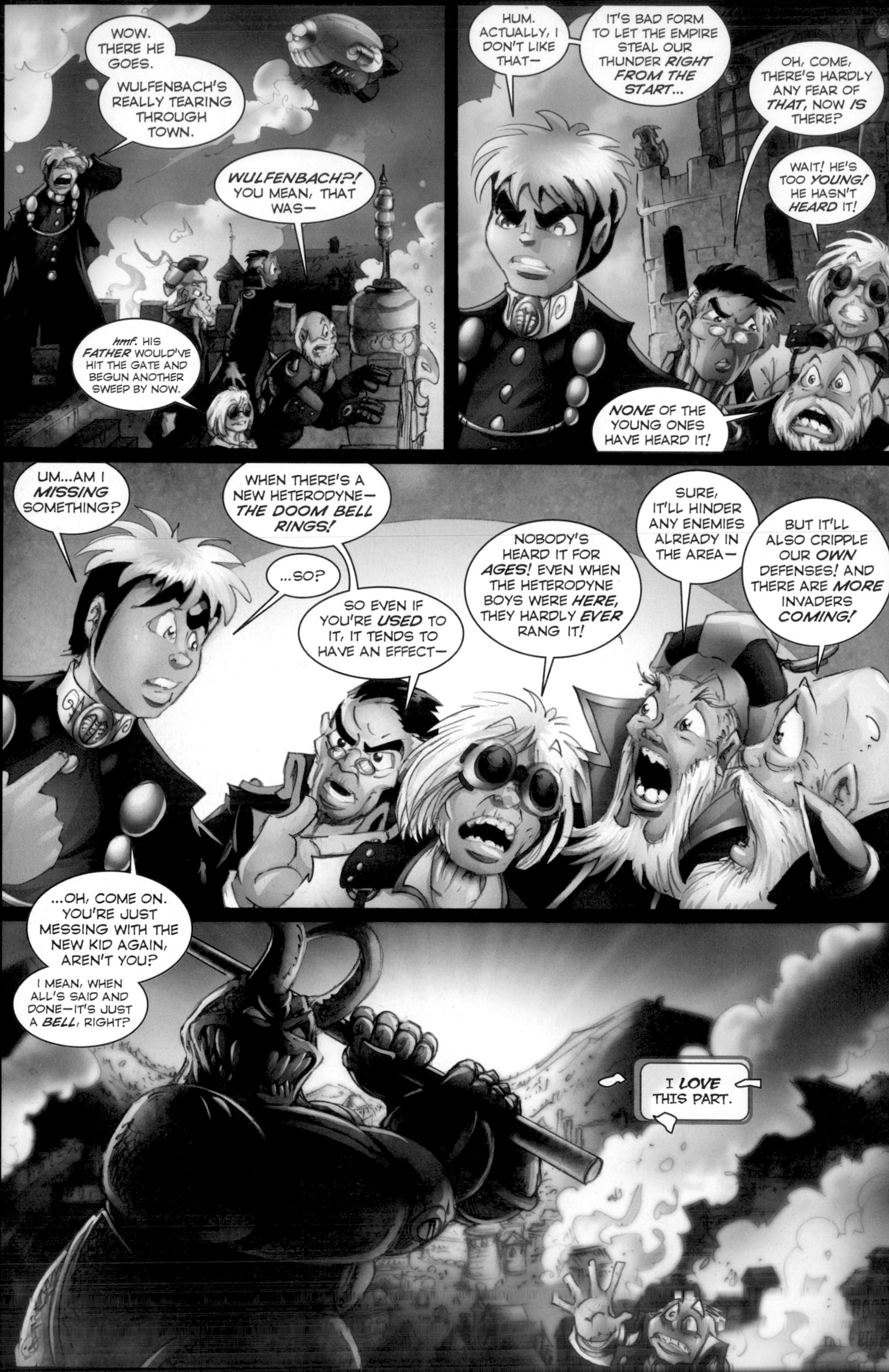

WOW. THERE HE GOES.
WULFENBACH'S REALLY TEARING THROUGH TOWN.
WULFENBACH?! YOU MEAN, THAT WAS—
hmf. HIS FATHER WOULD'VE HIT THE GATE AND BEGUN ANOTHER SWEEP BY NOW.
HUM. ACTUALLY, I DON'T LIKE THAT—
IT'S BAD FORM TO LET THE EMPIRE STEAL OUR THUNDER RIGHT FROM THE START...
OH, COME, THERE'S HARDLY ANY FEAR OF THAT, NOW IS THERE?
WAIT! HE'S TOO YOUNG! HE HASN'T HEARD IT!
NONE OF THE YOUNG ONES HAVE HEARD IT!
UM...AM I MISSING SOMETHING?
WHEN THERE'S A NEW HETERODYNE— THE DOOM BELL RINGS!
...SO?
SO EVEN IF YOU'RE USED TO IT, IT TENDS TO HAVE AN EFFECT—
NOBODY'S HEARD IT FOR AGES! EVEN WHEN THE HETERODYNE BOYS WERE HERE, THEY HARDLY EVER RANG IT!
SURE, IT'LL HINDER ANY ENEMIES ALREADY IN THE AREA—
BUT IT'LL ALSO CRIPPLE OUR OWN DEFENSES! AND THERE ARE MORE INVADERS COMING!
...OH, COME ON. YOU'RE JUST MESSING WITH THE NEW KID AGAIN, AREN'T YOU?
I MEAN, WHEN ALL'S SAID AND DONE—IT'S JUST A BELL, RIGHT?
I LOVE THIS PART.

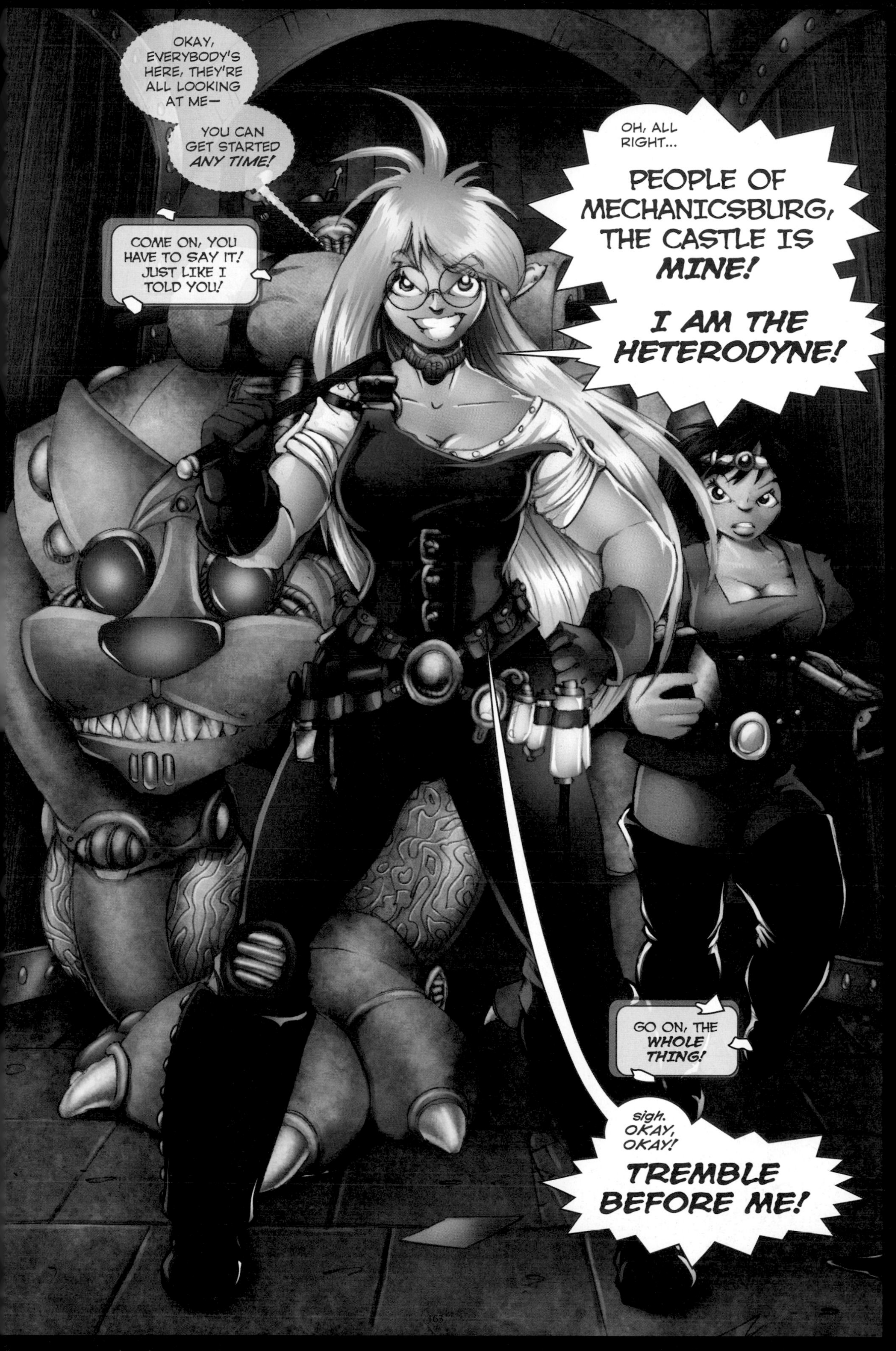

OKAY, EVERYBODY'S HERE, THEY'RE ALL LOOKING AT ME—
YOU CAN GET STARTED *ANY TIME!*
COME ON, YOU HAVE TO SAY IT! JUST LIKE I TOLD YOU!
OH, ALL RIGHT...
PEOPLE OF MECHANICSBURG, THE CASTLE IS *MINE!*
I AM THE HETERODYNE!
GO ON, THE *WHOLE THING!*
sigh. *OKAY, OKAY!*
TREMBLE BEFORE ME!

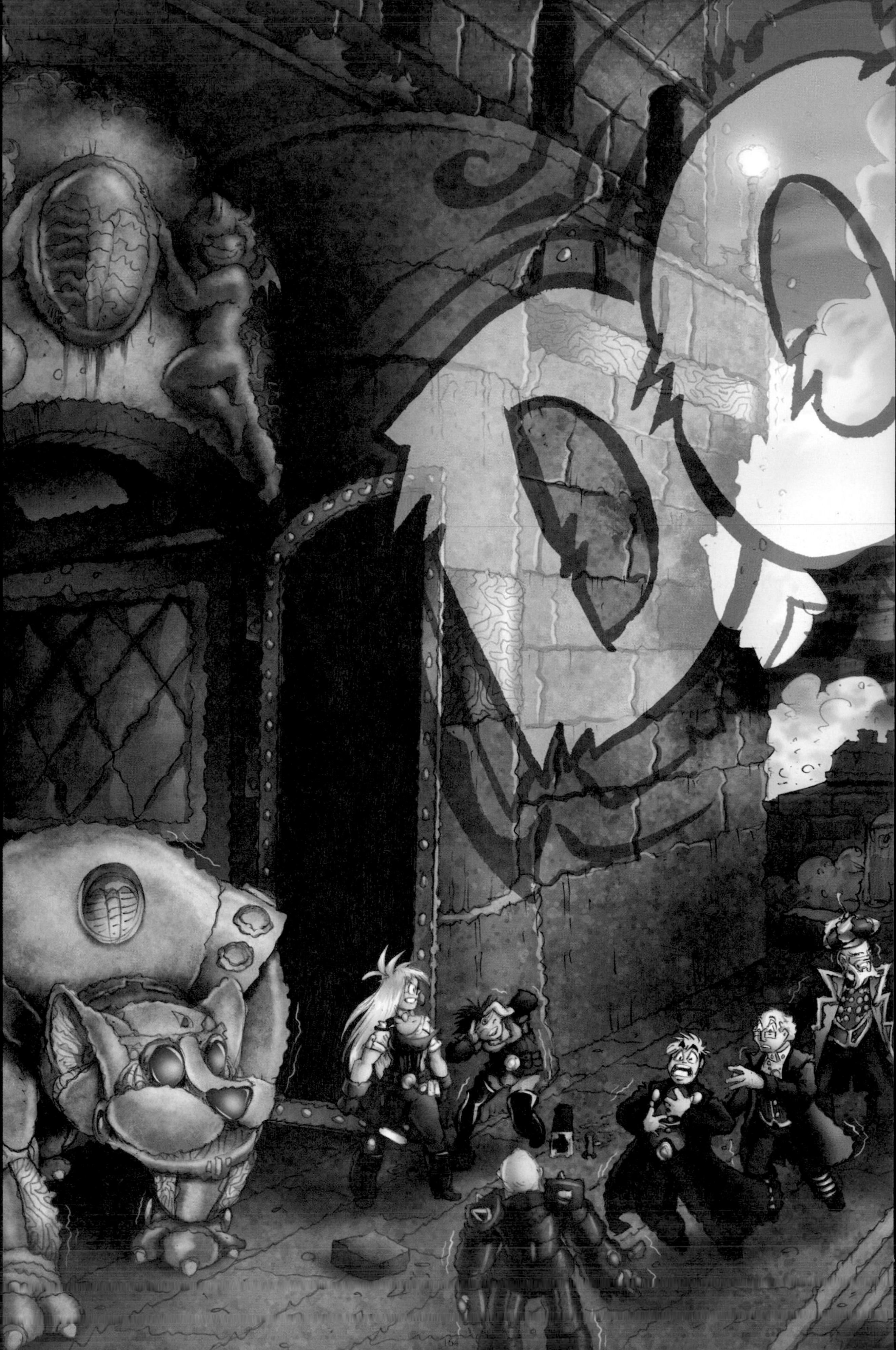

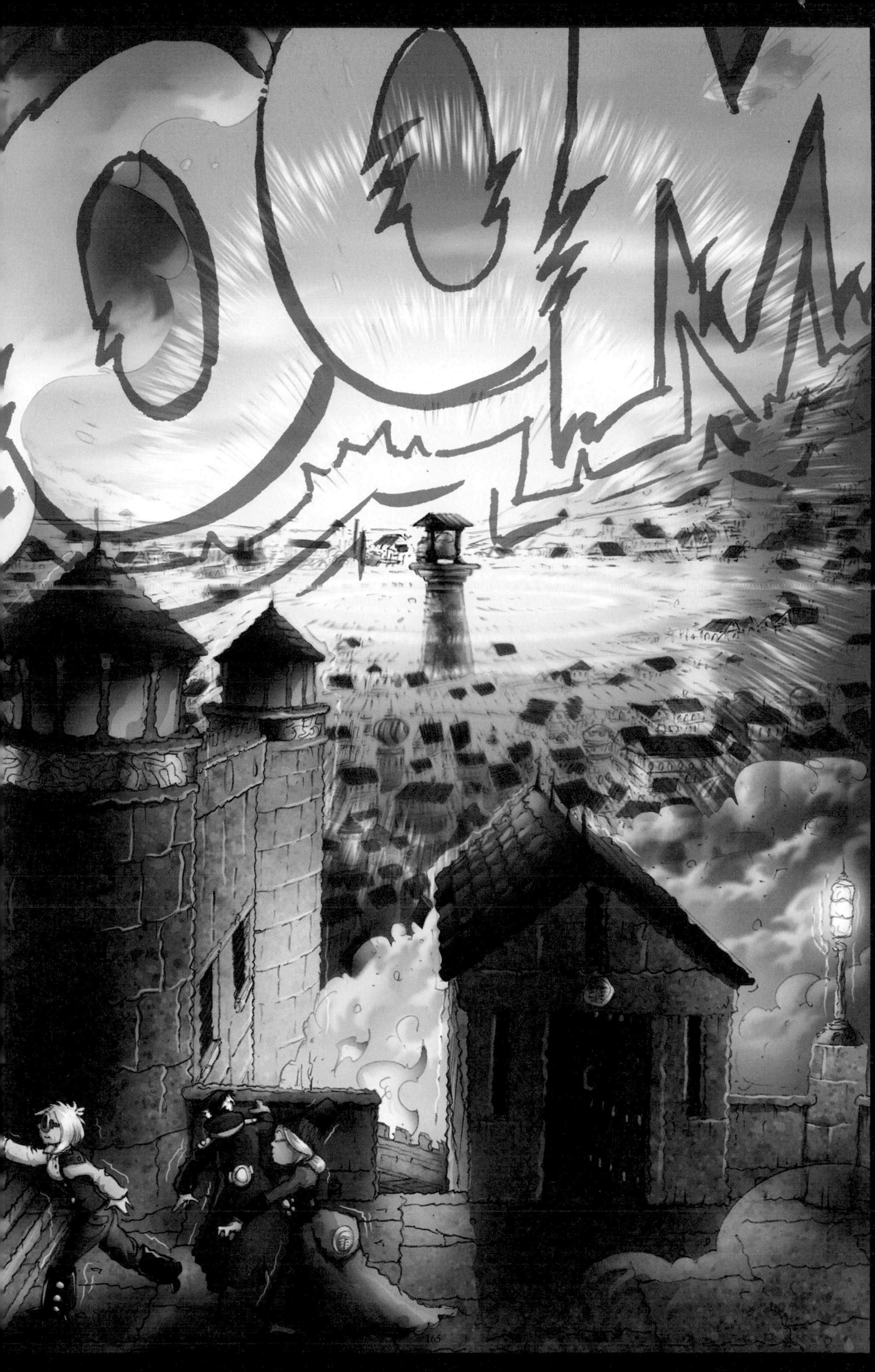

TO BE CONTINUED IN:

GIRL GENIUS® Book TWELVE

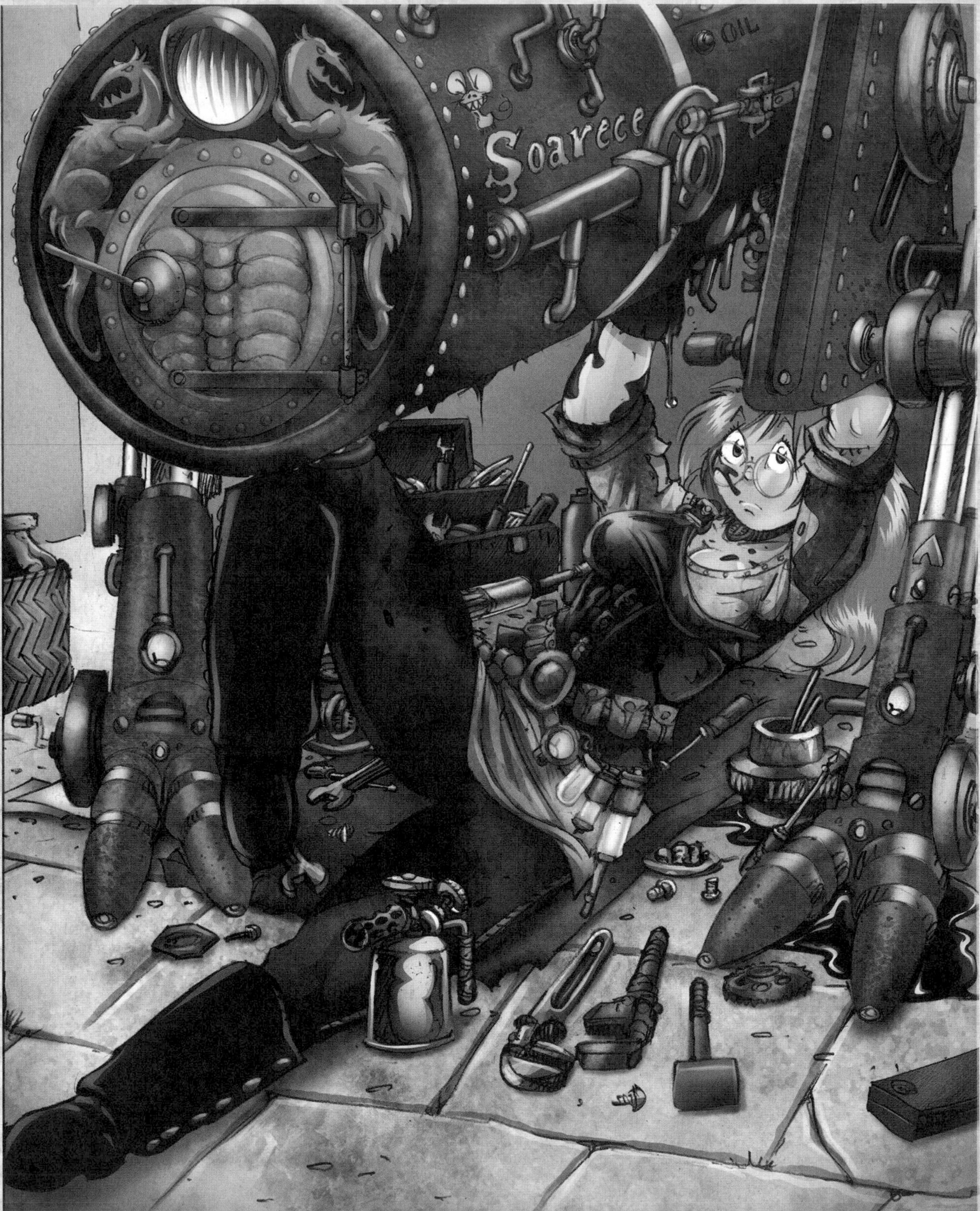
Soarece
OIL

KEEP UP WITH THE STORY! READ NEW COMICS THREE TIMES A WEEK AT:

www.GIRLGENIUS.NET

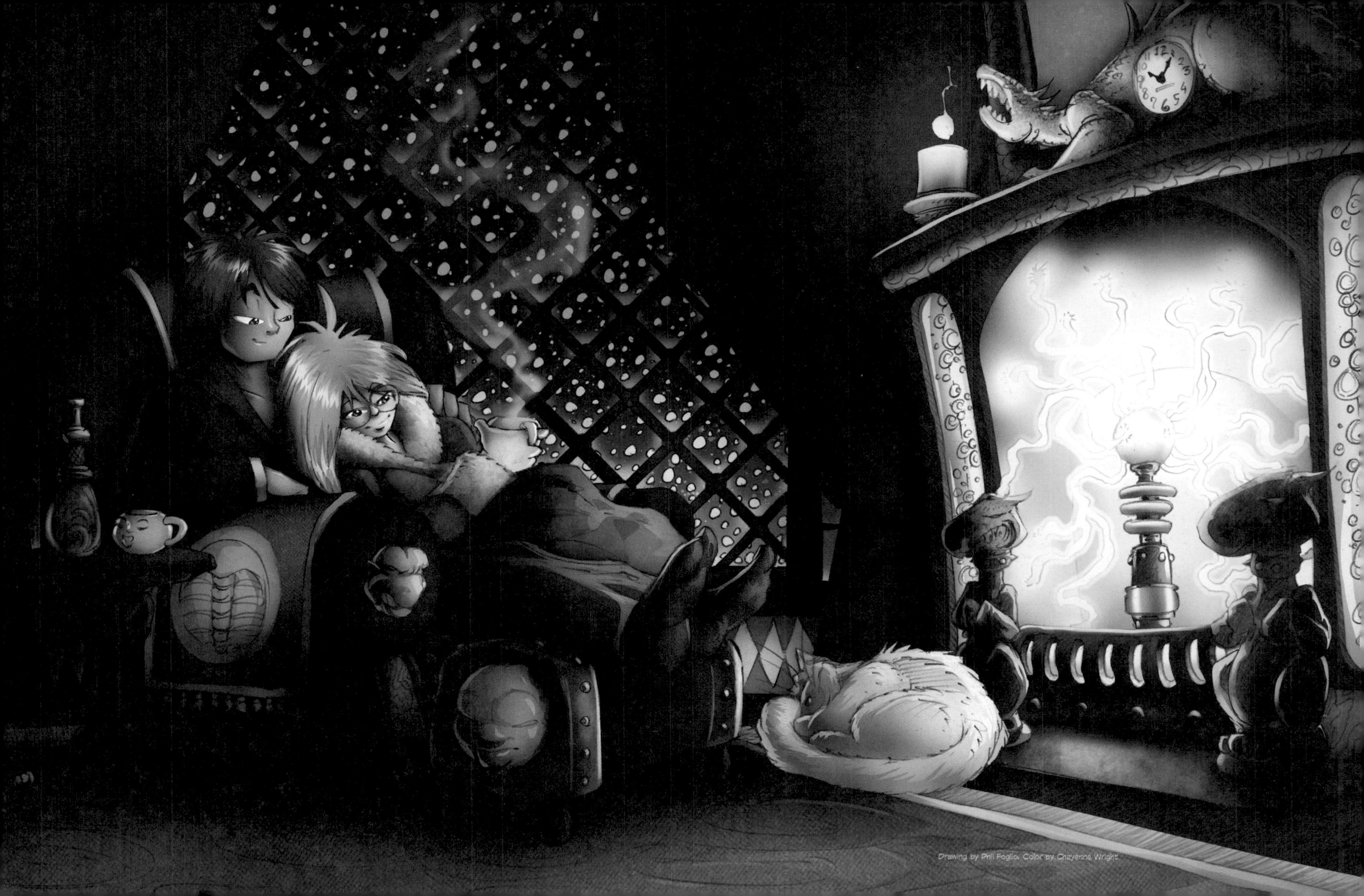
Drawing by Phil Foglio. Color by Cheyenne Wright

READ MORE COMICS ONLINE AT:

www.GIRLGENIUS.net

MONDAY · WEDNESDAY · FRIDAY